T0337648

LANDSCHAFTLICHKEIT als ARCHITEKTURIDEE
LANDSCAPE-NESS as ARCHITECTURAL IDEA

Margitta Buchert

a_ku jovis

LANDSCHAFTLICHKEIT LANDSCAPE-NESS
ALS ARCHITEKTURIDEE AS ARCHITECTURAL IDEA

PREFACE

The concept of landscape-ness is gaining increasing significance in architecture, not least due to climate change. Based on exemplary cases, the potential of architecture to deal with contemporary challenges is analysed, commented on and put forward here. Which understandings of architecture and which features flow into architectural and urbanistic projects through a consideration of landscape-ness? Which design processes are centrally associated with it; which qualities that define space are highlighted; and which types of awareness and capacities are enriched? In order to projectively stimulate future-orientated, positive and climate-effective potential in architecture and urban design, there is a focus on dimensions of landscape as nature (however they may have been shaped and reshaped by humans), as well as on the connection between architecture, the city, aesthetics and ecology. The concept of landscape-ness can be understood at the same time as a value that enhances aesthetic architectural quality. This book is written from the perspective of contemporary, primarily western-international architecture, urban design and landscape architectural design practices. Furthermore, it integrates impulses provided by architectural concepts in Singapore, as well as architecture ideas with a Japanese influence. By placing a spotlight on places, forms, spaces and effective qualities experienced as landscape, it pleads for a wide-ranging focus on and attentiveness to the living environment of people, as well as of design qualities in the conceptualisation, design creation and realisation of architectural ensembles. Not least, this can also enrich levels of understanding of the phenomenon of 'landscape' as a relative constant in people's existential and cultural environmental experience.

For his patient and competent work on the layout and assistance for corrections and image rights clarifications, I would like to cordially thank Julius Krüger, as well as Valerie Hoberg for the editing and translation of endnotes and Ferdinand Helmecke for image research. My thanks also go to all architecture offices and image copyright holders for their support. Many thanks to Lynne Kolar-Thompson for the translation into English and to jovis Verlag, especially Tim Vogel and Susanne Rösler for their reliable and dedicated support for the publication of this project.

VORWORT

Das Konzept der Landschaftlichkeit gewinnt nicht zuletzt durch den Klimawandel immer mehr an Bedeutung in der Architektur. Anhand exemplarischer Beispiele werden hier Potenziale der Architektur für den Umgang mit zeitgenössischen Herausforderungen analysiert, kommentiert und vorgeschlagen. Welche Architekturverständnisse und welche Eigenschaften fließen durch die Thematisierung von Landschaftlichkeit in architektonische und urbanistische Projekte ein? Welche gestalterischen Verfahren sind damit zentral verbunden, welche raumartikulierenden Qualitäten werden hervorgehoben, und welche Sensibilisierungen und Kapazitäten werden bereichert? Um zukunftsweisende positive und klimawirksame Potenziale in Architektur und Städtebau projektiv zu stimulieren, stehen dabei Dimensionen von Landschaft als Natur, wie geformt und überformt von Menschen sie auch sein mögen, ebenso im Fokus wie die Verbindung von Architektur, Stadt, Ästhetik und Ökologie. Das Konzept der Landschaftlichkeit kann gleichzeitig als eine Wertsetzung zur Erweiterung ästhetischer architektonischer Qualität verstanden werden. Dieses Buch ist geschrieben aus der Perspektive zeitgenössischer vor allem westlich-internationaler architektonischer, städtebaulicher und landschaftsarchitektonischer Entwurfspraktiken und integriert zudem impulsgebende Konzepte von Architekturen in Singapur sowie japanisch geprägte Architekturideen. Mit der Rahmung landschaftlich erfahrbarer Orte, Formen, Räume und Wirkqualitäten wird plädiert für eine vielfältige Aufmerksamkeit und engagierte Auseinandersetzung mit dem Lebensumfeld des Menschen sowie mit gestalterischen Qualitäten in der Konzeptualisierung, entwerferischen Kreation und Realisierung von architektonischen Ensembles. Nicht zuletzt können so auch Verständnisebenen des Phänomens ‚Landschaft' als relative Konstante in der existenziellen und kulturellen Umwelterfahrung des Menschen bereichert werden.

Für die geduldige und kompetente Mitarbeit am Layout sowie die Unterstützung bei Korrekturen und Bildrechteklärungen danke ich recht herzlich Julius Krüger sowie für das Korrektorat und Übersetzungen der Endnoten Valerie Hoberg und für Bildrecherchen Ferdinand Helmecke. Dank gilt an dieser Stelle auch allen Architekturbüros und Bildrechtegeber:innen für ihre Unterstützung. Vielmals bedanke ich mich bei Lynne Kolar-Thompson für die Übersetzung ins Englische und beim jovis-Verlag, insbesondere bei Tim Vogel und Susanne Rösler, für die bewährte und engagierte Begleitung des Publikationsprojekts.

LANDSCHAFTLICHKEIT
und ARCHITEKTUR. Einige Einblicke

LANDSCAPE-NESS
and ARCHITECTURE. Some insights

In the context of contemporary cultural conditions, 'landscape-ness as architectural idea' represents a multifaceted potentiality associated with positive values. Landscape-ness is thereby understood as an open question and projective task, not as a finished theory or retrospective narration; more as a research programme than as a research result, as well as a field with contradictory interpretations on how to find future-orientated, productive architectural qualities. Contrary to the search for a single or essential understanding of landscape, 'landscape-ness as architectural idea' focuses on a concept of theoretically and physically built discourses on continuities, transitions and spatial expansion; this includes built, structured and inhabited spaces, as well as site-specific solutions, 'green' technologies or new hybrids for urban landscapes, as well as explicitly aesthetic qualities.

Im Kontext zeitgenössischer kultureller Konditionen bildet ‚Landschaftlichkeit als Architekturidee' eine mit positiven Wertsetzungen verbundene Potenzialität mit vielfältigen Facetten. Landschaftlichkeit wird dabei als offene Frage und projektive Aufgabe, nicht als fertige Theorie oder retrospektive Nacherzählung verstanden, eher als Forschungsprogramm denn als Forschungsergebnis, und auch als ein Feld mit widersprüchlichen Interpretationen auf dem Weg, zukunftsweisende, produktive Architekturqualitäten zu finden. Im Unterschied zur Suche nach einem einzigen oder essenziellen Verständnis von Landschaft fokussiert ‚Landschaftlichkeit als Architekturidee' ein Konzept, das ideelle und physisch gebaute Diskurse zu Kontinuitäten, Übergängen und räumlicher Ausdehnung, das gebaute, strukturierte und gelebte Räume wie auch ortsspezifische Lösungen, ‚grüne' Techniken oder neue Hybride für urbane Landschaften sowie explizit ästhetische Qualitäten einschließt.

The notion of architectural idea focusses on concepts, intentions and plans, alternating somewhat between idea and ideal, as well as on actively defining strategies that give rise to creative activities and on concepts on a higher, abstract level, which serve as both guidance and model. In a philosophical sense, the connection between ideas and the essence of things and action and their effect, which is central for example in the ancient Greek noun 'idea', is the subject of controversial discussion.[1] In the following, architectural idea means both the guiding principles and basic thoughts that determine actions, and the perceivable phenomena that are created with the architectures and spaces and are associated with them. What is said, seen and experienced therefore forms the bases and the perspectives of the following considerations of phenomenological-hermeneutical nature.

LANDSCAPE AND LANDSCAPE-NESS   In the preamble of the European Landscape Convention, 'landscape' is described as an area perceived by people; and this area's character is the result of the action and interaction of natural and human factors.[2] There is also an emphasis on its significance in cultural, ecological, economic and social fields, as well as for human well-being in urban and rural environments, in any form of terrain regardless of whether the area is deemed beautiful or commonplace. Landscape is therefore described as a material substance, as scenery that can be experienced, as a public and social space, as a place of regeneration, and as a cultural asset and environmental system.

These stated properties have been increasingly discussed and elaborated on in various disciplines in recent decades.[3] This has also resulted in an extension of the notion of landscape, which integrates not only different layers of what is built and natural within various objects and spaces, but also the dynamic processes and events unfolding within them.[4]

Mit dem Begriff der Architekturidee werden, zwischen Idee und Ideal leicht changierend, Konzepte, Intentionen und Pläne fokussiert sowie aktiv bestimmende Strategien, aus denen die schöpferische Tätigkeit erwächst ebenso wie Vorstellungen auf einer höheren, abstrakten Ebene, die auch als Leitbild und Modell aufgefasst werden und wirken können. In der philosophischen Bedeutung wird der beispielsweise im altgriechischen Substantiv ‚idea' zentrale Zusammenhang von Ideen mit der Gestalt von Dingen und Handlungen und ihrer Wirkung kontrovers diskutiert.[1] Im Folgenden meint Architekturidee beides: die Leitbilder und Grundgedanken, die das Handeln bestimmen, und die wahrnehmbaren Phänomene, die mit den Architekturen und Räumen entstehen und verknüpft sind. Das Gesagte, das Gesehene und das Erfahrene bilden daher die Grundlagen und die Beobachtungebenen der nachfolgenden, phänomenologisch-hermeneutisch geprägten Ausführungen.

LANDSCHAFT UND LANDSCHAFTLICHKEIT   In der Präambel der European Landscape Convention wird ‚Landschaft' beschrieben als ein von Menschen wahrgenommenes Areal, dessen Charakter das Resultat der Aktion und Interaktion von natürlichen und menschlichen Faktoren ist.[2] Betont wird zudem ihre Bedeutung für kulturelle, ökologische, ökonomische und soziale Felder sowie das menschliche Wohlbefinden im städtischen wie in ländlichen Bereichen, in jeder Form von Gebiet und unabhängig davon, ob das Areal als schön oder alltäglich erachtet wird. Somit wird Landschaft als materielle Substanz, als erfahrbare Szenerie, als öffentlicher, sozialer Raum, als Regenerationsort, als Kulturgut und Umweltsystem beschrieben.

Die genannten Eigenschaften sind es auch, die in unterschiedlichen Disziplinen verstärkt in den letzten Jahrzehnten in sehr vielfältiger Weise diskutiert und differenziert wurden.[3] Dabei erfolgte auch eine Ausweitung des Begriffs Landschaft, die nicht nur unterschiedliche Schichten von Natürlichem und Gebautem verschiedener Objekte und Räume integrieren, sondern auch die sich in ihnen entfaltenden dynamischen Prozesse und Ereignisse.[4] Landschaft wird als vernetzende Matrix interpretiert, die alle diese Einzelphänomene integriert.

Landscape is interpreted as a networking matrix that integrates all these individual phenomena. This highlights a primacy of overarching connections in the surroundings and social environment, like those that have been developed in visionary projects by artists, intellectuals and architects since the late 1950s; for example, surrounding Team X, the International Situationists or the conceptual Land Art by Robert Smithson.[5] Since the 1990s, this has drawn the attention of architects and planners to existing elements in the sense of a combination of built structures, open space, memories and experiences – which must be viewed and termed differently to generate new forms, structures and ways of perception.[6] There is also a repeated emphasis in particular on the heterogeneity of types and elements contained in a landscape-like structured context.[7]

Imaginative and phenomenological potential gained renewed relevance, too, as did political dimensions that are closely connected to the Western-international history of notions of landscape and associated landscape design. The concept appears early on in relation to politically ordering structures. It spread widely after the Renaissance in connection with aesthetic characters presented in landscape painting and garden art, which are partly still present today; for example, the pastoral or picturesque landscape.[8]

The conventional (Western) landscape interpretations can form a starting point for exploring the ideas of other cultures and other places and for reflexively questioning landscape concepts anew.[9] Landscapes are interpretations of the environment; they show how people shape their geographies, territories and cities and how they can identify with them.[10] In the context of architecture, the question arises of 'landscape' as an idea, as a spatial composition, as articulation and as programme. Even so, it is not about replacing the notion of architecture with that of landscape. This is why a reference to 'landscape-ness' was chosen here, focussing on the genesis, presentation and effect of specific levels of understanding and of features.

Aktualisiert wird somit ein Primat übergeordneter Zusammenhänge der Um- und Mitwelt, wie sie auch in visionären Projekten von Künstler:innen, Intellektuellen und Architekt:innen seit den späten 1950er Jahren entwickelt wurden, beispielsweise im Umfeld des Team X, der Internationalen Situationisten oder der konzeptuellen Land Art von Robert Smithson.[5] Sie lenkten wie auch Architekt:innen und Planer:innen erneut seit den 1990er Jahren die Aufmerksamkeit auf die Felder des Vorhandenen im Sinne einer Verbindung von gebauten Strukturen, Freiraum, Erinnerungen und Erfahrungen, die differenziert beobachtet und benannt werden müssen, um neue Formen, Strukturen und Wahrnehmungsweisen zu generieren.[6] Immer wieder wird auch insbesondere die Heterogenität der in einem landschaftlich strukturierten Zusammenhang enthaltenen Spezies und Elemente hervorgehoben.[7]

Erneute Relevanz gewannen ebenso imaginative und phänomenologische Potenziale sowie politische Dimensionen, die mit der westlich-internationalen Geschichte der Landschaftsauffassungen und damit verbundener Landschaftsgestaltung eng verknüpft sind. Der Begriff findet sich früh in Bezug zu politisch ordnenden Strukturen und wurde seit der Renaissance weit verbreitet im Zusammenhang mit ästhetischen in der Landschaftsmalerei und Gartenkunst dargebotenen Charakteren, die in Teilen bis heute wirkmächtig sind wie die pastorale oder pittoreske Landschaft.[8]

Die konventionellen (westlichen) Landschaftsinterpretationen können einen Ausgangspunkt bilden, um Ideen anderer Kulturen und an anderen Orten zu untersuchen und dann nachfolgend reflexiv Landschaftskonzeptionen erneut zu befragen.[9] Landschaften sind Lesarten von Umwelt und zeigen auch, wie die Menschen ihre Geografien, Territorien und Städte formen und wie sie sich mit diesen identifizieren bzw. identifizieren können.[10] Im Kontext der Architektur stellt sich so die Frage nach ‚Landschaft' als Idee, als räumliche Komposition, als Artikulation und als Programm. Es geht aber dennoch nicht darum, den Begriff Architektur durch den der Landschaft zu ersetzen. Daher wurde hier eine Ausrichtung auf ‚Landschaftlichkeit' gewählt, mit der die Genese, Präsentation und Wirkung spezifischer Verständnisebenen und Eigenschaften fokussiert wird.

ARCHITECTURE AND LANDSCAPE   Descriptions and images of landscapes, as well as garden and park designs, have repeatedly incorporated individual architectures and architectural ensembles. Overall, however, these remain modest and subordinate in the spatial relation to wider environmental fabrics. Architecture is always a construction on a pre-existing site, which it changes and transforms irrevocably and whose individual character is influenced by the architectural object. The question of the locational relation as a parameter guiding the design is therefore of essential importance and has a long tradition in the theory and practice of architecture – and not only in relation to natural sites such as by rivers, forests, mountains or on plains.[11] In the contemporary fields of interpretation of landscape-ness in architecture, this basic constant is updated. It is linked with the potential to think, design and articulate the relations of buildings to their immediate surroundings and to the extension of a wider and more distant spatial continuum in new and different ways.[12] This is especially where one can see the interweaving with a changed perception of urban and urbanised contexts. The architectural projects are developed, observed and interpreted in relation to how they integrate into the surroundings or form landmarks; how they link indoor and outdoor space; how their transitions and continuums are articulated on an urban design or regional scale; and particularly how ecological interdependencies can be taken into account.[13]

ARCHITEKTUR UND LANDSCHAFT Beschreibungen und Bilder von Landschaften wie auch Garten- und Parkgestaltungen bezogen immer wieder einzelne Architekturen und architektonische Ensembles ein. Im Gesamten jedoch bleiben diese in der räumlichen Relation zu größeren Umgebungsgefügen zurückhaltend und untergeordnet. Architektur ist ihrerseits immer Konstruktion an einem präexistenten Ort, den sie unwiderruflich verändert, verwandelt und dessen individueller Charakter durch das architektonische Objekt mitgeprägt wird. Die Frage des Ortsbezugs als entwurfsleitendem Parameter hat daher essenzielle Bedeutung und eine lange Tradition in der Theorie und Praxis der Architektur – und das nicht nur bezogen auf naturräumliche Lagen beispielsweise an Flüssen, Wäldern, Bergen oder in Ebenen.[11] In den zeitgenössischen Deutungsfeldern des Landschaftlichen in der Architektur wird diese Grundkonstante aktualisiert, verbunden mit dem Potenzial, die Relationen von Gebäuden zur unmittelbaren Umgebung und zur Ausdehnung und Entfernung eines größeren räumlichen Kontinuums neu und anders zu denken, zu entwerfen und zu artikulieren.[12] Gerade darin zeigt sich die Verflechtung mit der veränderten Wahrnehmung urbaner und urbanisierter Kontexte. Die architektonischen Projekte werden entwickelt, beobachtet und gedeutet in Bezug auf die Weise, wie sie sich in die Umgebung einfügen oder Landmarken bilden, wie Innen- und Außenraum verbunden und ihre Übergänge und Kontinuen, auch im städtebaulichen oder regionalen Maßstab, artikuliert werden und nicht zuletzt wie ökologische Wirkungszusammenhänge berücksichtigt werden können.[13]

Overall, the widely ramified field of interpretations in the discourse about architecture and landscape also shows the attention to fundamental tectonic and aesthetic qualities of architectural volumes and spaces, especially since the 1990s. Specific terms have been proposed for some variants, such as landscrapers, groundscrapers, megaform or landform building.[14] A polarisation towards projects that seek a departure from familiar Cartesian and geometric building volume formulations through freely formed objects only presents one of the interpretations in this context.[15] Ideas and projects are thereby developed especially by means of an iterative process, with the possibilities of advanced software programmes. The external free forms and locational references correspond in the interior to continuities sought through the modulation of building components; for example, of the floors, walls and ceilings, which generate specific and also interpenetrating spatial arrangements.

It is the interweaving of complex spatial and physical appearances that guides the landscape analogies in association with natural physiognomies and fabrics.[16] This can also be observed in architectures that integrate fragmentations, irregular variety and complexity, free from the modulating organisation. Such projects are also interpreted as a landscape mode and, furthermore, are associated with newer natural science models of complexity, chaos theory or contemporary philosophical theories of the perception of reality, such as that of the rhizome of Gilles Deleuze and Felix Guattari.[17] This also shows how concepts can be historically and culturally contextualised and are formed depending on the interests and awareness of the time.

Insgesamt veranschaulicht das breit gefächerte Feld der Interpretationen im Diskurs um Architektur und Landschaft insbesondere seit den 1990er Jahren auch die Aufmerksamkeit für grundlegende tektonische und ästhetische Qualitäten architektonischer Körper und Räume. Für einige Varianten wurden spezifische Begriffe vorgeschlagen wie Landscrapers, Groundscrapers, Megaform oder Landform building.[14] Eine Polarisierung auf Projekte, die eine Loslösung von vertrauten kartesisch-geometrischen Baukörperformulierungen durch frei geformte Objekte suchen, bildet in diesem Kontext nur eine der Interpretationen.[15] Ideen und Projekte werden dabei vor allem durch einen iterativen Prozess mit den Möglichkeiten avancierter Softwareprogramme entwickelt. Den äußeren Freiformen und Lagebeziehungen entsprechen im Inneren durch Modulation von Bauteilen gesuchte Kontinuitäten beispielsweise von Boden, Wand und Decken, die spezifische, auch sich durchdringende Raumorganisationen erzeugen.

Es ist das Ineinandergreifen komplexer räumlicher und körperlicher Erscheinung, das in der Assoziation zu naturräumlichen Physignomien und Gefügen die Landschaftsanalogien leitet.[16] Dies kann ebenfalls bei Architekturen beobachtet werden, die, gelöst von der modulierenden Organisation, Fragmentierungen, irreguläre Vielfalt und Komplexität integrieren. Auch solche Projekte werden als Landschaftsmodus interpretiert und darüber hinaus verbunden mit neueren komplexitäts- und chaostheoretischen naturwissenschaftlichen Modellen oder zeitgenössischen philosophischen Theorien der Wirklichkeitserfassung wie der des Rhizoms von Gilles Deleuze und Felix Guattari.[17] Dies zeigt auch, wie Konzepte historisch-kulturell kontextualisiert sein können und sich abhängig von der Interessenlage und dem Bewusstsein einer Zeit bilden.

In the evolutionary process of modernity and industrialisation, one can already observe a latent attention to a variety of nature references. The garden city, the Broadacre City or the interweaving of cities and estates with green areas, light, air and sun are examples of this.[18] On the smaller scale of the architectural object, references to natural phenomena are expressed not only in the site-specific contextualisation of the building volume formulation. They are found also in the extension of building structures through outdoor walls; the integration of framed views out through windows and window-like wall openings; the layout of sunny terraces and roof gardens, as well as varying pathways into and within the buildings and the enrichment of the simple Cartesian space by means of more complex ensembles and the use of material features with a tactile or light effect. The theories and projects of Frank Lloyd Wright, Bruno Taut, Le Corbusier, and also of Mies van der Rohe, Hans Scharoun, Richard Neutra, Alvar Aalto or Oscar Niemeyer, to name just a few examples of so-called classical (Western) modernity and its early transformations, are multilayered, so that abbreviated interpretations cannot do them justice.[19] They were attempts to avoid making the connection of people and the environment unilaterally rationalistic and technical, as it can be the case in and through architecture. Architecture is the creation of a meaningful environment that is more than just necessary. Seen from this perspective, one can observe more differentiated analogies to landscape constructs in contemporary stances in architectural ideas, processes and projects. Answers that are all too quick should be avoided. The stated principal dimensions, however, are revealing with regard to what is possible.

Bereits im evolutionären Prozess der Moderne und Industrialisierung kann eine latente Aufmerksamkeit für Naturbezüge unterschiedlichen Charakters beobachtet werden. Die Gartenstadt, die Broadacre City oder die Durchdringung der Städte und Siedlungen mit Grünbereichen, Licht, Luft und Sonne sind Beispiele dafür.[18] Im kleineren Maßstab des architektonischen Objekts finden naturphänomenale Bezüge Ausdruck nicht nur in der ortsbezogenen Kontextualisierung der Baukörperformulierung. Sie finden sich auch in der Ausdehnung baulicher Strukturen durch Mauerzüge im Außenbereich, der Integration gerahmter Ausblicke durch Fenster und fensterartige Wandöffnungen, in der Anlage von Sonnenterrassen und Dachgärten, aber auch in wechselvollen Wegeführungen in die und innerhalb der Gebäude, in der Bereicherung des einfachen kartesischen Raums durch komplexere Gefüge sowie im Einsatz taktil wirkender Materialeigenschaften oder des Lichts.

Die Theorien und Projekte beispielsweise von Frank Lloyd Wright, Bruno Taut, Le Corbusier und auch Mies van der Rohe, von Hans Scharoun, Richard Neutra, Alvar Aalto oder Oscar Niemeyer, um nur einige Beispiele aus der sogenannten klassischen (westlichen) Moderne und ihrer frühen Transformationen zu nennen, sind vielschichtig und erschöpfen sich nicht in verkürzenden Interpretationen.[19] Es waren Versuche, die Verbindung von Menschen und Umwelt, wie sie auch in und durch Architekturen erfolgen kann, nicht rationalistisch und technisch zu vereinseitigen. Architektur ist die Schaffung einer bedeutungsvollen Umwelt, die mehr als nur notwendig ist. Aus dieser Perspektive betrachtet können Analogien zu Landschaftskonstrukten in zeitgenössischen Haltungen, in Ideen, Prozessen und Projekten der Architektur noch differenzierter beobachtet werden. Allzu schnelle Antworten sind hierbei zu vermeiden. Die angedeuteten prinzipiellen Dimensionen aber sind aufschlussreich im Hinblick auf das Mögliche.

LANDSCAPE-NESS AS ARCHITECTURAL IDEA   No 'grand narrative' is presented here but rather a future-relevant research programme for which a few different overlapping narratives are presented. This book is structured into three main chapters. Each of them seeks to illuminate a specific way of interpreting landscape-ness based on various international case studies and to present new design tasks and themes, along with their constellations, to reveal and sound out potential and to differentiate features.[20] Landscape-ness as architectural idea includes the idea and the artifact, as well as various manifestations and configurations. There is a focus on the three layers of 'Urban dimensions', 'Green architecture:Green city' and 'Space formation and material', which are presented together with the conceptual tool of discourse contextualisation. The contextualisation is by means of architectural and interdisciplinary themes that have emerged in recent decades in relation to landscape, environment, architecture and urban design, namely urban assemblage, urban landscape, sustainability and biophilia, as well as topology and atmosphere. On the one hand, these frameworks allow for the opening of various contexts of understanding and their incorporation into observations and analyses. On the other hand, their overlapping also generates iterative changes in perspective, which promote a process of ongoing adjustments. The reflexivity to which this relational field then leads can be a fertile ground for generating further insights and tools.

LANDSCHAFTLICHKEIT ALS ARCHITEKTURIDEE   Hier präsentiert wird keine ‚große Erzählung', eher ein zukunftsrelevantes Forschungsprogramm, von dem zunächst einige unterschiedliche Narrative vorgestellt werden, die noch dazu Überschneidungen aufweisen. Das vorliegende Buch ist in drei Hauptkapitel strukturiert. Jedes davon versucht eine spezifische Weise der Interpretation von Landschaftlichkeit an unterschiedlichen internationalen Case Studies zu erhellen und neue Entwurfsaufgaben und Themen sowie ihre Konstellationen vorzustellen, um Potenziale zu erschließen und auszuloten sowie Eigenschaften zu differenzieren.[20] Landschaftlichkeit als Architekturidee schließt die Idee und das Artefakt respektive verschiedene Manifestionen und Konfigurationen ein. Dabei erfolgt eine Konzentration auf die drei Layer ‚Urbane Dimensionen', ‚Grüne Architektur:Grüne Stadt', sowie ‚Raumformation und Material', die zusammen mit dem konzeptuellen Werkzeug der Diskurskontextualisierung dargeboten werden. Die Kontextualisierung erfolgt mit innerarchitektonischen und interdiziplinären Themen, die in den letzten Jahrzehnten in Bezug zu Landschaft, Umwelt, Architektur und Städtebau hervorgetreten sind: Urbane Assemblage, Urbane Landschaft, Nachhaltigkeit und Biophilie sowie Topologie und Atmosphäre. Diese Rahmungen ermöglichen einerseits, verschiedene Verstehenskontexte zu öffnen und in die Beobachtungen und Analysen einzubeziehen. Andererseits erzeugen deren Überschneidungen auch iterative Perspektivwechsel, die einen Prozess fortlaufender Justierungen befördern. Die Reflexivität, zu der dieses relationale Feld dann leitet, kann ein Nährboden sein, um weitere Erkenntnisse und Instrumente zu generieren.

'Urban dimensions' thematises currently increasing programmatic and spatial combinations of architecture and open spaces into architectural ensembles, often with hybrid programmes. 'Green architecture:Green city' thematises the use of plants for CO_2-balance, as well as for recreation purposes for people, using also technically researched, climate-effective high-tech compartments, while illuminating some design-related dimensions of biophilia. 'Spatial formation and material' focuses on various especially aesthetic and socially effective features of architecture, with their specifics and contextual relationships. This field comprises a whole range of visible, tangible spatial formations and can be associated with guiding principles of the modern tradition, such as those of fluid space, the architectural promenade or references to place in architecture and urban design. In contemporary examples, they are considered further and developed in a physical form with regard to their configurations, as well as to relational understandings of spatial formations and atmospheres.

Every variant can show different aspects. But they all illuminate the relevance of setting values in architectural design and in the product as well as in specific facets of landscape-ness as architectural idea. Even if the selected examples are not exhaustive, they still show a multifaceted spectrum that can be understood as a gravitational field that accentuates and highlights how new high quality habitats can be created through landscape-ness in the built environment. They also show seismographically which specific possibilities architects and architectures can take in relation to sustainable transformations. To understand the 'how' of these articulations, the theoretical resources of landscape-ness concepts as well as contexts of the building task are introduced, in order to then present the 'how' of the answers in descriptions, analyses and comments based on examples.

‚Urbane Dimensionen' thematisiert zeitgenössisch zunehmende programmatische und räumliche Verknüpfungen von Architekturen und Freiräumen
zu architektonischen Ensembles mit oftmals hybriden Programmen. ‚Grüne
Architektur:Grüne Stadt' thematisiert die Verwendung von Pflanzen zur
CO_2-Balance ebenso wie zur Erholung der Menschen auch mit ingenieur-
technisch erforschten, klimawirksamen Hightech-Kompartimenten und beleuchtet ebenfalls einige entwurfsbezogene Dimensionen von Biophilie.
‚Raumformation und Material' fokussiert verschiedene vor allem ästhetisch
und sozial wirksame Eigenschaften von Architekturen in ihrer Spezifik und
ihren kontextuellen Bezügen. Dieses Feld umfasst einen ganzen Fächer
sichtbarer, spürbarer Raumformationen und kann mit Leitideen der modernen Tradition wie der des fließenden Raumes, der architektonischen
Promenade oder der Ortsbezüge in Architektur und Städtebau verbunden werden. In den zeitgenössischen Beispielen werden sie weitergedacht
und in der physischen Gestalt entwickelt im Hinblick auf ihre Konfigurationen sowie in Bezug auf relationale Verständnisse räumlicher Formationen
und Atmosphären.

Jede Variante kann verschiedene Aspekte aufzeigen. Alle aber verdeutlichen
die Relevanz von Wertsetzungen im Architekturentwurf und im Produkt sowie
in spezifischen Facetten von Landschaftlichkeit als Architekturidee. Auch wenn
die ausgesuchten Beispiele zusammen nicht das Ganze enthalten, so zeigen
sie doch ein facettenreiches Spektrum, das als ein Gravitationsfeld verstanden
werden kann, das akzentuiert und pointiert, wie durch Landschaftlichkeit in der
gebauten Umwelt neue qualitätsvolle Habitate entstehen können. Sie zeigen
seismografisch ebenfalls, welche spezifischen Möglichkeitsräume Architekt:in-
nen und Architekturen in Bezug auf nachhaltige Transformationen einnehmen
können. Um das ‚Wie' dieser Artikulationen zu verstehen, werden jeweils zunächst die theoretischen Ressourcen der Landschaftlichkeitskonzepte sowie
Kontexte der Bauaufgabe vorgestellt, um dann das ‚Wie' der jeweiligen Antwort in Beschreibung, Analyse und Kommentierung an Beispielen vorzustellen.

As an introduction, the profile, stance and some exemplary projects of the office are outlined, finally concluding the specific repertoire that is fundamentally available as a potential for the architectural designs with a landscape character. The selection of examples was strategic and re-search-orientated, in order to illuminate various themes in a significant and multifaceted manner. In the majority of cases, examples were select-ed where an on-site analysis could be carried out with its cultural contex-tualisation corresponding to the field of competence of the author. There was no shying away from presenting international architecture examples that could also be viewed critically in connection with the relevant themes, because, for example, they could be associated as star architecture with the quick and conspicuous attention-seeking mode of the iconic, as well as with successful architects to whom innovative and responsible stances are only accorded to a limited extent. Due to this, approaches that pro-vide impulses for other relevant areas of architectural development are sometimes overlooked. The outlining of the repertoire makes it possible to trigger further questions and perspectives for research and practice.

The idea of landscape-ness prompts the question of which special features of architecture projects on different scales can show potentials and possibil-ities regarding the current challenges of the relations between humans and the environment, in contexts in which habitats are interpenetrated by digi-tal technologies and where climate change on a global scale has changed longstanding connections between architecture and landscape. Going be-yond the sustainable and measured handling of resources, which is con-stantly being addressed and developed further in a lot of in-depth research, the focus here is on qualities of the integration of architecture and open space; on the linking of various public, semi-public and private programme components as well as on the aesthetic connection of people, architecture and the environment. Not least, the impact of architectural articulations is addressed, which accords a higher importance to aesthetic sensitisa-tion and the differentiated promotion of an awareness of sustainability.

Einleitend werden jeweils das Profil, die Haltung und einige exemplarische Projekte des Büros sowie abschließend das jeweils spezifische Repertoire skizziert, das als Potenzial für landschaftlich geprägte Architekturentwürfe wie auch grundlegend zur Verfügung steht. Die Auswahl der Beispiele erfolgte forschungsorientiert, strategisch, um verschiedene Themen signifikant und facettiert zu erhellen. In den überwiegenden Fällen wurden Fallbeispiele gewählt, deren Vor-Ort-Analyse durchgeführt werden konnte und deren kulturelle Kontextualisierung dem Kompetenzbereich der Autorin entspricht. Es wurde dabei nicht gescheut, auch internationale Architekturbeispiele vorzustellen, die von anderer Seite möglicherweise im Zusammenhang mit der anstehenden Thematik auch kritisch betrachtet werden können, weil sie beispielsweise als Stararchitektur mit dem schnellen und auffälligen Aufmerksamkeitsmodus des Ikonischen in Zusammenhang gebracht werden könnten sowie mit erfolgreichen Architekturschaffenden, denen immer wieder innovative wie auch verantwortliche Positionen nur bedingt zugestanden werden. Dadurch werden impulsgebende Ansätze für andere relevante Bereiche der Architekturentwicklung manchmal geradezu übersehen. Die Skizzierung des Repertoires ermöglicht es, weitere Fragen und Perspektiven für Forschung und Praxis anzustoßen.

Mit der Idee von Landschaftlichkeit wird nach besonderen Merkmalen von Architekturprojekten in unterschiedlichen Maßstäben gefragt, die zu gegenwärtigen Herausforderungen der Relationen von Menschen und Umwelt Potenziale und Möglichkeitsräume aufzeigen können, in Kontexten, in denen Lebenswelten von digitalen Technologien durchsetzt sind und der Klimawandel im planetarischen Maßstab langwährende Verbindungen von Architektur und Landschaft veränderte. Hinausreichend über den nachhaltigen und maßvollen Umgang mit Ressourcen, der in zahlreichen profunden Forschungen stets erweitert thematisiert und entwickelt wird, richtet sich der Blick hier auf Qualitäten der Integration von Architektur und Freiraum, auf die Verknüpfung verschiedener öffentlicher, halb öffentlicher und privater Programmbausteine wie auch auf die ästhetische Verbindung von Menschen, Architektur und Umwelt. Nicht zuletzt ist dabei eine Wirksamkeit architektonischer Artikulationen angesprochen, die der ästhetischen Sensibilisierung und der differenzierten Förderung nachhaltigen Bewusstseins einen erhöhten Stellenwert beimessen.

1 Cf. | Vgl. Christian Schäfer, Idee/Form/Gestalt/Wesen, in: id. (ed.), Platon-Lexikon. Begriffswörterbuch zu Platon und der platonischen Tradition, Darmstadt: Wiss. Buchgesellschaft 2007, 157–165, 157; https://www.merriam-webster.com/dictionary/idea, 1.4.2022; https://www.merriam-webster.com/dictionary/ideal, 1.4.2022   **2** Cf. | Vgl. European Landscape Convention, on: | auf: https://www.coe.int/en/web/landscape, 1.4.2022; Meto J. Vroom, Landscape, in: id. (ed.), Lexicon of garden and landscape architecture, Basel: Birkhäuser 2006, 177–180, 177   **3** Cf. for example | Vgl. beispielsweise Kenneth R. Olwig, The meanings of landscape, London et al.: Routledge 2019, 9–12; Simone Linke, Die Ästhetik medialer Landschaftskonstrukte, Wiesbaden: Springer VS 2018, 22–27; Ed Wall/Tim Waterman, Introduction, in: ids. (eds.), Landscape agency. Critical essays, London: Routledge 2018, 1–6, 2–4; Ross Exo Adams, Landscapes of post-history, in: ibid., 7–17, 7–14; Marc Antrop/Veerle vam Eetvelde, Landscape perspectives. The holistic nature of landscape, Dordrecht: Springer 2017, 57, 62–71 and | und 331; Jane Bennett/Klaus K. Loenhart, Vibrant matter. Zero landscape (Interview), in: Klaus K. Loenhart (ed.), Zero landscape. Unfolding active agencies of landscape, Wien et al.: Springer 2011, 14–25, 23–24   **4** Cf. for example | Vgl. beispielsweise Pietro Valle, Wanderlust, in: Kristin Feireiss (ed.), Paradise-Remix, München: Prestel 2006, 350–356, 350; Anthony Vidler, The architectural uncanny, Cambridge, MA: MIT Press 1994, 130; Mirko Zardini, Green is the color, in: Arc en Rêve Centre d'Architecture/Rem Koolhaas (eds.), Mutations, Barcelona: ACTAR 2000, 434–437 or the interpretations in which the mentioned aspects are weighted differently in: | oder die die genannten Aspekte verschieden gewichtenden Interpretationen in: Moshen Mostafavi (ed.), Landscape urbanism. A manual for the machinic landscape, London: Architectural Association 2003   **5** Cf. | Vgl. Yorgos Simeoforidis, Notes for a cultural history. Between uncertainty and the contemporary urban condition, in: Arc en Rêve Centre d'Architecture/Rem Koolhaas (eds.) 2000, op. cit. (note | Anm. 4), 414–424; Aaron Betsky, Landscrapers. Building with the land, London: Thames & Hudson 2002, 10–12 and | und 18–19   **6** Cf. for example | Vgl. beispielsweise O.M.A./Rem Koolhaas/Bruce Mau, S,M,L,XL, New York, NY: Rizzoli 1995, 1238–1264; Karl Ganser cit. in | zit. in: Tom Sieverts, Zwischenstadt zwischen Ort und Welt, Raum und Zeit, Stadt und Land, Braunschweig et al.: Birkhäuser 1997, 68; Karl Ganser, Stadt frisst Landschaft - Landschaft frisst Stadt, in: Diethild Kornhardt/Gabriele Pütz/Thies Schröder (eds.), Mögliche Räume, Stadt schafft Landschaft, Hamburg: Junius 2002, 82–91, 88   **7** Cf. for example | Vgl. beispielsweise Hélène Frichot, Creative ecologies. Theorizing the practice of architecture, London et al.: Bloomsbury 2019, 38–43; Anna Tsing, The buck, the bull, and the dream of the stag. Some unexpected weeds of the Anthropocene, in: Suomen anthropologi 42(2017)/1, 3–21, 7 and | und passim; Olaf Bastian, Die Grundlagen der Landschaftsplanung als interdisziplinärer Forschungsansatz, in: Klaus Beyer/Dieter Scholz (eds.), Landschaft – Theorie, Praxis und Planung, Leipzig et al.: Hirzel 2000, 21–28   **8** Cf. | Vgl. Hilmar Frank, Landschaft, in: Karlheinz Barck (ed.), Ästhetische Grundbegriffe, Bd. 3, Stuttgart: Metzler 2001, 617–665, 618–620; on this in detail | hierzu ausführlich John Binkerhoff Jackson, Land-

schaften. Ein Resümee (1984), in: Brigitte Franzen/Stefanie Krebs (eds.), Landschaftstheorie, Köln: König 2005, 29–44, 32–38   **9** Cf. | Vgl. Peter Wynn Kirby, Lost in 'space'. An anthropological approach to movement, in: id. (ed.), Boundless worlds. An anthropological approach to movement, Oxford: Berghahn 2009, 1–27, 13–17   **10** Cf. | Vgl. James Corner, in: id. /Kim Megson, Interview, in: Cladmag (2017)2, on: | auf: https://www.clad-global.com/architecture-design-features?codeid=31801&source=home&p=11,   5.9.2021; Peter Jacobs, De/Re/In(form)ing landscape, in: Simon Swaffield (ed.), Theory in landscape architecture, Philadelphia, PA: University of Pennsylvania Press 2002, 116–122, 119–120   **11** Cf. | Vgl. Vittorio Gregotti, Il terrotorio dell'architettura, 2. ed. Mailand: Fetrinelli 1988; Christian Norberg-Schulz, Genius loci. Towards a phenomenology of architecture, New York, NY: Rizzoli 1980; Tomás Valena, Beziehungen. Über den Ortsbezug in der Architektur, Berlin: Ernst 1994   **12** Cf. on this also | Vgl. hierzu auch Aaron Betsky 2002, op. cit. (note | Anm. 5), 192; Richard Ingersoll, The critical picturesque. Auf der Suche nach einer Theorie der Architektur, Hamburg: Material-Verl. 2004, 9 and | und 20   **13** Cf. | Vgl. Eduard Bru/Museu d'Art Contemporani de Barcelona (eds.), Nuevos paisajes. New landscapes, Barcelona: ACTAR 1997   **14** Cf. | Vgl. Kenneth Frampton, Megaform as urban landscape. Ann Arbor, MI: The University of Michigan 1999, passim; Aaron Betsky, Landscrapers. Building with the land, New York, NY: Thames & Hudson 2002, passim; Andreas Ruby/Ilka Ruby, Groundscapes. The rediscovery of the ground in contemporary architecture, Barcelona: Gustavo Gili 2006; Stan Allen/Marc Mc Quade, Landform building. Architecture's new terrain, Baden: Lars Müller 2011   **15** Cf. for example | Vgl. beispielsweise Mark Lee, Die holländische Savanne. Architektur als topologische Landschaften, in: Daidalos 73 (1999), 9–15; Marc Angélil/Anna Klingmann, Hybride Morphologien. Infrastruktur, Architektur, Landschaft, in: ibid., 16–25   **16** Cf. on this also | Vgl. dazu auch Béatrice Simonot, Forces et forme, in: Marie-Ange Brayer/Béatrice Simonot (eds.), ArchiLab 2002: L'économie de la terre, Orléans: HXP 2002, 10–11; Manuel Gausa, Otras naturalezas urbanas, Barcelona: Generalitat Valenciana 2001, 40 and | und 265   **17** Cf. | Vgl. Susannah Hagan, Taking Shape. A new contract between architecture and nature, Oxford: Oxford Architectural Press 2001, 35; Aaron Betsky 2002, op. cit. (note | Anm. 5), 9–10; Charles Jencks, The new paradigm in architecture, New Haven, CT et al.: Yale University Press, 234–284   **18** Cf. on this also | Vgl. dazu auch Fritz Neumeyer, Im Zauberland der Peripherie. Das Verschwinden der Stadt in der Landschaft, in: Heinz Liesbrock/Westfälischer Kunstverein (eds.), Die verstädterte Landschaft, München: Aries 1995, 31–43, 34   **19** Cf. for example | Vgl. beispielsweise Marc Treib, Landscapes of modern architecture, New Haven, CT et al.: Yale University Press 2016, 140–145, 183–184 and | und passim; David Leatherbarrow, Topographical stories. Studies in landscape and architecture, Philadelphia, PA: University of Pennsylvania Press 2004, 94–97 and | und 246–250; Sarah Menin/Flora Samuel, Nature and space: Aalto and Le Corbusier, New York, NY: Taylor & Francis 2003   **20** Cf. on this also | Vgl. hierzu auch Hans Blumenberg, Theorie der Unbegrifflichkeit, Frankfurt a. M. 2007, 7

URBANE DIMENSIONEN
URBAN DIMENSIONS

Everyday notions of landscape and landscape-ness tend to be associated with harmonious and ideal places for recreation and leisure, as well as with spaces and areas that lie outside of cities. It may therefore appear unusual in the first instance to forge a connection with urbanity. However, it is precisely this that allows basic features of landscape-ness and its dimensions to become evident as an architectural idea, in association with everyday living environments as well as with special places.

For urban contexts, there have been a variety of proposals in recent decades for linking architecture, urban design and landscape architecture with a rich typological and dynamic character. The following approach is taken with reference to the urban theory perspective of 'urban assemblage' and the design theory concept of 'urban landscape'. As products of intellectual construction and as a basis or interpretation of design action, in particular in relation to aspects of programme, physical spatial design manifestation and associated appropriation potential, their combinations allow certain components and qualitative potentials of landscape-ness to be characterised, questioned and contextualised more specifically as an architectural idea in different impact fields.

In Alltagsauffassungen treten Vorstellungen von Landschaft und Landschaft-lichkeit immer wieder in Verbindung mit harmonischen idealen Orten der Erholung und Rekreation auf und mit Räumen und Orten, die außerhalb der Städte liegen. Daher mag es ungewöhnlich erscheinen, zunächst einen Zu-sammenhang mit Urbanität aufzuspannen. Gerade in dieser Weise jedoch können Grundzüge von Landschaftlichkeit als Architekturidee in ihren Di-mensionen deutlich werden, in Verbindung mit alltäglichen Lebensumwel-ten ebenso wie mit besonderen Orten.

Für städtische Kontexte wurden in den letzten Jahrzehnten unterschiedliche Varianten der Verknüpfung von Architektur, Städtebau und Landschaftsarchi-tektur mit einem reichhaltigen typologischen sowie dynamischem Charakter vorgeschlagen. Die folgende Annäherung wird hier im Blick auf die stadt-theoretische Perspektive ‚Urbane Assemblage' und das entwurfstheoretische Konzept ‚Urbane Landschaft' vorgenommen. Als Produkte intellektueller Konstruktion wie als Basis oder Interpretation entwerferischer Aktion ermög-lichen deren Mischungen, insbesondere bezogen auf Aspekte von Programm und physischer raumgestalterischer Manifestation sowie damit verbundener Aneignungspotenziale, einige Komponenten und qualitative Potenziale von Landschaftlichkeit als Architekturidee in unterschiedlichen Wirkungsfeldern spezifischer zu charakterisieren, zu befragen und zu kontextualisieren. 33

URBAN ASSEMBLAGE   In the fine arts, assemblage refers to works of art that include a combination of a variety of also non-artistic materials or objects with a three-dimensional effect, whereby the individual elements retain a certain degree of autonomy in relation to the other parts and the whole, despite the connections and transitions.[1] In a similar way, assemblage has also been interpreted for the characterisation of social complexity. Here interaction gains special importance, as opposed to a focus on individual subjects or the whole.[2] Prompted in addition by the interpretation of 'assemblage' according to the French philosophers Gilles Deleuze and Felix Guattari, in the sense of forming temporary constellations of different elements as well as of processuality instead of stable states, this view was not only incorporated into various sociocultural concepts such as the actor-network theory, New Materialism or scientific theory but also into urbanistic and architectural approaches.[3] The city is thereby viewed as a fabric of a wide range of relationships and networks, composed of elements that can be human and non-human, organic and inorganic, as well as technical and natural.[4] Actors and their behaviours, as well as the material and immaterial, can be just as much a part of it as the linking of the existing with future-orientated possibilities in the sense of urban transformation. Despite the vital power of the individual parts, urban assemblages can exert an overarching impact, formed by the potential of their joint presence.

URBANE ASSEMBLAGE   In den bildenden Künsten wird von Assemblage gesprochen, wenn die künstlerischen Werke aus einer Kombination verschiedenster, auch nicht-künstlerischer Materialien oder Gegenstände mit dreidimensionaler Wirksamkeit bestehen, wobei die einzelnen Elemente jeweils gegenüber anderen Teilen und dem Ganzen trotz der Verknüpfungen und Übergänge einen gewissen Grad an Autonomie bewahren.[1] In ähnlicher Weise wurde Assemblage auch zur Charakterisierung sozialer Komplexität interpretiert. Hier erhält gegenüber einem Fokus auf Einzelsubjekte oder die Gemeinschaft die Interaktion ein besonderes Gewicht.[2] Angeregt zudem durch die Interpretation von Assemblage im Denken der französischen Philosophen Gilles Deleuze und Felix Guattari im Sinne der Ausbildung provisorischer Konstellationen verschiedener Elemente sowie von Prozessualität anstelle von stabilen Zuständen fand diese Sichtweise nicht nur Aufnahme in unterschiedlichen sozio-kulturellen Konzepten wie der Akteur-Netzwerk-Theorie, dem Neuen Materialismus oder der Wissenschaftstheorie, sondern im Weiteren auch in urbanistischen und architektonischen Ansätzen.[3] Stadt wird dabei als ein Gefüge aus verschiedensten Beziehungen und Netzwerken gesehen, komponiert aus Elementen, die menschlich und nichtmenschlich, organisch und unorganisch sowie technisch und natürlich sein können.[4] Akteur:innen und ihre Verhaltensweisen sowie Materielles und Immaterielles können dabei ebenso Anteile bilden wie die Verknüpfung von Vorhandenem mit zukunftsweisenden Möglichkeitsräumen im Sinne urbaner Transformation. Trotz der vitalen Kraft der einzelnen Teile kann eine übergreifende Wirksamkeit urbaner Assemblagen entstehen, die sich aus den Potenzialen ihrer gemeinsamen Anwesenheit bildet.

URBAN LANDSCAPE   Like these urban theory analyses, the concept of 'Landscape Urbanism' also incorporates processes, methods and actors, as well as governance in the field of planning, while design potential and therefore also various structural-spatial forms, and the relevance of physical manifestations, also represent an emphasised point of focus. At the least since the beginning of the 21st century, prompted by Anglo-American impulses, the conceptualisation of urban landscapes has become one of the leading topics in spatial design professions. The focus is thereby shifted from the core/periphery model and the opposition of city and countryside to a notion that views the urban type as a more fragmented and discontinuous matrix in the sense of a topological field structure, as also comparably described in influential theoretical statements by Rem Koolhaas.[5] Furthermore, the appreciation of design culture, especially of landscape architecture in the context of urban developments, was high-lighted.[6] The work on process structures, across different scales and with the aim of adaptability, is described thereby as a guiding basis, orientated towards resilience and contextuality.[7] In addition, what appears relevant is the focusing of horizontal field conditions, which consider and deal with open space, infrastructure and architectural objects as environmentally constitutive and design-relevant factors in their interaction, in order to develop innovative habitats of the future through imagination and creative effort and to enable and stimulate social interaction in a rich urban diversity.[8] This updates one of the historical levels of meaning of landscape, in which sociocultural contexts, habitualised activities and dimensions of spaces are integrated.[9]

URBANE LANDSCHAFT   Wie in diesen stadttheoretischen Analysen sind auch im Konzept des ‚Landscape Urbanism' Prozesse, Methodiken und Akteur:innen sowie Governance im Planungsbereich einbezogen, doch bilden dabei entwerferische Potenziale und damit auch verschiedene baulich-räumliche Erscheinungsformen sowie die Relevanz physischer Manifestationen einen ebenfalls hervorgehobenen Fokus. Spätestens seit Beginn des 21. Jahrhunderts wurde, ausgehend von anglo-amerikanischen Impulsen, die Konzeptualisierung urbaner Landschaften zu einem der leitenden Themen in raumentwerferischen Professionen. Dabei wird der Fokus vom Kern/Peripherie-Modell sowie der Gegenüberstellung von Stadt und Land zu einer Vorstellung verschoben, die den urbanen Typus eher als fragmentiertere und diskontinuierliche Matrix im Sinne einer topologischen Feldstruktur auffasst wie sie vergleichbar auch in einflussreichen theoretischen Statements von Rem Koolhaas beschrieben wurde.[5] Zudem wurde die Aufwertung der Entwurfskultur insbesondere der Landschaftsarchitektur im Kontext urbaner Entwicklungen propagiert.[6] Das Arbeiten an Prozessstrukturen, über Maßstäbe hinweg und mit dem Ziel der Anpassungsfähigkeit, wird dabei als leitende auf Resilienz und Kontextualität ausgerichtete Grundlage beschrieben.[7] Wesentlich erscheint darüber hinaus die Fokussierung horizontaler Feldbedingungen, die Freiraum, Infrastruktur und architektonische Objekte als umweltkonstitutive und entwurfsrelevante Faktoren in ihrem Zusammenwirken denkt und behandelt, um mittels Imagination und kreativer Anstrengungen innovative Habitate der Zukunft zu entwickeln und soziale Interaktion in einer reichen urbanen Vielfalt zu ermöglichen und zu stimulieren.[8] Damit wird eine der historischen Bedeutungsebenen von Landschaft aktualisiert, in der sozio-kulturelle Kontexte, habitualisierte Aktivitäten und Dimensionen von Räumen integriert sind.[9]

LANDSCAPE-NESS   Various combinations of the two described concepts, which bypass strict and narrowly confined connotations, can be interpreted as variants of landscape-ness as an architectural idea. There is a particular focus on the formative and programmatic potential of architectural and urban concepts and projects. Multiple as well as competing relations of architecture and public space, architectural object and open space emerge, as well as spatial production through the interaction of various agencies of the natural, artistic, experienced, social and built environment. Which properties and entities play a special role in this and how differently such entities can be constituted are explored and reflected on in the following, based on the example of concepts and projects by the international architecture offices Diller Scofidio + Renfro, New York, along with BIG, Copenhagen and MVRDV, Rotterdam. The shifting of familiar perspectives and established concepts is differentiated through the analysis and comparison of different stances. These are coupled with different project ideas, which in their shape and programmatic mixing characterise the concepts and designs as well as their compatibility.

In accordance with the respective specific profile of the architects, the analysis and commenting of the exemplary stances have a differing structure. In the case of Diller Scofidio + Renfro, whose thinking and work is defined by a strong interweaving with artistic conception and articulation, this dimension is presented in greater detail in order to get to know the reflexive basic concept of the architecture. The relation to landscape-ness therein represents a special connection, amongst others, to contemporary cultural conditions and to conventions of the architecture discipline, which are questioned in the works. For architectural and urbanistic projects and combinations thereof, further dimensions also come into play, which can be associated in other ways with concepts of landscape-ness as an architectural idea.

LANDSCHAFTLICHKEIT   Diverse Kombinationen der beiden beschriebenen Konzepte, die starre und eng umgrenzte Konnotationen um-
gehen, können als Varianten von Landschaftlichkeit als Architekturidee
interpretiert werden. Insbesondere fokussiert wird das formative und programmatische Potenzial architektonischer und urbaner Konzepte und Projekte. Dabei treten multiple und auch konkurrierende Relationen von Architektur
und öffentlichem Raum, architektonischem Objekt und Freiraum hervor sowie
die Raumproduktion durch das Zusammenwirken unterschiedlicher Agencies
natürlicher, künstlicher, gelebter, sozialer und gebauter Umwelt. Welche
Eigenschaften und Gefüge dabei im Besonderen eine Rolle spielen und wie
unterschiedlich solche Gefüge konstituiert sein können, wird nachfolgend
am Beispiel von Konzepten und Projekten der international arbeitenden
Architekturbüros Diller Scofidio + Renfro, New York, BIG, Kopenhagen, und
MVRDV, Rotterdam, erkundet und reflektiert. Verschiebungen vertrauter Perspektiven und etablierter Konzepte zeichnen sich aus Analyse und Vergleich
verschiedener Positionen differenzierter ab. Diese sind mit unterschiedlichen
Projektideen gekoppelt, die gestalterisch und in der programmatischen Mischung die Konzepte und Entwürfe sowie ihre Anschlussfähigkeit prägen.

Dem jeweils spezifischen Profil der Architekturschaffenden entsprechend sind
Analyse und Kommentierung der exemplarischen Positionen unterschiedlich
aufgebaut. Bei Diller Scofidio + Renfro, deren Denken und Schaffen durch
eine starke Verflechtung mit künstlerischer Konzeption und Artikulation geprägt ist, wird diese Dimension zunächst ausführlicher vorgestellt, um die
reflexive Grundkonzeption des Architekturschaffens kennenzulernen. Der
Bezug zur Landschaftlichkeit bildet darin eine besondere unter anderen Verbindungen zu zeitgenössischen kulturellen Konditionen und zu Konventionen der Architekturdisziplin, die in den Arbeiten befragt werden. Bei architektonischen und urbanistischen Projekten bzw. deren Vermischung, treten
noch weitere Dimensionen hinzu, die noch in anderer Weise mit Konzepten von Landschaftlichkeit als Architekturidee verbunden werden können.   39

In the case of the Bjarke Ingels Group (BIG) with their interdisciplinary work, relations between architectural ideas and landscape-ness become evident especially in theoretical statements and media presence, as well as in the individual project concepts. In this case, therefore, positions and especially the concepts of various projects are presented in order to uncover the further exploration of the repertoire of landscape-ness as an architectural idea. And finally, for the architecture firm MVRDV, which has a similar pragmatic orientation to BIG, one can speak of a researching, experimental and pop-cultural approach. The spectrum of differentiated interpretations and articulations is extended in the process, especially in association with contemporary conditions of architecture and culture and questions about various impulses for a multifaceted spectrum of components for the imagination of landscape-ness as architectural idea.

The aim is to unfold a design-related practice theory through the invitation to understand landscape-ness as an architectural idea and as a relevant reading and design concept for different projects in urban space. The transdisciplinary constitution of the referenced theoretical models of 'urban assemblage' and 'urban landscape' is taken into consideration in this but is not the primary focus. Interest is directed towards architectural ideas and projects, respectively architectural aspects of projects, which are often also developed within a team and in cooperation with landscape architects or engineers, or are enriched by landscape architecture expertise and design. The question of landscape-ness as architectural idea emphasises the individual and collective agency of designers and planners, as well as of the projects themselves, with a view to generating, accompanying and triggering qualitative transformations in an urban context through the architectural interventions.[10] This catalytic role also includes the integration of thoughts on flexibility, openness to appropriation and continuous change, which are in part intended and may in part be informal.

Bei der ebenfalls interdisziplinär arbeitenden Bjarke Ingels Group werden Relationen von Architekturideen und Landschaftlichkeit insbesondere an theoretischen Statements und medialer Präsenz sowie in den einzelnen Projektkonzeptionen deutlich. Daher werden in diesem Fall Positionierungen und insbesondere die Vorstellung diverser Projekte dargeboten, um die weiterführende Erkundung des Repertoires von Landschaftlichkeit als Architekturidee zu eruieren. Und schließlich kann bei dem wie BIG pragmatisch orientierten Architekturbüro MVRDV von einem forschend experimentellen und popkulturellen Herangehen gesprochen werden. Das Spektrum differenzierter Interpretationen und Artikulationen wird dabei noch erweitert, insbesondere verknüpft mit zeitgenössischen Konditionen von Architektur und Kultur und Fragen nach verschiedenen Impulsen für ein facettenreiches Spektrum von Komponenten zur Imagination von Landschaftlichkeit als Architekturidee.

Ziel ist die Entfaltung entwurfsbezogener Praxistheorie mit der Einladung, Landschaftlichkeit als Architekturidee als eine relevante Lesart und Entwurfskonzeption unterschiedlicher Projekte im urbanen Raum zu begreifen. Die transdisziplinäre Verfasstheit der referenzierten theoretischen Modelle ‚Urbane Assemblage' und ‚Urbane Landschaft' wird dabei berücksichtigt, bildet aber nicht den primären Fokus. Das Interesse richtet sich auf architektonische Ideen und Projekte bzw. auf architektonische Anteile von Projekten, die oftmals auch im Team und in der Kooperation mit Landschaftsarchitekt:innen oder auch Ingenieur:innen entwickelt bzw. durch landschaftsarchitektonische Expertise und Gestaltung bereichert werden. Die Frage nach ‚Landschaftlichkeit als Architekturidee' betont dabei die individuelle und kollektive Agency von Entwerfenden und Planenden sowie der Projekte selbst im Hinblick darauf, qualitative Transformationen im urbanen Kontext durch die architektonischen Interventionen zu erzeugen, zu begleiten und anzustoßen.[10] Diese katalytische Rolle schließt auch die Integration des Denkens von Flexibilität, Aneignungsoffenheit und eines kontinuierlichen Wandels ein, die in Teilen intendiert werden, in Teilen aber auch informell erfolgen können.

LANDSCHAFTLICHKEIT ALS STADTRAUMERWEITERUNG
LANDSCAPE-NESS AS URBAN SPACE EXPANSION
DILLER SCOFIDIO + RENFRO

Even if landscape-ness is not explicitly referred to by Diller Scofidio + Renfro, their concepts and projects are characterised in a way that is interesting in the context of researching the potential of landscape-ness as architectural idea, among other things, because they open up various levels of understanding and possibilities for landscape-ness. What is special about this is a view of architecture that focuses on its interconnection with the surrounding space, as well as the wish to make a fundamental contribution to a 'democratisation of public space'. Aesthetic perception and participation, which are intended to be emphasised and stimulated by the spatial configuration as well as specific architectural elements of the buildings, are in the foreground. Diller Scofidio + Renfro (DS + R) conceive artistic installations, performances and buildings that display a wide variety of scales and functions, all the way up to large urban ensembles.

Auch wenn Landschaftlichkeit von Diller Scofidio + Renfro nicht explizit benannt wird, sind ihre Konzepte und Projekte in einer Weise charakterisiert, die im Kontext der Erforschung der Potenziale von Landschaftlichkeit als Architekturidee unter anderem deshalb interessant sind, weil sie verschiedene Verständnisebenen und Möglichkeitsräume des Landschaftlichen aufspannen. Das Besondere ist dabei eine Sicht auf Architektur, die ihre Verschränkung mit dem Umgebungsraum ebenso in den Mittelpunkt stellt wie den Wunsch, zu einer ‚Demokratisierung des öffentlichen Raums' grundlegend beizutragen. Ästhetische Wahrnehmung und Teilhabe, die durch die Raumkonfiguration sowie spezifische Architekturelemente der Gebäude in Szene gesetzt und stimuliert werden sollen, stehen dabei im Vordergrund. Diller Scofidio + Renfro (DS + R) konzipieren künstlerische Installationen, Performances und Bauwerke in verschiedensten Maßstäben und Funktionen bis hin zu großen urbanen Ensembles.

1–2 Slow House Long Island, NY 1991 Unbuilt

CONCEPTS   In the context of and influenced by the New York art scene, when their firm was first founded in New York in 1981, Elizabeth Diller and Ricardo Scofidio worked on projects with which they questioned architecture conventions through artistic means, as well as the relations between architecture, the human body, space and time, along with cultural conditions of the medially shaped perception of architecture and the environment.[11] They sought to open up analytical and catalytic fields of action.

The early artistic-conceptual projects by Diller + Scofidio displayed parallels to conceptual and performative constructions of exemplary situations as had been presented since the 1960s in Concept Art and Performance Art. In the way that Robert Smithson, Trisha Brown, Dan Graham or Gordon Matta-Clark questioned the real and virtual presence of spaces and called on viewers to see the rural, built, urban and medial environment in a new way, the works by Diller + Scofidio thematised the ways in which architecture and cultural spatial situations are created, perceived and conveyed.[12] A special role is accorded to dimensions of physical and mechanical movement, as well as to pictorial framing through real, virtual and technological 'windows'. In different configurations, these windows represent key ideas that are also important as perceptual tools also in their architectural and urbanistic projects. The uncompleted Slow House, designed on Long Island as a holiday home, features a curved formation like a sickle, whose rooms stretch dynamically from the door to a panoramic window facing the sea (fig. 1–2). With this analogous panoramic view, as well as with a virtual video image of the same view that can be played on a screen, Diller + Scofidio transform the environment of the house into a kind of 'ideal' view, which is preserved in the imagination of many people as a 'landscape' due to the plethora of media images.[13]

KONZEPTE   Im Kontext und beeinflusst von der New Yorker Kunstsze-
ne arbeiteten Elizabeth Diller und Ricardo Scofidio in ihrem 1981 in New
York gegründeten Büro anfänglich an Projekten, mit denen sie Architektur-
konventionen mit künstlerischen Mitteln ebenso befragten wie die Relationen von Architektur, menschlichem Körper, Raum und Zeit sowie kulturelle
Konditionen medial geprägter Wahrnehmung von Architektur und Umwelt.[11] Sie wollten analytisch und katalysatorisch Handlungsfelder öffnen.

Die frühen künstlerisch-konzeptuellen Projekte von Diller + Scofidio zeigten
darin Parallelen zu konzeptuellen und performativen Konstruktionen modell-
hafter Situationen wie sie seit den 1960er Jahren in der Concept Art und
Performance Art präsentiert wurden. Wie beispielsweise Robert Smithson,
Trisha Brown, Dan Graham oder Gordon Matta Clark reale und virtuelle
Präsenz von Räumen befragten und die Wahrnehmenden aufforderten, die
ländliche, gebaute, urbane und mediale Umgebung in neuer Weise zu sehen, thematisierten die Werke von Diller + Scofidio die Weisen, wie Architektur und kulturelle Raumsituationen geschaffen, wahrgenommen und vermittelt werden.[12] Eine besondere Rolle kommt Dimensionen der körperlichen
und mechanischen Bewegung sowie der bildhaften Rahmung durch reale,
virtuelle und technologische ,Fenster' zu. In unterschiedlichen Konfigurationen bilden diese ,Fenster' als Wahrnehmungsinstrumente wichtige Leitideen
auch in ihren architektonischen und urbanistischen Projekten. So zeigt das
auf Long Island als Ferienhaus entworfene und nicht vollendete Slow House
eine sichelartig gebogene Formation, deren Räume sich von der Tür bis zu
einem Panoramafenster zum Meer hin dynamisch erstrecken (Abb. 1–2).
Mit diesem analogen Panoramabild ebenso wie mit einem virtuellen Vi-
deobild desselben Ausblicks, das auf einem Bildschirm abgespielt werden
kann, wandeln Diller + Scofidio das Umfeld des Hauses in die Art von
,idealer' Aussicht, die aufgrund der vielfältigen Verbreitung in Medienbil-
dern in der Imagination vieler Menschen als ,Landschaft' gespeichert, ist.[13]

3 Blur Building Yverdon-les-Bains 2002

The Blur Building, designed for the Swiss Expo.02 and constructed in Yverdon-les-Bains in 2002, creates an artefact from water vapour in the form
of a cloud seemingly floating above the water of a lake. It represents an
example of creating an experience that goes beyond seeing and is interwoven with technologies on the one hand and location qualities on the
other (fig. 3).[14] Multisensory perception is heightened. Naturalness and artificiality overlap.[15] A picturesque landscape image, perception of the tides
and a wide range of sensory landscape perception through movement are
often associated with big parks within and outside of cities and are of particular importance in English and Japanese landscape garden traditions.[16]

Diller Scofidio + Renfro also reactivate landscape garden references in an
urban context with their designs. Some of their central projects can be referred to as crossings between architecture, landscape architecture, infrastructure and urban design, which furthermore also incorporate transdisciplinary approaches from the fine and performative arts in order to thematise and create cultures of perception and seeing. However, there is a
particular emphasis on the aim of extending public space. There is a repeated endeavour to counteract the increasing gentrification, privatisation
and commercialisation of the public sphere through designing spaces that
can act as forums and mediums of democratic publicness. The comprehensive restructuring and redesign at the campus of the Lincoln Center in New
York, as well as the High Line in New York conceived in collaboration with
the landscape architecture office James Corner Field Operations and the
garden designer Piet Oudolf, and not least projects such as the Museum of
Image and Sound in Rio de Janeiro that explicitly incorporate public spatial
structures, represent significant examples of this. Contrary to the rather more
free and artistically characterised installation, private house and pavilion
projects, these projects were defined by other framework conditions that
posed specific demands in relation to programme and design articulation.

Das für die Schweizer Expo.02 entworfene und im Jahr 2002 in Yverdon-les-Bains konstruierte Blur Building erzeugt aus Wasserdampf ein Arte-fakt in Form einer scheinbar über dem Wasser eines Sees schwebenden Wolke. Es bildet ein Beispiel für eine Erfahrungsgestaltung, die über das Sehen hinausgeht und mit Technologien einerseits und Standortqualitäten andererseits verwoben ist (Abb. 3).[14] Multisensorische Wahrnehmung wur-de geschärft.[15] Natürlichkeit und Künstlichkeit überlagerten sich. Solche pittoresken Landschaftsbilder, die Gezeitenwahrnehmung sowie die viel-fältige sinnliche Landschaftsraumwahrnehmung durch Bewegung werden oftmals mit großen Parks innerhalb und außerhalb der Städte verbunden und sind von besonderer Bedeutung in englischen und japanischen Land-schaftsgartentraditionen.[16]

Auch im urbanen Kontext re-aktivieren Diller Scofidio + Renfro mit ihren Entwürfen Landschaftsgartenreferenzen. Einige ihrer zentralen Projekte können als Kreuzungen von Architektur, Landschaftsarchitektur, Infrastruk-tur oder Städtebau bezeichnet werden, die zudem auch transdisziplinä-re Ansätze bildender und darstellender Künste einbeziehen, um Kulturen des Wahrnehmens und Sehens zu thematisieren und zu entfalten. Hervor-tretend ist aber insbesondere das Ziel, öffentlichen Raum zu erweitern. Wiederholt vorgetragen wird das Anliegen, der zunehmenden Gentrifi-zierung, Privatisierung und Kommerzialisierung des öffentlichen Raums mit dem Entwerfen von Orten entgegenzuwirken, die als Foren und Medien demokratischer Öffentlichkeit wirken können. Die umfangreichen Um- und Neugestaltungen am Campus des Lincoln Center in New York sowie die in Kollaboration mit dem Landschaftsarchitekturbüro James Corner Field Operations und dem Gartengestalter Piet Oudolf konzipierte High Line in New York und nicht zuletzt Projekte wie das Museum of Image and Sound in Rio de Janeiro, welche explizit die intentionale Ausprägung öf-fentlicher Raumstrukturen einbeziehen, können dafür als signifikante Bei-spiele stehen. Im Unterschied zu den eher freieren künstlerisch geprägten Projekten von Installation, Privathaus und Pavillon wurden diese Projekte von anderen Rahmenbedingungen geprägt, die spezifische Erfordernisse in Bezug auf Programm und gestalterische Artikulation mit sich brachten.

FIELD STRUCTURES: LINCOLN CENTER CAMPUS   With re-
gard to transformation and restructuring processes, as well as the specifics
of linking public buildings and public space, the many interventions carried
out successively by DS + R in various collaborations in the context of the
Lincoln Center in New York can demonstrate relevant and important components and effects that allow landscape-ness to come to the fore characteris-
tically as an architectural idea. The original ensemble of the Lincoln Center
was created as part of an urban renewal project in New York between 1955
and 1969 on a 61,000m² area between the 62nd and 65th Streets, Amsterdam and Columbus Avenues, as well as Broadway on the west side of
Manhattan. National and international architects renowned at the time such
as Wallace Harrison, Philipp Johnson, Eero Saarinen, Max Abramovitz and
Pietro Bellucci designed various buildings in this context for the performing
arts, ballet, opera, theatre performances and a dance academy, as well as
corresponding infrastructures and open spaces, in a modern architectural
language of expression inspired by abstract classical architecture traditions
(fig. 4). In time, especially the geometric-abstract, large-scale outdoor areas,
which in some cases had been subject to a series of restructuring measures,
proved to be inhospitable due to ageing processes. In addition, despite the
historical significance and symbolic character of the individual buildings,
the urban space situation overall was strongly influenced by transport, traffic
and pedestrian passages, with few connections to the surrounding areas.[17]

The restructuring and new planning realised by Diller Scofidio + Renfro
between 2003 and 2012 in the context of the Lincoln Center included
not only the redesign and extension of certain buildings – the Alice Tully
Hall, the renovation and extension buildings of the Juilliard School that
have been unified in one building, the extension building to the School
of American Ballet, the restructuring of the atrium of the New York State
Theater, the new building of the Hypar Pavilion – but also the redesigning
and restructuring of the outdoor areas, squares, pathways, stairs, roofing
and advertising surfaces in their vicinity (fig. 5–6).[18] This resulted overall
in an innovative constructional and spatial modification that combines architecture, landscape architecture and urban space.

The general development conditions and contexts that influenced the dynamics and development paths of the restructuring of this large-scale ensemble contributed significantly to stimulating, modifying and generating

4 Lincoln Center New York 2003-2012 Theatre, fountain and plaza with new street deck stairway and park

FELDSTRUKTUREN: LINCOLN CENTER CAMPUS   Im Hin-
blick auf Transformations- und Neuformulierungsprozesse sowie mit der
Spezifik der Verknüpfung von öffentlichen Gebäuden und öffentlichem
Freiraum können die zahlreichen sukzessive von DS + R in verschiedenen
Kollaborationen durchgeführten Interventionen im Kontext des Lincoln Center in New York relevante und wichtige Komponenten und Wirkorganismen
aufzeigen, die Landschaftlichkeit als Architekturidee charakteristisch hervortreten lassen. Das ursprüngliche Ensemble des Lincoln Center entstand
im Zuge eines Urban-Renewal-Projektes in New York zwischen 1955 und
1969 auf einem 61.000 m² großen Areal zwischen 62. und 66. Straße,
Amsterdam und Columbus Avenue sowie Broadway an der Westseite von
Manhattan. Damals renommierte nationale und internationale Architekten
wie Wallace Harrison, Philip Johnson, Eero Saarinen, Max Abramovitz
und Pietro Bellucci entwarfen für diesen Kontext verschiedenste Gebäude
für die darstellenden Künste, für Darbietungen von Ballett, Oper, Theater
und eine Tanzakademie wie auch entsprechende Infrastrukturen und Freiräume in einer durch abstrahierte klassische Architekturtraditionen inspi-
rierten modernen architektonischen Ausdrucssprache (Abb. 4). Mit der
Zeit erwiesen sich insbesondere die geometrisch-abstrakten weiträumigen
Außenbereiche, die teilweise mehrere Umgestaltungen erfahren hatten, vor
allem aufgrund von Alterungsprozessen als unwirtlich. Zudem war trotz der
historischen Bedeutung und symbolischen Wirksamkeit der Einzelbauten
die urbane Raumsituation insgesamt durch Transport, Verkehr und Transfer
stark überlagert und durch geringe Anbindungen an das Umfeld geprägt.[17]   49

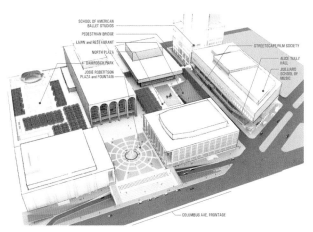

SCHOOL OF AMERICAN BALLET STUDIOS
PEDESTRIAN BRIDGE
LAWN and RESTAURANT
NORTH PLAZA
DAMROSCH PARK
JOSIE ROBERTSON PLAZA and FOUNTAIN
STREETSCAPE/FILM SOCIETY
ALICE TULLY HALL
JUILLIARD SCHOOL OF MUSIC
COLUMBUS AVE. FRONTAGE

5   Lincoln Center Campus Model of the redesign and extension building

design and appropriation qualities.[19] As regards the more complex cultures of the city, the aim of the architecture team was to emphasise, reinforce and supplement latent qualities of a complex that was not or was no longer 'perfect', as well as to invite urban integration and activation. The building ensemble that had been regarded as a cultural icon ever since its creation, which was designed originally like an urban acropolis on a plinthlike platform, was supposed to become a destination for a wider public with its outdoor spaces, especially also for the younger generation, and to open up the urban space here for the residents in the surrounding neighbourhood.[20] The reinterpretation of the streets and the platform for a permeable, flowing and linking spatial fabric creates an extension of the space into a continuous structure that is given a landscape-like character. The street coverings that remove barriers are worth a special mention, set out by the office of landscape architects Kim Mathews and Signe Nielsen as generous steps and passageways accompanied by a new design of green, urban forest-like and flower-landscaped outdoor spaces, as well as bridges, ramps and escalators, replacing the access points that previously led over busy roads (fig. 8–9).[21] The individual buildings and outdoor areas are thus much easier to access and the usage value is increased, especially for people who do not primarily just attend events in the evening. Orientation is positively supported through lighting and informative media panels as an extension to pathways, steps and bridges, roofing and entrance pavilions.[22] The outdoor areas become an urban space for everyday use for the many people working and studying here, for the local inhabitants, other city dwellers and tourists. This combined the physical transformation with a programmatic change.

In connection with the question of the significant contours of landscape-ness as an architectural idea, two reconstruction and redesign examples can be outlined here in more detail. The Hearst Plaza square situated in the north, originally designed by the landscape architect Dan Kiley, but then restructured

6   Alice Tully Hall and Juilliard School Extensions open up and interact on street level

Zu den von Diller Scofidio + Renfro zwischen 2003 und 2012 im Kontext
des Lincoln Center realisierten Um- und Neuplanungen zählen nicht nur
die Neugestaltung und Erweiterung einiger Gebäude – der Alice Tully
Hall, die Erneuerung und der Erweiterungsbau der Juilliard School, die in
einem Gebäude zusammengefasst sind, der Erweiterungsbau der School
of American Ballet, der Umbau der Vorhalle des New York State Theater,
das neue Gebäude des Hypar Pavilion –, sondern auch die Neukonzipie-
rung und Umgestaltung der Außenräume, der Plätze, Gehwege, Treppen,
Überdachungen und Werbeflächen in deren Umfeld (Abb. 5–6).[18] Damit
erfolgte insgesamt eine baulich-räumlich innovative Modifikation, die Architektur, Landschaftsarchitektur und urbanen Raum verbindet.

Die allgemeinen Entstehungsbedingungen und Kontexte, welche die Dynamik und die Entwicklungspfade der Umbauten dieses Großensembles
beeinflussten, trugen hier wesentlich dazu bei, Gestaltungs- und Aneig-
nungsqualitäten zu stimulieren, zu modifizieren und schließlich zu generieren.[19] Im Zusammenhang mit den komplexeren Kulturen der Stadt war
es das Ziel des Architekturteams, latente Qualitäten eines nicht bzw. nicht
mehr ‚perfekten' Komplexes hervorzuheben bzw. zu unterstreichen und zu
ergänzen sowie zu urbaner Integration und Aktivierung einzuladen. Das
bereits seit seiner Entstehung als kulturelle Ikone betrachtete Gebäudeensemble, das auf einer plinthenartigen Plattform ursprünglich wie eine urbane Akropolis gestaltet war, sollte mit seinen Freiräumen diesen Ort zu einer
Destination für ein breiteres Publikum werden lassen, insbesondere auch
für eine jüngere Generation, und den Stadtraum hier für die Bewohner:in-
nen der umliegenden Nachbarschaft öffnen.[20] Die Uminterpretation des
Straßenraums und der Plattform zu einem durchlässigen, fließenden und
verknüpfenden Raumgefüge erzeugt eine Ausdehnung des Raums zu einem
kontinuierlicheren Gefüge, das damit einen landschaftlichen Charakter erhält. Hervorzuheben sind hier insbesondere die Barrieren beseitigenden

7   Hearst Plaza Water basin and added trees with seating

many times and used little, was not a total reconstruction, as emphasised by
Elizabeth Diller.[23] It was more of a revitalisation of Kiley's design intentions: a
tranquil, geometrical 'landscape' as well as the originally chosen tree species
(fig. 7). A rectangular water basin with a sculpture by Henry Moore, which
had already been placed on the square by Dan Kiley, was now renovated. An
equally rectangular plant podium with three parallel rows of trees and a pavilion rising like a pitched roof were modified and extended. This resulted in
a balanced dosage of order, orientation and sensory richness. The newly arranged podium is now surrounded by long, continuous seating benches, offering spaces to sit and relax on the platform, also in shaded areas under the trees.

The Hypar Pavilion (2010), a new detached structure in the form of an excep-
tionally robust, hyperbolic paraboloid, unfolds from the square as a diagonally rising, grass-covered roof surface open to appropriation, housing a café,
a bar and flexible usages for research, studios and events (fig. 10). The roof
planted with grass reinforces the outdoor space qualities in this area and opens
up the possibility of new views of the surroundings (fig. 11–12). The balance
of tranquillity and activity gives rise to the 'feeling' of briefly departing from
everyday life into a different situation, as well as reinforcing the identity of the
location.[24] Elizabeth Diller refers to the proposal for this outdoor area of the
former North Plaza as an 'ensemble of landscape-like elements', through the
merging of architecture and landscape architecture, and sees a sculpted and
enhanced landscape in the design of the public spaces of the Lincoln Center.[25]

8–9   Street deck stairway on Columbus Ave. and pedestrian passage as public space

Straßendeckel, ausgeführt als großzügige Treppen und Passagen, die begleitet werden durch eine neue Gestaltung grüner stadtwaldähnlicher und blumenbepflanzter Außenräume vom Büro der Landschaftsarchitektinnen Kim Mathews und Signe Nielsen sowie Brücken, Rampen und Aufzüge, die insgesamt nun die zuvor über vielbefahrene Straßen führenden Zugänge ersetzen (Abb. 8–9).[21] So sind die einzelnen Gebäude und Außenbereiche viel besser zu erreichen, der Gebrauchswert erhöht sich insbesondere für die Menschen, die nicht vorrangig abends zu Veranstaltungen kommen. Durch Lichtführung und informative Medientafeln in Erweiterung von Gehwegen, Treppen und Brücken, Überdachungen sowie Eingangspavillons wird Orientierung positiv unterstützt.[22] Die Außenbereiche werden für die alltägliche Nutzung zum urbanen Freiraum für die zahlreichen hier arbeitenden und studierenden Menschen, für die Bewohnenden der Umgebung sowie weitere Stadtbewohner:innen und Tourist:innen. Damit wurde die physische Transformation mit einem programmatischen Wechsel verbunden.

Im Zusammenhang mit der Frage nach signifikanten Konturen von Landschaftlichkeit als Architekturidee können hier zudem zwei Um- und Neugestaltungsbeispiele differenzierter skizziert werden. Der im Norden gelegene, ursprünglich von dem Landschaftsarchitekten Dan Kiley entworfene, aber mehrfach umgestaltete und dann wenig genutzte Platz wurde, wie Elizabeth Diller betont, nicht als totale Rekonstruktion ausgeführt.[23] Re-vitalisiert wurden vielmehr Entwurfsintentionen Kileys: die ruhige, geometrische ‚Landschaft' und die ursprünglich gewählten Baumspezies (Abb. 7). Ein rechteckiges Wasserbecken mit einer Skulptur von Henry Moore, das sich bereits auf dem Platz von Dan Kiley befand, wurde nun renoviert. Modifiziert bzw. ergänzt wurden ein neu arrangiertes ebenfalls rechteckiges Pflanzpodest mit drei parallelen Baumreihen und ein satteldachartig ansteigender Pavillon. So entstand eine balancierte Dosierung von

10   Hearst Plaza Hypar Pavilion and basin

A further, equally overarching conceptual idea contributes to reinforcing connections through spatial continuities. Visual presence on the streets is enabled through transparency, through views into the buildings, out from the buildings and on the lower levels even through them. In this manner, additional spatial continuities are created visually, with connections at the perception level of pedestrians, users and car traffic, for example through previously opaque ground-level areas of buildings being modified by means of morphological restructuring and transparent zones. The brutalist building of The Juilliard School and Alice Tully Hall by the Italian architect Pietro Bellucci from the year 1968 was restructured, for example, not only by means of a spatial extension on the upper level towards Broadway but through the creation of a triangular public outdoor area by means of a diagonal underpass and a generous glazed foyer.[26] Furthermore, a new double stairway was added in the street corner which people can sit on, forming a transition between the street and the square (fig. 13–15). Another connection between the cultural centre and public space is presented by a bridge over 65th Street, which links the building with the Lincoln Theater.

11–12 Hypar Pavilion lawn on Hearst Plaza

Ordnung, Orientierung und sensitivem Reichtum. Das Pflanzpodest wird nun von neuen, langen kontinuierlichen Sitzbänken eingefasst und bietet auf der Plattform Aufenthalt auch in schattigen Bereichen unter den Bäumen.

Der Hypar Pavillon (2010), als eine neue, frei stehende Struktur in Form eines äußerst belastbaren hyperbolischen Parboloids, faltet sich als diagonal ansteigende, rasenbedeckte aneignungsoffene Dachfläche aus der Platzfläche auf und beherbergt ein Café, eine Bar sowie flexible Nutzungen für Forschung, Studio und Veranstaltungen (Abb. 10). Das rasenbepflanzte Dach stärkt und erweitert die Freiraumqualitäten an diesem Platz und eröffnet die Möglichkeit von zuvor nicht bestehenden Ausblicken auf den Umgebungsraum (Abb. 11–12). Durch die Balance von Ruhe und Aktivität können sowohl das Gefühl, aus dem Alltag kurzzeitig in eine andere Situation enthoben zu sein, als auch die Identität des Ortes gesteigert werden.[24] Elizabeth Diller bezeichnet den Vorschlag für diesen Freiraum des ehemaligen North Plazas als ‚Ensemble von landschaftlichen Elementen', in dem Architektur und Landschaftsarchitektur verschmelzen, und sieht in der Gestaltung der öffentlichen Räume des Lincoln Center insgesamt eine skulptierte und erhöhte Landschaft.[25]

Eine weitere, ebenfalls übergreifende konzeptuelle Idee trägt außerdem dazu bei, Verknüpfungen durch Raumkontinuitäten zu verstärken. Die visuelle Präsenz an den Straßen wird durch Transparenz ermöglicht, durch die Blicke in Gebäude hinein, aus ihnen heraus und in den unteren Bereichen auch durch sie hindurch. Visuell entstehen in dieser Weise weitere räumliche Kontinuitäten, Verbindungen auf der Wahrnehmungsebene der Fußgänger:innen, der Nutzenden und der des Autoverkehrs, indem beispielsweise vormals opake Basisbereiche von Gebäuden modifiziert wurden mittels morphologischer Umbauten und durch transparente Zonen. Das brutalistische Gebäude der Juilliard School und Alice Tully Hall des italienischen Architekten Pietro Bellucci aus dem Jahr 1968 gestalteten sie beispielsweise nicht nur durch eine räumliche Erweiterung im oberen Bereich zum Broadway hin

13–14 Alice Tully Hall extension Entrance to Juilliard School and new plaza with stairwell seating

The interventions in the context of the Lincoln Centre therefore clearly show how the designing of spaces for the public can be interpreted. Participation, appropriation, interaction and gathering can be stimulated by free and easy access to open spaces that invite appropriation and lingering by linking indoors and outdoors through various architectural transition elements, as well as through transparent building parts that generate visual references. The many people working at the cultural institutes can subsequently view themselves more as part of an active urban public and contribute to forging an identity here. It remains an open question, subject to the test of time, as to what extent what is created will be effective in its formal and informal aspects, whether those previously uninvolved will become integrated here and whether conflict situations can also be taken into consideration.[27] Potential is offered, however, for a variety of scenarios and actions regarding democratic participation through the ensemble of structural and spatial outdoor space design and infrastructure. The city landscape is regarded as a public resource, in which the conglomerate of projects and its individual constituents contribute to urban life. The design activity associated with these spatial concepts is repeatedly described by Elizabeth Diller as a 'democratisation of public space' and also as a landscape.[28]

15 Alex Tully Hall Lobby facing the new triangular stairwell seating

um, sondern schufen hier mittels einer diagonal geführten Unterschneidung einen triangulär zugeschnittenen öffentlichen und frei zugänglichen Außenbereich und ein großzügiges verglastes Foyer.[26] Außerdem wurde eine ebenfalls frei zugängliche Doppeltreppe, auf der die Menschen sitzen können, in die Straßenecke eingefügt, die einen Übergang zwischen der Straße und dem Platz bildet (Abb. 13–15). Eine weitere Verbindung des Kulturzentrums mit dem öffentlichen Raum bildet eine Brücke über die 65. Straße, durch die das Gebäude mit dem Lincoln Theater verbunden wird.

Die Interventionen im Kontext des Lincoln Center zeigen damit signifikant, wie das Entwerfen von Räumen für die Öffentlichkeit interpretiert werden kann. Teilhabe, Aneignung, Interaktion und Versammlung können stimuliert werden durch einen freien und leichten Zugang zu Freiräumen, die zur Aneignung und zum Aufenthalt einladen, durch Verknüpfung von Innen und Außen mittels unterschiedlicher architektonischer Übergangselemente, durch transparente Gebäudeteile, die visuelle Bezugnahmen generieren. Auch die hier in großer Zahl in den kulturellen Institutionen Arbeitenden und die Kulturschaffenden können sich so stärker als Teil einer aktiven urbanen Öffentlichkeit verstehen und zur Identitätsbildung an diesem Ort beitragen. In welchem Grad das so Geschaffene mit seinen formalen und informellen Anteilen Wirksamkeit entfalten wird, ob auch bislang Anteilslose nun hier integriert und auch Konfliktsituationen einbezogen werden können, bleibt dabei eine noch offene Frage, die dem Test der Zeit ausgesetzt ist.[27] Ein Potenzial aber für verschiedenste Szenen und Performanzen demokratischer Teilhabe wird hier durch das Ensemble baulich-räumlicher Freiraumgestaltung und Infrastruktur dargeboten. Stadtlandschaft wird als öffentliche Ressource aufgefasst, in der das Konglomerat der Projekte wie auch seine einzelnen Konstituenten einen Beitrag zum urbanen Leben erbringen. Das mit diesen Raumkonzepten verbundene Entwurfshandeln wird von Elizabeth Diller wiederholt als ‚Demokratisierung öffentlichen Raums' und ebenfalls als Landschaft beschrieben.[28]

16–17 High Line Park New York 2004 and ongoing

URBAN LANDSCAPE: HIGH LINE PARK   The openness to be able to flexibly accommodate a wide spectrum of public activities and interaction – from recreation, strolling, dining, playing, talking and relaxing to cultural performances – also represents a prominent programmatic feature of the High Line Park. Together with the landscape architecture office James Corner Field Operations and the Dutch garden designer Piet Oudolf, they had since 2004 been drawing up a concept for this restructuring project and redesign of a former infrastructure building, a 2.4-kilometre-long raised stretch of rail from the Whitney Museum of American Art to Hudson Yards by the water, integrating proposals, wishes and ideas of the community 'Friends of the High Line' (fig. 16–19). Awareness of the potential of this open space in the middle of the city had been raised by the informal use of the grassy areas over the disused and ruinous track, as well as by the documentary images of various aspects of this open space by the photographer Joel Sternfeld.[29] Today the High Line with its immediate surroundings forms a rich urban assemblage and urban landscape, which display various facets of landscape-ness.

Inspired also by the 'Promenade plantée' opened in Paris in 1998, where a railway track was transformed into a park pathway that crosses a variety of areas, the design team developed the aim of achieving a transformation with as little 'architecture' as possible in the project.[30] The new ensemble of public spaces was generated out of the existing substance with a variety of connections to the respective surrounding urban areas. The characteristics of the overgrown rail track, built from 1929 to 1934, and which closed down in 1980 and remained in disuse until around 2000, were reinterpreted

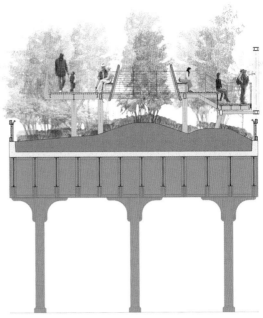

18　High Line as a park pathway　　　19　Section with different levels for plantings, walking and seating

STADTRAUMLANDSCHAFT: HIGH LINE PARK　Die Offenheit, eine große Bandbreite von Ereignissen öffentlicher Aktivität und Interaktion flexibel aufnehmen zu können, von der Rekreation, dem Flanieren, über Essen, Spielen, Reden und Ausruhen bis hin zu kultureller Performanz, bildet eine programmatisch hervortretende Eigenschaft auch des High Line Park. Zusammen mit dem Landschaftsarchitekturbüro James Corner Field Operations und dem niederländischen Gartengestalter Piet Oudolf konzipierten DS + R seit 2004 unter Integration von Anregungen, Wünschen und Ideen der Community ‚Friends of the High Line' diese Um- und Neugestaltung eines ehemaligen Infrastrukturbauwerks, einer 2,4 km langen, aufgeständerten Bahnstrecke vom Whitney Museum of American Art bis zu den Hudson Yards am Wasser (Abb. 16–19). Die Aufmerksamkeit für das Potenzial dieses Freiraums mitten in der Stadt war durch die informelle Nutzung der Wiesenflächen über der stillgelegten ruinösen Trasse sowie durch die dokumentarischen Bilder verschiedener Situationen dieses Freiraums des Fotografen Joel Sternfeld geweckt worden.[29] Heute bildet die High Line mit ihrem unmittelbaren Umfeld eine reichhaltige urbane Assemblage und urbane Landschaft, die unterschiedliche Facetten von Landschaftlichkeit erkennen lässt.

Angeregt auch durch die 1998 in Paris eröffnete Promenade plantée, wo eine Eisenbahntrasse zu einem Parkwanderweg transformiert wurde, der eine Vielzahl von Bereichen durchquert, entwickelte sich die Absicht des Entwurfsteams, im Projekt eine Transformation mit möglichst wenig ‚Architektur' zu erreichen.[30] In vielfältigen Bezügen zu den jeweils umgebenden Stadträumen wurde das neue Ensemble öffentlicher Räume aus dem Bestand heraus

21–23   Different spatial situations along the High Line park pathway

imaginatively and enhanced. Every section has remained in situ or has re-interpreted a certain aspect of the former ambience – such as self-seeding plants and dilapidated iron structures (fig. 21–23).

A path system was created out of ready-mixed concrete panels as a central element, with a slightly meandering course and interrupted at intervals with lower areas of planted grass and flowers, in some cases enclosed with corten steel, and in other areas lined by high mature trees and bushes (fig. 24). Raised seating with wood and deckchairs, as well as viewpoints, resting niches and meeting points with a wide range of outdoor furniture, enrich the linear park, as does the path system as a passage through existing building structures or alongside the upper floors and roofs of the surrounding urban development (fig. 25–28). The promenade is thus activated three-dimensionally as a pathway and is perceived overall as a sequence of different spatial situations that also includes layering and areas that can serve as flexible exhibition sites for art objects and platforms for events.

Seen from street level, the original iron structure is in the foreground. Especially at the intersections with the stair and escalator accesses, the park, with the naturalistic, seasonal and varied garden art designs by Piet Oudolf, can be clearly made out.[31] The High Line Park also acts as a catalyst for the surrounding urban areas.[32] In the Meatpacking District, for example, additional small-scale public spatial situations were created replacing car traffic, and alongside the park an architectural development was prompted by the high popularity of the High Line, with buildings by international architects such as Zaha Hadid, Shigeru Ban or Neil Denari.The criticism of the associated gentrification of this part of the city is countered by the idea

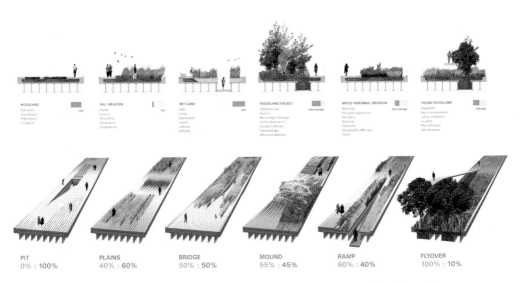

MOSSLAND | TALL MEADOW | WETLAND | WOODLAND THICKET | MIXED PERENNIAL MEADOW | YOUNG WOODLAND

PIT	PLAINS	BRIDGE	MOUND	RAMP	FLYOVER
0% : 100%	40% : 60%	50% : 50%	55% : 45%	60% : 40%	100% : 10%

24 James Corner Field Operations Different scenes of greenery are created on the High Line Park

generiert. Die Charakteristik der 1929 bis 1934 errichteten, 1980 stillgelegten und bis um 2000 brachliegenden und verwilderten Bahnstreckenanlage wurde einfallsreich neu interpretiert und bereichert. Jeder Abschnitt hat einen gewissen Teil des Bestandsambientes – selbstaussäende Pflanzung und korrodierte Eisenkonstruktion – in situ bewahrt oder neu interpretiert (Abb. 21–23).

Als zentrales Element wurde ein Wegesystem aus Fertigbetonpaneelen kreiert, das in seinem Verlauf leicht mäandrierend und in Teilen aufgebrochen wird von niedrigeren, teilweise von Cortenstahl eingefassten Gras- und Blütenpflanzungen und in anderen Bereichen gerahmt wird von hohen mehrjährigen Bäumen und Büschen (Abb. 24). Erhöhte Sitzmöglichkeiten und Liegestühle mit Holz wie auch Aussichtspunkte, Erholungsnischen und Treffpunkte mit verschiedenstem Freiraummobiliar bereichern die lineare Parkanlage wie auch die Wegeführung als Passage durch bauliche Bestandsstrukturen hindurch oder entlang von Obergeschossen und Dächern der städtischen Umgebungsbebauung (Abb. 25–28). Die Promenade wird so dreidimensional als Wegraum aktiviert und insgesamt als Sequenz unterschiedlicher Raumsituationen wahrnehmbar, die auch Überlagerungen einschließt und zudem Bereiche, die als flexible Ausstellungsplätze für Kunstobjekte und Tribünen für Aktionen dienen können.

Von der Straßenebene aus wahrgenommen, steht die ursprüngliche Eisenstruktur im Vordergrund. Insbesondere an den Schnittstellen mit den erschließenden Treppen und Aufzügen kann jedoch die Parkanlage mit den naturalistischen und von Diversität geprägten, in Wirkung jahreszeitlich wechselnden gartenkünstlerischen Gestaltungen von Piet Oudolf klar erkannt werden.[31] Der High Line Park wirkt auch als Katalysator für die umliegenden städtischen Bereiche.[32]

25–27 Spatial situations from dense greenery to leisure spaces

that, firstly, this is often associated with a successful restructuring of urban areas and is therefore inevitable, and secondly, that the restructuring and redesign of the High Line has multiple facets of impact, acting in particular as an urban catalyst that raises the attractiveness of the surrounding urban areas that have benefitted from the developments (fig. 29).[33] In addition, possibilities remain for the appropriation of the public space by the wider population. Many programmatic dimensions can be incorporated. Furthermore, the park opened up new and unusual perspectives on the urban space nearby and the wider surroundings.[34] The design interventions by James Corner Field Operations, Piet Oudolf and Diller Scofidio + Renfro and their pathway constellations encourage looking, observing and resting, as well as performing and participating in urbanity and the future development of culture and urban life.[35]

Context references and participative aspects, as well as the configuration of different and varied impressions, alternations and the contrast between for example denser and darker or lighter and more open areas, between more narrowly limited and more open spatial situations and between more ordered and wilder areas, as well as visual connections into the urban space and the integration of post-industrial existing buildings, evoke James Corner's theoretical concepts of Landscape Urbanism. The appropriation dynamics of the platforms and the panoramic views highlighted variously by framing as big as screens (fig. 30–31), with differently nuanced visual axes onto everyday scenes of Manhattan, such as the flow of traffic or the variable 'normality' of built structures, as well as diversely scaled depths of spatial perception, especially reveal certain aspects that run centrally through the thinking and work of Diller Scofidio + Renfro: imagination

28 Diverse recreational areas invite to linger   29 Redeveloped street neighbouring the High Line

Im Meatpacking District beispielsweise entstanden weitere kleinere öffentliche Raumsituationen anstelle von Verkehr, und entlang der Parkstrecke wurde eine architektonische Entwicklung mit Bauten international tätiger Architekt:innen wie Zaha Hadid, Shigeru Ban oder Neil Denari durch die hohe Popularität der High Line angestoßen. Der Kritik an der damit einhergehenden Gentrifizierung dieses Stadtbereichs ist der Gedanke zur Seite zu stellen, dass dies einerseits oftmals mit einer gelungenen Neugestaltung von Stadtbereichen verbunden ist und damit unvermeidbar und andererseits die Um- und Neugestaltung der High Line multiple Wirkungsfacetten aufweist und insbesondere als urbaner Katalysator wirkt, durch den die umliegenden Stadtbereiche an Attraktivität gewonnen und von den Entwicklungen profitiert haben (Abb. 29).[33] Darüber hinaus bleiben die Aneignungsmöglichkeiten des öffentlichen Raums durch die breite Bevölkerung erhalten. Viele programmatische Dimensionen können aufgenommen werden. Zudem eröffnete der Parkparcours neue und ungewöhnliche Perspektiven auf den Stadtraum im näheren und weiteren Umfeld.[34] Die gestalterischen Interventionen von James Corner Field Operations, Piet Oudolf und Diller Scofidio + Renfro evozieren mit ihren Wegraumkonstellationen neben dem Blicken, dem Schauen und Ausruhen auch das Performen, das Partizipieren im urbanen Leben und die zukünftige Entfaltung von Kultur und Stadtleben.[35]

Kontextbezüge und partizipative Anteile, die Konfiguration unterschiedlicher und abwechslungsreicher Eindrücke, mit dem Wechsel und Kontrast beispielsweise von dichteren, dunkleren zu helleren und offeneren Bereichen, von enger begrenzten zu weiter aufgespannten Raumsituationen, vom Geordneteren ins stärker Wildere, sowie die Sichtbezüge in den Stadtraum und die Integration postindustrieller Bestandstrukturen erinnern an James Corners theoretische Konzeptionen des ‚Landscape Urbanism'. 63

30 Visual connections into the city fabric   31 Screens framing panoramic views of the city

and sentiment, as well as perceptions of the city and environment are addressed and questioned; spatial conventions are reinterpreted; and innovative ways of participation and possibly also of identification in the urban space are stimulated.[36] The actual narrowness of the park is thereby extended into the urban spaces and the respective location is linked variously with the wider urban space, with different degrees of contrast and similarity, as well as proximity and distance. The mental perception of Manhattan, strongly influenced by the cartographic image of the city, is thus extended into a more diverse spatial perception and also prompts an understanding of one's own location within an urban fabric (fig. 32).[37]

Separate from the hectic hustle and bustle of the city, the High Line Park created a fabric of open space, infrastructure, architectural objects and art; an ensemble of architecture, nature and culture, comprising a park, squares, forums, social spaces, cultural facilities and a recreational area: a typologically innovative urban space for appropriation and development, with a landscape-like feel. This comprises urban microclimates with a variety of atmospheres. James Corner emphasises that the assemblage of organic and constructional 'material', in a mix of different proportions, incorporates the wild, the cultivated, the intimate and the hyper-social.[38] In the merging of what already exists and the creative imagination, the urban spaces were staged as urban landscape and as future-orientated fields of possibility.

32   View points extend the perception into the city fabric

Insbesondere mit der Aneignungsdynamik der Tribünen und den durch lein-
wandgroße Rahmungen (Abb. 30–31) verschieden inszenierten Panorama-
ausblicken mit unterschiedlich nuancierten Sichtachsen auf Alltagsszene-
rien Manhattans wie den Verkehrsfluss oder die verschiedene ,Normalität'
baulicher Strukturen sowie mit den verschieden skalierten Tiefenausdeh-
nungen der Raumerfahrung können einige das Denken und Schaffen Diller
Scofidio + Renfros zentral durchziehende Anliegen erkannt werden: Imagination und Empfindung, Stadt- und Umweltwahrnehmung werden angesprochen und befragt, Raumkonventionen neu interpretiert, innovative
Weisen der Partizipation und potenziell auch Identifikation im urbanen
Raum werden angeregt.[36] Die eigentliche Schmalheit des Wegeparks wird
damit in die Staträume hinein erweitert, der jeweilige Standort mit dem
weiteren Stadtraum je unterschiedlich verknüpft in verschiedenen Graden
von Kontrast und Annäherung sowie Nähe und Ferne. Die sehr stark durch
die stadtkartografische Abbildung mental geprägte Wahrnehmung von
Manhattan wird so zu einer vielfältigeren räumlichen Wahrnehmung erweitert, und es wird auch dazu angeregt, den eigenen Standort innerhalb
eines urbanen Gefüges zu verstehen (Abb. 32).[37]

Vom hektischen Treiben der Großstadt separiert, entstand mit dem High Line
Park ein Gefüge aus Freiraum, Infrastruktur, architektonischen Objekten und
Kunst, ein Ensemble aus Architektur, Natur und Kultur, aus Park, Plätzen, Foren,
sozialen Räumen, kulturellen Einrichtungen und Erholungsgebiet, ein landschaftlich geprägter, typologisch innovativer Stadtraum für Aneignung und Entfaltung. Dieser umfasst urbane Mikroklimata mit unterschiedlichen Atmosphären.
James Corner betont, dass die Assemblage von organischem und baulichem
,Material' in einer Mischung unterschiedlicher Proportionen das Wilde, das
Kultivierte, das Intime und das Hyper-Soziale aufnimmt.[38] In der Verknüpfung
von Vorhandenem und entwerferischer Imagination wurden die Staträume
als urbane Landschaft und als zukunftweisende Möglichkeitsräume inszeniert.   65

33 Museum of Image and Sound Rio de Janeiro 2009 and ongoing

The presented themes, as well as the associated design repertoire, can be found in many of the built, planned and presented concepts and works by Diller Scofidio + Renfro. It is the project-specific and situation-specific variations that then give each respective realisation its distinctiveness. The act of designing starts with the human being and is linked to multi-sensory modalities of perception that include focused and peripheral guided attention. In this way, routes with pathways and square-like situations at the Vagelos Education Center on the medical campus of Columbia University in New York, which are programmatically flexible as large study areas for informal learning and cooperation, as well as social spaces for encountering wide panoramic views of the Hudson River and New York, are described by Elizabeth Diller as a vertical landscape.[39] Wide zigzagged stairs and ramps featured along the façade of the Museum of Image and Sound in Rio de Janeiro lead as an outdoor space up to the roof terrace with an open-air cinema, bar and restaurant, opening up curated views of the city and of the expanse of the sea (fig. 33–35).[40] The landscape-like architectural idea becomes in practice a tool for opening up ways of perception for all the inhabitants of the city that were previously reserved for privileged classes and tourists from villas, restaurants and hotels on the shore promenade, as well as furthermore encouraging a new way of perceiving the city and the surroundings.

34–35   Roof terraces as social spaces giving publicly accessible views onto the promenade

Die aufgezeigten Themen sowie das damit verbundene gestalterische Repertoire sind in vielen der gebauten, projektierten und dargebotenen Konzeptionen und Werke von Diller Scofidio + Renfro wiederzufinden. Es sind die Variationen, die je projekt- und situationsspezifisch der jeweiligen Realisierung dann ein besonderes Gepräge geben. Das Entwerfen wird ausgehend vom Menschen gedacht, mit multisensorischen Wahrnehmungs-modalitäten verknüpft, die fokussierte und periphere Aufmerksamkeitslen-kungen einschließen. So werden im Vagelos Education Center auf dem medizinischen Campus der Columbia University in New York Routen mit Wegräumen und platzartigen Situationen als programmatisch flexible, gro-ße Studienbereiche für informelles Lernen und Kooperation sowie als so-ziale Begegnungsorte konzipiert. Sie geben weite Panoramablicke auf den Hudson River und New York frei und werden von Elizabeth Diller als vertika-le Landschaft beschrieben.[39] Eine zickzackförmig geführte breite Treppen- und Rampenanlage entlang der Fassade des Museum of Image and Sound in Rio de Janeiro wird als öffentlicher Raum nach oben geführt zur Dachter-rasse mit Freiluftkino, Bar und Restaurant und öffnet dabei kuratierte Blicke auf die Stadt und auf die Weite des Meeres (Abb. 33–35).[40] Die landschaft-lich geprägte architektonische Idee wird in der Praxis zum Instrument, um für alle Bewohner:innen der Stadt Wahrnehmungsweisen zu öffnen, die bislang privilegierten Schichten und Tourist:innen aus Villen, Restaurants und Hotelanalagen an der Uferpromenade vorbehalten waren und zudem dazu ermuntern, die Stadt und Umwelt in neuer Weise wahrzunehmen. 67

REPERTOIRE   No doubt the most conspicuous component of the projects by Diller Scofidio + Renfro is the proposal to increase the extent of public space. The mixing of architecture and landscape architecture substance and infrastructure can be interpreted as a condition and component of events. The elements in the fabric, in the open mesh, reinforce each other. Apart from various usage and sojourn qualities, the physical space displays the potential for promoting democratic forms of social interaction.[41] The invitation to diversified appropriation and interaction as an urban life practice appears to be decisive. The juxtaposition and mingling of spaces that open up towards each other and towards external neighbouring spaces as extended spatial continuums is characteristic for levels that can be formulated as architectural ideas also in connection with landscape-ness. Architecture is then not primarily interpreted and experienced as an object but more as a component of an overarching whole. More specific design elements present, alongside the aim of generating spatial continuums, an invitation to linger for a longer or shorter period as well as overlapping with transfer areas that are expressed as stairs, ramps, platforms and benches, creating distinctions such as lighter and darker, as well as more open and denser areas. These design elements also achieve this, in particular, by means of visual axes through porous spaces and transitions, whereby transparent facades and window motifs in buildings and open spaces serve as frames and the latest technologies are used as structural-spatial elements of expression. Overall, the design interventions open

up various participatory and thereby also performative possibilities.

Die wohl auffälligste Komponente der Projekte von Diller Scofidio + Renfro ist der Vorschlag, den Anteil des öffentlichen Raumes zu erhöhen. Dabei kann die Vermischung von architektonischer und landschaftsarchitektonischer Substanz sowie Infrastruktur als Voraussetzung und Komponente von Ereignissen interpretiert werden, wobei sich diese einzelnen Elemente im Gefüge, in der offenen Verflechtung miteinander, gegenseitig verstärken. Der physische Raum zeigt neben den verschiedenen Nutzungs- und Aufenthaltsqualitäten das Potenzial, demokratische Formen sozialer Interaktion zu befördern.[41] Ausschlaggebend erscheint die Einladung zu unterschiedlicher Aneignung und Interaktion als urbane Lebenspraxis. Als charakteristisch für Ebenen, die zudem in Verbindung mit Landschaftlichkeit als Architekturidee formuliert werden können, wirkt das Neben- und Ineinander von Räumen, die sich zueinander und zu äußeren, benachbarten Räumen zu weiter gespannten Raumkontinuen öffnen. Architektur wird dann nicht vorrangig als Objekt, vielmehr als Bestandteil eines übergreifenden Ganzen interpretiert und erfahrbar. Neben dem Anliegen, Raumkontinuen zu erzeugen, gibt es auch spezifischere architektonische Komponenten. So finden die Einladungen zu längerem oder kürzerem Aufenthalt sowie Überschneidungen mit Transferbereichen Ausdruck in Treppen, Rampen, Podesten, Bänken. Auch Unterscheidungen wie beispielsweise von helleren und dunkleren, offeneren und dichteren Bereichen wie auch insbesondere Blickführungen durch poröse Räume und Übergänge werden eingesetzt, wobei auch transparente Fassaden sowie Fenstermotive in Gebäuden und Freiräumen als Rahmungen wirken sowie neueste Technologien als baulich-räumliche Ausdruckselemente Verwendung finden. Insgesamt öffnen die gestalterischen Interventionen diverse partizipative und damit ebenfalls performative Möglichkeitsräume.

LANDSCHAFTLICHE ZUKUNFTSRÄUME
FUTURE LIVING LANDSCAPES
BJARKE INGELS GROUP

The notion that cities are more than buildings and infra-structure is shown in a variety of ways by the projects by the Bjarke Ingels Group, founded in Copenhagen in 2005. Particular attention is given to the qualities that are attributed significance as being performative and multiscalar. This is associated with and distinguished by a typological mixing of architecture and landscape architecture and the development of unfamiliar urban programme hybrids. These hybrids were developed by the architecture firm BIG as a cooperation between architects and landscape architects as an internal team, as well as in cooperation with external architects, landscape architects and artists. The office's founder, Bjarke Ingels, takes a committed stance, characterised equally by realism and a pragmatic optimism; one could even say hedonistic pragmatism.[42]

Die Vorstellung, dass Städte mehr sind als Gebäude und Infrastruktur, zeigen Projekte der 2005 in Kopenhagen gegründeten Bjarke Ingels Group in unterschiedlicher Weise. Die Eigenschaften, denen als performative und multiskalare Qualitäten Bedeutung beigemessen wird, erhalten dabei besondere Aufmerksamkeit. Eine gleichzeitig signifikante Prägung durch typologische Vermischung von Architektur und Landschaftsarchitektur und die Entwicklung unvertrauter urbaner Programmhybride sind damit verbunden. Sie wurden von dem Architekturbüro BIG als Zusammenarbeit von Architekt:innen und Landschaftsarchitekt:innen im internen Team und auch in Kooperation mit externen Architekt:innen, Landschaftsarchitekt:innen und Künstler:innen entwickelt. Die Position des Bürogründers Bjarke Ingels ist engagiert und gleichermaßen von Realismus wie von einem pragmatischen Optimismus geprägt, man könnte auch sagen von hedonistischem Pragmatismus.[42]

CONCEPTS   A strong interest in everyday culture is associated with the aim of creating socially, ecologically and economically 'perfect' places, which is also clearly shown in the manner in which the projects, partly playfully developed, are conceptualised and conveyed.[43] In the combination of pragmatism and hedonism, they see a new notion of a social infrastructure, as a proactive way of designing the cities of the future as a world in which people would like to live.[44] In this they also work with the system within which architecture is created, with rules of play, norms and regulations, and reinterpret these both logically and with playful innovation. This basic stance is combined with a self-defined interest in creating model projects for urban landscapes, which evolve in the context of ambitious climate goals of Danish politics and economics and flow into internationally realised projects.

In a short time, the architect Bjarke Ingels achieved global recognition with his BIG team, with many major assignments and a wide-ranging media presence. The titles of the books brought out in the last decade in connection with exhibitions of the internationally realised projects by BIG and their speculative future concepts clearly express the conceptual stance: 'Yes is More,' an optimistic impetus, 'Hot to Cold', an orientation towards context and climate, as well as 'Formgiving', a specific architec-

KONZEPTE   Mit dem Ziel sozial, ökologisch und ökonomisch ‚perfekte' Orte zu schaffen, ist ein starkes Interesse an Alltagskultur verbunden, welches sich auch in der Weise der teils spielerisch entwickelten Konzeptualisierung und Vermittlung der Projekte deutlich zeigt.[43] In der Kombination von Pragmatismus und Hedonismus sehen sie eine neue Auffassung sozialer Infrastruktur, als proaktiven Weg, um die Städte der Zukunft als eine Welt zu entwerfen, in der die Menschen gerne leben möchten.[44] Dabei arbeiten sie auch mit dem System, innerhalb dessen Architektur entsteht, mit Spielregeln, Normen und Regulierungen und interpretieren diese gleichermaßen logisch wie spielerisch innovativ um. Diese Grundhaltung verbindet sich mit einem selbstgesteckten Interesse, Modellprojekte für urbane Landschaften zu kreieren, die im Kontext ambitionierter Klimaziele der dänischen Politik und Wirtschaft entstehen und in international realisierte Projekte einfließen.

In kurzer Zeit erreichte der Architekt Bjarke Ingels mit seinem BIG-Team globale Anerkennung, viele große Aufträge und eine breit gefächerte Medienpräsenz. Die Titel der in der letzten Dekade im Zusammenhang mit Ausstellungen zu den international realisierten Projekten von BIG und ihren spekulativen Zukunftskonzepten entstandenen Bücher bringen signifikant

1–2 BIG Publications Hot to Cold, 2015 & Formgiving, 2021

ture, landscape architecture and urban development design competence which lies in giving a form to what is not yet existent (fig. 1–2).[45] The projects by the firm headquartered in Copenhagen and with branches in New York, London and Barcelona are targeted towards appropriation potential and mixing, through a strong orientation towards programming. They are linked to system thinking and are often combined with environmental analyses such as light and heat relations, wind and traffic influences and thermal qualities.[46] They are carried out with cost and resource awareness and also include futuristic visions, such as a floating city or a master plan on a planetary scale.[47] In the visionary project 'Masterplanet', for example, BIG applied this way of thinking to the whole earth and presented how the planet could be restructured to reduce emissions, save resources and actively counteract climate change.[48] Referred to as a worldwide leading visionary, in 2019 Bjarke Ingels received the internationally renowned prize from the Stiftung Deutscher Nachhaltigkeitspreis (German Sustainability Prize Foundation), which is awarded to encourage the economy and the communal sector to act sustainably and to anchor principles of sustainable development more deeply in public perception.[49] It especially emphasises the socio-cultural and aesthetic dimensions of sustainability, beyond the aforementioned aspects. With the intention of improving the quality of life of people and society, their design proposals are targeted towards promoting integrative public spaces.[50] For BIG, the driving force of every design is the wish to find new possibilities and to imaginatively extend the repertoire of spatial concepts.[51]

die konzeptuelle Grundhaltung zum Ausdruck: ‚Yes is more' einen optimistischen Impetus, ‚Hot to cold' eine Orientierung an Kontext und Klima
sowie ‚Formgiving' eine spezifische architektonische, landschaftsarchitektonische und städtebauliche Entwurfskompetenz, die darin liegt, dem noch
nicht Vorhandenen Form zu geben (Abb. 1–2).[45] Die Projekte des Büros
mit Sitz in Kopenhagen und Niederlassungen in New York, London und
Barcelona sind durch eine starke Orientierung auf das Programmieren, auf
Aneignungspotenziale und Vermischungen unterschiedlicher Art geprägt.
Sie sind mit Systemdenken verknüpft und werden oftmals verbunden mit
Umweltanalysen wie unter anderem zu Licht- und Wärmerelationen, Wind-
und Verkehrsflüssen und thermischen Qualitäten.[46] Sie werden kosten- und
ressourcenbewusst ausgeführt und schließen auch futuristische Visionen
ein, wie beispielsweise eine schwimmende Stadt oder einen Masterplan
im planetarischen Maßstab.[47] In dem visionären Projekt ‚Masterplanet' beispielsweise hat BIG diese Denkweise auf die gesamte Erde bezogen und
dargestellt, wie der Planet umgestaltet werden könnte, um Emissionen zu
verkleinern, Ressourcen zu schonen und dem Klimawandel aktiv entgegenzuwirken.[48] Bezeichnet als weltweit führender Visionär erhielt Bjarke Ingels
2019 den international renommierten Ehrenpreis der Stiftung Deutscher
Nachhaltigkeitspreis, der vergeben wird, um die Wirtschaft und den kom-
munalen Sektor zu nachhaltigem Handeln zu ermuntern sowie Grundsätze
nachhaltiger Entwicklung in der öffentlichen Wahrnehmung besser zu ver-
ankern.[49] In der Begründung werden insbesondere die über die benannten
Aspekte hinausreichenden sozio-kulturellen und ästhetischen Dimensionen
von Nachhaltigkeit betont. Mit der Intention, Lebensqualität von Menschen
und Gemeinschaft zu verbessern, sind diese darauf gerichtet, mit ihren
Gestaltungsvorschlägen integrative öffentliche Räume zu fördern.[50] Die treibende Kraft jedes Entwurfs ist für BIG der Wunsch, neue Möglichkeiten zu
erfinden und das Repertoire von Raumkonzepten fantasievoll zu erweitern.[51]

3–4   Harbour Bath   PLOT (BIG & JDS) Copenhagen 2003

An early project, the harbour in Copenhagen, already showed these incli-
nations. In an area densely built up with six-storey residential buildings,
the public space was extended into the water in the centrally situated
harbour area, Islands Brygge (fig. 3–4). In the formerly industrially used
42-kilometre-long area, architecture and landscape architecture projects
are designed to support the transformation of the harbour facilities into
a cultural and social centre of the city.[52] The bath's construction, built in
2003 as the first in a series of harbour baths and later extended by a
winter bath, is directly adjacent to the harbour's edge and a linear park
behind it, which was created in the 1980s through participatory processes,
with lawns crossed diagonally by several paths and with trees on the wider
paths. The city area is one of the most densely built up in Copenhagen,
consisting mostly of 6-storey residential buildings with little space for leisure
activities and regeneration. The team from the former firm PLOT (now separated into the firms BIG and JDS, Brussels) designed a stepped, elongated
area parallel to the edge of the embankment made of Scandinavian wood
and supported by movable pontoons. It serves as a delimitation and enclo-
sure of water basins for swimming, rising up as a roof and diving tower, as
well as a plateau for social use with various performative options (fig. 5).
The project represents an enrichment of the public space and recreational
possibilities and has become a social and cultural anchor point in the middle of the city.[53] There are plans for an extension to the successful site with
saunas and thermal baths. Soil sealing was avoided here, creating a space
with a high sojourn quality amidst the city by the water, enabling a perception of interaction with the water landscape nearby and further away.

5 The pool serves for social use with various performative options

Ein frühes Projekt, das Hafenbad in Kopenhagen, zeigte bereits Ansätze hierzu. In einem mit sechsgeschossigen Wohngebäuden dicht bebauten Gebiet wurde im zentral gelegenen Hafenareal Island Brygge der öffentliche Raum ins Wasser hinein fortgesetzt (Abb. 3–4). In dem vormals industriell genutzten, 42 km langen Gebiet sollen architektonische und landschaftsarchitektonische Projekte die Transformation der Hafenanlagen zu einem kulturellen und sozialen Zentrum der Stadt wesentlich fördern.[52] Die 2003 als erste einer Reihe von Hafenbädern entstandene Badkonstruktion, die später noch durch ein Winterbad erweitert wurde, grenzt direkt an die Hafenkante und einen dahinterliegenden linearen Park an. Er entstand in den 1980er Jahren in partizipativen Prozessen, mit Rasenflächen, die diagonal von mehreren Wegen durchquert werden und Baumbestand an den breiteren Wegen aufweisen. Der Stadtbereich ist einer der dichtbebautesten in Kopenhagen mit meist sechsgeschossigen Wohnbauten mit engen Höfen und wenig Raum für Freizeitaktivitäten und Regeneration. Das Team vom damaligen Büro PLOT (heute getrennt in den Büros BIG und JDS, Brüssel) entwarf eine parallel zur Uferkante abgestufte, lang gestreckte Platzfläche aus skandinavischen Hölzern und getragen von beweglichen Pontons. Sie dient als Begrenzung und Umrandung von Wasserbecken zum Schwimmen, ansteigend als Dach und Sprungturm sowie als Plateau für sozialen Gebrauch mit unterschiedlichen perfomativen Optionen (Abb. 5). Das Projekt bildet eine Bereicherung des öffentlichen Raums und Freizeitangebots und wurde zu einem sozialen und kulturellen Ankerpunkt inmitten der Stadt.[53] Eine Erweiterung der erfolgreichen Anlage mit Saunen und Thermalbad ist geplant. Hier wurde Flächenversiegelung vermieden, Raum mit hoher Aufenthaltsqualität mitten in der Stadt am Wasser geschaffen und die Wahrnehmung einer Verknüpfung mit der näheren und weiteren Wasserlandschaft ermöglicht.

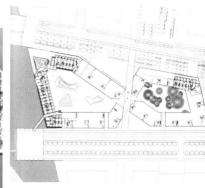

6–7   8-House Copenhagen 2010 South façade and ground floor plan

LANDSCAPE-NESS URBAN: 8-HOUSE   In relation to the idea of landscape-ness, it is the buildings often referred to as inhabited 'mountains' that display an exponentiated mixing to a high degree. An example of this can be found in the 8-House project in Copenhagen – Ørestad. It was constructed in 2010 as the first new build of a new district at the southern tip of Amager Island, in front of the Kalvebod Fælled nature reserve and the Køge Bay behind it.[54] A significant and high density is to be achieved with four large complexes in the new city district with its excellent connections to Copenhagen's inner city, in order to keep other parts of this area free for greenery and water (fig. 6). The building conceived by the BIG team together with the landscape architecture office KLAR, with a variety of residential, office and open space typologies plus additional functions (retailing, playschool, café, communal facilities) evokes a perimeter development formed in the shape of an eight, with a wide public traverse leading through its constricted middle as a connection to and between the urban spaces situated to the west and east (fig. 7). This formation creates two inner areas that were designed differently by KLAR. In the south, areas of lawn create a geometrically curved stepped relief (fig. 8). A children's playground was integrated later. In the northern courtyard, round hillocks of grass, criss-crossed by meandering paths, provide areas that can be freely used.

8   South courtyard giving views to the Kalvebod Fælled natural reserve

LANDSCHAFTLICHKEIT URBAN: 8-HOUSE   In Bezug zur
Idee von Landschaftlichkeit sind es die oftmals als bewohnte ‚Berge' bezeichneten Gebäude, die eine in hohem Maße potenzierte Vermischung zeigen.
Ein Beispiel dafür findet sich im Projekt 8-House in Kopenhagen-Ørestad.
Es entstand 2010 als erster Neubau eines neuen Stadtteils an der südlichen
Spitze auf der Insel Amager vor dem Naturschutzgebiet Kalvebod Fælled
und der dahinterliegenden Köge Bucht.[54] In dem neuen, hervorragend an
die Innenstadt Kopenhagens angebundenen Stadtbereich soll in vier größeren Komplexen eine große und hohe Dichte erreicht werden, um andere
Teile dieses Gebiets für Grün- und Wasserflächen freizuhalten (Abb. 6).
Das BIG-Team konzipierte das Gebäude zusammen mit dem Landschaftsarchitekturbüro KLAR mit unterschiedlichen Wohn-, Büro- und Freiraumtypologien sowie ergänzenden Funktionen (Einzelhandel, Kindergarten, Café,
Gemeinschaftseinrichtungen). Es ähnelt einer Blockrandbebauung, die in
Form einer Acht entwickelt wurde, durch deren eingeschnürte Mitte eine
breite öffentliche Traverse führt als Verbindung zu und zwischen den westlich und östlich gelegenen Stadträumen (Abb. 7). Durch diese Formation
entstehen zwei Innenbereiche, die von dem Landschaftsarchitekturbüro
KLAR verschieden gestaltet wurden. Im Süden erzeugen Rasenflächen ein
geometrisch geschwungenes Stufenrelief (Abb. 8). Ein Kinderspielplatz
wurde später integriert. Im Nordhof bilden runde Rasenhügel, durchzo-
gen von geschwungenen Wegen und Flächen, Areale zur freien Nutzung.

9   Square and café at south end

In addition, two squares were formed. One of them, which has a café, lies towards the water, where the building was lowered to one storey to bring the south sun and the view of the expansive adjoining meadow landscape to the south into the rooms and yards (fig. 9).[55] A second square lies diagonally opposite towards the successively constructed areas, where the 8-House rises partially up to thirteen storeys and has shops on the ground floor. Around the building, alternately on the inner and outer sides, leads a wide promenade that ascends and descends like uphill and downhill slopes.

From top to bottom, there is a mix of different residential typologies: penthouses, apartments and row houses with their own front garden, as well as commercial spaces and offices. The building units and spaces organised additively from various basic modules are characterised diversely by cantilevered elements and recesses, by layering and stepping. The ramp-like promenade is a special element, with grey and white patterned floor ornaments, accessible from different corners of the building both from outside, from the street, and from inside, from the courtyard. It culminates on the roof in a mixture of hillside path and roof garden. In connection with some stair sequences and passageways lined with a golden yellow colour, the whole building complex is surrounded by an open space for movement with various performative options (fig. 10–11). This results in a mix of indoor and outdoor spatial situations, as well as topographies, typologies and properties known from landscape spaces and city spaces.

10 Promenade along row houses facing south

11 Promenade crossing in a passageway

Zudem wurden zwei Platzsituationen ausgebildet. Eine davon mit einem Café liegt zum Wasser hin, wo das Gebäude auf ein Geschoss abgesenkt wurde, um die Südsonne und die Aussicht auf die nach Süden anschließende weite Wiesenlandschaft in die Höfe und Räume zu bringen (Abb. 9).[55] Ein zweiter Platz ist diagonal gegenüberliegend zu den nachfolgend bebauten Arealen hin orientiert, wo das 8-House partiell bis zu 13 Geschossen aufsteigt und im Erdgeschoss mit Geschäften ausgestattet ist. Um das Gebäude herum, Innen und Außen im Wechsel, wird eine breite Promenade geführt, die berg- und hangartig auf- und absteigt.

Von oben nach unten findet sich eine Mischung unterschiedlicher Wohntypologien: Penthouses, Apartments und Reihenhäuser mit eigenem Vorgarten sowie kommerzielle Bereiche und Büros. Die aus verschiedenen Grundmodulen additiv organisierten Baukörper- und Raumbildungen sind durch Auskragungen und Rücksprünge, durch Schichtung und Abtreppung vielfältig charakterisiert. Als besonderes Element ist die von verschiedenen Gebäudeecken jeweils außen von der Straße und innen vom Hof zugängliche, rampenartige Promenade mit grau-weiß-gemusterten Bodenornamenten ausgebildet. Diese kulminiert auf dem Dach in einer Mischung aus Bergpfad und Dachgarten. In Verbindung mit einigen Treppensequenzen und in goldgelber Farbigkeit gefassten Durchgängen umgibt so ein offener Bewegungsraum mit unterschiedlichen performativen Optionen den gesamten Gebäudekomplex (Abb. 10–11). Dabei vermischen sich innen- und außenräumliche Situationen ebenso wie Oben und Unten sowie aus Landschaftsräumen und aus Stadträumen bekannte Topografien, Typologien und Eigenschaften.

12   Promenade, northern courtyard

Adaptable public spaces were formed in different ways, as an invitation to linger, stroll, cycle, play and communicate, and are also used in this way. Ideals were developed further or modified here that had been proposed in the 1950s and 1960s, for example by Peter and Alison Smithson, for large residential complexes in London, referred to as 'Streets in the air' and in their part inspired by the public spaces to be found in Le Corbusier's residential blocks.[56] The promenade links the 150 front gardens of comparatively low-priced row houses and apartments and invites use of the street area as an active meeting place to forge contacts (fig. 12–13). The materials and patterns of the promenade design evoke the Copacabana, which the renowned Brazilian landscape architect Roberto Burle Marx had designed in the 1970s in Rio de Janeiro.[57] It is reminiscent of a place for leisure, recreation, encounters and enjoyment.

A property mix of landscape-ness and urbanity is generated through various spatial relations and public promenades, paths, steps and interior courtyards, which also allow a range of appropriation possibilities, highlighting a series of potential spatial-temporal movement sequences, coupled with a variety of scales, rhythms and situations of opening up and views out into the expanse of the surrounding nature and culture landscapes. Qualities of suburban life in the context of large natural areas are mixed with dynamic experience qualities of the city so as to become an urban landscape. Like these, many of the architectural formations of BIG evoke mountains, hills, oases and harbours, which appear to emerge as landscape elements on a city scale. They have an influence on urban silhouettes, on shorelines and aerial perspectives of the city.[58] Also due to their scale and their connections to a wider territory than that of the immediate urban context, they gain a landscape-like character.

13   Row houses with private gardens have access to the promenade

Es wurden in verschiedener Weise adaptierbare öffentliche Räume gebildet, die zum Aufenthalt, zum Promenieren, Fahrradfahren, Spielen und Kommunizieren einladen und auch in dieser Weise genutzt werden. Weiterentwickelt bzw. modifiziert wurden hier Ideale, die in den 1950er und 1960er Jahren vorgeschlagen worden waren, beispielsweise von Peter und Alison Smithson für Londoner Großwohnkomplexe, bezeichnet als ‚Streets in the air', die ihrerseits inspiriert waren durch die in Wohnblöcken Le Corbusiers zu findenden öffentlichen Räume.[56] Die Promenade verbindet die 150 Vorgärten der im städtischen Vergleich kostengünstigen Reihenhäuser und Apartments und lädt dazu ein, den Straßenraum als aktiven Treffpunkt zu nutzen und Kontakte zu knüpfen (Abb. 12–13). In der Materialität und Musterung erinnert die Promenadengestaltung an die Copacabana, die der renommierte brasilianische Landschaftsarchitekt Roberto Burle Marx in den 1970er Jahren in Rio de Janeiro gestaltet hatte.[57] Sie erinnert an einen Ort der Freizeit, Erholung, Begegnung und des Vergnügens.

Es wird so eine Eigenschaftsmischung von Landschaftlichkeit und Urbanität erzeugt: Eine Abfolge von potentiellen raum-zeitlichen Bewegungssequenzen tritt in den Vordergrund in Form verschiedener Raumrelationen und über die öffentlichen Promenaden, Wege, Treppen und Innenhöfe, die zudem vielfältige Aneignungsmöglichkeiten bieten, sowie mittels unterschiedlicher Maßstäbe, Rhythmen und Stiuationen der Öffnung und des Ausblickens in die Weite der umgebenden Natur- und Kulturlandschaften. Qualitäten suburbanen Lebens im Kontext großer naturräumlicher Bereiche werden mit dynamischen Erfahrungsqualitäten der Großstadt gemischt zu urbaner Landschaft. Wie diese evozieren zahlreiche der architektonischen Formationen von BIG Erinnerungen an Berge, Hügel, Oasen und Häfen, die im Maßstab der ganzen Stadt als landschaftliche Elemente hervorzutreten scheinen. Sie haben eine Auswirkung auf städtische Silhouetten, auf Uferlinien und die Luftperspektiven der Stadt.[58] Auch aufgrund ihres Maßstabs und ihrer Verbindungen zu einem größeren Territorium als dem des direkten urbanen Kontextes erhalten sie einen landschaftlichen Charakter.

14 CopenHill Copenhagen 2017 View towards the centre of Copenhagen

CITY TOPOGRAPHY: WASTE-TO-ENERGY   This can be found in a further project with even more evident mixing of design and programmatic qualities. The waste-to-energy site in Amager Bakke, which was established as the largest project built in the centre of Copenhagen near the yacht harbour and the water skiing areas, and which opened in 2017, is a novel mixed typology formed out of the technical facility of an infrastructure building, artificial landscape and public space (fig. 14).[59] It was designed by BIG with the teams from the landscape architecture office Topothek and Man Made Land, based in Berlin, as well as the architecture and media art firm realities:united. Through the restructuring, the building from the 1960s was turned into a technologically renewed and extended refuse incinerating site, which provides wide areas of Copenhagen with energy and produces more clean water than is used. An inclined and undulating roof forming a big curve was conceived by the Copenhagen landscape architecture firm SLA. Designed with an artificial grass surface, as well as hills, individual indigenous groups of trees and the planting of bushes and shrubs like a hill landscape, it spanned the volume of the building and the 100-metre-high chimney (fig 15–16).[60] This new urban ecosystem serves a wide range of activities all year round. As a ski piste, climbing wall, walking area and public space, the 'CopenHill' can offer a range of possibilities to the inhabitants of Copenhagen, who do then not need to drive to the faraway mountains of southern Sweden.

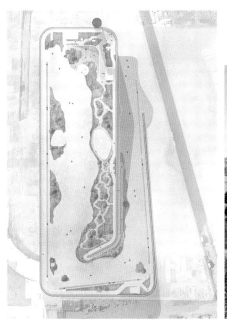

15–16   SLA landscaping Landscape design forms a roof landscape for various outdoor activities

STADTTOPOGRAFIE: WASTE-TO-ENERGY Dies findet sich in einem weiteren Projekt mit noch deutlicheren Vermischungen der gestalterischen und programmatischen Qualitäten. Die Waste-to-energy-Anlage in Amager Bakke, die als größtes von BIG gebautes Projekt im Zentrum Kopenhagens nahe des Yachthafens und der Wasserskibereiche entstand und 2017 eröffnet wurde, bildet eine neuartige Mischtypologie aus der technischen Anlage eines Infrastrukturgebäudes, artifizieller Landschaft und öffentlichem Raum (Abb. 14).[59] Sie wurde von BIG mit den in Berlin ansässigen Teams der Landschaftarchitekturbüros Topotek 1 und Man made land sowie des Architektur- und Medienkunstbüros realities:united entworfen. Durch den Umbau entstand aus dem Bau der 1960er Jahre eine nun technologisch erneuerte und erweiterte Müllverbrennungsanlage, die große Bereiche Kopenhagens mit Energie versorgt und mehr sauberes Wasser produziert als verbraucht wird. Über dem Gebäudevolumen wurde eine die notwendigen Baukörper sowie den 100 m hohen Schornstein mit Aufzug überfangende schräge, in einer großen Kurve geschwungene Dachform konzipiert. Sie ist mit künstlicher, ganzjährig befahrbarer Grasfläche sowie mit Hügeln, vereinzelten indigenen Baumgruppen und Busch- und Bodenbepflanzungen wie eine Berglandschaft von dem Kopenhagener Landschaftsarchitekturbüro SLA gestaltet (Abb. 15–16).[60] Dieses neue urbane Ökosystem ist ganzjährig für verschiedenste Aktivitäten nutzbar.   85

17   SLA landscaping   Different paths allow for hiking

The 'alpine' park is thus formed as a literal extension to the topography of Copenhagen, an infrastructure with public benefit, which is associated with well thought out, positive social and environmental side effects (fig. 17–19). It shows the many possibilities that sustainability harbours, which in an urban context can be associated with various dimensions of landscape-ness, with physically present and referentially conveyed elements. The effect of this rather object-like leisure and event landscape as an analogy to hill landscapes is reinforced further through greenery that promotes biodiversity and the landscape architecture design of the surrounding areas, as a park with an artificial topography of hills of various heights and a pond. The planned signal effect of smoke rings rising in certain CO_2 contamination situations, which is intended to make the excessive production and transformation of refuse a visible sign in the sky for the city dwellers and tourists, has not yet been realised. With this 'social infrastructure' characterised by the evocation of experiential density, which can also act as a transferable prototype, a new type of landscape-ness is created within the metropolitan field, in which it can act from afar as a landmark with visual connecting properties.[61] Not only are indoors and outdoors, top and bottom semantically interwoven but also familiar notions of natural space and urban space. The mix proposed here of ecosystematic properties and a new urban way of life forges visionary horizons for the structural-spatial design.

18–19   SLA landscaping   Idyllic landscapes contrast the surrounding industrial sites

Als Skipiste, Kletterwand, Wandergebiet und öffentlicher Raum kann der CopenHill vielfältige Möglichkeitsräume für die Bewohnerschaft Kopenhagens erzeugen, die dann nicht mit Autos bis zu den weit entfernt gelegenen Gebirgen nach Südschweden fahren muss. Der ‚alpine' Park wird so als buchstäbliche Erweiterung der Topografie Kopenhagens geformt, eine Infrastruktur mit öffentlicher Nützlichkeit, die mit zuvor überlegten positiven sozialen und umweltbezogenen Nebeneffekten verbunden ist (Abb. 17–19). So wird veranschaulicht, wie Nachhaltigkeit viele Möglichkeiten birgt und im urbanen Kontext mit verschiedenen Dimensionen von Landschaftlichkeit verbunden sein kann, mit physisch präsenten ebenso wie mit referenziell vermittelten. Die Wirkung dieser eher objekthaften Freizeit- und Eventlandschaft in Analogie zu Berglandschaften wird durch eine Biodiversität fördernde Begrünung und die landschaftsarchitektonische Gestaltung der umgebenden Flächen zu einem Park mit künstlicher Topografie aus verschieden hohen Hügeln und einem Teich noch gestärkt werden. Die geplante Signalwirkung von in bestimmten CO_2-Belastungssituationen aufsteigenden Rauchringen, die eine übermäßige Produktion und Transformation von Müll als am Himmel sichtbares Zeichen für die Stadtbewohner:innen und Tourist:innen wahrnehmbar machen sollten, wurde bislang nicht realisiert. Mit dieser durch die Evokation von Erlebnisdichte charakterisierten ‚sozialen Infrastruktur', die auch als transferfähiger Prototyp wirken kann, entsteht eine neue Art Landschaftlichkeit innerhalb des metropolitanen Felds, in dem sie weiträumig als Landmark mit visuellen Verknüpfungseigenschaften wirken kann.[61] Es werden nicht nur Innen und Außen, Oben und Unten semantisch verwoben, sondern auch vertraute Vorstellungen von Naturraum und Stadtraum. Die hier vorgeschlagene Mischung von ökosystematischen Eigenschaften und neuer urbaner Lebensform zeichnet für die baulich-räumliche Gestaltung visionäre Horizonte.

20 BIG U flood protection New York 2021 and ongoing

INFRASTRUCTURE ARCHITECTURE LANDSCAPE: BIG U

By means of a proactive cross between architecture and a social programme with leisure qualities, the BIG team seeks to promote new urban lifestyles in the city, along with its major project, BIG U, in New York. With this project, which was commissioned as a flood prevention measure for Lower Manhattan by the Department of Housing and Urban Development (HUD) of New York City after a restricted architecture competition, a prototype was created for rebuilding and as a prophylaxis against flood disasters, here based on the example of a metropolis.[62] Invisible flood barriers were to be developed in various locations on the embankment. For Manhattan, this competition was won by BIG with ONE Architecture & Urbanism (ONE). The flood barriers present a 13-kilometre-long, continuous protective wall with various zones (fig. 20). Incorporating findings from workshops with the local population, the project includes programmatic elements for culture, leisure and sports, parks, pavilions and sports areas, as well as a marine museum, all with a sustainable design with green roofs, photovoltaic systems, electric charging stations and reused materials.[63] In this way, the life of the city is not separated from the water; instead leisure and recreation areas by the water are created for the various city areas accordingly (fig. 21–22). Here one can speak of an infrastructural space that exceeds individual typological articulations. It is characterised in its relationality by landscape-ness, whereby architecture directly links infrastructure and landscape architecture and is characterised by overlapping and layering. The configuration is subject to a systematic thinking that has an urban character.[64] In addition, the necessary resilient infrastructure is combined not only with structural-spatial manifestations but also harbours the potential for a variety of appropriations and interpretations by the users.

21–22   Diverse programmatic elements cover the flood barriers

INFRASTRUKTUR ARCHITEKTUR LANDSCHAFT: BIG U

Mittels einer proaktiven Kreuzung von Infrastruktur und sozialem Programm mit Erholungsqualitäten möchte das BIG-Team auch mit dem Großprojekt BIG U in New York neue urbane Lebensformen in der Stadt befördern. Mit diesem Projekt, das als Hochwasserschutzmaßnahme für Lower Manhattan vom Department of Housing and Urban Development (HUD) der Stadt New York City nach einem beschränkten Architekturwettbewerb beauftragt wurde, entstand ein Prototyp für den Wiederaufbau und die Prophylaxe gegen Flutkatastrophen für Städte am Wasser, hier am Beispiel einer Metropole vorgestellt.[62] An verschiedenen Standorten sollten am Ufer unsichtbare Flutbarrieren entwickelt werden. Für Manhattan wurde dieser Wettbewerb von BIG mit ONE Architecture & Urbanism (ONE) gewonnen. Sie präsentierten einen 13 km langen, kontinuierlichen Schutzwall mit diversen Zonen (Abb. 20). Unter Einbezug der Erkenntnisse aus Workshops mit der lokalen Bevölkerung sind programmatische Bausteine aus Kultur, Freizeit- und Sportangeboten, mit Parks, Pavillons und Sportbereichen und einem Meeresmuseum vorgesehen. Sie sollen nachhaltig gestaltet werden beispielsweise mit Gründächern, Fotovoltaik, elektrischen Ladestationen und wiederverwendeten Materialien.[63] In dieser Weise wird das Leben der Stadt nicht vom Wasser getrennt, vielmehr entstehen für die verschiedenen Stadtbereiche angepasste Freizeit- und Naherholungsgebiete am Wasser (Abb. 21–22). Hier kann von einem Infrastrukturraum gesprochen werden, der einzelne typologische Artikulationen überschreitet. Er ist in seiner Relationalität durch Landschaftlichkeit geprägt, wobei Architektur, Infrastruktur und Landschaftsarchitektur unmittelbar verschränkt sowie durch Überschneidungen und Überlagerungen charakterisiert sind. Die Konfiguration unterliegt hier einem urban geprägten Systemdenken.[64] Darüberhinaus wird die notwendige resiliente Infrastruktur nicht nur mit baulich-räumlichen Manifestationen kombiniert, sondern enthält zudem das Potenzial für verschiedenste Aneignungen und Interpretationen durch die Nutzenden.

REPERTOIRE   The presented projects by BIG show how an event-ori
entated and narrative design orientation generates novel urban space
formations of a hybrid nature with the mixing of architecture, open space
and landscape architecture, which can be associated with experiences of
landscape-ness on different scales and in differing manifestations. Diverse
schemata, which are repeatedly incorporated in the project designs in many
variants, may prove in some cases to be pithy or adapted to mass media,
but are fundamentally based on both serious and playful experimental
approaches to contemporary challenges. They form distinctive and because
of this also potentially identity-forging locations and spaces.[65] The repertoire comprises the emphasis, differentiated articulation and high relevance
of the access areas as public spaces of movement, interaction and leisure
activity. Passageways, promenades, ramps, steps, interior courtyards and
roof surfaces have varied designs and are articulated as communal public
spaces that can stimulate a variety of events and situations. The formations
analogous to mountains and hills do not only forge an allusion to landscape
topographies but also hint at an architectural ideal that already appeared in
ancient descriptions and found a more explicit conceptualisation and formulation in Renaissance architectures. Thus, views out into the nearer and further
surroundings were incorporated, which are shaped in a targeted manner in
the building formation.[66] This thematises important layers of ordering architecture composition and their connections to surrounding areas, as well as
reinterpreting and updating them in specific familiar and unfamiliar ways.
In addition, it is the strong programmatic mixes of the combined parts of
architecture, landscape architecture and infrastructure, of architecture object
and open space, as well as natural area and urban area that form the central
design approach and open up new perspectives in the context of various
everyday perceptions and actions, of memories and experiences, as well as
of wishes and fictions. This creates a mix of features of landscape-ness and
urbanity. Qualities of suburban life in the context of large natural areas are
mixed with dynamic experience qualities of the city into an urban landscape.
This results in ambivalent and multivalent hybrid urban formations. Typologically, spatially and in relation to usage, a design diversity unfolds that can
mix up orientation as well as open up new possibilities.[67] Landscape-ness as
architectural idea is understood in particular here as a design of potential
actions and interactions, in the sense of active formations of urban spaces.

Die vorgestellten Projekte von BIG zeigen, wie eine ereignisorientierte und narrative Entwurfsorientierung mit der Vermischung von Architektur, Freiraum und Landschaftsarchitektur neuartige Stadtraumgebilde hybriden Charakters erzeugt, die in unterschiedlichen Maßstäben und Manifestationen mit Erfahrungsbereichen von Landschaftlichkeit verbunden sein können. Vereinfachte Schemata, die in diversen Varianten wiederholt in den Projektentwürfen Aufnahme finden, mögen sich dabei in manchen Fällen als massenmedial angepasst oder plakativ erweisen, beruhen aber grundlegend auf gleichermaßen ernsthaften wie spielerisch-experimentell vorgenommenen Auseinandersetzungen mit zeitgenössischen Herausforderungen. Sie bilden einprägsame und gerade dadurch auch potenziell identitätsstiftende Orte und Räume aus.[65] Das Repertoire umfasst dabei die Betonung, differenzierte Artikulation und hohe Relevanz der Erschließungsbereiche als öffentliche Räume der Bewegung, Interaktion und Freizeitaktivität. Passagen, Promenaden, Rampen, Treppen, Innenhöfe und Dachflächen werden differenziert gestaltet, als gemeinschaftliche öffentliche Räume artikuliert, die viele unterschiedliche Ereignisse und Situationen stimulieren können. Schließlich wird mit den berg- und hügelanalogen Formbildungen nicht nur eine Anspielung auf landschaftliche Topografien erzeugt, vielmehr auch auf ein Architekturideal, das bereits in antiken Beschreibungen auftaucht und in Renaissancearchitekturen explizitere Konzeptualisierung und Ausformulierung fand. So werden auch die Ausblicke in die nahe und fernere Umgebung einbezogen, die gezielt in der baulichen Formation mitgestaltet werden.[66] Dadurch werden wichtige Layer ordnender Architekturkomposition und ihrer Verbindungen zu umgebenden Räumen thematisiert und in spezifischen vertrauteren und unvertrauten Weisen neu interpretiert und aktualisiert. Darüber hinaus sind es die starken programmatischen Vermischungen der kombinierten Teile aus Architektur, Landschaftsarchitektur und Infrastruktur, aus Architekturobjekt und Freiraum sowie Naturraum und Stadtraum, die dabei den zentralen Entwurfsansatz bilden und neue Perspektiven eröffnen im Kontext verschiedener alltäglicher Wahrnehmungen und Aktionen, von Erinnerungen und Erfahrungen wie auch von Wünschen und Fiktionen. Damit wird eine Eigenschaftsmischung von Landschaftlichkeit und Urbanität erzeugt. Qualitäten suburbanen Lebens im Kontext großer naturräumlicher Bereiche werden mit dynamischen Erfahrungsqualitäten der Großstadt gemischt zu urbaner Landschaft. Es entstehen ambivalente und multivalente hybride Stadtraumgebilde. Typologisch, räumlich und nutzungsbezogen wird eine gestalterische Mannigfaltigkeit wirksam, die ebenso zu Orientierungsbrüchen führen kann wie zur Öffnung neuer Möglichkeitsräume.[67] Landschaftlichkeit als Architekturidee wird dabei insbesondere auch als Entwurf potenzieller Aktionen und Wechselwirkungen verstanden im Sinne aktiver Formationen urbaner Räume.

GEBAUTE LANDSCHAFTEN
BUILT LANDSCAPES
MVRDV

Notions of architecture as a built landscape, presented in the thinking and works of the Dutch architecture firm MVRDV, enable the extension on various levels of the previously analysed means of interpretation and articulation of landscape-ness as an architectural idea, especially with regard to conceptual architecture components and landscape interpretations. Theoretical and built examples of these appeared very early on in the work of the firm founded in 1993 in Rotterdam by the Dutch architects Winy Maas, Jacob van Rijs and Nathalie de Vries who now work internationally with further branches in Shanghai and Paris.[68] From the beginning, the specific working method of MVRDV has been characterised predominantly by a coevolutionary development of speculative research and building projects at the intersection of architecture and urban design.

Vorstellungen von Architektur als gebauter Landschaft, wie sie im Denken und Schaffen des niederländischen Architekturbüros MVRDV dargeboten werden, ermöglichen es, die bisher analysierten Weisen der Interpretation und Artikulation von Landschaftlichkeit als Architekturidee um weitere Ebenen insbesondere im Hinblick auf konzeptuelle Architekturkomponenten und Landschaftsinterpretationen zu erweitern. Ideelle und gebaute Beispiele dafür waren sehr früh aufgetreten im Werk des 1993 in Rotterdam von den niederländischen Architekt:innen Winy Maas, Jacob van Rijs und Nathalie de Vries gegründeten und mittlerweile international arbeitenden Büros mit weiteren Standorten in Shanghai und Paris.[68] Übergreifend ist die spezifische Arbeitsweise von MVRDV von Beginn an charakterisiert durch eine koevolutionäre Entwicklung von spekulativer Forschung und baulichen Projekten an der Schnittstelle von Architektur und Städtebau.

Their numerous publications do not only present an invitation to communication. They correlate with individual project ideas by examining particular aspects of questions about the future from a transdisciplinary point of view that at the same time has a perspective focused on the built environment. The influence of Rem Koolhaas and his office OMA/AMO provided these impulses. Their ambitious, internationally developed and published research on programmatic architecture, and on the current conditions of contemporary cities and urbanised territories were introduced to the later MVRDV partners as students at TU Delft, and to Winy Maas and Jacob van Rijs also as employees at this office.[69] Theory and practice are linked with a reflexive stance also in the basic approach by MVRDV. It can be described as pragmatic and provoking. The condition of the Netherlands as a physically and spatially constructed, artificially manufactured landscape also feeds the ongoing enthusiasm of MVRDV to create contemporarily relevant and future-orientated architecture in an unusual and innovative manner with their approaches to landscape-ness in architecture and urban development.[70]

CONCEPTS   One of the fundamental and consistent themes in the thinking and works of MVRDV is density as a central challenge of the contemporary world, which occurs not only in the densely populated Netherlands but in many metropolises and metropolitan regions. Density is thereby understood as population density and resource-related density.[71] It is sounded out experimentally in various ways how architecture and urban development can affect these developments as means and mediums. The smallest common denominator of the various studies by the office and

Ihre zahlreichen Veröffentlichungen bilden nicht nur eine Einladung zur Kommunikation. Sie stehen in Wechselwirkung mit einzelnen Projektideen, indem sie Einzelaspekte zu Fragen der Zukunft aus einer transdisziplinären und gleichzeitig auf die gebaute Umwelt fokussierten Perspektive untersuchen. Impulsgebend wirkte der Einfluss von Rem Koolhaas und seinem Büro OMA/AMO. Deren ambitionierte, international entwickelte und publizierte Forschungen zu programmatischer Architektur, zu aktuellen Konditionen zeitgenössischer Städte und verstädterter Territorien lernten die späteren MVRDV-Partner:innen als Studierende an der TU Delft und Winy Maas und Jacob van Rijs zudem als Mitarbeiter in diesem Büro kennen.[69] Auch in der Grundhaltung von MVRDV werden Theorie und Praxis mit einer reflexiven Haltung verknüpft, die als pragmatisch und provokant beschrieben werden kann. Die Kondition der Niederlande als physisch und räumlich konstruierte, künstlich manufakturierte Landschaft nährt zudem den anhaltenden Enthusiasmus von MVRDV, mit ihren Ansätzen zur Landschaftlichkeit in Architektur und Städtebau zeitgenössisch relevante und zukunftsfähige Architektur in ungewöhnlicher und innovativer Weise zu schaffen.[70]

KONZEPTE   Eines der grundlegenden und durchgängigen Themenfelder im Denken und Schaffen von MVRDV bildet Dichte als zentrale Herausforderung der zeitgenössischen Welt, die nicht nur in den dicht besiedelten Niederlanden, sondern in vielen Metropolen und Metropolregionen weltweit auftritt. Dichte wird dabei verstanden als Bevölkerungsdichte und als ressourcenbezogene Verdichtung.[71] Wie Architektur und Städtebau als Mittel und Medien in diesen Entwicklungen wirken können, wird experimentell in verschiedener Weise ausgelotet. So kann als kleinster gemeinsamer

1 Metacity Datatown 1999

the think tank 'The Why Factory' directed by Winy Maas at TU Delft can be described as the researching of stacked, layered and vertical constructional density for a wide range of usage types and in many places around the world. These studies present reference points for decision-making processes and impulses for the spatial formations of building projects.[72] In the office's research, projects are developed from hypotheses and condensed with the 'Datascapes' tool. Datascapes are conceptual visualisations that link abstract and concrete representational means. As a methodological approach to research and design projects, given parameters and data are visualised in order to create unexpected formations of dynamic systems.[73] They serve as potential for rethinking themes and tasks in architecture and urban design and for evoking input for projects, even if no general conclusions can be drawn from them. Examples of this are the studies 'Metacity Datatown' from 1999 with extreme scenarios for the future densification of urbanised re-gions and 'PoroCity' from 2018 with the researching of the possibilities of porous open spaces in dense buildings (fig. 1–3). The spectrum of associated design solutions is extended rather than restricted. Datascapes enable the testing of various scenarios in combination with different design parameters, in order to design more sustainable, efficient and adaptable buildings.

The gently folded continuity of the levels of the compact five-storey office and studio building VPRO in Hilversum, Netherlands, from 1997, with patios in the building that let light in and open up views, as well as ramps, wide stairs and slightly terraced areas, displays a formation that in the interior morphologically resembles topographical conditions (fig. 4–6). This evokes

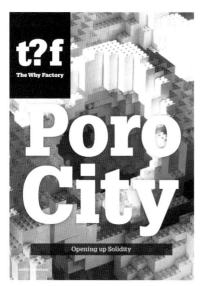

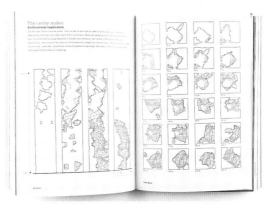

2–3 The Why Factory PoroCity 2018

Nenner der diversen Studien des Büros und des von Winy Maas an der TU Delft geleiteten Thinktanks ‚Why Factory' die Erforschung gestapelter, geschichteter vertikaler baulicher Dichte für unterschiedlichste Nutzungsarten und an verschiedensten Orten der Welt beschrieben werden. Diese Untersuchungen bilden Bezugspunkte für Entscheidungsprozesse und Impulse für die räumlichen Formationen baulicher Projekte.[72] In den Forschungsprojekten des Büros werden aus Hypothesen Projekte entwickelt und mit dem Instrument der Datascapes komprimiert. Datascapes sind konzeptuelle Visualisierungen, die abstrakte und anschauliche Darstellungsweisen verknüpfen. Als methodische Ausrichtung für Forschungs- und Entwurfsprojekte werden damit gegebene Parameter und Daten visualisiert, um unerwartete Formationen dynamischer Systeme zu kreieren.[73] Sie dienen als Potenzial, um Themen und Aufgaben von Architektur und Städtebau neu zu überdenken und Input für Projekte zu evozieren, auch wenn daraus keine generellen Schlüsse zu ziehen sind. Beispiele dafür bilden die Studien ‚Metatacity Datatown' von 1999 mit extremen Szenarios zur zukünftigen Verdichtung verstädterter Regionen oder ‚PoroCity' von 2018 mit der Erforschung der Möglichkeiten poröser offener Räume in verdichteten Gebäuden (Abb. 1–3). Das Spektrum der daran anknüpfenden gestalterischen Lösungen wird eher ausgeweitet als beschränkt. Datascapes ermöglichen, verschiedene Szenarien in Kombination mit unterschiedlichen Entwurfsparametern zu testen, um Gebäude nachhaltiger, effizienter und anpassungsfähiger zu entwerfen. Die weich gefaltete Kontinuität der Ebenen des kompakten fünfgeschossigen Büro- und Studiogebäudes VPRO im niederländischen Hilversum von 1997 veranschaulicht mit lichteinlassenden und ausblicköffnenden Patios im Gebäude sowie Rampen, breiten Treppen und leicht terrassierten Bereichen als frühes

4 VPRO Building Hilversum 1997

a type of continuation of a potential site formation, which can be used flexibly as an open, adaptive environment and is rounded off by a roof garden with views and an additional sojourn quality.[74] Compactness in combination with varied spatial differentiation, as well as the distinctively spatially articulated connection with the outdoor area, are design components that are interpreted variously in further concepts and projects by MVRDV, often in connection with a mix of functions, with sustainable technological solutions, imaginative building volumes and spatial designs. Clients, users and various experts are also included in the creative processes.[75] Standards of sustainable, energy-efficient and resource-efficient building are not only taken into consideration in the projects but are also thematised, questioned, uncommonly interpreted and transgressed in order to find innovative, extravagant and extrapolative solutions, as well as to take social, cultural and aesthetic dimensions into account. The focus of the numerous international urban design and residential projects, as well as of other construction tasks, are land use within the metropolitan region, the relations between city and countryside, residential forms of the future, inclusive social culture and not least the economy and ecology. Their designs are alluring, sustainable and community orientated. Fundamentally associated with various types of built landscape, many of the projects by MVRDV are characterised by analytical seriousness as well as by playful innovative power.

5–6   Inner patios and interior spaces form a continuous space

gebautes Beispiel eine Formation, die im Innern morphologisch an topografische Gegebenheiten erinnert (Abb. 4–6). Dies evoziert eine Art Fortsetzung
einer potenziellen Grundstücksformation, die als offene adaptive Umgebung
flexibel nutzbar wird und von einem Dachgarten mit Ausblicken und zusätz-
licher Aufenthaltsqualität abgeschlossen ist.[74] Kompaktheit in Verknüpfung
mit vielfältiger räumlicher Differenzierung wie auch die dezidiert räumlich
artikulierte Verbindung mit dem Außenraum sind Gestaltungskomponenten,
die in weiteren Konzepten und Projekten von MVRDV variantenreich interpretiert werden, oftmals verknüpft mit Funktionsmischung, mit nachhaltigen
technologischen Lösungen und imaginativen Baukörper- und Raumgestaltungen. In die kreativen Prozesse werden zudem Klient:innen, Nutzende sowie
diverse Expert:innen einbezogen.[75] Standards nachhaltigen, energie- und
ressourcensparenden Bauens sind dabei nicht nur in den Projekten berücksichtigt, sondern werden thematisiert, befragt, ungewöhnlich interpretiert
und überschritten, um innovative, extravagante und extrapolierbare Lösungen zu finden sowie soziale, kulturelle und ästhetische Dimensionen einzubeziehen. Im Mittelpunkt der zahlreichen internationalen Städtebau- und
Wohnprojekte, aber auch bei anderen Bauaufgaben stehen die Flächen-
nutzung im städtischen Raum, die Relationen von Stadt und Land, Wohn-
formen der Zukunft, inklusive Soziokultur und nicht zuletzt Ökonomie und
Ökologie. Ihre Entwürfe sind verführerisch, nachhaltig und gemeinschafts-
orientiert. Grundlegend mit verschiedenen Varianten gebauter Landschaft
verbunden, zeichnen sich zahlreiche der Projekte von MVRDV durch analytische Ernsthaftigkeit ebenso aus wie durch spielerische Innovationskraft.

7 Dutch Pavilion Hanover 2000

STACKED LANDSCAPE   With the Dutch Pavilion 'Holland creates Space', MVRDV realised a model of a densified built landscape at
Expo 2000 in Hanover (fig. 7). The building is currently being transformed
according to designs also by MVRDV and extended into a larger urban
ensemble. The first world exhibition in its 150-year history to be held in
Germany had the intention of presenting future developments and problems,
and formulating future issues of world society and solutions. The concepts
of the pavilions are designed to show and sound out the dimensions of the
theme 'People – nature – technology'.[76] The Dutch contribution thematised
the feasibility and artificiality of landscape, the interweaving of nature and
technology.[77] The vertical stacking of different landscape types – dunes,
greenhouses, forest and embankment landscape – formed the key idea of
the concept (fig. 8–10). The levels were networked into an artificial ecosystem with a self-contained water and energy cycle. The individual storeys of
the open pavillion showed how plants gain biomass, produce food and can
clean the water. The 47-metre-high pavilion also presented a stacked public
space in the sense of a dense outdoor area that forms an indoor space here.
In this manner, the building became the framework for a continuity of the
site on the various floors, representing a landscape type respectively from
the support structure to the interior design and accessed from circulating
outdoor stairs.[78] The upper level, which was designed as a Dutch marsh, especially became an expressive representation medium with its wind wheels.

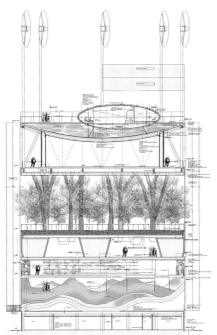

8–10 Section showing different spatial situations and types of landscape

GESTAPELTE LANDSCHAFT   Mit dem niederländischen Pavillon ‚Holland creates space' hatte MVRDV ein Modell verdichteter gebauter Landschaft auf der Expo 2000 in Hannover realisiert (Abb. 7). Zurzeit wird das Gebäude ebenfalls nach Entwürfen von MVRDV transformiert und zu einem größeren urbanen Ensemble erweitert. Die in der 150-jährigen Geschichte der Weltausstellungen erste, die in Deutschland stattfand, hatte die Intention, zukünftige globale Entwicklungen und Probleme dazustellen, Zukunftsfragen der Weltgesellschaft zu formulieren und Lösungen aufzuzeigen. In den Konzepten der Pavillons sollten Dimensionen des Themas ‚Mensch – Natur – Technik' aufgezeigt und ausgelotet werden.[76] Mit dem niederländischen Beitrag wurde die Machbarkeit und Künstlichkeit von Landschaft, die Verschränkung von Natur und Technologie thematisiert.[77] Die vertikale Stapelung unterschiedlicher Landschaftstypen – Dünen, Gewächshäuser, Wald- und Deichlandschaft – bildete die Leitidee des Konzepts (Abb. 8–10). Die Ebenen wurden vernetzt zu einem künstlichen Ökosystem mit geschlossenem Wasser- und Energiekreislauf. Die einzelnen Geschosse des offenen Pavillons veranschaulichten, wie Pflanzen Biomasse gewinnen, Lebensmittel erzeugen und Wasser reinigen können. Der 47 m hohe Pavillon bot zugleich einen gestapelten öffentlichen Raum dar im Sinne eines verdichteten Außenraums, der hier ein Innen bildet. In dieser Weise wurde das Gebäude zum Rahmen einer Kontinuität der Standortfläche in den verschiedenen Geschossen, die ihrer-seits vom Tragwerk bis zur inneren Gestaltung jeweils einen Landschaftstyp der Niederlande repräsentierte und von einer außen liegenden

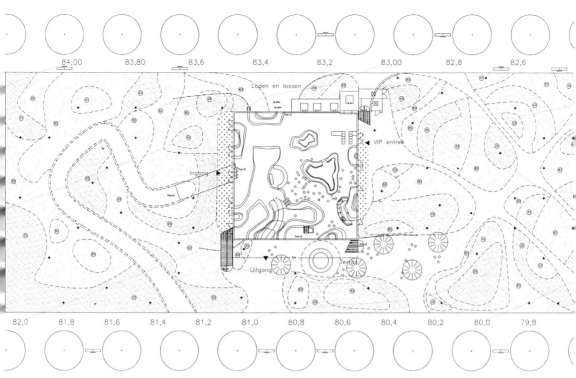

11   Bureau B+B Landscape design

Through the densification and stacking, only part of the site is built on and the Amsterdam landscape architecture and urban design office Bureau B+B designed planting here that was precisely planned and technologically advanced, changing over the course of the year (fig. 11–13).[79] With various types of flowers and four different degrees of plant density, it defined the outdoor area around the pavilion. The design principle of stacking, adding a variety of functions, dimensions, proportions and facades, was to become a variously recurring topic among many later buildings by MVRDV, combined with various requirements of the situational context.

The experimental character of the Expo pavilion, which communicated the overarching complex themes of people, nature and technology through architectural design with a specific reference to the Netherlands in a simplified manner through a walkable sensory experience, showed the contemporary close link between nature and artificiality, nature and technology with the use of the latest technologies in the architectural-conceptual and landscape architectural design. It is precisely this physically and conceptually compressed 'pictoriality' that was subject to strong criticism in specialist circles, whilst at the same time bringing about the popularity of the architecture among the wider public.[80] Alternatives to conventional ways of acting and perceiving were shown here, for example the potential of resource-efficient building or perceptions of the environment, relationality and processuality that often go beyond notions of the landscape as harmonious arcadian scenarios. With its stacked landscapes, the Dutch Pavilion remained memo-

12–13 Bureau B+B Plantings changing over the course of the exhibition

Treppe ringförmig erschlossen wird.[78] Insbesondere die als niederländische Marsch gestaltete obere Ebene wurde mit ihren Windrädern zudem zu einem wirkkräftigen Repräsentationsmedium. Durch die Verdichtung und Stapelung wurde nur ein Teil der Grundfläche bebaut und das Amsterdamer Landschaftsarchitektur- und Städtebaubüro B+B gestaltete hier eine mit offenen Prozessqualitäten präzise geplante, technologisch forcierte Pflanzung, die sich im Verlauf des Jahres veränderte (Abb. 11–13).[79] Mit verschiedenen Blumenarten und vier verschiedenen Pflanzendichtegraden prägte sie den Außenraum um den Pavillon herum. Das Gestaltungsprinzip des Stapelns, des Addierens unterschiedlicher Funktionen, Dimensionen, Proportionen und Fassaden wurde bei vielen späteren Bauten von MVRDV, kombiniert mit verschiedenen Anforderungen des situativen Kontexts, variiert und insgesamt zu einem wiederkehrenden Topos.

Der Expo-Pavillon kommunizierte das übergreifende komplexe Thema ‚Mensch – Natur – Technik‘ durch architektonische Gestaltung in spezifischem Bezug auf die Niederlande vereinfacht über begehbare, sinnlich wahrnehmbare Veranschaulichung. Dieser experimentelle Charakter zeigte unter Einsatz neuester Technologien in der architektonisch-konzeptuellen und der landschaftsarchitektonischen Gestaltung die zeitgenössisch enge Verknüpfung von Natur und Künstlichkeit, Natur und Technologie. Genau diese physisch und konzeptuell komprimierte ‚Bildhaftigkeit‘ unterlag starker Kritik in Fachkreisen und bedingte zu gleicher Zeit die Popularität der Architektur beim breiten Publikum.[80] Es wurden hier Alternativen zu konventionellen Handlungs- und Wahrnehmungsweisen aufgezeigt, beispielsweise Potenziale ressourcenschonenden Bauens oder Wahrnehmungen von Umwelt, Relationalität und Prozessualität, die über oftmals auf harmonisch arkadische Szenerien bezogene Landschaftsvorstellungen hinausreichen.

Mit seinen gestapelten Landschaften blieb der niederländische Pavillon nach der Weltausstellung lange Zeit im Gedächtnis, während die physische Struktur ungenutzt alterte. Mit dem neuen Stadtteil Kronsrode wird im Umfeld des Standorts eine Stadterweiterung erfolgen. Gegenwärtig wird die Struktur

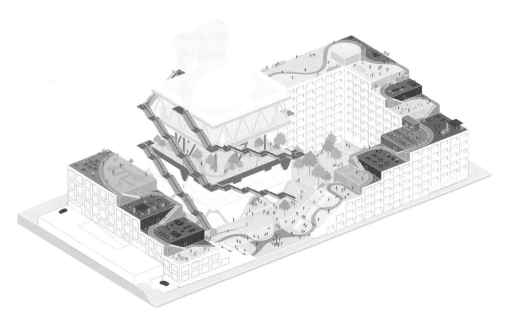

14 Dutch Pavilion Extension Hanover 2021 The roof surface is designed as a continuous active space

rable for a long time after the world exhibition, while the physical structure aged through disuse. With the new city district of Kronsrode, an urban expansion will be carried out in the vicinity of the site. The structure is currently being reactivated and extended by MVRDV themselves together with the local landscape architecture office lad+ Landschaftsarchitektur Diekmann from Hanover (fig. 14).[81] A mixed use of residence, work and leisure is striven for. The former landscape levels are being encased with glass facades and transformed into co-working offices with micro apartments, preserving existing elements. The forest landscape level on the fourth floor is being maintained as a recreational area (fig. 15). In addition, the pavilion is being structurally extended into an open perimeter block development with apartments in a large U-shaped block. Additional offices with parking spaces for cars and bicycles are housed in a smaller block. Various communal areas and public usages such as a café and exhibition rooms on the ground floor are also integrated. The new buildings, rising like stepped terraces on either side of the pavilion, surround a square-like entrance area to the buildings on the street side, as well as an interior courtyard with landscape architectural greenery. The roof areas of the upper floors are accessed by means of terracing in the form of interim platforms, each with specific programmatic usages such as gardens, sports and study areas or a cinema (fig. 16). They are marked by colour coding on the floors and walls. Together with the pavilion, this forms an urban ensemble and a new synthetic landscape-ness, which builds on the original effect, reinterpreting and programmatically extending it in a transformed usage matrix. The theme of the stacking of landscape in the sense of open space components is also spatially reinterpreted. The large proportion of public space that is proposed with this programme hybrid can especially act as an activating, innovative urban building block.

15–16 Dutch Pavilion reactivation and extension

von MVRDV selbst zusammen mit dem Landschaftsarchitekturbüro lad+ Landschaftsarchitektur Diekmann aus Hannover reaktiviert und erweitert (Abb. 14).[81] Dabei wird eine Mischnutzung aus Wohnen, Arbeiten und Erholung angestrebt. Die ehemals landschaftlichen Ebenen werden mit Glasfassaden umhüllt und unter Beibehaltung von Bestandselementen zu Co-Working-Büros mit Mikroapartments transformiert. Die Waldlandschaftsebene im vierten Obergeschoss bleibt als Rekreationsbereich erhalten (Abb. 15). Zudem wird der Pavillon baulich zu einer offenen Blockrandbebauung erweitert mit Wohnungen in einem U-förmigen größeren Block. Weitere Büros mit Parkmöglichkeiten für Pkw und Fahrrad sind in einem kleineren Block untergebracht. Diverse Gemeinschaftsbereiche und öffentliche Nutzungen wie Café und Ausstellungsräume im Erdgeschoss sind ebenfalls integriert. Die sich beidseitig des Pavillons terrassenartig gestuft erhebenden Neubauten umgeben straßenseitig einen platzartigen Eingangsbereich zu den Gebäuden sowie einen mit landschaftsarchitektonischem Grün ausgestalteten Innenhof. Über die Abstufungen werden die Dachflächen der Obergeschosse erschlossen. Diese sind in Form von Zwischenpodesten ausgebildet und erhalten jeweils spezifische programmatische Nutzungen, beispielsweise Gärten, Sport- und Studienbereiche oder ein Kino (Abb. 16). Sie werden durch farbige Codierungen der Boden- und Wandflächen markiert. Zusammen mit dem Pavillon wird so ein urbanes Ensemble und eine neue synthetische Landschaftlichkeit gebildet, die an die ursprüngliche Wirkkraft anknüpft und diese in einem transformierten Nutzungszusammenhang neu interpretiert und pragmatisch erweitert. Dabei wird auch das Thema der Stapelung von Landschaft im Sinne von Freiraumkomponenten räumlich neu interpretiert. Insbesondere der große Anteil öffentlichen Raums, der mit diesem Programmhybrid vorgeschlagen wird, kann hier als aktivierender innovativer Stadtbaustein wirken.

17 Depot Boijmans Van Beuningen Rotterdam 2021

CITY : LANDSCAPE   The basic idea incorporated in many projects by MVRDV of viewing and interpreting the city as a landscape can also be found in the 39.5-metre-high ovoid building they designed on the edge of the museum park in the centre of Rotterdam (fig. 17).[82] The platform Architectenweb lauded the Depot Boijmans Van Beuningen as 'Public Building of the Year 2021'.[83] In the ground-floor area, the bowl-shaped, mirrored architectural artefact, which is surrounded by many cultural and medical establishments and the museum park, has a footprint 40m in diameter that is small for its size. This allows views and the pathways at street level to be guided smoothly into the museum park, which represented an important starting and reference point of the design.[84] At the same time, the circular flat roof surface is thereby enlarged to a perimeter of 60m (fig. 18). The building comprises publicly accessible showrooms and store rooms for the art and design inventory of the 170-year-old Museum Boijmans van Beuningen. On the roof there is also a cross-shaped, glazed restaurant and event pavilion (fig. 19–20). It is surrounded by a birch and pine grove planted with grass, which enables water reserves, supports biodiversity and can contribute to balancing potential heat accumulation. The motif of the coordinate axes surrounded by a circle appears repeatedly in relation to the four points of the compass in architecture and urban design tradition, for example for ideal city designs or Palladian villas.[85]

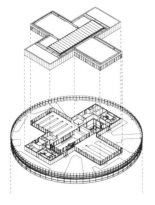

18–20 Rooftop pavilion

STADT:LANDSCHAFT   Die in vielen Projekten von MVRDV mitschwingende Grundidee, die Stadt als Landschaft aufzufassen und zu interpretieren, kann auch in dem von ihnen entworfenen 39,5 m hohen, ovoid
gebildeten Gebäude am Rand des Museumsparks im Zentrum Rotterdams
wiedergefunden werden (Abb. 17).[82] Von der Plattform Architectenweb wurde das Depot Bojmans Van Beuningen ausgezeichnet als ‚Öffentliches Gebäude des Jahres 2021'.[83] Im Erdgeschossbereich hat das schüsselförmige,
verspiegelte architektonische Artefakt, das von vielen kulturellen und medizinischen Einrichtungen und dem Museumspark umgeben ist, einen für seine
Größe geringen Fußabdruck von 40 m Durchmesser. So können die Blicke
und die Wegeführung auf Straßenniveau geschmeidig in den Museumspark
gelenkt werden, der einen wichtigen Ausgangs- und Bezugspunkt des Ent-
wurfes bildete.[84] Gleichzeitig vergrößert sich die kreisförmige Flachdach-
fläche dadurch auf einen Perimeter von 60 m (Abb. 18). Das Gebäude
umfasst öffentlich zugängliche Schau- und Lagerräume für die Kunst- und
Designbestände des 170-jährigen Museums Bojmans Van Beuningen. Auf
dem Dach befindet sich zudem ein kreuzförmiger, gläserner Restaurant- und
Veranstaltungspavillon (Abb. 19–20). Er ist umgeben von einem Birken- und
Kiefernhain mit Graspflanzungen, die Wasserreserven ermöglichen, Biodiversität fördern und zum Ausgleich potenzieller Hitzestaus beitragen können. Das Motiv des von einem Kreis umgebenen Achsenkreuzes erscheint
wiederholt mit Bezug auf die vier Himmelsrichtungen in der Architektur- und
Städtebautradition, etwa bei Idealstadtentwürfen oder Palladio-Villen.[85]

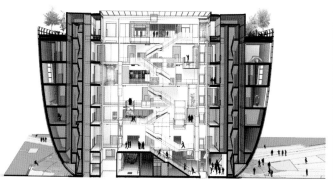

21–22 The central atrium and staircase functions as an exhibition space

All routes through the seven main levels of the depot are linked by means of large zigzagging stairs and bridges in the central, narrow and at the same time deep, high and very light atrium space, from the lobby on the ground floor to the roof level (fig. 21–22). This can also be accessed directly via a glass lift, without entering the showrooms. The public space of the city is thus extended. The area reclaimed from the park is made available again here with the additional potential of a viewing platform.[86] A variety of extensive panoramic views are opened up towards the city and the port of Rotterdam as far as the sea. This allows both an exploration of the city and enjoyable outlooks onto expansive areas, as described by Francesco Petrarca in 1335 after his ascent of Mont Ventoux.[87] Of course, in order to reduce high energy consumption, technical solutions were implemented such as heat exchangers, photovoltaic systems, innovative climate regulation systems and a rainwater cistern.[88] Even so, it was the architecturally specific design articulation that was the main focus of interest. The result was an unusual, in its specific form no doubt also disputable site reference of the building.[89] The project was designed to show its situatedness as a component of a wider whole, of a spatial relationship in terms of its effect on the surroundings, which at the same time can bring about reinterpretations of the surrounding urban areas and spaces and their relations.[90] An effect impact that had already been described in the 18th century by the philosopher Christian Cay Hirschfeld in his garden art theory is brought up to date here by the building that enters into reciprocal relations with the surrounding spaces (fig. 23).[91] The depot architecture appears as if it is formed out of urban landscape panoramas and reflections of the sky

23　The façade reflects the immediate and further surroundings, extending the public space

Alle Routen durch die sieben Hauptebenen des Depots sind verknüpft über große, im Zickzack geführte Treppen und Brücken im zentralen, schmalen und gleichzeitig tiefen, hohen und sehr lichterfüllten Atriumraum von der Lobby im Erdgeschoss bis zur Dachebene (Abb. 21–22). Diese kann zudem, ohne Eintritt in die Schauräume, über einen gläsernen Aufzug direkt erreicht werden. In dieser Weise wird der öffentliche Raum der Stadt erweitert. Die dem Park abgewonnene Grundfläche wird hier mit dem zusätzlichen Potential einer Aussichtsplattform wieder zur Verfügung gestellt.[86] Rundum werden verschiedene weiträumig ausgespannte, fernräumliche Panoramablicke auf die Stadt und den Hafen von Rotterdam bis zum Meer geöffnet. Stadterkundung und das genießende Schauen auf weite Gegenden, wie es bereits Francesco Petrarca 1335 nach seinem Aufstieg auf den Mont Ventoux beschrieb, können sich dabei verbinden.[87] Selbstverständlich wurden zur Linderung des hohen Energieverbrauchs technische Lösungen eingesetzt wie Wärmetauscher, Fotovoltaik, innovative Klimaregelungssysteme sowie ein Regenwasserspeicher.[88] Dennoch war es die architektonisch besondere gestalterische Artikulation, der das Hauptinteresse galt. So entstand ein ungewöhnlicher, in der spezifischen Formation sicher auch streitbarer Ortsbezug des Baukörpers.[89] Das Projekt wurde entworfen, um seine Situiertheit als Kompartiment eines größeren Ganzen, eines räumlichen Wirkungs- und Weltzusammenhangs zu veranschaulichen, der gleichzeitig Re-Interpretationen der umgebenden städtischen Orte und Räume und ihrer Relationen bewirken kann (Abb. 23).[90] Eine Wirkkraft, die bereits im 18. Jahrhundert von dem Philosophen Christian Cay Hirschfeld in seiner Gartenkunsttheorie beschrieben worden ist, wird hier aktualisiert, indem

24   The convex reflections open new spatial perceptions on the car park and square designed by OMA

and weather situations. Its continuous façade reflects the surrounding situations in inconclusive, changeable and multifaceted conglomerates, but without reflecting them completely (fig. 24). Reality can be experienced as the potential sum of possible appearances, whereby the indistinctness can have a particularly fascinating effect. The viewers are incorporated, even if on a small scale. Their actions and interactions form parts of the perceptible spatial situations. In the reflections, which also create a certain lightness, they are surrounded by the wider spatial continuity of the park, buildings, infrastructure, traffic, people and sky. In the landscape-ness constructed in this manner, materially prescribed – and not just associated – aspects of the urban landscape area are emphasised. Physical reality and figurative reality are interwoven. The question of whether the changeably reflecting building shell creates a neoliberal, 'shining' spectacle here, through which the image of the city supports consumer tendencies and superficiality, can be countered by the gaining of a sensory quality that is generally accessible, as well as by public possibilities for recreation and identification.[92] The reflections evoke a spatially extended perception of the city. In addition, the effect of limits is reduced. The idea of seeing the city as a landscape is therefore given a location-specific interpretation. City-landscape is therefore experienced under quite particular architecturally constructed perception conditions and as an ensemble with the 'natural' aspects of the planted trees and grass it gains an imaginative impact as a positive resource. The surrounding rectangular area is also designed to provide space for alternating installations of contemporary art.

das Gebäude wechselseitige Relationen mit den Räumen im Umfeld eingeht.[91] Die Depotarchitektur erscheint als eine aus Stadtlandschaftspanoramen sowie von Reflexionen der Himmels- und Wettersituationen gebildete Architektur. Ihre kontinuierliche Fassade gibt die umgebenden Situationen in unbestimmten, wandlungsfähigen Konglomeraten facettenreich wieder, ohne sie jedoch in diesen jeweils ganz zu zeigen (Abb. 24). Wirklichkeit wird als Summe von Erscheinungsmöglichkeiten erfahrbar, wobei die Undeutlichkeit als spezifisches Faszinosum wirken kann. Dabei sind die Schauenden einbezogen, wenn auch sehr klein. Ihre Aktionen und Interaktionen bilden Anteile der wahrnehmbaren Raumsituationen. In den Spiegelungen, die gleichzeitig eine gewisse Helligkeit bewirken, werden sie umgeben von der größeren räumlichen Kontinuität aus Park, Gebäuden, Infrastruktur, Verkehr, Menschen und Himmelsbereichen. In der so konstruierten Landschaftlichkeit werden materiell vorgegebene – und nicht nur assoziierte – Aspekte der stadtlandschaftlichen Gegend hervorgehoben. Physische Wirklichkeit und Bildwirklichkeit verschränken sich. Der Frage, ob die changierend spiegelnde Gebäudehülle hier ein neoliberales, ‚glänzendes' Spektakel erzeugt, durch welches das Bild der Stadt Konsumtendenzen und Oberflächlichkeit unterstützt, kann hier der Gewinn einer sinnlichen, allgemein zugänglichen Wirkqualität zur Seite gestellt werden, sowie von öffentlichen Möglichkeitsräumen für Rekreation und Identifikation.[92] Die Spiegelungen evozieren eine raumerweiternde Stadtwahrnehmung. Zudem wird die Wirkung von Grenzen verringert. Der Idee, die Stadt als Landschaft zu sehen, wird damit eine ortsspezifische Interpretation gegeben. Stadt:Landschaft wird so unter ganz bestimmten, architektonisch konstruierten Wahrnehmungsbedingungen erfahren und gewinnt im Ensemble mit dem ‚Natürlichen' der Baum- und Grasbepflanzung imaginative Wirkkraft als positive Ressource. Die umgebende rechteckige Platzfläche soll zudem wechselnden Installationen zeitgenössischer Kunst Raum geben.

REPERTOIRE   With the aim of maintaining open ground surfaces as far as possible and generating synergy effects from the density of programmatic hybrids, MVRDV has often used layering, stacking and verticalisation of the city as overarching guiding ideas for research, research-based design and constructional realisations. This is also combined with the striving to create structural-spatial settings that stimulate public activity and interaction. Change and dynamics are also incorporated through the typological richness and openness to appropriation. Specific characteristics of landscape-ness can thereby be created as properties. The invitation to gain an extended perception of the specific city landscape and location situation in combination with various open space typologies and landscape spaces forms a special aspect. Added to this are mixings of natural phenomena and artificiality, as well as of proximity and distance, and finally of pictorial reality and experienced reality.

This results in many project ideas that can also be understood as prototypical conceptualisation with various dimensions. The use of plants as material and as an outdoor space quality is given increasing importance in current projects, along with sustainable technologies such as photovoltaic systems, rainwater collection or the use of recycled materials. Responses to local circumstances and their application to the project as assemblage-like structural-spatial configurations are also decisive. This is shown exemplarily in the low-tech transformation, currently in progress, of the former film studio of BUFA (Berliner Union Film Ateliers) in the southern area of the Tempelhof Airport in Berlin, with planted roof surfaces, plant tendrils in the façade area, as well as alleys, existing trees and new planting in the outdoor spaces. The primary motivation to develop contemporary and forward-looking architecture for urban conditions through the link with the idea of landscape appears in the often surprisingly different designs for imaginary and concrete spaces of possibility.

Mit dem Ziel, offene Grundflächen möglichst zu erhalten und aus der Dichte programmatischer Hybride Synergieeffekte zu erzeugen, sind bei MVRDV oftmals Überlagerung, Stapelung und Vertikalisierung der Stadt als übergreifende Leitideen für Forschung, forschungsbasiertes Entwerfen und bauliche Realisierungen zu finden. Dies verbindet sich zudem mit dem Anliegen, baulich-räumliche Settings zu gestalten, die zu öffentlicher Aktivität und Interaktion anregen. Über die typologische Reichhaltigkeit und Aneignungsoffenheit werden zudem auch Wandel und Dynamik einbezogen. Spezifische Ausprägungen von Landschaftlichkeit können dabei als Eigenschaft erzeugt werden. Einen besonderen Aspekt bildet zudem die Einladung zur erweiterten Wahrnehmung der jeweils spezifischen Stadtlandschaft und Ortssituation in Verbindung mit unterschiedlichen Freiraumtypologien und landschaftlicher Räumlichkeit. Vermischungen von Naturphänomenen und Artifizialität sowie von nahem Raum und Ferne und schließlich von bildlicher Wirklichkeit und gelebter Wirklichkeit treten hinzu.

Dabei entstehen wiederholt Projektideen, die auch als prototypische Konzeptualisierung mit unterschiedlichen Dimensionen verstanden werden können. Dem Einsatz von Pflanzungen als Material und Freiraumqualität kommt in aktuellen Projekten neben nachhaltigen Techniken wie Fotovoltaikanlagen, Regenwassersammlung oder dem Einsatz recycelter Materialien zunehmende Bedeutung zu. Zudem sind Reaktionen auf die lokalen Gegebenheiten und deren Anwendung auf das Projekt als assemblageartige baulich-räumliche Konfigurationen ausschlaggebend. Dies zeigt exemplarisch die in der Realisierung befindliche Lowtech-Transformation der ehemaligen Filmstudios von BUFA (Berliner Union Film Ateliers) im südlichen Bereich des Tempelhofer Flughafens in Berlin mit begrünten Dachflächen, Pflanzenranken im Fassadenbereich sowie Alleen, weiteren Baumbeständen und neuen Pflanzungen in den Freiraumbereichen. Die primäre Motivation, zeitgemäße und zukunftsoffene Architekturen für urbane Konditionen durch die Verknüpfung mit der Idee von Landschaft zu entwickeln, zeigt sich in den immer wieder überraschend andersartigen Entwürfen imaginärer und konkreter Möglichkeitsräume.

AUSBLICK: LANDSCHAFTLICHKEIT UND URBANE ARCHITEKTUR
OUTLOOK: LANDSCAPE-NESS AND URBAN ARCHITECTURE

Landscape-ness as architectural idea includes wide-ranging conceptual and compositional approaches that with a focus on 'urban assemblage' and 'urban landscape' can be described as an integrative orientation. Architecture, landscape architecture and infrastructure are mixed also in a trans-scalar manner in different conglomerates. Artistically conceptual and researching procedures were also associated with the projects presented here through the design teams. Beyond given understandings and routines, cultural as well as architectural, landscape architecture and urban design concepts are questioned and linked with innovative typological, and certainly disputable morphological, ecological and programmatic ideas. They are supported by optimistic basic attitudes and offer, in particular, public spaces and capacities for interaction in an extended way.

Sensory experiences form not only important bases for the designs but also for the perception and interpretation of the structural-spatial realisations with their range of performative potential. In the formations, in particular, the distinctions between object and space, volume and ground, as well as the 'above' and 'below', are challenged. Horizontal and vertical transitions, continuities, layering and connections become a focus, in the sense of spatial and experience extensions that appear as qualities of perception, of sojourn and appropriation of urban space, as well as of the wide territorial context. This can result in spatial sequences of differing intensity, which are formed specifically in connection with local conditions and situations.

Landschaftlichkeit als Architekturidee beinhaltet weitgespannte konzeptuelle und kompositorische Annäherungen, die mit dem Fokus auf ‚Urbane
Assemblage' und ‚Urbane Landschaft' als integrative Ausrichtung beschrieben werden können. Architektur, Landschaftsarchitektur, Infrastruktur vermischen sich in unterschiedlichen Konglomeraten auch transskalar. Mit den
hier vorgestellten Projekten waren durch die Entwurfsteams auch künstlerisch konzeptuelle und forschende Verfahren verbunden. Über gegebene
Verständnisse und Routinen hinausgehend werden sowohl kulturelle als
auch architektonische, landschaftsarchitektonische und städtebauliche
Konventionen befragt und mit innovativen typologischen, durchaus streit-
baren, morphologischen sowie mit ökologischen und programmatischen
Ideen verknüpft. Sie werden von optimistischen Grundhaltungen getragen
und bieten insbesondere öffentlichen Raum und Kapazitäten zur Interaktion in erweiterter Weise.

Sinnliche Erfahrungen bilden dabei nicht nur wichtige Grundlagen für
die Entwürfe, sondern auch für die Wahrnehmung und Interpretation der
baulich-räumlichen Realisierungen mit ihren unterschiedlichen performativen Potenzialen. In den Formationen werden insbesondere Unterscheidungen von Objekt und Raum, von Figur und Grund sowie Oben und
Unten entgrenzt. Horizontale und vertikale Übergänge, Kontinuitäten,
Stapelungen und Erschließungen treten in den Fokus im Sinne von Raum-
und Erfahrungserweiterungen, die als Qualitäten der Wahrnehmung, des
Aufenthalts und der Aneignung des urbanen Raums sowie des weiter aufgespannten territorialen Kontextes erscheinen. So können Raumsequen-
zen unterschiedlicher Intensität entstehen, die im Zusammenhang lokaler Bedingungen und Situationen jeweils spezifisch ausgebildet werden.

According to this, the city forms an autonomous type of landscape, a city:landscape, an urban landscape. It is characterised on the one hand by building volumes and spatial volumes, as well as their dimensions and relations, and by the interaction of different structures. On the other hand, it is generated by the dynamics of human actions in the sense of social and cultural aspects of assemblages, which generate particular urban atmospheres, stimulated by these textures that open up potential for a range of scenes, performances and figurations of publicness, as well as forms of participation. The distribution and density of urban form is then influenced by the various actions and processes that take place there. What the landscape architect and urbanist James Corner describes as 'landscape imagination' can be comprehended here: beyond signs loaded with meaning and representations of landscapes, it is instrumental practices that make up their qualities, what they enable and bring forth, and how they can challenge cultural habits and conventions with regard to their relations with the environment.[93]

As an ordering means of composition by imagining landscape-ness as an architectural idea, programme hybrids for a multiple publicness and various interactions will come to the fore, as well as the 'flowing' urban space landscape, which is characterised by porosity, connections and low-threshold transitions, as well as by gestures of verticalisation and the combination of building substance with planting, in consideration of the receptivity to atmospheres determined by times of day and seasons. But what is more: connections of a visual and sensory nature to the nearby surroundings and wider spatial territories – even those that only end at the horizon – are especially activated and stimulated in the process of design and in the later perception and experience. Perception levels of landscape as a picture to be looked at and landscape as a multimodal phenomenon that can be experienced

through movement and interaction in space and time then come to the fore.

Stadt bildet demnach eine eigenständige Art von Landschaft, eine Stadt:Landschaft, eine urbane Landschaft. Sie ist einerseits charakterisiert durch Baukörper- und Raumkörperformen sowie deren Dimensionen und Relationen und durch die Wechselwirkung unterschiedlicher Strukturen. Andererseits wird sie generiert durch Dynamiken menschlicher Aktionen im Sinne sozialer und kultureller Ebenen von Assemblagen, die besondere urbane Atmosphären erzeugen, stimuliert durch diese Texturen, die das Potenzial für eine Vielzahl von Szenen, Performanzen und Figurationen von Öffentlichkeit sowie Formen der Teilhabe eröffnen. Die Verteilung und Dichte urbaner Form wird dann mitgeprägt durch die verschiedenen Aktionen und Prozesse, die sich darin vollziehen. Das, was der Landschaftsarchitekt und Urbanist James Corner als ‚landscape imagination' beschreibt, kann hier nachvollzogen werden: Jenseits bedeutungsgeladener Zeichen und Repräsentationen von Landschaften sind es instrumentelle Praktiken, die ihre Qualitäten ausmachen, das, was sie ermöglichen und hervorbringen, und wie sie kulturelle Gewohnheiten und Konventionen herausfordern können im Hinblick auf ihre Relationen zur Umwelt.[93]

Als ordnende Kompositionsmittel der Imagination von Landschaftlichkeit als Architekturidee werden dann Programmhybride für eine multiple Öffentlichkeit und verschiedene Interaktionen hervortreten sowie die ‚fließende' Stadtraumlandschaft, die durch Porosität, Verknüpfungen und niederschwellige Übergänge geprägt ist wie auch durch Gesten der Vertikalisierung und der Verknüpfung von baulicher Substanz mit Pflanzungen unter Einbezug der Aufmerksamkeit für tages- und jahreszeitlich bedingte Atmosphären. Doch mehr noch: Insbesondere visuell-sinnlich erfahrbare Verbindungen, zum nahen Umraum wie auch zu weiten räumlichen Territorien – auch solchen, die erst am Horizont enden –, werden im Prozess des Entwerfens wie auch der späteren Wahrnehmung und Erfahrung aktiviert und stimuliert. Wahrnehmungsebenen von Landschaft als anzuschauendes Bild und Landschaft als multimodal durch die Bewegung und Interaktion in Raum und Zeit erlebbares Phänomen treten dann in den Vordergrund.

1 Cf. on this | Vgl. hierzu Stephan Geiger, The art of assemblage, München: Silke Schreiber 2008, 176–182
2 Cf. | Vgl. Manuel de Landa, A new philosophy of society. Assemblage theory and social complexity, London: Continuum 2006, 5–12   **3** Cf. on this | Vgl. hierzu Thomas Bender/Ignazio Farias (eds.), Urban assemblages. How actor network theory changes urban studies, Abingdon: Routledge 2010, 13–15; Jane Bennett/Klaus K. Loenhart, Vibrant matter – Zero landscape (Interview), in: Klaus K. Loenhart (ed.), Zero landscape. Unfolding active agencies of landscape, Wien et al.: Springer 2011, 14–25; Ross Exo Adams, Landscapes of post-history, in: Ed Wall/Tim Waterman (eds.), Landscape agency, London et al.: Routledge 2018, 7–17, 8–9; Jan Buchanan, Assemblage theory and method, London et al.: Bloomsbury Academic 2021, 4–6 and | und passim   **4** Cf. | Vgl. Thomas Bender/Ignazio Farias (eds.) 2010, op. cit. (note | Anm. 3), 13; Ben Anderson/Colin McFarlane, Assemblage and geography, in: Area 43(2011)/2, 124–127, 124   **5** Cf. for example | Vgl. beispielsweise Rem Koolhaas, What ever happened to urbanism?, in: id./Bruce Mau/OMA, S,M,L,XL, Rotterdam: 010 1995, 958–971, 969   **6** Cf. | Vgl. Charles Waldheim, Landscape as urbanism, A general theory, New York: Princeton University Press 2016, passim   **7** Cf. | Vgl. James Corner, Terra fluxus, in: Charles Waldheim, The Landscape urbanism reader, Princeton, NJ: Princeton Architectural Press 2006, 20–33, 28–32; Moshen Mostafavi, Landscapes of urbanism, in: id. (ed.), Landscape urbanism. A manual for the machinic landscape, London: Architectural Association 2003, 5–9, 9   **8** Cf. | Vgl. James Corner, The landscape imagination, New York, NY: Princeton Architectural Press 2014, 7–9; Stan Allen, Field conditions. Points + Lines: Diagrams and projects for the city. New York, NY: Princeton Architectural Press 1999, 90; Alex Wall, Programming the urban surface, in: James Corner (ed.), Recovering landscape. Essays in contemporary landscape architecture, New York, NY: Princeton Architectural Press 1999, 233–250, 247   **9** Cf. on this | Vgl. hierzu James Corner, Eidetic operations and new landscapes, in: ibid. 1999, 153–169, 154–155   **10** Cf. on this also | Vgl. hierzu auch Annika Agger/Catherine Durose/Oliver Escobar/Merlijn van Hulst/Mark van Ostaijen, Working the urban assemblage. A transnational study of transforming practices, in: Urban Studies 58(2021)/9, 1–18, 5 and | und 12; Janet Newman, Landscapes of antagonism, in: Urban Studies 51(2014)/15, 3290–3305, 3293   **11** Cf. | Vgl. Elizabeth Diller/Ricardo Scofidio, Flesh. Architectural probes, New York, NY: Princeton Architectural Press 1994, passim   **12** Cf. on this | Vgl. hierzu Elizabeth Diller, quoted at | zit. bei Edwin Heathcote, A critical dialogue, in: Luis Fernández Galiano (ed.), Diller Scofidio Renfro 2000-2020, Madrid: Arquitectura Viva 2020, 4–7, 5; Margitta Buchert, Kunst in der Architektur. Spurensuche am Ende des 20. Jahrhunderts, in: Maike Kozok (ed.), Architektur, Struktur, Symbol, Petersberg: Imhof 1999, 467–478, 468–470; Whitney Moon, Staging architecture. The early performances of Diller and Scofidio, on: | auf: https://www.acsa-arch.org/proceedings/Annual%20Meeting%20Proceedings/ ACSA.AM.103/ACSA.AM.103.52.pdf, 17.8.2021   **13** For this form of landscape perception cf. also | Zu dieser Form der Landschaftsperzeption vgl. auch Simon Schama, Landscape and memory, 1995, 6–10   **14** Cf. | Vgl. Diana Murphy (ed.), Diller + Scofidio, Blur. The making of nothing, New York: Harry M. Abrams 2002, passim; Edward Dimendberg, Diller Scofidio + Renfro. Architecture after images, Chicago: The University of Chicago 2013, 150–155   **15** Cf. on this also | Vgl. hierzu auch Elizabeth Diller, in: Elizabeth Diller/Ricardo Scofidio/Anna Winston, The High Line is a pulling back from architecture, say Diller and Scofidio (Interview), in: Dezeen (2014) 14.11., on: | auf: https://www.dezeen.com/2014/11/03/elizabeth-diller-ricardo-scofidio-interview-high-line-new-york, 30.9.2021   **16** Cf. | Vgl. Michael Symes, The English landscape garden in Europe,

Swindon: Historic England 2016, 1–20; Wybe Kuitert, Japanese gardens and landscapes, Philadelphia: University of Philadelphia Press 2016, 6–17, 32–33, 182–185   **17** On history cf. | Zu Geschichte vgl. Diller, Scofidio + Renfro (eds.), Lincoln Center inside out. An architectural account, Bologna: Daminai 2012, 11–14   **18** Cf. | Vgl. ibid., 10 and | und passim   **19** In on-site studies in July 2019, the diverse qualities of use could be observed in all their plurality. | In Vor-Ort-Studien im Juli 2019 konnte die verschiedensten Nutzungsqualitäten in ihrer Vielfalt beobachtet werden.   **20** Cf. on this | Vgl. hierzu Elizabeth Diller (2006), What they forgot to teach you in architecture school (lecture | Vortrag 1.2.2006) New York, NY: GSAPP Columbia University on: | auf: https://www.dailymotion.com/video/x4rm6fe 18.10.2021   **21** Cf. on this | Vgl. hierzu Diller, Scofidio + Renfro, Columbia Avenue Entrance, in: ids. (eds.), Lincoln Center inside out. An architectural account, Bologna: Daminai 2012, 66-74; Mathews Nielsen Landscape Architects, in: ibid. 300   **22** Cf. on this | Vgl. hierzu Diller, Scofidio + Renfro, Identity, in: ibid., 59   **23** Cf. on this | Vgl. hierzu Elizabeth Diller 2006, op. cit. (note | Anm. 20); Diller Scofidio + Renfro, North Plaza, in: ids. (eds.) 2012, op. cit. (note | Anm. 21), 106–117   **24** Cf. on this | Vgl. hierzu Stephen Kaplan, The restorative benefits of nature. Towards an integrative framework, in: Journal of Environmental Psychology 15(1995)/3 169–182, 173–174   **25** Cf. on this | Vgl. hierzu Elizabeth Diller 2006, op. cit. (note | Anm. 20); Diller Scofidio + Renfro 2012, op. cit. (note | Anm. 23), 52 und 123   **26** Vgl. hierzu auch Nobuyuki Yoshida, The Juilliard School and Alice Tully Hall at Lincoln Center fo the Performings Arts, in: id. (ed.), Diller Scofidio + Renfro, Tokio: a+u 2019, 110–129, 112; Diller Scofidio + Renfro 2012, op. cit. (note | Anm. 23), 162–165 and | und 202–298   **27** For these aspects of an understanding of democracy cf. | Zu diesen Aspekten eines Demokratieverständnisses vgl. Eric Hazan/Jacques Rancière, Democracies against democracy, in: Giorgio Agamben/Alain Badiou et al. 2011, Democracy in what state?, New York, NY: Columbia University Press 2011, 76–81   **28** Elizabeth Diller, in: id./Ricardo Scofidio/Charles Renfro/Benjamin Gilmartin/Nobuyuki Yoshida, Democratizing space (Interview), in: Nobuyuki Yoshida (ed.) 2019, op. cit. (note | Anm. 26), 7–17, 8   **29** Cf. | Vgl. Joel Sternfeld, Walking the High Line, New York: Steidl/Pace/MacGill Gallery 2002   **30** Cf. | Vgl. Elizabeth Diller/Ricardo Scofidio/Anna Winston 2014, op. cit. (note | Anm. 15)   **31** On Piet Oudolfs naturalistic design cf. | Vgl. zu Piet Oudolfs naturalistischer Gestaltung Noel Kingsbury/Piet Oudolf, Design trifft Natur. Die modernen Gärten des Piet Oudolf, Stuttgart: Ulmer 2013, passim   **32** Cf. in detail | Vgl. hierzu ausführlich Steffen Bösenberg, Plastizität. Konzeptionen postindustrieller Transformation, Diss. Ing. Leibniz Universität Hannover: unpublished 2021, 305–330   **33** Cf. | Vgl. Elizabeth Diller/Ricardo Scofidio/Anna Winston 2014, op. cit. (note | Anm. 15)   **34** Cf. in detail | Vgl. hierzu ausführlich Steffen Bösenberg 2021, op. cit. (note | Anm. 32), 277–279   **35** Cf. | Vgl. James Corner, Hunt´s haunts, in: Christoph Lindner/Brian Rosa (eds.), Deconstructing the High Line. Postindustrial urbanism and the rise of the elevated park, New Brunswick: Rutgers University Press 2017, 23–27, 26   **36** Elizabeth Diller specifically names the reference to the Japanese garden | Elizabeth Diller benennt konkret den Bezug zum japanischen Garten, in: id./Ricardo Scofidio/Charles Renfro/Benjamin Gilmartin/Nobuyuki Yoshida 2019, op. cit. (note | Anm. 28)   **37** Cf. on this also | Vgl. hierzu auch Ricardo Scofidio, in: ibid., 8, 11   **38** Cf. | Vgl. Elizabeth Diller, in: ibid., 8   **39** Cf. | Vgl. Elizabeth Diller, in: ibid.,12   **40** Cf. on this also | Vgl. hierzu auch Davis Baker, Design Awards 2016. Best building site. Museum of Image and Sound, in: Wallpaper 213 (2016)14.1., on: | auf: https://www.wallpaper.com/architecture/design-awards-2016-best-building-site-diller-scofidio-renfro-museum-of-image-and-sound-rio-de-janeiro-brazil,

2.10.2021 **41** Cf. on this | Vgl. hierzu Moshen Mostafavi, Why ecological urbanism? Why now?, in: id. (ed.), Ecological urbanism, Rev. ed. Zürich: Lars Müller 2016, 12–51, 48 **42** Cf. | Vgl. Bjarke Ingels, Pragmatic pleasures, in: Luis Fernández-Galiano (ed.), BIG 2001-2013. Madrid 2013, 4–11,11 **43** Cf. | Vgl. BIG, Hot to cold. An odysee of architectural adaptation, 2.ed. Köln: Taschen 2021, 9 **44** Cf. | Vgl. BIG, Infrastructure, in: BIG, Hot to cold. An odyssey of architectural adaptation, 2. ed. Köln: Taschen 2021, 652–653 **45** Cf. | Vgl. Bjarke Ingels (ed.), Yes is more. Köln: Taschen 2010; ibid.; BIG (ed.), Formgiving. An architectural future history, Köln: Taschen 2020 **46** Cf. | Vgl. Bjarke Ingels 2021, op. cit. (note | Anm. 43), 654–655 and | und passim. **47** Cf. on this | Vgl. hierzu BIG 2020, op. cit. (note | Anm. 45), 7–28, 18–24 and | und passim **48** Cf. | Vgl. ibid., 632-671 **49** Cf. | Vgl. https://www.nachhaltigkeitspreis.de/presse/pressemitteilungen/news/deutscher-nach-haltigkeitspreis-fuer-stararchitekt-bjarke-ingels, 19.10.2021 **50** Cf. explanation of the honory award winner on: | Vgl. Ehrenpreisträgerbegründung auf: ibid. **51** Cf. | Vgl. BIG, From fact to fiction, in: BIG 2020, op. cit. (note | Anm. 45), 692–707, 693 **52** Cf. | Vgl. Bjarke Ingels, Harbor pool and winter baths, in: Luis Fernández-Galiano (ed.) 2013, op. cit. (note | Anm. 42) 14–19, 14 **53** Cf. | Vgl. Lars Gemzøe, Swimming in the city, in: Magda Anglès/Antoni Faguè Moya (eds.), In favour of public space, Barcelona: Actar 2010, 149–151, 150 **54** For characterization cf. | Vgl. zur Charakterisierung Verena Brehm, Komplexe Morphologie in der Architektur der Gegenwart. Morphogenese. Physiognomie. Ästhetik. Hannover: TIB 2015, 132–137 **55** Cf. | Vgl. Carsten Thau, in: Kristoffer Linhardt Weiss (interview | Interview), Architecture that opens the world, in: Kjeld Vindum/Kristofer Linhardt Weiss, The new wave in Danish architecture, Copenhagen: Arkitektens Forl. 2012, 220–235, 231 **56** Vgl. Bjarke Ingels (2012), Hedonistic sustainability (lecture | Vortrag 15.2.2012) Stockholm: KTH School of Architecture,on: | auf: https://www.youtube.com/watch?v=PpMDkQbye0A, 26.1.2016; on the 'streets in the air' cf. | zu den ‚Streets in the air‘ vgl. Alan Powers, Robin Hood Gardens. A critical narrative, in: Max Risselada (ed.), Alison and Peter Smithson. A critical anthology. Barcelona: Ediciones Polígrafa 2011, 228–245, 233–243 **57** Cf. on this also | Vgl. hierzu auch Verena Brehm 2015, op. cit. (note | Anm. 54) 136; on Copacabana cf. | zur Copacabana vgl. Lauro Cavalcanti/Farés El-Dadah/Leonardo Finotti, Robert Burle Marx. The modernity of landscape. Barcelona: Actar 2011, 246–254 **58** Cf. on this | Vgl. hierzu Emmanuel Petit, Metropolis now, in: Log 39(2017), 11–19, 11–12 **59** Cf. | Vgl. BIG 2021, op. cit. (note | Anm. 44), 624–651 **60** Cf. | Vgl. Rasmus Grandelag, Amager Bakke Rooftop Park. Turning technical infrastructure into a social, sustainable and biodiverse asset for the entire city of Copenhagen, on: | auf: https://www.sla.dk/cases/amager-bakke 19.9.2021 **61** Cf. | Vgl. BIG, Social infrastructure, in: id. (ed.) 2021, op. cit. (note | Anm. 43), 653; Bjarke Ingels 2012, op. cit. (note | Anm. 56) **62** On competition and workshops cf. | Zu Wettbewerb und Workshops vgl. Henk Ovink, Transformative capacity of resilience. Learning from rebuild by design, in: Andreas Ruby/Ilka Ruby, Infrastructure space, Berlin: Ruby Press 2017, 337–344, 338–339; BIG et al. (eds.), The big 'U'. Rebuild by design. Promoting resilience post-Sandy through innovative planning, design and programming, Copenhagen: BIG 2014, 2–21, on: | auf: http://www.rebuildbydesign.org/data/files/675.pdf, 20.9.2021 **63** Cf. | Vgl. BIG 2021, op. cit. (note | Anm. 44), 262–275 **64** Cf. on this in general | Vgl. hierzu allgemein Elizabeth Mossop, in: Charles Waldheim (ed.), The Landscape urbanism reader, New York: Princeton University Press 2006, 165–177, 176 **65** Cf. on this also | Vgl. hierzu auch Verena Brehm 2015, op. cit. (note | Anm. 54), 137 **66** On parallels in antiquity and the Renaissance cf. | Zu Parallelen in der Antike und Renaissance vgl. Gerd Blum, Fenestra prospectiva. Berlin et al.: De Gruyter 2015, 67–68 and | und 77–

79   **67** Cf. on this project | Vgl. zu diesem Projekt MVRDV, Ateliergardens, on: | auf: https://www.mvrdv.com/projects/594/atelier-gardens, 18.11.2021   **68** Cf. on datascapes in general | Vgl. zu Datascapes allgemein Brett Steele, Data(E)Scape. Entwurf als Forschung, in: Daidalos 69/70(1998), 54–59, 57   **69** Cf. | Vgl. MVRDV/Laura F. Suárez; Three voices. One vision. (Interview), in: Luis Fernández-Galiano (ed.), MVRDV. Dream Works, Madrid: Arquitectura Viva 2016, 6–17, 7; Winy Maas, in: Marcus Fairs/Winy Maas, (Interview), Dezeen Virtual Design Festival 17.6.2020, on: | auf: https://www.youtube.com/watch?v=9VF2G6FTNzM, 28.10.2021   **70** Cf. on this | Vgl. hierzu Hans Ibelings, Machbarkeit, in: id. (ed.), Die gebaute Landschaft, München: Prestel 2000, 8–18, 10   **71** Cf. on this | Vgl. hierzu Winy Maas, in: MVRDV/Laura F. Suárez 2016, op. cit. (note | Anm. 69), 9 and | und 13   **72** Cf. on this also | Vgl. hierzu auch James Corner 1999, op. cit. (note | Anm. 9), 165   **73** Cf. | Vgl. Winy Maas, Datascape. The final extravaganza, in: Daidalos 69/70(1999) 48–49; Bart Lootsma, Synthetic regionalization. The Dutch landscape toward a second modernity, in: James Corner (ed.) 1999, op.cit. (note | Anm. 8), 251–273, 266–272   **74** Cf. | Vgl. Bart Lootsma 1999, ibid. 263–264; Nobuyuki Yoshida, VPRO, in: id. (ed.), MVRDV Files 1, Tokio: a+u 2002, 18   **75** Cf. for example | Vgl. beispielsweise Stefan De Koning/Inger Kammeraat/Jan Knikker/Fokke Moerel/Bertrand Schippan, A round tabel discussion among the new partners of MVRDV, in: Nobuyuki Yoshida (ed.), MVRDV, Files 4, Tokio 2020, 54–59, 54   **76** Cf. | Vgl. Expo 2000 Hannover (ed.), Die Pavillons der Expo 2000, Hannover 2000   **77** Cf. on this | Vgl. hierzu Laura F. Suárez 2016, op. cit. (note | Anm. 69), 13   **78** Cf. | Vgl. MVRDV, Niederländischer Pavillon EXPO 2000, in: Archplus 149/150(2000), 60–65   **79** Cf. | Vgl. https://bplusb.nl/en/work/expo-2000-dutch-garden, 11.11.2021   **80** Cf. | Vgl. hierzu Andreas Ruby/Ilka Ruby, Introduction, in: ids. (eds.), MVRDV, Rotterdam: NAI 010 2015, 8–13, 9   **81** Cf. | Vgl. https://www.mvrdv.nl/projects/432/expo-pavilion-2.0, 13.11.2021   **82** Cf. | Vgl. Winy Maas in: id./Jacob van Rijs/Nathalie de Vries, Designing with idea(l)s for growing complexity in the built environment, in: Nobuyuki Yoshida (ed.) 2020, op. cit. (note | Anm. 75), 5–9, 6   **83** For the jury's reasoning cf. | Zur Jurybegründung vgl. Depot Boijmans Van Beuningen uitgeroepen tot Publiek gebouw van het Jaar 2021, on: | auf: https://architectenweb.nl/nieuws/artikel.aspx?ID=51073, 15.11.2021   **84** Cf. Arjen Ketting at: | Vgl. Arjen Ketting bei: Benedikt Crone/Arjen Ketting, Von der Nachbarschaft verkleidet (Interview), in: Bauwelt 10(2020), 56–59, 58   **85** On this motif in the history of architecture and town planning cf. | Zu diesem Motiv in der Architektur- und Städtebaugeschichte vgl. Gerd Blum, Fenestra perspectiva, Berlin et al.: De Gruyter 2015, 58–59 and | und 67   **86** Cf. Arjen Ketting at: | Vgl. Arjen Ketting bei: Benedikt Crone/Arjen Ketting 2020, op. cit. (note | Anm. 84), 57   **87** Cf. | Vgl. Francesco Petrarca: Die Besteigung des Mont Ventoux, Frankfurt am Main et al.: Insel 1996, 11   **88** On structural engineering cf. | Zur Bautechnik vgl. Benedikt Crone/ Arjen Ketting 2020, op. cit. (note | Anm. 84), 58   **89** Cf. on this | Vgl. hierzu (stu), Spiegelei in Rotterdam. Schaulager Boymans Van Beuningen von MVRDV, in: Baunetz (2020)25.9., on | auf: https://www.baunetz.de/meldungen/Meldungen-Schaulager_Boijmans_Van_Beuningen_von_MVRDV_7418058.html 15.11.2021   **90** Cf. Vgl. Winy Maas in: id./Jacob van Rijs/Nathalie de Vries 2020, op. cit. (note | Anm. 82), 5–9, 6   **91** Cf. | Vgl. Christian C. L. Hirschfeld, Theorie der Gartenkunst, Leipzig: M.G. Weidmanns Erben und Reich 1780, 41   **92** For similar reviews cf. | Zu vergleichbaren Kritiken vgl. Tom Fischer/Nicolas P. Maffei, Historizing shining. Finding meaning in an unstable phenomenon, in: Journal of Design History 26(2013), 131–240, 239–240   **93** Cf. | Vgl. James Corner 2014, op. cit. (note | Anm. 8), 8–9 and | und 111–113 and | und 291–297

GRÜNE ARCHITEKTUR: GRÜNE STADT
GREEN ARCHITECTURE: GREEN CITY

The term 'green architecture' or 'green city' does not inevitably have to be associated with the integration of vegetation. As it is described by the World Green Building Council and its national subgroups, 'green' as an attribute can also be understood as energy-conscious and sustainable, in the sense of a low-resource consumption, and of architecture and built spatial habitats with characteristics that have little negative impact on the environment and climate.[1] The specific notions of the concepts and projects presented in the following take up and focus on both the aforementioned aspects: vegetation as well as the preservation of the climate and resources. These perspectives involve rationally developed, research-based technological and environmentally friendly solutions, and are also associated with the integration of natural elements and processes, with organisms and systems that are only partly created and controlled by humans. Intersections of architecture and technology are extended here by climate-related and biological dimensions. Plants become integral conceptual components of the technological-constructional and space-shaping architectural design. The various technologies do not only represent useful tools but rather media that are linked with the design of possibilities.[2] With connotations of sustainability and biophilia as a background to the widely ramified field of 'Green Architecture:Green City', the possibility emerges to map out and qualify elements, properties and various facets of landscape-ness as architectural idea in different contexts, in an individual building or ensemble, or on a wider urban scale and within wider climatic conditions.

Die Bezeichnung ‚Grüne Architektur' oder ‚Grüne Stadt' muss nicht zwangsläufig mit der Integration von Vegetation verbunden sein. Wie es nicht nur vom World Green Building Council und dessen nationalen Untergruppen beschrieben wird, kann das Attribut ‚grün' vielmehr auch verstanden werden als energiebewusst und nachhaltig im Sinne eines niedrigen Ressourcenverbrauchs und einer Umwelt und Klima wenig beeinträchtigenden Charakteristik von Architektur und baulich-räumlichen Habitaten.[1] Die spezifischen Dimensionen der nachfolgenden vorgestellten Konzepte und Projekte liegen darin, beide der zuvor genannten Aspekte aufzugreifen und in den Vordergrund zu stellen: die Vegetation und die Klima- und Ressourcenschonung. Diese Perspektiven haben ebenso mit rational entwickelten, forschungsbasierten technologischen und umweltschonenden Lösungen zu tun wie sie graduell mit integrierten Naturelementen und -prozessen zusammenhängen, mit Organismen und Systemen, die vom Menschen nur in Teilen geschaffen und kontrolliert werden können. Schnittstellen von Architektur und Technologie werden hierbei erweitert um klimabezogene und biologische Dimensionen. Pflanzen werden zu integralen konzeptuellen Komponenten des technologisch-konstruktiven und räumlich-gestalterischen Architekturentwurfs. Die verschiedenen Technologien bilden dabei nicht nur nützliche Instrumente, vielmehr Medien, die mit dem Entwurf von Möglichkeiten verknüpft sind.[2] Mit Konnotationen zu Nachhaltigkeit und Biophilie als Hintergrund des weitverzweigten Feldes ‚Grüne Architektur:Grüne Stadt' öffnet sich die Möglichkeit, Elemente, Eigenschaften und diverse Facetten von Landschaftlichkeit als Architekturidee im Hinblick auf unterschiedliche Verknüpfungen zu eruieren und zu qualifizieren, im Einzelgebäude oder Ensemble ebenso wie im größeren urbanen Maßstab sowie innerhalb weiter reichender klimatischer Konditionen.

SUSTAINABILITY   The widespread discourses about the bases, intentions and strategies surrounding sustainability concepts have grown consistently since the first UN conference in Stockholm in 1972 about the risks of human influence on the environment, the United Nations Conference on the Human Environment (UNCHE) and the report by the Club of Rome in 1972. These revealed growth tendencies and limits as well as states of balance in the context of the rapid increase in the world population and global industrial production.[3] The Brundtland report by the World Commission on Environment and Development (WCED) in 1987 explicitly formulated the goal of sustainable development for the first time: The demands of the present day should not compromise the opportunities of future generations, which means generating and implementing sustainable ways of thinking and acting for the responsible management of global resources.[4] The Agenda 21 that was then decreed in Rio de Janeiro in 1992 along with the Kyoto Protocol in 1997, and the subsequent conferences in Copenhagen 2009 and Paris 2015, placed a focus on the aim of securing natural bases of existence, economic stability and social tolerance.

A wide variety of sustainability models was developed around the interpretation of these aspects, whereby notions and definitions from different disciplines and research traditions were and are associated with different understandings of nature, notions of value and interests.[5] The exploding global population, increasing awareness of the limited fossil resources and in particular climate change had posed an increasing need for sustainable development since the beginning of the 21st century and had strengthened the scientific and practical effort to preserve the integrity of the non-human world for its survival, as well as for the survival of humanity. The aims, referred to as Sustainable Development Goals by the international community of states in the Agenda 2050, are wide-ranging and relate to a variety of fields of action.[6]

NACHHALTIGKEIT   Die breitgestreuten Diskurse zu Grundlagen, Intentionen und Strategien, die um Nachhaltigkeitskonzepte kreisen, sind stetig angewachsen seit der ersten Konferenz der Vereinten Nationen zu den Risiken menschlicher Umweltbeeinflussung 1972 in Stockholm, der United Nations Conference on the Human Environment (UNCHE), und dem Bericht des Club of Rome von 1972, der über die Wachstumstendenzen und -grenzen sowie Gleichgewichtszustände im Kontext des rapiden Anstiegs der Weltbevölkerung und der Weltindustrieproduktion aufklärte.[3] Mit dem Brundtland-Bericht der Weltkommission für Umwelt und Entwicklung (WCED) wurde 1987 erstmals explizit das Ziel nachhaltiger Entwicklung formuliert: Die Bedürfnisse der Gegenwart sollten die Möglichkeiten zukünftiger Generationen nicht beeinträchtigen, und das bedeutet, nachhaltige Denk- und Handlungsweisen für eine verantwortungsvolle Verwaltung planetarischer Ressourcen zu generieren und umzusetzen.[4] Die dann in Rio de Janeiro 1992 beschlossene Agenda 21 und ihre Ergänzung durch das Kyoto-Protokoll von 1997 sowie die Folgekonferenzen in Kopenhagen 2009 und Paris 2015 hatten die Ziele der Sicherung natürlicher Lebensgrundlagen, der wirtschaftlichen Stabilität und der sozialen Verträglichkeit in den Mittelpunkt gerückt.

Um die Interpretation dieser Dimensionen wurden verschiedenste Nachhaltigkeitsmodelle entwickelt, wobei Vorstellungen und Definitionen aus diversen Disziplinen und Forschungstraditionen heraus mit verschiedenen Naturverständnissen, Wertvorstellungen und Interessen verbunden wurden und werden.[5] Die explodierende Weltbevölkerung, zunehmende Erkenntnisse zu den beschränkten fossilen Ressourcen und insbesondere der Klimawandel hatten seit Beginn des 21. Jahrhunderts die Notwendigkeit nachhaltiger Entwicklung noch stärker herausgefordert und die wissenschaftlichen wie praktischen Bemühungen verstärkt, die Integrität der nicht humanen Welt für deren Überleben ebenso wie für das Überleben der Menschheit zu bewahren. Die Ziele, wie sie in der Agenda 2050 mit den Sustainable Development Goals von der internationalen Staatengemeinschaft differenzierter benannt wurden, sind weitgefächert und beziehen sich auf unterschiedlichste Aktionsfelder.[6]

In architectural discourse and in building practice, the described general historical developments and sustainability discourses were not so much a clearly defined field of guiding ideas but more of a generator of various courses of action, projects and regulations. To be highlighted here are the approaches of those architects who were initially associated with the label of high tech and whose later projects were then referred to as eco tech architecture. These pioneers primarily include Norman Foster, Richard Rogers, Nicholas Grimshaw and Renzo Piano, as well as Ken Yeang and Hideo Sasaki.[7] Their intentions in this respect were especially directed towards fundamentally improving the environmental performance of buildings by means of structural-technical strategies.

The use of technical, technological and material innovations that are quantifiable and certifiable spread more generally with quality seals such as BREEAM (UK), LEED (US), Green Mark (Singapore) and DGNB (Germany). The initial criteria and evaluation dimensions were extended over time. In addition, the attention to constructional elements and to the use of materials contributed to finding more sustainable solutions. The handling of natural shade, lighting and ventilation, the avoidance of waste and preservation of resources in the production process, as well as the reuse of existing building stock and materials, are relevant aspects of this. Alongside this, certain typological developments and new interpretations of historical typologies such as interior courtyards, atria, wind catchers or dense building structures can contribute to preserving resources and reducing energy consumption.[8] The sustainability interpretations in architecture repeatedly criticised as too high technology orientated were also extended to various relational ecological perspectives. On many levels also, spatial-temporal, socio-political and gender differences are incorporated, as well as the impulse to think of and deal with human and non-human collective life as more strongly intertwined in this context.[9] These specifics form integral aspects of the inhabiting of environments.

Im Architekturdiskurs und der baulichen Praxis wirkten die beschriebenen allgemeinen historischen Entwicklungen und Nachhaltigkeitsdiskurse weniger im Sinne eines klar und eindeutig definierten Felds von Leitideen, sondern vielmehr als Generator:innen verschiedener Handlungsweisen, Projekte und Regulierungen. Hervorzuheben sind hier die Ansätze derjenigen Architekturschaffenden, die zunächst mit dem Label Hightech verbunden und deren spätere Projekte dann als Eco-Tech-Architektur bezeichnet wurden. Zu diesen Pionieren zählen vorrangig Norman Foster, Richard Rogers, Nicholas Grimshaw und Renzo Piano sowie Ken Yeang oder Hideo Sasaki.[7] Ihre Intentionen sind in diesem Zusammenhang vor allem darauf gerichtet, mit bautechnischen Strategien die Umweltperfomance von Gebäuden grundlegend zu verbessern.

Der Einsatz technischer, technologischer und materialbezogener Innovationen, die quantifizierbar und zertifizierbar sind, wurde beispielsweise in Gütesiegeln wie BREEAM (UK), LEED (US), Green Mark (Singapur) oder DGNB (D) allgemeiner verbreitet. Anfängliche Kriterien und Bewertungsdimensionen wurden mit der Zeit erweitert. Zudem trug auch die Aufmerksamkeit für bauliche Elemente und Materialgebrauch dazu bei, nachhaltigere Lösungen zu finden. Der Umgang mit natürlicher Verschattung, Belichtung und Belüftung, Abfallvermeidung und Ressourcenschonung im Produktionsprozess und auch die Weiterverwendung von Baubestand und Baumaterial sind Aspekte, die dabei Relevanz besitzen. Daneben können auch bestimmte typologische Entwicklungen und Neuinterpretationen historischer Typologien wie Innenhöfe, Atrien, Windtürme oder verdichtete Baustrukturen dazu beitragen, Ressourcen zu schonen und Energieverbrauch zu reduzieren.[8] Die wiederholt als zu hochtechnologieorientiert kritisierte Nachhaltigkeitsinterpretationen in der Architektur wurden zudem erweitert zu diversen relationalen ökologischen Perspektiven (ecology). Vielschichtig werden dabei auch raum-zeitliche, soziopolitische und Genderdifferenzen einbezogen sowie der Impuls, in diesem Kontext das menschliche und nichtmenschliche kollektive Leben als stärker verwoben zu denken und zu behandeln.[9] Diese Spezifiken verweisen auf essenzielle Verknüpfungen mit dem Bewohnen von Umwelten.

BIOPHILIA   Within the concept of biophilia this is also addressed and associated on the one hand with empirical findings and on the other hand with design aspects. This theoretical approach has increasingly gained attention in recent decades in a wide range of disciplines, as well as in architecture, landscape architecture and urban development design.[10] The notion of biophilia, introduced into philosophy and psychology by Erich Fromm in the middle of the 20th century, initially referred generally to the 'love of the living'.[11] The interpretations by the biologist Edward O. Wilson, influential since the 1980s, extended the scope of the notion beyond the human connection.

Since then, biophilia has been associated with the preservation of the biodiversity of the environment and therefore also with the relationship of people to neighbouring species and habitats.[12] In more recent research, especially in environmental sciences, psychology, medicine and neurosciences, the concept of biophilia now goes hand in hand with various physiological, psychological, cognitive and mental health benefits, which furthermore also promise economic gain.[13] High relevance is thereby accorded to the built environment. Apart from qualities of light, air and water, aspects such as 'living' architecture, vertical green, greenery in skyscrapers and facades, as well as green urban corridors, are thematised.[14] Overall, these 'green' properties are characterised as climate-positive, sustainable and healthy. They are associated with the intentions of promoting appropriation and direct connections between people and 'nature', using natural resources on-site responsibly, as well as planning and designing in accordance with climatic conditions and local ecological processes.[15] With the international 'WELL standards' developed by medics, scientists and architects based on empirical evaluations, biophilia strategies and criteria have also been taken up in the certification taxonomies for sustainable architecture since 2013.[16] These are aimed towards design components for the promotion of health, a sense of safety and well-being.

BIOPHILIE   Im Konzept der Biophilie wird dies ebenfalls angesprochen und einerseits mit empirischen Erkenntnissen und andererseits mit gestalterischen Aspekten verbunden. Dieser Theorieansatz hat in den letzten Dekaden in einem breiten Feld von Disziplinen zunehmend an Aufmerksamkeit gewonnen, und auch für das architektonische, landschaftsarchitektonische und städtebauliche Entwerfen.[10] Mit dem von Erich Fromm Mitte des 20. Jahrhunderts in die Philosophie und Psychologie eingeführten Begriff der Biophilie wurde zunächst übergreifend die ‚Liebe zum Lebendigen' bezeichnet.[11] Die seit den 1980er Jahren einflussreichen Interpretationen des Biologen Edward O. Wilson erweiterten das begriffliche Bedeutungsfeld über den humanen Bezug hinaus.

Biophilie wurde seitdem mit der Erhaltung der Biodiversität der Umwelt und damit auch mit den Relationen von Menschen zu benachbarten Spezies und Habitaten in Verbindung gebracht.[12] In jüngeren, insbesondere von Umweltwissenschaften, Psychologie, Medizin und Neurowissenschaften getragenen, Forschungen sind mit dem Konzept der Biophilie nun verschiedene physiologische, psychologische, kognitive und mentale gesundheitliche Benefits benannt, die zudem im weiteren auch wirtschaftliche Gewinne versprechen.[13] Der gebauten Umwelt wird dabei eine hohe Relevanz beigemessen. Neben Qualitäten von Licht, Luft und Wasser werden Aspekte thematisiert wie ‚lebendige' Architektur, vertikales Grün, Begrünung in Wolkenkratzern und Fassaden sowie grüne städtische Korridore.[14] Insgesamt sind diese ‚grünen' Eigenschaften als klimapositiv, nachhaltig und gesund charakterisiert. Sie werden verbunden mit den Intentionen, Aneignung und direkte Verbindung von Mensch und ‚Natur' zu fördern, natürliche Ressourcen am Standort verantwortlich zu nutzen und entsprechend der klimatischen Konditionen und lokalen ökologischen Prozesse zu planen und zu gestalten.[15] Mit den von Mediziner:innen, Wissenschaftler:innen und Architekt:innen aufgrund empirischer Evaluationen entwickelten internationalen ‚Well-Standards' wurden seit 2013 auch in die Zertifizierungstaxonomien für nachhaltige Architektur biophile Strategien und Kriterien aufgenommen.[16] Diese sind auf Gestaltungskomponenten zur Förderung von Gesundheit, Sicherheitsgefühl und Wohlbefinden gerichtet.

LANDSCAPE-NESS   'Green Architecture:Green City' as a seemingly obvious dimension of landscape notions will provide a multifaceted extension of qualities and potentials of the concept of landscape-ness as architectural idea and contribute to introducing and stimulating both calculable and unusually creative solutions. This dimension is similar to a rational and technologically characterised approach to the controlled and economically orientated production of landscapes, as associated for example with agricultural landscapes and forestry, and in general with a natural science and engineering logic.[17] The overlapping of systematic conceptions with architecture, landscape architecture and urban development design competence constitutes the creative potential in this regard. This can result in approaches and artefacts that contribute to extending the possibilities of qualitatively distinguishing built spaces in the living environment of people and in cohabitation with the environment.[18] It is especially in connection with an understanding of landscape that goes beyond a distanced perception of the environment, in which multisensory, physiological and mental-perception dimensions are integrated, that one can see how mixings drive the design imagination forwards. This includes disciplinary traditions while generating transdisciplinary novelties, thereby contributing fundamentally to further developments.

The presented models are based on the systematic inclusion of vegetation in the conceptual framework of the architecture design. This is associated with a corresponding technical specialisation of the firms in greenery for buildings and the inclusion of various experts who help to qualify the architectural, landscape architectural and urban design projects as models for sustainable architectures and cities, as is the case for Ingenhoven Architects, WOHA and Stefano Boeri Architetti.[19] The projects that are also strongly characterised by economic factors were repeatedly criticised as being subjugated to the laws of the market.[20] It is to be taken into consideration here that with their search for a balance of ecological sustainability, economic feasibility and biophile orientation, as well as with experimental and exemplary aspects and the aspiration to design architectural quality, they actively seek to go beyond one-sided orientations.

LANDSCHAFTLICHKEIT ,Grüne Architektur:Grüne Stadt' als scheinbar naheliegende Dimension von Landschaftsvorstellungen wird das Spektrum von Qualitäten und Potenzialen des Konzepts der Landschaftlichkeit als Architekturidee facettenreich erweitern und dazu beitragen, sowohl kalkulierbare als auch ungewöhnliche kreative Lösungen differenzierter kennenzulernen und anzuregen. Diese Dimension kommt einem rational und technologisch geprägten Ansatz der kontrollierten und ökonomisch ausgerichteten Produktion von Landschaften nahe wie sie beispielsweise im Zusammenhang mit Agrarlandschaften und Forstwirtschaft und allgemein mit natur- und ingenieurwissenschaftlicher Logik verbunden zu finden sind.[17] Die Überlagerung systematischer Konzeptionen mit architektonischer, landschaftsarchitektonischer und städtebaulicher Entwurfskompetenz ist dabei das kreative Potenzial. So können Ansätze und Artefakte entstehen, die dazu beitragen, die Möglichkeiten zu erweitern, um gebaute Räume im Lebensumfeld des Menschen und in Ko-Habitation mit der Umwelt qualitativ auszuzeichnen.[18] Insbesondere in der Verknüpfung mit einem über distanzierte Wahrnehmung von Umwelt hinausreichenden Landschaftsverständnis, in dem multisensorische, physiologische und mentale Wahrnehmungsdimensionen integriert sind, zeigt sich, wie Vermischungen die entwerferische Imagination vorantreiben. Diese schließt disziplinäre Traditionen ebenso ein wie sie transdisziplinär neue generiert, und damit grundlegend zu Weiterentwicklungen beiträgt.

Die vorgestellten Modelle gehen dabei von einer systematischen Inklusion von Vegetation in das konzeptuelle Rahmenwerk des Architekturentwurfs aus. Damit verbunden sind eine entsprechende technische Spezialisierung der Büros auf Gebäudegrün und der Einbezug diverser Expert:innen, welche die architektonischen, landschaftsarchitektonischen und städtebaulichen Projekte als Modelle für nachhaltige Architekturen und Städte mitqualifizieren wie dies bei Ingenhoven Architects, WOHA und Stefano Boeri Architetti der Fall ist.[19] Die ebenfalls stark durch ökonomische Faktoren geprägten Projekte wurden wiederholt kritisiert als Unterwerfung unter die Gesetze des Marktes.[20] Dem ist der Gedanke zur Seite zu stellen, dass sie mit der Suche nach einer Balance aus ökologischer Nachhaltigkeit, wirtschaftlicher Machbarkeit und biophiler Orientierung sowie mit experimentellen, modellhaften Anteilen und architektonischem Gestaltungsanspruch Ansätze aufzeigen, die einseitige Ausrichtungen engagiert zu überschreiten suchen.

The individual examples are presented in their respective specific context. Ingenhoven Architects, Dusseldorf, counts as one of the protagonists of sustainable construction in Europe and is shown with projects in Europe and internationally. Besides the dominant orientation towards a researching and constructional development of sustainable architectural solutions, it is a humanistic orientation that accompanies the thinking and works of this firm. The projects integrate vegetation in different areas, which in the built context are evocative of landscape types such as jungles, rice terraces or vineyards. The architecture office WOHA, Singapore, and their architectural and urban building ideas are very strongly bound up with the development of the island state Singapore and its specific climatic and cultural conditions, characterised at the same time by the production of innovative typological hybrids of green areas, architecture and urban space. For the office of Stefan Boeri in Milan, Tirana and Shanghai, which also works with model concepts and projects, integrating the idea of landscape-ness in architectural and urbanistic projects, notions of forest, forest/city and agriculture (kitchen gardens) are associated with the architectural and urban development articulations that are immediately evocative of landscape formations. Landscape-ness as architectural idea is presented in the mentioned concepts and projects in particular with the use of vegetation and the multilayered references to climatic and bio-physiological location qualities, which can form instigating dimensions for future yet unknown variants of a sustainable, biophile landscape-ness.

Die einzelnen Beispiele werden in ihrem jeweils spezifischen Kontext vorgestellt. Ingenhoven Architects, Düsseldorf, zählen zu den Protagonisten nachhaltigen Bauens in Europa und werden mit europäischen und internationalen Projekten dargeboten. Neben der dominierenden Orientierung auf die forschende und bauende Entwicklung nachhaltiger architektonischer Lösungen ist es eine humanistische Ausrichtung, die das Denken und Schaffen dieses Büros begleitet. Die Projekte integrieren Vegetation in unterschiedlichen Bereichen, die im gebauten Kontext an Landschaftsypen erinnern wie Dschungel, Reisterrassen oder Weinberge. Das Architekturbüro WOHA, Singapur, ist mit seinen architektonischen und städtebaulichen Ideen sehr stark mit der Entwicklung des Inselstaates Singapur und dessen spezifischen klimatischen und kulturellen Konditionen verknüpft und zugleich charakterisiert durch die Produktion innovativer typologischer Hybridisierungen von Grünräumen, Architektur und Stadtraum. Bei dem ebenfalls mit modellhaften Konzepten und Projekten arbeitenden Büro von Stefano Boeri in Mailand, Tirana und Shanghai sind mit der Idee von Landschaftlichkeit in architektonischen und urbanistischen Projekten Vorstellungen von Wald, Wald/Stadt und Landwirtschaft (Nutzgarten) verbunden, deren architektonische und städtebauliche Artikulationen unmittelbar landschaftliche Formationen nahelegen. Landschaftlichkeit als Architekturidee wird in den genannten Konzepten und Projekten insbesondere mit dem Einsatz von Vegetation und der vielschichtigen Bezugnahme auf klimatische und bio-physiologische Standortqualitäten dargeboten, die impulsgebende Dimensionen für zukünftige noch unbekannte Varianten einer nachhaltigen, biophilen Landschaftlichkeit bilden können.

SUPER GRÜN
SUPER GREEN
INGENHOVEN ARCHITECTS

Ingenhoven Architects was founded by Christoph Ingenhoven, who since 1985 has emerged with sustainable,
environmentally friendly concepts and building designs.
The RWE headquarters built in Essen in 1996 was one of
the first ecological high-rises worldwide. Further exceptional high-rise projects were built in Japan, Australia and
Singapore.[21] In addition, the realised projects comprise
urban development designs, infrastructure, industrial,
residential and hospital buildings, as well as a variety of
hybrids and numerous projects within existing building
stock, in various climate zones and on different scales.
Many of them have been awarded renowned national
and international certifications and sustainability prizes.

Ingenhoven Architects wurde von Christoph Ingenhoven gegründet, der seit 1985 mit nachhaltigen, umweltschonenden Konzepten und Gebäudeentwürfen hervorgetreten ist. Das in Essen entstandene RWE-Hauptquartier von 1996 war eines der ersten ökologischen Hochhäuser weltweit. Weitere ausgezeichnete Hochhausprojekte entstanden in Japan, Australien und Singapur.[21] Die realisierten Projekte umfassen darüber hinaus in verschiedenen Klimazonen und Maßstäben städtebauliche Entwürfe, Infrastruktur, Industrie-, Wohnungs- und Krankenhausbau ebenso wie unterschiedliche Hybride und zudem zahlreiche Projekte im Bestand. Viele davon wurden mit renommierten nationalen und internationalen Zertifizierungen und Nachhaltigkeitspreisen ausgezeichnet.

The firm works with engineering companies, landscape architects and biologists to constantly further develop the application-related and often research-based approaches and solutions. Christoph Ingenhoven is a co-founder of the German Sustainable Building Council (DGNB) and was involved in the establishment and further development of the respective certification system. The highly technologically characterised construction hardware is combined to green methods with the goal of increasing the potential of what is built through aesthetic and social dimensions.[22] This results in site-specific projects that are exceptional typologically and with regard to the use of greenery, combined with compositional and social space qualities.

CONCEPTS   In reference to concepts and projects by Buckminster Fuller, Frei Otto and Werner Sobek, as well as to vernacular architecture, Christoph Ingenhoven repeatedly indicates the fundamental intention to develop environmentally friendly architectural and infrastructural projects with limited resources.[23] As could already be seen in the early high-rise project of the RWE headquarters in Essen, the compact building method that enabled a generous park and an entrance square, as well as the element of the thermal buffer – here as a double-layer, naturally ventilated, fully glazed façade – were essential means of providing the best possible response to the requirement of a low use of resources and energy (fig. 1).[24] The use of sunlight, geothermal energy and rainwater, as well as the possibility of natural ventilation of the buildings and views of the surroundings, become fundamental aspects of the further building designs. Different key

Das Büro arbeitet mit Ingenieurbüros, Landschaftsarchitekt:innen und Biolog:innen zusammen, um die anwendungsbezogenen und oft forschungsbasierten Ansätze und Lösungen stetig weiterzuentwickeln. Christoph Ingenhoven ist Mitbegründer der Deutschen Gesellschaft für Nachhaltiges Bauen (DGNB) und war engagiert an der Entstehung und Fortentwicklung des entsprechenden Zertifizierungssystems beteiligt. Die hochtechnologisch geprägte bauliche Hardware wird verknüpft mit grünen Techniken und zudem mit dem Ziel, die Kapazität des Gebauten durch ästhetische und soziale Dimensionen zu erhöhen.[22] In dieser Weise entstehen typologisch und in Bezug auf den Einsatz von Grün außergewöhnliche, ortsbezogene Projekte, verknüpft mit sozialräumlichen und kompositorischen Qualitäten.

KONZEPTE   In Referenz zu Konzepten und Projekten von Buckminster Fuller, Frei Otto und Werner Sobek sowie zu vernakulärer Architektur verweist Christoph Ingenhoven immer wieder auf die grundlegende Intention, mit begrenzten Ressourcen umweltschonende architektonische und Infrastrukturprojekte zu entwickeln.[23] Bereits bei dem frühen Hochhausprojekt des RWE-Hauptsitzes in Essen waren die kompakte Bauweise, die einen großzügigen Park und einen Eingangsplatz ermöglichte, und das Element des thermischen Puffers, hier als zweischalige natürlich belüftete Ganzglasfassade, essenzielle Mittel, um mit einem geringen Ressourcen- und Energieverbrauch bestmöglich auf Umweltbedingungen zu antworten (Abb. 1).[24] Die Nutzung von Sonnenlicht, Erdwärme, und Regenwasser sowie die Möglichkeit natürlicher Be- und Entlüftung der Gebäude und Ausblicke in die Umgebung werden zu grundlegenden Aspekten der weiteren

1 RWE headquarters building Essen 1997

concepts are developed for the respective projects, which are adapted to the surrounding 'natural' landscape and urban structure. The use of materials evaluated according to the specific climate and location forms part of this. From the outset, outdoor areas and the integration of plants and gardens are part of the architectural concepts. Landscape-ness is highly valued by Ingenhoven and particular attention is paid to the development of landscape architectural aspects.[25] In 2018, a comprehensive practical handbook on 'Green building' was published that was significantly influenced by the thinking and work of the office.[26] It deals with architecture, law and technical aspects as decisive factors. The architect Christoph Ingenhoven therein propagates an architectural stance that goes beyond mere environmental standards, which he denotes as 'supergreen' and to which he gave the 'R'-logo as trademark protection.[27] Even so, it is not a stance that adheres to a one-sided, neoliberal, quantifying market logic, but rather the innovative, highly technological, rational approach is associated with the humanistic dimension of a design attitude centred on people. The aims of raising the well-being and comfort of the users, as well as of inviting informal communicative encounters indoors and outdoors, are just as much part of it as technological innovations regarding the use of regenerative energies and resources, spatial efficiency and multifaceted contextualisation. All these aspects are associated with the basic stance of research and development, whereby every building task represents an opportunity to constantly work further on the typology of such projects, as well as

on the overarching idea of creating qualitatively valuable public spaces.

Gebäudeentwürfe. Für die Projekte werden jeweils verschiedene Schlüsselkonzepte entwickelt, die an das Klima, die umgebende ‚natürliche' Landschaft und urbane Struktur angepasst werden. Klima- und ortsspezifisch evaluierter Materialeinsatz bilden einen Teil davon. Von Anfang an sind Außenanlagen und die Integration von Pflanzen und Gärten Teil der Architekturkonzeptionen. Landschaftlichkeit wird von Ingenhoven sehr geschätzt und Landschaftsarchitekturanteile werden mit besonderer Aufmerkamkeit entwickelt.[25] 2018 wurde ein maßgeblich durch das Denken und Schaffen des Büros geprägtes, umfangreiches Praxishandbuch zum ‚Green building' publiziert.[26] Darin werden Architektur, Recht und technische Faktoren als ausschlaggebende Faktoren behandelt. Der Architekt Christoph Ingenhoven propagiert darin eine über bloße Umweltstandards hinausgehende Architekturposition, die er als ‚supergreen' bezeichnet und mit dem R-Logo als Markenschutz versah.[27] Dennoch ist es nicht eine einseitig neoliberale, quantifizierender Marktlogik folgende Haltung, vielmehr wird mit der innovativen hochtechnologischen, rationalen Herangehensweise die humanistische Dimension einer menschenzentrierten Entwurfshaltung verknüpft. Die Ziele, das Wohlbefinden und den Komfort der Nutzer:innen zu befördern sowie zu informellen kommunikativen Begegnungen im Innen- wie im Außenraum einzuladen, finden darin ebenso Aufnahme wie technologische Innovationen zur Nutzung regenerativer Energien und Ressourcen, räumliche Effizienz und facettenreiche Kontextbezüge. Mit all diesen Aspekten verbunden ist die Grundhaltung von Forschung und Entwicklung, wodurch jede Bauaufgabe einen Anlass bildet, an dem Typus solcher Projekte sowie an der übergreifenden Idee, qualitativ wertvolle öffentliche Orte zu schaffen, stetig weiterzuarbeiten.

2 Kö-Bogen II Dusseldorf 2019 forms a hinge between a park area and the dense business district

GREEN FACADES AS A RESOURCE: KÖ-BOGEN II   Built as an inner-city extension to retail space and office buildings on the Dusseldorf shopping strip of Schadowstraße, the Kö-Bogen II of 2019 is generally based on a reformulation of the inner-city urban area (fig. 2). It replaces a disorderly situation due to war and post-war destruction with a car park and a flyover. The new ensemble forms a hinge and a connection between the commercial business centre of the city and the cultural context, between Königsallee, Schadowstraße, the Dreischeibenhaus and the theatre, furthermore creating new open space situations.[28] The two iconic post-war buildings, the Dreischeibenhaus by HPP Hentrich-Petschnigg & Partner (1960) and the theatre by Bernhard Pfau (1969) renovated by Ingenhoven Architects, are framed by the new building and seen in the urban space in a new way. Along the shopping street, the 27-metre-high and 120-metre-long building volume is fully glazed. It is structured at varying intervals by fronting lamellae of different lengths made of expanded metal. In the upper area, an animated LED screen was integrated along the full length and protruding plant trays are visible (fig. 3). Towards the Hofgarten park with water areas and old mature trees, as well as towards the theatre, the building is enclosed by green facades. Rising in steep terraces here, the rows of hornbeam hedges, 1.3 metres high, span the

3 High street glazing and LED screens

GRÜNFASSADEN ALS RESSOURCE: KÖ-BOGEN II Dem als innerstädtische Erweiterung von Einzelhandelsfläche und Bürogebäude an der Düsseldorfer Einkaufsmeile der Schadowstrasse entstandenen Kö-Bogen II von 2019 liegt übergreifend eine Neuformulierung des innerstädtischen Stadtraums zugrunde (Abb. 2). Sie tritt an die Stelle einer durch Kriegs- und Nachkriegszerstörungen ungeordneten Situation mit Parkplatz und Hochstrasse. Das neue Ensemble bildet ein Scharnier und eine Wegeverbindung zwischen dem kommerziellen Geschäftszentrum der Stadt und dem kulturellen Kontext, zwischen Königsallee, Schadowstraße, Dreischeibenhaus und Schauspielhaus, und es werden zudem neue Platzsituationen ausgebildet.[28] Die beiden ikonischen Nachkriegsbauten, das Dreischeibenhaus von HPP – Hentrich-Petschnigg und Partner (1960) sowie das von Ingenhoven Architects sanierte Schauspielhaus von Bernhard Pfau (1969), werden durch den Neubau gerahmt und in neuer Weise im Stadtraum sichtbar. Entlang der Einkaufsstraße ist das 27 Meter hohe und 120 Meter lange Gebäudevolumen vollständig verglast (Abb. 3). In variierenden Abständen wird es durch vorgesetzte, unterschiedlich lange Lamellen aus Streckmetall gegliedert. Im oberen Bereich wurde auf ganzer Länge ein bespielter LED-Bildschirm integriert und auskragende Pflanztröge werden sichtbar. Zum Hofgarten mit Wasserflächen und alten

4 The staggered horn beam hedges resembles vineyards on hills

whole height of the building and over the inclined roof. Only the glazed office floors in the upper area become visible and interrupt the rhythm of the hedges (fig. 4–5). Properties of the vegetation were established by a variety of phytotechnological research that accompanied the realisation process. The constructional, biotechnological and design concept was developed in cooperation with the botanist Karl-Heinz Strauch and the engineering office of Werner Sobek; the structure, form and care of the hornbeam hedges were pre-cultivated and tested over a period of years.[29] In a landscape perspective, this type of planting is reminiscent of vineyards on slopes (fig. 6). In the context of architecture, it is the stepped terraces of the ACROS building built in 1995 in Fukuoka, Japan, by Emilio Ambasz that are evoked. There, however, the whole building has more monumental dimensions and the steps in the threshold area towards the building volume next to the rows of vegetation include terrace-like ambulatories.[30]

It is not only the façade material that is reduced by the plant shell. The green façades become micro-climatically positive as an air-cooling reservoir that mildens urban heat islands and acts as CO_2 binding, noise reduction and as a natural wind barrier. In addition, they allow the settlement

5–6   The glazed office floor interrupts the vegetation which forms a green wall

Baumbestand hin ebenso wie zum Theater wird der Baukörper von grünen Fassaden umfasst. Die hier steil terrassiert aufsteigenden, 1,3 Meter hohen Hainbuchenheckenreihen erstrecken sich über die gesamte Gebäudehöhe und über das geneigte Dach. Nur die verglasten Bürogeschosse im oberen Bereich werden sichtbar und unterbrechen den Heckenrhythmus (Abb. 4–5). Eigenschaften der Vegetation wurden durch differenzierte phytotechnologische Forschungen, die den Realisierungsprozess begleiteten, ermittelt. Das konstruktive, bio-technologische und gestalterische Konzept entstand in Kooperation mit dem Botaniker Karl-Heinz Strauch und dem Ingenieurbüro Werner Sobek; die Struktur, Form und Pflege der Hainbuchenhecken wurde über Jahre vorkultiviert und getestet.[29] Landschaftlich erinnert diese Art der Bepflanzung an Weinberge in Hanglagen (Abb. 6). Im Kontext der Architektur sind es die abgestuften Terrassen des von Emilio Ambasz 1995 in Fukuoka, Japan, errichteten ACROS-Gebäudes, die erinnert werden. Dort allerdings hat das gesamte Gebäude monumentalere Ausmaße und die Stufen enthalten im Schwellenbereich zum Gebäudevolumen hin neben den Vegetationsreihen terrassenartige Wandelgänge.[30]

Nicht nur das Fassadenmaterial wird durch die Pflanzenhülle reduziert. Mikroklimatisch positiv werden die Grünfassaden zum Luftkühlungsreservoir, das urbane Hitzeinseln mildert, und wirken als CO_2-Bindung, als Lärmreduzierung sowie als natürliche Windbarriere. Zudem ermöglichen sie die Ansiedlung von Habitaten bestimmter Vogel- und Kleintierarten.[31] Die charakteristische, je nach Jahreszeit wechselnde Farbigkeit der laubhaltenden Hainbuchenhecken trägt darüber hinaus dazu bei, dass hier verschiedene Naturfacetten wahrgenommen werden können. Am westlichen Ende des

7 The hornbeam hedges and the walkable roof extend the public green spaces

of habitats for certain species of birds and small animals.[31] The characteristic colours of the deciduous hornbeam hedges that change with the seasons also contribute to the visibility of various nature facets. At the western end of the building ensemble, a triangular glazed pavilion rises out of the square surface, with restaurants, a supermarket and a gourmet shop in the interior, whose diagonally inclined roof is covered with grass. This is walkable and open to appropriation, thus extending the public green spaces (fig. 7–8). In the perception of the urban space, a green corridor emerges towards the Hofgartenpark and the boulevards of Königsallee. The Kö-Bogen II can be interpreted as a pilot project of inner-city greenery and landscape-ness as architectural idea. The project elements supported, developed and tested by clients, architects and all cooperation partners on an urban scale contribute to enabling urban public life, individual well-being and habitat potential for urban flora and fauna. They can be modified and extended site-specifically in further projects. The perceptual continuum with neighbouring urban green spaces, the visual relations within the urban composition, the sequencing of buildings and spaces, as well as the climate-friendly green building envelope generate in total the effective qualities of landscape-ness throughout. The biophilic properties, to which the architecture office also accorded a special relevance, contribute additionally to not understanding landscape-ness and urbanity as a contradiction.[32]

8   A triangular pavilion offers a walkable grass covered area.

Gebäudeensembles erhebt sich aus der Platzfläche ein dreieckiger verglaster Pavillon mit Restaurants, Supermarkt und Gourmetshop im Innern, dessen diagonal ansteigendes Dach mit Rasen bedeckt ist. Dieser ist begehbar und aneignungsoffen und erweitert so die öffentlichen Grünräume (Abb. 7–8). In der stadträumlichen Wahrnehmung entsteht ein grüner Korridor zum Hofgartenpark und zu den Alleen der Königsallee. Der Kö-Bogen II kann als Pilotprojekt innerstädtischer Begrünung und Landschaftlichkeit als Architekturidee interpretiert werden. Die hier von Auftraggebenden, Architekt:innen und allen Kooperationspartner:innen im Maßstab des Städtischen geförderten, entwickelten und erprobten Projektbausteine tragen dazu bei, urbanes öffentliches Leben, individuelles Wohlbefinden sowie Habitatpotenziale für urbane Flora und Fauna zu ermöglichen. Sie können in weiteren Projekten ortsspezifisch modifiziert und weitergeführt werden. Das Wahrnehmungskontinuum mit benachbarten städtischen Grünräumen, die Blickbeziehungen in der stadträumlichen Komposition, die Sequenzierung von Baukörpern und Raumkörpern sowie die klimawirksamen grünen Gebäudehüllen erzeugen im Gesamten Wirkungsqualitäten von Landschaftlichkeit. Die biophilen Eigenschaften, denen von dem Architekturbüro ebenfalls eine besondere Relevanz beigemessen wurde, tragen darüber hinaus dazu bei, Landschaftlichkeit und Urbanität nicht als Gegensätze zu begreifen.[32]

9 Marina One Singapore 2018

URBAN GREEN OASIS: MARINA ONE   In another project by Ingenhoven Architects with much larger dimensions, this characteristic is articulated even more widely. The Marina One complex was created in the financial district of Singapore, which since the 1970s has been developed into the urban quarter Marina Bay through clearing and land filling and with financial real estate, hotels, conference centres, theatres and residential buildings. Singapore is a small country with limited resources. For this reason, the attraction of external investors is regarded as important and the city state is planning a long-term, sustainable urban development with the aim of a higher quality of life for the population.[33] This is associated with the concept of the 'city in the garden', with the biophilic idea of becoming the greenest, healthiest and most liveable metropolis in the world.[34] The building ensemble opened in 2018 and has a hybrid usage with apartments and offices, a kindergarten, cafes and restaurant, as well as commercially used and freely accessible public areas in the lower areas. Adapted externally to the perimeter developments and planning grids, it is formed out of four cubic 30-storey high-rise volumes (fig. 9). A volume of space cuts through the middle like a canyon, opening up a generous outdoor space with lush vegetation (fig. 10). A range of additional green areas are integrated into the complex. Apart from roof gardens, on the 4th, 15th and 32nd floors there are so-called sky gardens, up to two storeys high and either roofed or open to the sky.

10 In the center a generous outdoor space with lush vegetation opens up

URBANE GRÜNOASE: MARINA ONE   In einem anderen, in den Dimensionen viel größeren Projekt von Ingenhoven Architects ist diese Charakteristik in noch vielfältigerer Weise artikuliert. Im Finanzdistrikt Singapurs, der seit den 1970er Jahren durch Rodung und Landaufschüttung mit Finanzimmobilien, Hotels, Konferenzzentren, Theatern und Wohnungsbau zum urbanen Quartier Marina Bay entwickelt wird, entstand der Komplex Marina One. Singapur ist ein kleines Land mit begrenzten Ressourcen. Aus diesem Grund wird die Attraktion für externe Investoren für wichtig erachtet, und der Stadtstaat plant eine langfristige, nachhaltige Stadtentwicklung mit dem Ziel höchster Lebensqualität für die Bevölkerung.[33] Diese ist mit dem Konzept der ‚Stadt im Garten' verknüpft, mit der biophilen Vorstellung, die grünste, gesündeste und lebenswerteste Metropole der Welt zu werden.[34] Das 2018 eröffnete Gebäudeensemble wird mit Wohnungen und Büros, Kindergarten, Cafes und Restaurant sowie kommerziell genutztem und in den unteren Bereichen frei zugänglichen öffentlichen Räumen hybrid genutzt. Nach außen den Blockrändern und Planungsrastern angepasst, wird es aus vier kubischen 30-geschossigen Hochbaukörpern gebildet (Abb. 9). In deren Mitte ist ein Raumvolumen canyonartig eingeschnitten und öffnet so einen großzügigen Freiraum mit üppiger Vegetation (Abb. 10). Eine Vielfalt von weiteren Grünräumen ist in den Komplex integriert. Neben Dachgärten sind es im vierten, 15. und 32. Geschoss sogenannte Skygardens, die bis zu zwei Geschosse hoch, überdacht oder himmeloffen gestaltet sind.   149

11–13   Walkways and shading in curved forms enhance the idea of an inner landscape designed by Kathryn Gustafson

14　Section with green areas distributed on different levels

Über mehrere Geschosse erstreckt sich die landschaftliche Anlage im unteren Bereich. Ein Wasserfall, verschiedene Wasserbecken, Steinsetzungen und üppige Vegetation, die, so die am Entwurf beteiligte anglo-amerikanische Landschaftsarchitektin Kathryn Gustafson, in Anlehnung an asiatische Reisfelder mit regionaltypischer tropischer Bepflanzung gestaltet und hangartig nach oben ausgedehnt wurde (Abb. 11–13).[35] Hier war die Zusammenarbeit mit dem lokalen Landschaftsarchitekturbüro ICN inspirierend und hilfreich. Die über mehrere Geschosse terrassiert durch das Gebäude hindurchgeführte Vegetation kann auf unterschiedlichen Höhen erlebt werden. Über Stege, die freigeformt und spiralartig nach oben verlaufen, wird es ermöglicht, das Areal zu durchqueren. Bänke ermöglichen zudem den weiteren Aufenthalt. Zuvor waren die Pflanzen in überdachten Bereichen und im offenen Freiraum in ihrem Wachstum beobachtet worden, um zu eruieren, ob und wie sie gedeihen können und wie die Bepflanzung einem Dschungel ähnlich werden kann, der sich hier befand und bestehen würde, wenn es die Stadt nicht gäbe. Gleichzeitig sollte sie einer Oase vergleichbar sein.[36] Mit all den direkt und vermittelt verbundenen Grünbereichen hat das Architekturteam eine multidimensionale Landschaft integriert, deren Wirkung auch der eines Waldes gleicht, so Kathryn Gustafson.[37] Christoph Ingenhoven wählte zudem die Charakterisierung ‚gestaffelte Landschaft'.[38] Die Vegetation benötigt Licht, Wasser, Luft und Erde, um zu gedeihen, und dies ist eine technische und gestalterische Herausforderung für jeden Architekturentwurf, der Vegetation integriert (Abb. 14). Beschreibungen wie terrassierte Reisfelder, Wald, Oase oder Dschungel verbildlichen deutlich

15 Outer façades with specific glazing and façade lamellae

The landscaping in the lower area stretches across several floors. A waterfall, various water basins, decorative stones and lush vegetation which, according to the Anglo-American landscape architect Kathryn Gustafson, who was involved in the design, is shaped in a way that evokes Asian rice paddies with typical regional tropical planting and is extended upwards like a slope (fig. 11–13).[35] Here the cooperation with the local landscape architecture office ICN was inspiring and helpful. The vegetation terraced through the building across several floors can be experienced at different levels. Walkways that are freely formed and spiral upwards allow passage through the area. Benches in addition make it possible to linger. The plants in roofed areas and in the open space had been previously observed regarding their growth, to establish whether and how they can flourish and how the planting can be similar to a jungle that would exist if the city did not. At the same time, it was to be comparable to an oasis.[36] With all the directly and loosely connected green areas, the architecture team integrated a multidimensional landscape whose effect also resembles a forest, according to Kathryn Gustafson.[37] Christoph Ingenhoven also chose the term 'staggered landscape'.[38] The vegetation needs light, water, air and earth to flourish, and this is a technical and design challenge for any architectural plan that integrates vegetation (fig. 14). Descriptions such as terraced rice paddies, forest, oasis or jungle clearly show the landscape ideas and analogies for this metropolitan green oasis, referred to as the green heart of the urban area.

In Singapore there is a landscape replacement strategy that dictates that up to 100% of the site area must be replaced or restored by greenery in the building context, i.e. the creation of green areas is mandatory. Altogether 125% of the plot are here generated as green areas. Many species of tree,

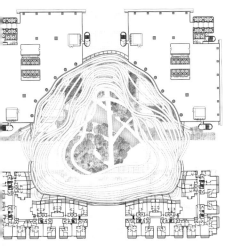

16–17 Internal open space in ondulated, canyon-like form allows for greenery and ventilation

die landschaftlichen Ideen und Analogien für diese als Green Heart, grünes Herz, des Stadtbereichs bezeichnete metropolitane Grünoase. In Singapur gibt es eine Landscape-Replacement-Strategie, die vorschreibt, dass bis zu 100 Prozent der Standort-/Grundstücksfläche durch Grün im Gebäudekontext ersetzt bzw. zurückgegeben werden müssen, d.h. das Schaffen von Grünbereichen ist vorgegeben. Insgesamt wurden hier 125 Prozent der Standortfläche als Grünräume geschaffen, die mit zahlreichen Baum-, Strauch- und weiteren Pflanzenspezies ausgestattet sind. Es kann hier nicht nur Biodiversität entstehen, sondern die Gärten wirken auch luftkühlend, reduzieren Oberflächentemperaturen und Feinstaubanteile, absorbieren CO_2, produzieren Sauerstoff und ermöglichen Fauna-Habitate.[39] Zudem wurden hier zahlreiche energie- und ressourcenschonende Verfahren eingesetzt wie eine Regenwasseranlage, Fotovoltaikzellen (PV), Windturbinen, geothermische Anlagen und spezifische, Sonneneinstrahlung reduzierende Verglasungen. Zusammen mit außen liegenden Fassadenlamellen verringert die üppige Vegetation durch Verschattungen und Luftströme Hitzestaus, ermöglicht Verschattungen etc., die auch den Energieverbrauch und den Einsatz von Klimaanlagen wesentlich reduzieren (Abb. 16).[40] Zugleich wird damit der Anteil an öffentlichem Raum in der hochverdichteten Stadt erhöht. Es wurden verschiedene Milieus generiert für Aktivitäten, Bewegung, Erholung und Interaktion. Die programmatische Strategie ist zugleich eine technologische wie biophile und sozialräumliche. Sie vermischt Grünraum und urbanen, metropolitanen Raum zu einem innovativen Hybrid (Abb. 17–18). Er kann international als Prototyp und Modell weitere Entwicklungen befördern, nicht nur für vergleichbar dichte Agglomerationen Asiens, Afrikas oder Südamerikas.

shrub and other plants were planted here. In this way not only biodiversity is enabled but also gardens that cool the air, reduce surface temperatures and fine dust, absorb CO_2, produce oxygen and allow fauna habitats.[39] In addition, numerous energy-conscious and resource-saving measures were used here, such as a rainwater collector, photovoltaic cells, wind turbines, geothermal systems and specific glazing that reduces sun radiation. Together with external façade lamellae, the lush vegetation reduces heat accumulation through shading and air flows that also significantly reduce energy consumption and the use of air conditioning units (fig. 16).[40] At the same time, the proportion of public space in the highly densified city is increased. Various milieus were generated for activities, exercise, leisure and interaction. The programmatic strategy is at the same time a technological, biophilic and socio-spatial one. It combines green space and urban, metropolitan space into an innovative hybrid (fig. 17–18). This project can stimulate further developments internationally as a prototype and model, not only for comparably dense agglomerations in Asia, Africa or South America.

REPERTOIRE   The technical and technological design catalogue of Ingenhoven Architects forms a solid repertoire for sustainable building. Furthermore, it is associated with experimental and forward-looking processes, which is also expressed with being accorded exceptional certifications, awards and respective prizes. The combination with biological design elements forms a fundamentally relevant basis for 'green' architecture and urban construction with a positive effect on the climate. Both building shells and complex large areas of vegetation in the buildings with various morphologies and species, as an overarching composition, become the specifics and biophile attraction of the architecture that promises lifestyle, comfort and recreation. It is to be emphasised that the specific design approach draws attention to the location and climate. The term 'supergreen', which was chosen as branding for the architectural stance, also comprises the linking of circulation and leisure spaces, of public and private areas, of commercial and democratic, i.e. freely accessible areas and 'shared space' as contents of the design processes. Landscape-ness is thereby developed in a sustainable and climatic, contemporarily location-specific and biophile context. Different types of physiological and sensory aspects are incorporated. These components become the respective guiding idea of a wide range of design interactions and compositions, which also integrate social implications. A wide spectrum of human-environment-interactions is thereby included, which take on a specific cultural and geographical form in relation to the location and situation.

Der technische und technologische Entwurfsbestand von Ingenhoven Architects bildet ein solides Repertoire zum nachhaltigen Bauen. Darüber hinaus werden damit experimentelle und zukunftsweisende Prozesse verbunden, was auch in Würdigungen mit exzeptionellen Zertifizierungen, Auszeichnungen und entsprechenden Preisen zum Ausdruck kommt. Die Verknüpfung mit biologischen Entwurfsbausteinen bildet eine grundlegend relevante Position für positiv klimawirksame ,grüne' Architektur- und Stadtgestaltung. Hierbei werden sowohl Gebäudehüllen als auch komplexe große Vegetationsbereiche im Gebauten mit verschiedenen Morphologien und Spezies in einer übergreifenden Komposition zur Spezifik und biophilen Attraktion der Architekturen, die Lifestyle, Komfort und Rekreation versprechen. Hervorzuheben ist die jeweils standort- und klimabezogene entwerferische Herangehensweise. Mit dem Begriff ,Supergreen', der als Branding für die Architekturhaltung gewählt wurde, wird dabei zudem die Verknüpfung von Zirkulations- und Aufenthaltsräumen, von öffentlichen und privaten Bereichen, von kommerziellen und demokratischen, d.h. frei zugänglichen Räumen und ,shared space', als Inhalt der Entwurfsprozesse benannt. Landschaftlichkeit wird dadurch in einem nachhaltigen und klimatischen, zeitgenössisch ortsbezogenen und einem biophilen Kontext entwickelt. Dabei sind physiologische und sensorische Aspekte unterschiedlicher Art einbezogen. Diese Komponenten werden zur jeweiligen Leitidee verschiedenster gestalterischer Interaktionen und Kompositionen verknüpft, die zudem soziale Implikationen integrieren. Ein breites Spektrum von Mensch-Umwelt-Interaktionen ist damit integriert, die sich kulturell und geografisch, d.h. orts- und situationsbezogen spezifisch, ausbilden. 155

GRÜNES PROTOTYPING
GREEN PROTOTYPING
WOHA

The aspect of a site-specific approach to climate control and spatial design can be seen in concepts and projects by the Singapore architecture and urban design office WOHA with a different procedure, presented in developed and also in published strategies and components. WOHA Architects was founded in 1994 by the Singapore architect Wong Mun Summ and the Australian architect Richard Hassell. Operating mainly in the Southern Hemisphere, in Singapore, Australia, China and other Southeast Asian countries, this approach involves the prototyping of 'green' stances and design elements, presenting innovative dimensions for the concept of landscape-ness as architectural idea for other regions of the world. Their intention of creating integrative architectural and urban development solutions to the challenges of the 21st century, such as climate change, population growth and increasing urbanization flows into visionary and built projects on different scales, from interiors to master plans.[41]

Der Aspekt einer ortsspezifischen Annäherung an Klima-
kontrolle und Raumentwurf wird in Konzepten und Projekten des Singapurer Architektur- und Städtebaubüros
WOHA in einer weiteren Vorgehensweise ablesbar, die
sich in herausgebildeten und auch in publizierten Strategien und Komponenten darbietet. Gegründet wurde
WOHA Architects 1994 von den Architekten Wong Mun
Summ aus Singapur und dem gebürtigen Australier
Richard Hassell. Mit hauptsächlichem Wirkungsbereich
auf der Südhalbkugel, in Singapur, Australien, China
und anderen südostasiatischen Ländern, verbindet
sich ihr Ansatz mit der Prototypisierung ‚grüner' Positionen und Bausteine, die auch für andere Regionen
der Welt innovative Dimensionen für das Konzept von
Landschaftlichkeit als Architekturidee präsentieren.
Ihre Intention, integrative architektonische und städtebauliche Lösungen für die Aufgaben des 21. Jahrhunderts wie Klimawandel, Bevölkerungswachstum
und zunehmende Urbanisierung zu kreieren, fließt
ein in visionäre und gebaute Projekte in unterschiedlichen Maßstäben vom Interieur bis zum Masterplan.[41]

Guided by the notion of perceiving the world overall as a landscape to take into consideration, they seek to dissolve boundaries between landscape and architecture. In particular, large building complexes with an urban design contextualisation in megacities, which integrate vegetation in various ways and are often described as 'green' architecture in the national and international resonance, are characteristic of the projects by this firm. Their attitude of thinking of a building as a landscape, working on the possibilities of dissolving the boundaries between architecture and landscape and of preserving 'nature' by integrating it into the built environment, is understood by the architects as a contemporary 'super critical' stance.[42]

CONCEPT   For the Architecture Biennale 2016, WOHA Architects presented the exhibition contribution 'Fragments of an urban future' and published the book 'Garden City Mega City: Rethinking Cities for the Age of Global Warming', together with the photographer, writer and publisher Patrick Bingham-Hall (fig. 1–3).[43] In about a quarter of the volume of the book, problems that cities are currently confronted with are articulated in texts and photographs regarding megacities such as Mumbai, Delhi, Jakarta and Manila, showing the need for architectural ideas and urban design models. Possible answers to this are presented in the larger part of the book as fundamental strategies and principles for the creation of highly dense urban ensembles for long-term growth and sustainability. There is also a presentation of how the architects try to combine this approach with highly qualified sojourn and living qualities. In particular, it is to be highlighted how they have developed design systematics over time for innovative design

1　Garden City Mega City　Venice 2016　Exhibition at Architecture Biennale

Geleitet von der Vorstellung, die Welt im Gesamten als eine zu berücksichtigende Landschaft zu begreifen, möchten sie Grenzen zwischen Landschaft und Architektur auflösen. Insbesondere große Gebäudekomplexe mit städtebaulicher Kontextualisierung in Megastädten, die in unterschiedlicher Weise Vegetation integrieren und in der nationalen und internationalen Resonanz oft als ‚grüne' Architektur beschrieben werden, sind charakteristisch für die Projekte dieses Büros. Ihre Haltung, ein Gebäude als Landschaft zu denken, an den Möglichkeiten zur Auflösung der Grenzen zwischen Architektur und Landschaft zu arbeiten und ‚Natur' zu bewahren, indem sie in die gebaute Umwelt integriert wird, verstehen die Architekten als eine zeitgenössisch ‚superkritische' Position.[42]

KONZEPT　Zur Architekturbiennale 2016 präsentierten WOHA Architects den Ausstellungsbeitrag ‚Fragments of an urban future' und publizierten zusammen mit dem Fotografen, Schriftsteller und Verleger Patrick Bingham-Hall dazu das Buch ‚Garden City Mega City. Rethinking cities for the age of global warming' (Abb. 1–2).[43] Etwa in einem Viertel des Buchumfangs werden Probleme, mit denen die Städte aktuell konfrontiert sind, in Texten und Fotografien zu Megastädten wie Mumbai, Delhi, Jakarta oder Manila artikuliert, womit der Bedarf an architektonischen Ideen und städtebaulichen Modellen übergreifend aufgezeigt wird. Mögliche Antworten darauf werden im größeren Teil des Buchs vorgestellt als grundlegende Strategien und Prinzipien zur Erzeugung hochverdichteter urbaner Ensembles für langfristiges Wachstum und Nachhaltigkeit. Artikuliert wird ebenfalls, wie die Architekten versuchen, diesen Ansatz mit hochqualifizierten Aufenthalts- und Lebensqualitäten zu verbinden. 159

2 Garden City Mega City 2016

elements and for evaluations of the performance of buildings. These had an internationally influential effect. It goes without saying that the density of the Southeast Asian island state of Singapore, due to population growth and physical architectural density, as well as the necessity to extend the limited building surface through land reclamation by means of backfilling, are driving forces of the concepts of the office located in Singapore and thereby also the topic of the vertical city. Project designs include luxury hotels, villas and office high-rises, as well as social housing and urban models. They collaborate with experts from different specialist fields, including landscape architects, mechanical engineers, ecologists, horticulturalists and hydrologists. In the book, they systematically present the strategies and components hitherto gleaned from the collective design, realisation and evaluation processes. Therefore, they used descriptive renderings, axonometries, photographs, diagrams and infographics, showing realisation variants in a more specific way based on the example of the built projects.

Green façades and green walls with climbing plants, roof gardens (sky gardens) and roof parks (sky parks) are among the design elements; green areas, communal areas and resource saving are among the exemplary criteria of evaluation.[44] They also describe this systematisation as a toolbox with which they produce performative greenery that counteracts heat islands and dust pollution, while also enabling biodiversity.[45] In addition, they work with students to develop and integrate concepts, master plans and visions of how future cities can be formed self-sustainably and three-dimensionally out of several layers. This urban landscape idea, also conceived as socially sustainable, comprises a flat roof layer with a sunroof spanning it for

Insbesondere hervorzuheben ist, wie sie über die Zeit Entwurfssystematiken entwickelt haben für innovative Bausteine und für Bewertungen der Performance von Gebäuden. Diese wirkten international einflussreich. Es ist nur naheliegend, dass die Dichte des südostasiatischen Inselstaates Singapur durch Bevölkerungswachstum und physische bauliche Dichte aufgrund der Notwendigkeit, die beschränkte Baufläche durch Landgewinnung mittels Aufschüttung zu erweitern, als treibende Kräfte der Konzepte des in Singapur angesiedelten Büros wirken und damit auch das Thema der vertikalen Stadt äußerst relevant ist. Die Projektkonzeptionen schließen Luxushotels, Villenbau und Bürohochhäuser ebenso ein wie Sozialwohnungsbau und urbane Modelle. Dabei arbeiten sie mit Experten aus unterschiedlichen Fachgebieten zusammen, die neben Landschaftsarchitekt:innen und mechanischen Ingenieur:innen auch Ökolog:innen, Gartenbauer:innen und Hydrolog:innen einschließen. Die bislang aus den kollektiven Entwurfs- und Realisierungs- sowie Evaluierungsprozessen gewonnenen Strategien und Komponenten stellen sie im Buch systematisiert vor. Dafür nutzen sie beschreibende Renderings, Axonometrien, Fotografien, Diagramme und Infografiken und zeigen Realisierungsvarianten am Beispiel der gebauten Projekte konkreter auf.

Grüne Fassaden und Kletterpflanzenwände, Dachgärten (skygardens) und Dachparks (skyparks) sind einige der Bausteine; Grünflächenanteile, Gemeinschaftsflächen sowie Ressourcenschonung einige exemplarische Kriterien der Evaluation.[44] Sie beschreiben diese Systematik auch als einen Werkzeugkasten, mit dem sie performatives Grün hervorbringen, das urbanen Hitzeinseln und Staubbelastung entgegenwirkt und Biodiversität ermöglicht.[45] Zudem sind Konzepte integriert, die sie mit Studierenden entwickeln,

3　Visions for future cities show layers of various functions and activities

energy production and urban farming, a layer for living and working consisting of perforated buildings of a medium size, which minimise energy consumption with natural lighting and ventilation, a layer that encourages human activities and biodiversity, a layer comprising parks, as well as a transport and service layer running through the park landscape (fig. 3–4). The ecological footprint is thereby to remain restricted to the current physical size of the cities and the boundaries of densification are to be tested.[46] By developing individual building blocks, which they generate with projects in Singapore as types, the architects from WOHA and their teams always seek to take account of the human scale and good adaptation potential. The architectural and urban development objectives are set within the aim of creating networked environments that correspond to a human scale, as well as of protecting nature, activating resilient and active ecosystems, promoting a sense of community and finally generating biophilic qualities. In reference to the garden city idea of the late 19th and early 20th century, as well as to utopian and realised major architecture and urban development projects of the 1960s and 1970s, they seek to update and merge these concept ideas and to develop the 'green' garden city of the future. The latter should be pleasant, comfortable, natural and homely. Their ideal is to develop a comfortable garden suburb experience and to add it vertically as a megastructure that everyone can enjoy.

4 Large green areas span the roof surfaces of the city visions

Masterpläne sowie Visionen dazu, wie zukünftige Städte dreidimensional aus mehreren Layern gebildet und selbstversorgend gestaltet werden können. Diese auch sozial nachhaltig konzipierte Stadtlandschaftsidee umfasst einen von einem Sonnendach überspannten Flachdach-Layer für Energieproduktion und Urban Farming, einen Layer für Wohnen und Arbeiten aus perforierten Gebäuden mittlerer Größe, die mit natürlicher Belichtung und Ventilation Energieverbrauch minimieren, einen Layer, der menschliche Aktivitäten und Biodiversität fördert, einen Layer aus Parks sowie einen Transport- und Service-Layer, der sich durch die Parklandschaft zieht (Abb. 3–4). Der ökologische Fußabdruck soll damit auf die aktuelle physische Größe der Städte beschränkt bleiben, und die Grenzen von Verdichtung sollen getestet werden.[46] In der Entwicklung einzelner Bausteine, die sie mit Projekten in Singapur typenbildend generieren, versuchen die Architekten von WOHA mit ihren Teams immer auch den menschlichen Maßstab und gute Adaptionspotenziale zu berücksichtigen. Die architektonisch-städtebaulichen Ziele sind gefasst in dem Anliegen, vernetzte Umwelten zu erzeugen, die dem menschlichen Maßstab entsprechen, Natur zu schützen, resiliente und aktive Ökosystemleistungen zu aktivieren, Gemeinschaft zu fördern sowie schließlich biophile Qualitäten zu generieren. In Referenz zur Gartenstadtidee des späten 19. und frühen 20. Jahrhunderts sowie zu utopischen und realisierten architektonisch-städtebaulichen Großprojekten der 1960er/70er Jahre möchten sie deren Konzeptideen vermischt aktualisieren und die ‚grüne' Gartenstadt der Zukunft entwickeln. Diese soll angenehm, komfortabel, natürlich und häuslich sein. Ihr Ideal ist es, eine komfortable Gartenvorstadterfahrung zu entwickeln und diese vertikal zu addieren zu einer Megastruktur, die alle genießen können.

5–6 Singapore Pavilion Expo 2020 Dubai 2022

CITY IN THE GARDEN: SINGAPORE PAVILION EXPO 2020

The thinking and work of WOHA Architects can be viewed as an example of the visions of the cultural context, within which they develop their ideas and strategies. The theme of the Singapore pavilion for Expo 2020 in Dubai, 'Nature, nurture and future', significantly represents the vision of the city state as a city in nature, in which both people and ecologies are nurtured, maintained and cultivated. This is associated with the notion of playing an exemplary role among contemporary cities of the world as a 'city in the garden', and with showing Singapore's expertise in the development and realisation of urban visions, reinforcing Singapore's profile in order to attract talent, technology, tourism and investment.[47] This green branding in the sense of a neoliberal market economy orientation goes hand in hand with city state regulations and concrete directives for the reclamation and creation of sustainable green areas.

Appointed by Singapore's state Urban Redevelopment Authority (URA), WOHA designed the Singapore pavilion for Expo 2020, which due to the coronavirus pandemic was then held in 2021–22. The pavilion exemplifies the notion of integrating natural and built-spatial systems (fig. 5–7). This occurs in urban development by means of controlled assignments and especially with building regulations, such as the internationally influential programme for the revegetation of high-rises, which prescribes that 100% of the built surface area in the new construction should be restored as a green area.[48]

7 Lush tropical greenery is placed along an internal circulation route

STADT IM GARTEN: SINGAPUR PAVILLON EXPO 2020

Das Denken und Schaffen von WOHA Architects kann als Beispiel für die Visionen des kulturellen Kontexts gesehen werden, innerhalb dessen sie ihre Ideen und Strategien entwickeln. Das Thema des Singapur-Pavillons für die Expo 2020 in Dubai ,Nature, nurture and future' repräsentiert signifikant die Vision des Stadtstaates, eine Stadt in der Natur zu sein, in der sowohl Menschen als auch Ökologien gehegt, gepflegt und kultiviert werden. Damit verbunden ist die Vorstellung, für die zeitgenössischen Städte der Welt als ,Stadt im Garten' modellhaft zu wirken, Singapurs Expertise in der Entwicklung und Umsetzung urbaner Visionen aufzuzeigen und nicht zuletzt, Singapurs Profil zu stärken, um Talent, Technologie, Tourismus und Investment anzuziehen.[47] Dieses Green Branding im Sinne einer neoliberalen Marktwirtschaftsorientierung steht in Verbindung mit stadtstaatlicher Regulierung bzw. konkreten Vorgaben für die Wiedergewinnung und Erzeugung von nachhaltigen Grünräumen.

Beauftragt von Singapurs staatlicher Urban Redevelopment Authority (URA) entwarfen WOHA den Singapur-Pavillon für die Expo 2020, die aufgrund der Corona-Pandemie dann 2021/22 stattfand. Der Pavillon veranschaulicht die Vorstellung, natürliche und baulich-räumliche Systeme zu integrieren (Abb. 5–7). Dies erfolgt in der Stadtentwicklung mittels gesteuerter Beauftragung und insbesondere mit Bauvorschriften wie etwa dem international einflussreichen Programm zur Begrünung von Hochhäusern, das vorschreibt, dass 100 Prozent der bebauten Grundfläche in der neuen Konstruktion als

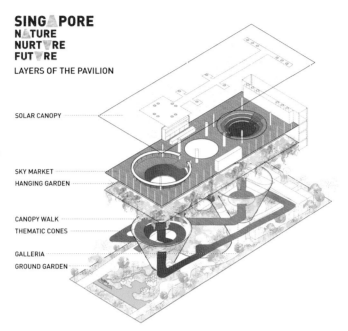

SINGAPORE
NATURE
NURTURE
FUTURE

LAYERS OF THE PAVILION

SOLAR CANOPY

SKY MARKET
HANGING GARDEN

CANOPY WALK
THEMATIC CONES

GALLERIA
GROUND GARDEN

8 Singapore Pavilion Expo 2020 Axonometry with different layers of the pavilion

In the design by WOHA and the landscape architecture firm Salad Dressing, this aim is experimentally implemented and combined with a circulation route spiralling upwards through various levels with an open layout, in a construction with lush tropical vegetation running through it inside and outside (fig. 8–9).[49] Three large cones with greenery are set into the lower pavilion area that is not closed to the outside. This and other zones show Singapore's path as a pioneer for sustainable and biophile urban development, as does the pavilion itself. In addition, a plant maintenance system developed by the firm Oceania Robots from Singapore and carried out by robots shows possibilities for how vertical greenery and high-rise gardens can be technologically cultivated (fig. 10). Natural shading and transverse ventilation, as well as a solar and water desalination system on the top floor, enable the net zero energy balance of the pavilion. The energy, climate and water concept has been developed with the German climate and energy technology company Transsolar.[50] In this pavilion, the focus is on movement and the experience of nature, making it clear that, beyond balcony planting and parks, nature in architecture and the city is thought of as an environmental space of encounter that can bring numerous environmental benefits in combination with technology and biological expertise.

9 Greenery dominates the pavilion's appearance

10 The robotic plant maintenance system

Grünfläche zurückgegeben werden sollen.⁴⁸ Im Entwurf von WOHA und dem Landschaftsarchitekturbüro Salad Dressing wird dieses Anliegen experimentell umgesetzt und verbunden mit einer spiralförmig über verschiedene Ebenen mit offenem Grundriss nach oben führenden Zirkulationsroute in einer von tropischer Vegetation innen und außen üppig durchzogenen Konstruktion (Abb. 8–9).⁴⁹ Drei große begrünte Kegel sind in den unteren, nach außen nicht geschlossenen Pavillonbereich eingestellt. Darin und in anderen Arealen wird wie mit dem Pavillon selbst Singapurs Weg als Vorreiterin für nachhaltige und biophile Stadtentwicklung aufgezeigt. Zudem zeigt ein vom Büro Oceania Robots aus Singapur entwickeltes, durch Roboter ausgeführtes Pflanzenpflegesystem Möglichkeiten auf, wie vertikales Grün und Hochhausgärten technologisch kultiviert werden können (Abb. 10). Natürliche Verschattung und Querlüftung sowie eine Solar- und Wasserentsalzungsanlage auf der obersten Ebene ermöglichen die Netto-Null-Energiebilanz des Pavillons. Das Energie-, Klima- und Wasserkonzept wurde mit dem deutschen Klima- und Energietechnikunternehmen Transsolar entwickelt.⁵⁰ In diesem Pavillon stehen die Bewegung und das Erleben von Natur im Mittelpunkt, wobei verdeutlicht wird, dass Natur in Architektur und Stadt über Balkonbepflanzungen und Parks hinaus landschaftlich als Umgebungs- und Begegnungsraum gedacht wird, der zudem in Verknüpfung mit Technologie und biologischer Expertise zahlreiche Umweltbenefits mit sich bringen kann.

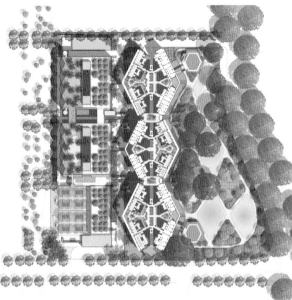

11   Skyville @ Dawson Singapore 2015

12   Site plan with greenery on different building levels

POROSITY AND OPEN SPACE: SKYVILLE   In the projects
realised in Singapore, WOHA Architects also already managed to integrate
a variety of the mentioned aspects. The project Skyville @ Dawson, publicly
funded by the Housing Development Board (HDB), is a hybrid megastructure
with 960 apartments for the middle class.[51] A high-rise structure of twelve
47-storey towers was realised with diamond-shaped and interconnected atria.
They stand on a multi-layered and multifunctional base zone, where the public park with preserved mature trees stretches as far as under the residential
towers (fig. 11–12). This creates interstices for wind permeability as well as
for additional shaded outdoor spaces. Two-storey communal rooms with seating groups are integrated in the ground floor zone, for leisure time, communication and views out towards the park (fig. 13–14). In Singapore, one can
often find multipurpose ground levels with residential usage above in building complexes of the 1970s, such as at the Golden Mile Complex by Design
Partnership Architects (1973), which has a large communal terrace for the
residential tower residents above the commercially used ground floor zone.[52]

At Skyville @ Dawson, the height of the volume is furthermore divided into
sections of 11 floors, each of which is allocated shared access and open
areas. The purpose is to allow the development of village community structures, analogous to rural settlements, the traditional kampung.[53] Each apartment with an open layout is flexible for various forms of usage and belongs
to a cluster of 80 apartments, grouped around so-called sky gardens.[54] The
open spaces were designed and realised with the Singapore landscape

13 Open communal rooms on ground floor   14 Sky gardens on higher levels

POROSITÄT UND FREIRAUM: SKYVILLE Auch in den in Singapur realisierten Projekten konnten WOHA Architects bereits verschiedenste der genannten Aspekte integrieren. Das vom Housing Development Board (HDB) öffentlich geförderte Projekt Skyville @ Dawson ist eine hybride Megastruktur mit 960 Wohnungen für die Mittelschicht.[51] Realisiert wurde eine Hochhausstruktur aus zwölf 47-geschossigen Türmen mit diamantförmig gebildeten und miteinander verbundenen Atrien. Sie sitzen auf einer mehrgeschossigen multifunktionalen Sockelzone auf, wo sich der öffentliche Park mit erhaltenem Baumbestand bis unter die Wohntürme erstreckt (Abb. 11–12). So entstehen Zwischenräume für Winddurchlässigkeit ebenso wie für zusätzliche verschattete Außenräume. Im Sockelbereich sind zudem zweigeschossige Gemeinschaftsräume mit Sitzgruppen integriert, die Aufenthalt, Kommunikation und Ausblicke zum Park ermöglichen (Abb. 13–14). In Singapur sind Multigroundlevels mit darüber befindlicher Wohnnutzung mehrfach in Gebäudekomplexen der 1970er Jahre anzutreffen, wie beim Golden Mile Complex von Design Partnership Architects (1973), bei dem oberhalb der gewerblich genutzten Sockelzone eine große Gemeinschaftsterrasse für die Bewohnenden der Wohntürme liegt.[52]

Im Falle von Skyville @ Dawson ist zudem die Höhenentwicklung des Volumens in Abschnitte aus elf Geschossen unterteilt, denen jeweils eine gemeinsame Erschließung und Freibereiche zugeordnet sind. Sie sollen ermöglichen, in Analogie zu ländlichen Wohnsiedlungen, den traditionellen Kampung, dorfgemeinschaftliche Strukturen zu entwickeln.[53] Jedes Apartment ist mit offenem Grundriss flexibel für verschiedene Nutzungsformen zugeschnitten und gehört zu einem Cluster von 80 Wohnungen, die um sogenannte Skygardens gruppiert sind.[54] Die Gestaltung der Freiräume wurde mit dem Singapurer Landschaftsarchitekturbüro ICN Design International entworfen und realisiert. Ein großer, 24 Stunden geöffneter öffentlicher Park auf dem Dach mit teils überdachtem Boulevard und Joggingstrecke lädt zu

15–16 Skygardens allow for meeting and ventilation

architecture firm ICN Design. A large public park on the roof open 24 hours, with a partly roofed boulevard and jogging path, invite exercise and leisure and enable sweeping views of the city and landscape. The various areas of greenery act as environmental filters by absorbing carbon and reducing heat accumulation. Rainwater collection and photovoltaics, together with the natural ventilation and shade, contribute to reducing energy consumption. In addition, the scale and the inhospitable effect of the external repetitive appearance of the large building complex are mitigated by the porosity. The multiplication of the green outdoor areas with a landscape architectural design thus also generates a variety of horizontal public and semi-public spaces even on the vertical, which beyond access functions also contribute to individual and communal use for recreation, informal encounters and interaction, and overall well-being, as post-occupancy evaluations have shown (fig. 15–16).[55] Together with the clustering, which allows an overview of the individual village unit, neighbourly connections, productive cohabitation and a variety of social relations are potentially strengthened further.[56] Artworks in the building also contribute to this, their motifs and contents evoking the history of the location and its surroundings.[57] The ground-level green areas and the publicly accessible roof garden park contribute to the link with the city in the natural surroundings and on a wider scale, also through closer and more distant visual connections (fig. 17–18). All the outdoor areas, the greenery and the visual axes not least also allow the stimulation of biophile effects such as recreation and well-being through the mental and physical balance of the residents and the visitors of Skyville @ Dawson.

17 Green roof garden park   18 The public roof garden connects with the city

Bewegung und Erholung ein und ermöglicht weite Ausblicke über die Stadt und Landschaft. Die verschiedenen Grünflächen wirken nicht nur als Umweltfilter, indem sie CO_2 absorbieren und Hitzestaus reduzieren. Regenwassersammlung und Fotovoltaik tragen zusammen mit der natürlichen Belüftung und Verschattung dazu bei, den Energieverbrauch zu reduzieren. Zudem werden die Maßstäblichkeit und auch die unwirtliche Wirkung der äußeren repetitiven Erscheinung des großen Gebäudekomplexes durch die Porosität gemildert. Die Multiplizierung der begrünten und landschaftsarchitektonisch gestalteten Außenbereiche erzeugt so auch in der Vertikalen unterschiedliche horizontale öffentliche und halb öffentliche Räume, die über Erschließungsfunktionen hinaus zur individuellen und gemeinschaftlichen Nutzung für Rekreation, zur informellen Begegnung und Interaktion sowie zum Wohlergehen beitragen, wie Post-Occupancy-Evaluierungen gezeigt haben (Abb. 15–16).[55] Zusammen mit der Clusterung, die es ermöglicht, die einzelne Village-Einheit zu überblicken und auch akustisch wahrnehmen zu können, werden nachbarschaftliche Verbindungen und das produktive Nebeneinander unterschiedlicher sozialer Beziehungen potenziell noch verstärkt.[56] Dazu tragen auch Kunstwerke am Bau bei, deren Motive und Inhalte an die Geschichte des Standorts und seiner Umgebung erinnern.[57] Die ebenerdigen Grünräume und der öffentlich zugängliche Dachgartenpark tragen durch nahe und ferne Blickbeziehungen zur Verbundenheit mit der Stadt im natürlichen Umfeld und im weiteren Maßstab bei (Abb. 17–18). Mit all den Außenräumen, der Begrünung und den Blickbeziehungen können nicht zuletzt auch biophile Wirkungen wie Rekreation und Wohlbefinden durch psychisches und physisches Gleichgewicht der Bewohnenden und Besuchenden von Skyville @ Dawson stimuliert werden.

19 Hotel Parkroyal Collection Pickering facing Hong Lim Park Singapore 2012

GREEN VARIATIONS: PARKROYAL I OASIA HOTEL

In later projects, the architects have further developed and tested their strategies and components for the idea of combining architecture and landscape in varying designs. This refers to the possibilities of passive ventilation and shading and the reduction of the use of artificially generated energy, as well as vertical, horizontal and diagonal ventilation techniques that enable wind channels and air movement, along with a variety of shading and especially an increase in the proportion of vegetation and of morphological properties, in order to ultimately develop models for a landscaped garden city of the future with large, green, urban gestures.[58]

In the project Parkroyal Collection Pickering of 2012 in the Central Business District of Singapore, for example, the proportion of greenery in relation to the site surface was doubled. It represents a variant of what the architects call 'topographical architecture'. It is designed with a five-storey, partially organoid formed base zone with a landscaped and lushly planted roof terrace (fig. 19).[59] A market hall, medical centre, childcare, parking deck and other functions are integrated on this ground-floor level. The sculptural, cascade-like design towards the street evokes geological formations, rocky landscapes by the sea and in the desert, or rice terraces (fig. 20–21). Even the parking deck levels were given plants growing lushly over the railings (fig. 22–23). The intention is to allow more pleasant experiences of this

20–21   Base zone with organoid forms and lush greenery on roof terrace

GRÜNE VARIATIONEN: PARKROYAL I OASIA HOTEL

In weiteren Projekten haben die Architekten ihre Strategien und Komponenten zur Idee, Architektur und Landschaft zu verbinden, in variierten Gestaltungen weiter entfaltet und getestet. Dies bezieht sich auf die Möglichkeiten zu passiver Ventilation und Verschattung und die Reduktion des Gebrauchs künstlich erzeugter Energie, auf vertikale, horizontale und diagonale Belüftungstechniken, die Windwege und Luftbewegung ermöglichen, auf diverse Verschattungen und insbesondere auf die Erhöhung des Vegetationsanteils sowie auf morphologische Eigenschaften, um schließlich mit großen grünen urbanen Gesten Modelle zu entwickeln für eine landschaftliche Gartenstadt der Zukunft.[58]

Bei dem Projekt Parkroyal Collection Pickering von 2012 im Central Business District Singapurs beispielsweise wurde der Grünflächenanteil in Relation zur Standortfläche verdoppelt und mit verschiedenen Bausteinen verknüpft. So repräsentiert es beispielsweise eine Variante der von den Architekten sogenannten ‚topographischen Architektur'. Es ist mit einer in Teilen organoid geformten fünfgeschossigen Sockelzone mit üppig bepflanzter und landschaftsarchitektonisch gestalteter Dachterrasse gestaltet (Abb. 19).[59] In diesen Sockel sind Markthalle, Medical Center, Kinderbetreuung, Parkhaus und weitere Funktionen integriert. Die skulpturale kaskadenartige Gestaltung zum Straßenraum erinnert weitläufig an geologische Formationen, an Felsenlandschaften am Meer und in der Wüste oder an Reisterrassen (Abb. 20–21). Selbst die

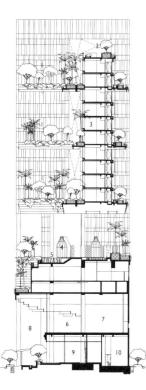

22–23   Section and view onto the sky gardens on four levels

infrastructure building from inside, from the street and from the park, compared to standard parking decks.[60] The project also contributed to upgrading the neighbouring Hong Lim Park and the urban space in this district, not only by creating flowing transitions from green outdoor space to the indoors but by demonstrating overall that dense and green do not have to be contradictory.[61]

The guest rooms have views out on equally curvaceous sky gardens, which extend between the tower blocks rising over the base zone on every fourth floor, lushly planted with palm trees and jasmin and other tropical species (fig. 24–25). Here the foliage also spills over the railings and grows downwards. Like the terrace on the base zone roof, these sky gardens integrate planted areas, walls and water basins with greenery, as well as outdoor furniture. Like the other outdoor space, they were realised with the Singapore landscape architecture firm Tierra Design.[62] They allow appropriation for a variety of activities, as well as new experiences of the urban space and architecture. With rainwater catchment basins and solar elements on the roof, they also ensure the building's own energy production, reinforcing the environmental performance of the building. This reduces the effects of urban heat islands, air pollution and noise.

24–25   Green gardens are situated on multiple levels

Parkhausebenen wurden hier mit üppig über die Balustraden hinweg wachsenden Pflanzen versehen (Abb. 22–23). Dadurch sollen im Vergleich zum Standardparkhaus von innen, von der Straße und vom Park aus, angenehmere Erfahrungen dieses Infrastrukturbaus ermöglicht werden.[60] Das Projekt hat zudem dazu beigetragen, den benachbarten Hong-Lim-Park und den urbanen Raum in diesem Stadtteil aufzuwerten, indem es nicht nur fließende Übergänge von begrüntem Außenraum und Innenraum erzeugt, sondern insgesamt auch aufzeigt, dass dicht und grün keine Gegensätze bilden müssen.[61]

Die Gästezimmer haben Ausblicke auf ebenfalls kurvenreich angelegte Skygardens, die sich zwischen den sich über dem Sockel erhebenden Turmblöcken auf jedem vierten Geschoss erstrecken, und mit Palmbäumen und Jasmin und weiteren tropischen Spezies üppig bepflanzt sind (Abb. 24–25). Das Blattwerk übergreift auch hier die Balustraden und wächst nach unten. Wie die Terrasse auf dem Sockelzonendach integrieren diese Skygardens bepflanzte Flächen, begrünte Mauern und Wasserbecken sowie Outdoor-Mobiliar. Sie wurden wie die anderen Freiräume mit dem Singapurer Landschaftsarchitekturbüro Tierra Design realisiert.[62] Sie ermöglichen die Aneignung für unterschiedliche Tätigkeiten und Aktivitäten sowie neue Erfahrungen der Stadträume und Stadtarchitektur. Mit Regenwasserauffangbecken und Solarelementen auf dem Dach sorgen sie zudem für eine gebäudeeigene Energieproduktion, um die Umweltperformance des Gebäudes zu verstärken. So werden Auswirkungen urbaner Hitzeinseln, Luftverschmutzung und Lärmaufkommen reduziert.

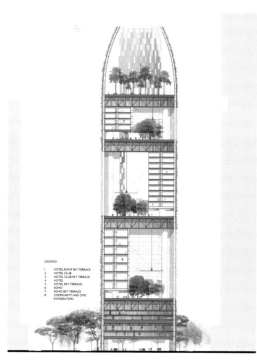

26　Section　Sky gardens and guest rooms

27　Climbing plants lushly cover the red mesh

The building for the Oasia Hotel Downtown (2016) shows an even stronger permeability of outdoors and indoors, as well as of vegetation and architecture. It rises over a square site as a 27-storey architectural formation with mixed office and hotel usage. The high-rise tower in a dense business district of steel and glass towers opens up in four places on the vertical to multistorey plenums, to big high verandas designed as sky gardens, and is rounded off at the top by a high, semi-open crown with a roof terrace (fig. 26–27). The sky gardens with water basins, planted areas and outdoor furniture were realised with the Singapore landscape architecture office STX Landscape Architects and the Milan design office of Patricia Urquiola.[63] The perforation of a building and the letting in of light and air have traditionally played a special role in tropical architecture.[64] Together with the atria on the ground floor and the roof gardens, a high degree of blending of outdoor space and architecture is achieved. The façade design is also a significant contributing factor. The microperforated aluminium façade construction in a red colour is penetrated by 21 different types of climbing plants, plus a further 33 plant and tree species in other areas (fig. 28–30).[65] Overall the building therefore promotes biodiversity in the inner city of Singapore and appears as an iconic high green building in the city in an innovative way.[66] 'Landscaping' surfaces and spaces, according to the architects, allows the harsh appearance of the abstract cityscape to be mitigated and a more pleasant design of the environment for the people. Trees and plants form important elements of scale and biophile qualities can encourage humans to feel more strongly bound to nature.[67]

28–30 Greenery creates various atmospheres throughout the building

Das Gebäude für das Oasia Hotel Downtown (2016) zeigt eine noch stärkere Durchdringung von Außen und Innen sowie von Vegetation und Gebäude. Es erhebt sich über einem quadratischen Grundstück als 27-geschossige architektonische Formation mit gemischter Büro- und Hotelnutzung. Der Hochhausturm in einem dichten Businessquartier aus Stahl-Glas-Hochhäusern öffnet sich an vier Stellen in der Vertikalen zu mehrgeschossigen Lufträumen, zu großen hohen Veranden, die als Skygarden ausgebildet sind, und wird von einer hohen halb offenen Krone mit Dachterrasse nach oben abgeschlossen (Abb. 26–27). Die Skygardens mit Wasserbecken, Pflanzflächen und Outdoor-Mobiliar wurden mit dem Singapurer Landschaftsarchitekturbüro STX Landscape Architects und dem Mailänder Designbüro von Patricia Urquiola realisiert.[63] In der tropischen Architektur spielte die Perforation eines Gebäudes und das Hereinlassen von Licht und Luft traditionell eine besondere Rolle.[64] Zusammen mit den Atrien im Erdgeschoss und den Dachgärten wird ein hoher Grad an Vermischung von Aussenraum und Architektur erzeugt. Dazu trägt auch die Fassadengestaltung wesentlich bei. Die mikrogelochte Aluminiumfassadenkonstruktion in roter Farbigkeit wird durchdrungen von Kletterpflanzenbewuchs mit 21 verschiedenen Arten, zu denen in den anderen Bereichen weitere 33 Pflanzen- und Baumarten kommen (Abb. 28–30).[65] So fördert das Gebäude insgesamt die Biodiversität in der Innenstadt Singapurs und kann als hohes grünes Gebäude in der Stadt in innovativer Weise ikonisch wirken.[66] Oberflächen und Räume zu ‚verlandschaftlichen‘ ermöglicht es, so die Architekten, die harsche Erscheinung der abstrakten Stadtbildlichkeit zu mildern und die Umwelt für Menschen angenehmer zu gestalten. Bäume und Pflanzen bilden dabei wichtige Maßstabselemente und können die Menschen im Sinne biophiler Qualitäten dazu ermutigen, sich mit der Natur stärker verbunden zu fühlen.[67]

REPERTOIRE   In the process of the synthesis of different sustainability aspects with the wish to conceive residential and living culture based less on the individual and more on the habitat, as well as of attributing relevance to the relations of an environment that is also climatically and biologically formed, WOHA Architects create prototypes for an idealised, sustainable and social architecture and city of the future. This consists also in reference to the pattern language approaches of Christopher Alexander, of strategies and components of what is called 'macro-architecture micro-urbanism'.[68] The explicitly three-dimensionally conceived city and architecture concept is associated with the reduction of the footprint as well as with energy production that is as self-sufficient as possible. It prioritises the vertical with multistorey base zones, as well as in some cases large, high openings towards open air to create porosity. Climate-related and vegetation-related design elements are integrated systematically into green shields, especially green facades and in horizontal circulation at a variety of building heights, which are situated within the building complex or on the building as public spaces or smaller private spaces with gardens and can also link several buildings. Finally, the architects generally thematise the idea of thinking of architecture topographically as an inhabited landscape.[69] References are also made to the specific local building culture.

As the structures can be perceived as environments, the habitual delineations of indoors and outdoors and of landscape and architecture only appear to be partially fixed.[70] Even if the large dimensions do not disappear from the perceptions of the inhabitants and users, they are mitigated by attempts to find a more human scale, for example through clustering and division into smaller units, through plenums and the addition of open spaces on the vertical axis, as well as in particular through the widespread use of lush vegetation. WOHA's strategies provide the possibility of being applied, adapted and modified accordingly, on various scales, in different places and in various climate zones. Plants also become a means of spatial definition, of wall structuring and of support for the various functions of a building. With programmatic building blocks and creative imagination, in the designs they become syntheses that can have a differentiated socio-spatial and biophile effect.

REPERTOIRE   Im Prozess der Synthese unterschiedlicher Nachhaltigkeitsaspekte mit dem Wunsch, Wohn- und Lebenskultur weniger vom Individuum und mehr ausgehend vom Habitat zu konzipieren sowie den Relationen einer auch klimatisch und biologisch gebildeten Umwelt Relevanz beizumessen, schaffen WOHA Architects eine Prototypologie für eine idealisierte, nachhaltige und soziale Architektur und Stadt der Zukunft. Diese besteht, auch in Referenz zu den Pattern-Language-Ansätzen von Christopher Alexander, aus Strategien und Komponenten dessen, was sie ‚Macro-Architecture – Micro-urbanism' nennen.[68] Das explizit dreidimensional gedachte Stadt- und Architekturkonzept ist mit der Reduktion des Fußabdrucks ebenso verbunden wie mit einer möglichst selbstversorgenden Energieproduktion. Es priorisiert die Vertikale mit mehrgeschossigen Sockelzonen sowie Porosität erzeugenden zum Teil großen, hohen Öffnungen zu Lufträumen. Klima- und vegetationsbezogene Entwurfsbausteine werden systematisiert in grüne Schirme, insbesondere grüne Fassaden und in horizontale Zirkulation auf verschiedenen Gebäudehöhen, die sich als öffentliche Räume oder kleinere private Räume mit Gärten innerhalb des Gesamtkomplexes oder auf dem Dach befinden und auch mehrere Gebäude verbinden können. Schließlich thematisieren die Architekten übergreifend die Idee, Architektur topografisch zu denken als bewohnte Landschaft.[69] Dabei werden auch Bezüge zur ortsspezifischen Baukultur aufgenommen.

Da die Strukturen als Umgebungen wahrgenommen werden können, erscheinen die üblichen Begrenzungen von Innen und Außen und von Landschaft und Architektur nur in Teilen fixiert.[70] Auch wenn die Großdimensionalität nicht aus dem Erfahrungsbereich der bewohnenden und nutzenden Menschen verschwindet, wird sie durch Versuche, humanere Maßstäblichkeit zu finden, gemildert, beispielsweise durch Clusterung und die Unterteilung in kleinere Einheiten, durch Lufträume und Freiraumaddition in der Vertikalen sowie insbesondere durch umfangreichen Einsatz üppiger Vegetation. WOHAs Strategien bieten die Möglichkeit, in verschiedenen Maßstäben, an verschiedenen Orten und in verschiedenen Klimazonen, jeweils entsprechend angepasst und modifiziert, angewandt zu werden. Pflanzen werden dabei auch zum Mittel der Raumdefinition, der Wandstrukturierung und der Unterstützung der verschiedenen Funktionen eines Gebäudes. Mit den programmatischen Bausteinen und gestalterischer Imagination werden sie in den Entwürfen zu Synthesen geführt, die differenzierte sozialräumliche und biophile Wirksamkeit entfalten können.

URBANE WÄLDER
URBAN FORESTS
STEFANO BOERI ARCHITETTI

With ambitious architectural and urban design projects, Stefano Boeri also seeks with multidisciplinary teams to not only mitigate the influence of a building on natural systems but to make them a part of these systems, of the surroundings and of the environment. He thereby pleads for a green city of the 21st century. In 1993, Boeri had founded Multiplicity, a committed multidisciplinary office for the study of urban settlement structures and of the unstable, constantly evolving conditions of contemporary cities.[71] Also in the architectural office Studio Boeri, opened in 1999 in Milan with Gianandrea Barrenca and Giovanni La Varra, which was later renamed Stefano Boeri Architetti, the architectural and urban development design activities are continually accompanied by research, now with a focus on biodiversity and sustainability, as well as on the future of metropolises from a planetary perspective.

Mit ambitionierten architektonischen und städtebaulichen Projekten versucht auch Stefano Boeri in multidisziplinären Teams nicht nur den Einfluss eines Gebäudes auf natürliche Systeme zu mildern, sondern sie zu einem Teil dieser Systeme, der Umgebung und der Umwelt werden zu lassen. Er plädiert dabei für eine grüne Stadt des 21. Jahrhunderts. 1993 hatte Boeri Multiplicity gegründet, ein engagiertes, multidisziplinäres Büro zur Untersuchung urbaner Siedlungsstrukturen und instabiler und sich stets entwickelnder Konditionen zeitgenössischer Städte.[71] Auch im 1999 in Mailand zusammen mit Gianandrea Barrenca und Giovanni La Varra eröffneten Büro Studio Boeri, das später in Stefano Boeri Architetti umbenannt wurde, begleitet Forschung, nun mit Schwerpunkt auf Biodiversität und Nachhaltigkeit sowie fokussiert auf die Zukunft von Metropolen in planetarischer Perspektive, fortlaufend die architektonische und städtebauliche Entwurfstätigkeit.

The work of the office with branches in Milan, Tirana and Shanghai comprises architecture and urban design, interior and landscape architecture. Apart from the usual cooperations, it must be pointed out that the Milan environment expert and landscape planner Laura Gatti is intensely integrated in the research, design and realisation processes. The international attention, resonance and commissioning is targeted towards projects such as the green highrise towers complete with greenery realised in Milan, as well as towards future visions that present, for example, fully forested cities with high biodiversity as an answer to climate change. Not least, Stefano Boeri's work as a publicist, also in a leading function between 2004 and 2011, at the magazines Domus and Abitare, as well as his involvement in international exhibitions, contributed to the wide public relations work and media presence of the office.[72]

CONCEPT   Especially the forward-looking openness and the impetus for the improvement of current conditions expressed in the concepts and projects, as well as the belief in their feasibility, strengthen both the concept ideas themselves and their popularity. Already in the 1990s, specific observation perspectives and means of representation characterised Boeri's explorations for the development of cities and territories.[73] With the network Multiplicity that he co-founded, these artistic, graphic and photographic analyses of various territories were gathered through on-site visits and research and were then developed to explore further, alongside the ways in which cities are described and presented, as well as geopolitical, socio-economic urban design and political relations.[74] The results were presented in exhibitions and publications, with the aim of promoting the transformation of the studied areas. Stefano Boeri's interest in the 'citta diffusa', especially the fragmented parts on the periphery and the suburban area around Milan, remained in further urban design concepts. Prior to and in the context of the planning for Expo 2015 in Milan, together with the Swiss architect Jacques Herzog, the London urbanist Richard Burdett, and the American architect William McDonough, Boeri developed the general guidelines and a master plan.[75] The latter proposes – instead of the national country pavilions on a large site northwest of the city, each on a plot of land – to present on a country-specific basis forms of biodiversity, technology and suggestions that improve food and supplies

Das Schaffen des Büros mit Standorten in Mailand, Tirana und Shanghai umfasst Architektur und Städtebau, Innen- und Landschaftsarchitektur. Neben den üblichen Kooperationen ist hervorzuheben, dass die Mailänder Umweltexpertin und Landschaftsplanerin Laura Gatti in Forschung, Entwurf und Realisierungsprozessen intensiv integriert ist. Die internationale Aufmerksamkeit, Resonanz und Auftragsvergabe richtet sich auf Projekte wie die in Mailand realisierten, vollständig begrünten Hochhaustürme, aber auch auf Zukunftsvisionen, die zu Fragen des Klimawandels beispielsweise vollständig durchwaldete Städte mit hoher Biodiversität vorstellen. Nicht zuletzt hat wohl Stefano Boeris Arbeit als Publizist, auch in leitender Funktion zwischen 2004 und 2011 bei den Zeitschriften ‚Domus' und ‚Abitare', sowie seine Beteiligung an internationalen Ausstellungen zu einer umfangreichen Öffentlichkeitsarbeit und Medienpräsenz des Büros beigetragen.[72]

KONZEPT   Insbesondere die Zukunftsoffenheit und der in den Konzepten und Projekten zum Ausdruck kommende Impetus zur Verbesserung gegenwärtiger Konditionen und der Glaube an deren Realisierbarkeit stärken sowohl die Konzeptideen selbst als auch deren Popularität. Schon in den 1990er Jahren waren es spezifische Beobachtungsperspektiven und Darstellungsweisen, durch die Boeris Erforschungen zur Entwicklung von Städten und Territorien charakterisiert waren.[73] Mit dem von ihm mitbegründeten Netzwerk Multiplicity wurden diese in Vor-Ort-Begehungen und Recherchen künstlerisch, grafisch, fotografisch erhobenen Analysen zu verschiedenen Territorien weiterentwickelt, um neben der Art, wie Städte beschrieben und dargestellt werden, geopolitische, sozioökonomische städtebauliche und politische Relationen zu erforschen.[74] Die Ergebnisse wurden in Ausstellungen und Publikationen präsentiert und sollten die Transformation der untersuchten Gebiete fördern. Das Interesse Stefano Boeris an der ‚città diffusa', insbesondere der Zwischenstadt an der Peripherie und dem suburbanen Raum um Mailand, blieb auch in weiteren städtebaulichen Konzepten erhalten. Im Vorlauf und Kontext der Planungen für die Expo 2015 in Mailand entwickelte er zusammen mit dem Schweizer Architekten Jacques Herzog, dem Londoner Urbanisten Richard Burdett sowie dem amerikanischen Architekten William McDonough die allgemeinen Leitlinien und einen Masterplan.[75] In diesem wird vorgeschlagen, anstelle der nationalen Länderpavillons auf

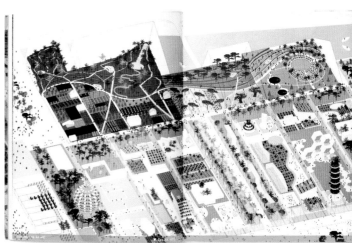

1–2 Biomilano, 2011 Cover and inside pages with axonometric drawings

worldwide, whereby greenhouses are also included, to show the agri-cultural products for the extreme climate zones of the world. In general, the use of solar energy and water resources, biodegradable materials and 'green' transport also formed part of the overall project of a large global garden.

Stefano Boeri developed these approaches further with other architects, urban planners, artists and his students at the Politechnico di Milano. With 'Biomilano' in 2011, he presented the ideas and concepts in significant axonometric drawings with a glossary entitled 'Social Landscapes', which thematises agricultural aspects in an urban context, biodiversity, ecological sequences and relations of metropolises and forest (fig. 1–2). In addition, a kind of verbal-visual dictionary with building blocks, means of production and application of the individual emerging components was integrated.[76] The idea was not only to integrate the urban rural areas and farms around Milan into the urban development to a greater extent but also to show a forest belt called 'Metrobosco' around Milan with three million trees – as well as forest houses and the prototype Bosco Verticale, a green high-rise with greenery – as part of an urban development scenario referred to as 'Biomilano'. Overall, this was to be characterised by a new type of city. It could be referred to as a city-landscape and is characterised as a network of green spaces designed to increase urban biodiversity and also to include autonomous, 'wild' developments of vegetation. The concepts of urban forestry and biodiversity presented by Stefano Boeri, which he also researches with students for example at Tongji University in Shanghai, also form a driving force of the World Forum on Urban Forests founded in 2018. The relevance of green areas and trees for achieving global sustainability goals is examined and postulated to promote biodiversity, urban habitats for flora and fauna, as well as biophilic properties of cohabitation.[77]

einem großen Gelände nordwestlich der Stadt auf je einem Stück Land For-men von Biodiversität sowie Technologie und Vorschläge, die Ernährung und Versorgung weltweit zu verbessern, länderspezifisch zu präsentieren, wobei auch Gewächshäuser einbezogen sind, die agrikulturelle Produkte für die extremen Klimazonen der Welt aufzeigen sollten. Insgesamt bilde-ten auch die Nutzung von Solarenergie und Wasserressourcen, biologisch abbaubare Materialien und ‚grüner' Transport Anteile des Gesamtprojekts eines großen globalen Gartens.

Stefano Boeri entwickelte diese Ansätze zusammen mit anderen Archi-tekt:innen, Städtebauer:innen, Künstler:innen und seinen Studierenden am Politecnico di Milano weiter. 2011 präsentierte er die Ideen und Konzepte unter dem Titel 'Biomilano' in signifikanten axonometrischen Zeichnungen mit einem ‚soziale Landschaften' bezeichneten Glossar, das agri-kulturelle Aspekte im städtischen Kontext, Biodiversität, ökologische Sequenzen und Relationen von Metropolen und Wald thematisiert (Abb. 1–2). Zusätzlich ist eine Art verbal-visuelles Wörterbuch mit Bausteinen, Produktions- und Anwendungsweisen der einzelnen herauskristallisierten Komponenten inte-griert.[76] Dabei sollten nicht nur die städtischen ländlichen Gegenden und die Bauernhöfe um Mailand herum stärker in die Stadtentwicklung integriert werden, vielmehr werden ein ‚Metrobosco' genannter Waldgürtel rund um Mailand mit drei Millionen Bäumen sowie Waldhäuser und der Prototyp Bosco Verticale, das begrünte Hochhaus, als Teil eines ‚Biomilano' bezeich-neten Szenarios für die Stadtentwicklung aufgezeigt. Insgesamt soll diese charakterisiert sein durch eine neue Art von Stadt. Sie könnte als Stadt-landschaft bezeichnet werden und ist charakterisiert als Netzwerk grüner Räume, die städtische Biodiversität vermehren sollen und auch autonome, ‚wilde' Entwicklungen von Vegetation einschließen. Die von Stefano Boeri vorgestellten Konzepte zu urbaner Forstwirtschaft und Biodiversität, die er auch mit Studierenden unter anderem an der Tongji Universität in Shanghai erforscht, bilden ebenfalls eine treibende Kraft in dem 2018 gegründeten ‚World Forum on Urban Forest'. Dabei wird die Relevanz von Grünflächen und Bäumen bei der Erreichung globaler Nachhaltigkeitsziele untersucht und postuliert, um mit dieser Idee Biodiversität, urbane Lebenswelten für Flo-ra und Fauna sowie biophile Eigenschaften der Ko-Habitation zu fördern.[77]

3 Bosco Verticale Milan 2014 within the redeveloped Porta Nuova district and adjacent park Parco Biblioteca degli Alberi

VERTICAL FOREST: BOSCO VERTICALE   In the project 'Bosco Verticale', Boeri sees a means that enables the regeneration of the linking of urban biodiversity to the constructional-spatial environment as an urban forest, without extending the territory of the city.[78] In addition, with this the idea of a new type of city as city/forest and of the vertical densification of 'nature' in the city is developed as a model. The prototype modified later in numerous variations was realised for the first time in Milan. It involves two high-rise towers completed in 2014 for classy residential use, whose external appearance is fully encased by an elaborately designed green façade (fig. 3–4). The vegetation of trees, shrubs, bushes and ground cover plants grows in big plant pots on balconies that protrude variously (fig. 5). It corresponds in sum to around a hectare of forest.[79] The planting was developed over a long period with the involvement of experts in botany, ethology and sustainability. It was then composed by plant expert and landscape architect Laura Gatti and Emanuela Borio and realised after precultivation and testing of the plants and plant ensembles. The two apartment towers are linked to the revitalisation project of the city of Milan, the 'Metrobosco' programme proposed by Multiplicity. They were built in a deindustrialised urban area near the second-largest railway station of the city with the name Porta Nuova, in connection with the large-scale restructuring of this area in the neighbourhood of various residential districts and new high-rise complexes, as well as the Parco Biblioteca degli Alberi. There the 80- and 112-metre-high towers

4–5 Diverse greenery is distributed in big plant pots on the green façade

VERTIKALER WALD: BOSCO VERTICALE

In dem Projekt ‚Bosco Verticale' sieht Boeri ein Mittel, das es ermöglicht, die Re-Generation der Verbindung urbaner Biodiversität mit der baulich-räumlichen Umwelt zu einem urbanen Wald zu erreichen, ohne die Stadt auf dem Territorium zu erweitern.[78] Zudem wird mit diesem die Idee einer neuen Art von Stadt als Stadt/Wald und für die vertikale Verdichtung von ‚Natur' in der Stadt modellbildend entwickelt. In Mailand wurde der später in zahlreichen Variationen modifizierte Prototyp zum ersten Mal realisiert. Es handelt sich um zwei 2014 fertiggestellte Hochhaustürme für gehobene Wohnnutzung, deren Äußeres vollständig ummantelt ist von einer aufwendig gestalteten begrünten Fassade (Abb. 3–4). Die Vegetation aus Bäumen, Stauden, Sträuchern und Bodendeckern wächst in großen Pflanzkübeln auf unterschiedlich weit auskragenden Balkonen (Abb. 5). Sie entspricht in der Summe etwa 1 Hektar Wald.[79] Die Bepflanzung wurde unter Einbezug von Expert:innen für Botanik, Ethologie und Nachhaltigkeit über längere Zeit entwickelt. Sie wurde dann mit den Pflanzenexpertinnen und Landschaftsarchitektinnen Laura Gatti und Emanuela Borio komponiert und nach Vorkultivierung und Testung der Pflanzen und Pflanzensembles realisiert. Die beiden Apartmenttürme sind mit dem Revitalisierungsprojekt der Stadt Mailand, dem von Multiplicity vorgeschlagenen Programm ‚Metrobosco' verbunden. Sie wurden in einem deindustrialisierten Stadtbereich in der Nähe des zweitgrößten Bahnhofs der Stadt mit Namen Porta Nuova im Zusammenhang

6   Section Interconnection of apartments and green balconies

7–8   Sliding doors connect to the private gardens

9 The appearance of 400 individual gardens changes according to the seasons

mit der großmaßstäblichen Restrukturierung dieses Areals errichtet und befinden sich im Umfeld verschiedener Wohnviertel und neuer Hochhauskomplexe sowie des Parco Biblioteca degli Alberi. Dort ragen die sich in ihrem Erscheinen mit den Jahreszeiten in Form und Farbe verändernden, 80 und 112 Meter hohen Türme als besondere Solitäre aus der Stadtstruktur in die Vertikae auf, bilden einen Anziehungspunkt und können mit ihrer dichten grünen Ummantelung identitätsstiftend wirksam werden.[80] Mit der unmittelbaren Umgebung und dem Alltagsleben sind sie darüber hinaus räumlich teilweise verbunden. Die Erdgeschossbereiche dienen dem Zutritt für die Bewohner:innen. Die Wohnungen selbst sind über deckenhohe Schiebetüren großzügig mit dem Außenraum verbunden (Abb. 6–8). Die Pflanzen wurden so ausgewählt, dass sie je nach Anforderung der verschiedenen Arten und abhängig von den mikroklimatischen Bedingungen gut gedeihen können und für ein angenehmes Klima in den Wohnungen sorgen: immergrüne an der Süd- und Westseite, laubabwerfende an der Nord- und Ostseite. Die Palette der Spezies umfasst beispielweise Rotbuche und Feldahorn, niedriger wachsende Pflanzen wie Olivenbäume und noch kleinere Bäume und Sträucher wie Granatapfelgewächse.[81] Entsprechend der Pflanzkomposition entstanden so 400 verschiedene, sich von Frühling bis Winter verändernde Gärten (Abb. 9).

Die Pflanzenfassade ersetzt moderne Klimatechnik. Das Laub der Bäume schützt im Sommer vor der Sonne. Im Winter ist durch das herabfallende Laub dennoch Helligkeit gewährleistet. Wind- und Fotovoltaikenergie sowie geothermische Grundwassernutzung werden zur Selbstversorgung der beiden Türme beitragen. Die Pflanzenmasse des vertikalen Waldes produziert

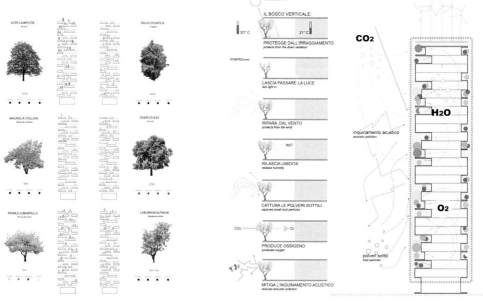

10–11   The plant facade acs as and replaces air-conditioning systems

rise vertically as notable solitaires out of the city structure, their appearance changing with the seasons in terms of form and colour, forming a centre of attraction and forging an identity with their dense green envelope.[80] Furthermore, they are linked spatially with the immediate surroundings and everyday life. The ground-floor areas serve as access for the residents. The apartments themselves are generously connected with the outdoor space by means of floor-to-ceiling sliding doors (fig. 6–8). The plants were selected so that they can flourish depending on the requirements of the different types and on the microclimatic conditions, ensuring a pleasant climate in the apartments: evergreens on the south and west side, deciduous ones on the north and east side. The palette of species comprises, for example, common beech and field maple, those growing low like olive trees and even smaller trees and bushes like pomegranate.[81] In accordance with the plant composition, this resulted in 400 different gardens changing from spring to winter (fig. 9).

The plant facade replaces modern air conditioning technology. The foliage of the trees provides protection from the sun in summer, while in winter lightness is still assured due to the loss of foliage. Wind and photovoltaic energy, as well as geothermal groundwater usage, will contribute to the self-sufficiency of the two towers. The plant mass of the vertical forest produces oxygen, binds fine dust, protects against noise and enables a new format of urban biodiversity, in which new relations can emerge between people and other living species (fig. 10–11).[82] The green facade therefore brings about an improvement of the climate balance of the nearer and further surroundings, as post-project analyses show.[83] This also stands in contrast to criticism that

12　Bosco Verticale and Parco Biblioteca degli Alberi form a restorative green appearance in densely built Milan

Sauerstoff, bindet Feinstaub, schützt vor Lärmbelastung und ermöglicht ein neues Format urbaner Biodiversität, bei der neue Relationen zwischen Menschen und anderen lebenden Spezies entstehen können (Abb. 10–11).[82] Damit bewirkt die Grünfassade eine Verbesserung der Klimabilanz der näheren und ferneren Umgebung, wie Postprojektanalysen zeigen.[83] Diese stehen auch in Kontrast zu Kritiken, die den ‚Bosco verticale' als Greenwashing, ästhetische Spielerei und Luxusprojekt bezeichneten, insbesondere aufgrund der Stahlbetonstruktur, die den inneren Gebäudekern bildet, und der Hochpreisigkeit der Wohnungen.[84] Die beiden Hochhaustürme avancierten zu Ikonen der Fassadenbegrünung in Europa und wurden als Modell von unterschiedlichen Disziplinen im Hinblick auf ihr Transferpotenzial untersucht. Für die Bewohnenden des Umfelds und die Mailänder Bevölkerung konnten empirische Untersuchungen zeigen, dass die begrünten Türme zusammen mit den kleinen Grünräumen und dem Parco Biblioteca degli Alberi zu ihren Füßen, trotz des eher kritisch betrachteten ausschließlich luxuriösen Wohnungsangebots in den Türmen, als besonderer und erholsamer Ort in Mailand erfahren werden (Abb. 12). In dessen Umgebung würden viele Menschen gerne wohnen, auch, weil hier eine Vermischung von Moderne und Natur wahrnehmbar sei.[85]

Das Konzept für die Wald/Stadt beinhaltet auch die Multiplikation und Evolution des Vertical Forest im globalen Kontext, unter verschiedenen Umweltbedingungen und in lokalen Klimazonen, die jeweils die Entwicklung lokaler Kriterien beispielsweise für die Pflanzschemata oder die behausten

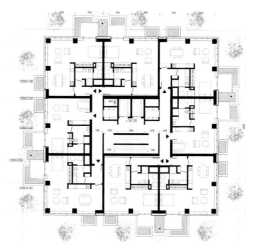

13   Trudo Tower Eindhoven 2021 Regular floor plan

referred to the 'bosco verticale' as greenwashing, an aesthetic dalliance and luxury project, especially due to the ferroconcrete structure that forms the inner building core and to the high price of the apartments.[84] The two high-rise towers became icons of facade greenery in Europe and were studied by different disciplines as a model with regard to their transfer potential. For the local residents and the Milan population, empirical studies were able to show that the green towers, together with the small green areas and the Parco Biblioteca degli Alberi at their feet, were perceived as a special and restorative place in Milan, despite the rather critically viewed, exclusively luxurious apartment offer in the towers (fig. 12). Many people would be happy to live in its environs, also because of the mix of modernity and nature.[85]

The concept for the forest/city also contains the multiplication and evolution of the vertical forest in a global context, in different environmental conditions and local climate zones, intended to include the development of local criteria, for example for the plant scheme or the housed animal species.[86] Stefano Boeri Architetti realised and planned the concept of the vertical forest in different contexts and in modified variants, for example in Utrecht, Eindhoven, Antwerpen, Lausanne and Paris, as well as in Nanjing and Hun Agang in China.[87] Some of these cities integrate this 'vertical landscape-ness' into the city marketing concept of 'green city'. An example of this is Eindhoven in the Netherlands, where in 2021 the Trudo Vertical Forest was completed as a nine-storey residential tower with a controlled rental price and a densely planted façade envelope, in collaboration with Studio Laura Gatti and the Amsterdam architecture firm Inbo (fig. 13–14).[88] The tower with greenery forms part of the large-scale regeneration project in the Strijp-S district on a deindustrialised site of the electrical company Philips. In the context of the master plan designed by the international landscape architecture and urban development firm West 8 for housing with low rents, as well as a big skate park, co-working spaces, shops, trades and flexible open spaces,

14   The Trudo Tower is located within the dense regeneration project Strijp-S

Tierspezies einschließen sollen.[86] Stefano Boeri Architetti haben das Konzept des vertikalen Waldes in unterschiedlichen Kontexten in modifizierten Varianten realisiert und geplant, in Utrecht, Eindhoven, Antwerpen, Lausanne oder Paris beispielsweise sowie in Nanjing und Hunagang in China.[87] Verschiedene dieser Städte integrieren diese ‚vertikale Landschaftlichkeit' in das Stadtmarketingkonzept ‚grüne Stadt'. Ein Beispiel dafür ist Eindhoven in den Niederlanden, wo 2021 der Trudo Vertical Forest als ein mietpreiskontrollierter, 19-geschossiger Wohnturm mit hochverdichtet bepflanzter Fassadenhülle in Kollaboration mit Laura Gatti Studio und mit dem lokalen Architekturbüro Inbo fertiggestellt wurde (Abb. 13–14).[88]

Dort bildet der begrünte Turm einen Teil des großflächigen Regenerationsprojekts im Strijp-S-Viertel auf dem deindustrialierten Gelände des Elektrounternehmens Philips. Im Kontext der von dem internationalen Landschaftsarchitektur- und Städtebaubüro West 8 entworfenen Masterplans für Wohnungen mit niedrigen Mieten und einen großen Skatepark sowie Co-Working-Spaces, Geschäfte, Handwerksbetriebe und flexible Freiräume ist er eines der Beispiele, die aufzeigen, wie der Prototyp Vertical Forest an unterschiedliche Kontextbedingungen angepasst und weiterentwickelt werden kann. Im transparenten Erdgeschoss sind neben dem Eingang ein Fahrradparkbereich sowie Büros und eine Bäckerei integriert und im dritten Obergeschoss eine Gemeinschaftsküche und eine große Terrasse. Materialwahl, Präfabrikation und die Beschränkung der Pflegekosten für die Pflanzen haben es dabei ermöglicht, Baukosten zu reduzieren.[89] Auch hier wird der auf den unterschiedlich weit auskragenden und von weißen

15 Densely planted façade with a wide range of plants and trees

this is an example of how the prototype of a vertical forest can be adapted to different contextual conditions and developed further. On the transparent ground floor, a bicycle parking space, offices and a bakery are integrated next to the entrance, and on the third floor there is a communal kitchen and a big terrace. The choice of materials, prefabrication and the limitation of maintenance costs for the plants allowed the reduction of building costs.[89] Here the planted area on the variously protruding balconies encased in white concrete strips also comprises many regionally specific trees, shrubs and smaller plants (fig. 15). A wide-ranging choice of foliage colours, leaf shapes and blossoms were used. For the residents of the apartments of less than 50 square metres, these outdoor spaces create an enriching microenvironment, even though the plant care is handled by external experts (fig. 16). How far the link between people and flora and fauna can be achieved to the desired extent is discussed just as controversially as the ecological overall balance.[90] Through a more resource-saving use of building materials and through plant combinations that increase the biodiversity further, this could be changed. This corresponds to the aspiration of the designers to constantly improve and adapt the prototype. For example, for the more recent highrise projects in Milan and Paris, combinations of concrete and wooden structures are already being planned.[91] Biophilic effects in the sense of a contribution to individual and communal well-being, as well as the raising of awareness for the environmental contexts, are also achieved in the formation like that realised in Eindhoven. It is to be emphasised here that this variant enables a wide layer of the population to be in connection in the immediate residential surroundings with this landscape-orientated architecture idea.

16 Open plan apartment opening onto green balconies

Betonbändern ummantelten Balkonen angelegte Pflanzraum aus zahlreichen, vor allem regionalspezifischen Bäumen, Sträuchern und kleineren Pflanzen gebildet (Abb. 15). Dabei wurde eine vielfältige Auswahl an Laubfarben, Blattformen und Blüten eingesetzt. Für die Bewohnenden der weniger als 50 Quadratmeter großen Apartements wird mit diesen Außenräumen eine bereichernde Mikroumwelt erzeugt, obwohl auch hier die Pflanzenpflege durch externe Expert:innen erfolgt (Abb. 16). Inwieweit damit die Verbindung von Menschen mit Flora und Fauna im angestrebten Maße erreicht werden kann, wird dabei ebenso kontrovers diskutiert wie die ökologische Gesamtbilanz.[90] Durch einen ressourcenschonenderen Materialeinsatz von Baustoffen und durch Pflanzkombinationen, die Biodiversität noch steigern, könnte das verändert werden. Dies entspricht der Vorstellung der Gestaltenden, den Prototyp beständig zu verbessern und anzupassen. So beispielsweise werden für die neueren Hochhausprojekte in Mailand und Paris bereits Kombinationen von Beton- und Holzstrukturen geplant.[91] Biophile Wirksamkeit im Sinne eines Beitrags zum individuellen und gemeinschaftlichen Wohlbefinden sowie zur Sensibilisierung für Umweltrelationen wird in der Formation, wie sie in Eindhoven realisiert wurde, erreicht. Hervorzuheben ist, dass mit dieser Variante einer breiten Bevölkerungsschicht ermöglicht wird, in der unmittelbaren Wohnumgebung mit dieser landschaftlich orientierten Architekturidee in Verbindung zu sein.

17 Tirana Riverside master plan 2020 Biodiversity is integrated through parks and building greenery

FOREST CITY: TIRANA RIVERSIDE   A 'project for reclaiming landscape' is how Stefano Boeri referred to the overarching master plan of his office for the redefinition of the Albanian capital Tirana by 2030.[92] The Tirana Riverside project is one of the areas that will contribute to the realisation of the planned tripling of the public green space (fig. 17). It can also represent an example of the urban design dimension of the forest/city concept, as had been articulated since the Biomilano project. Contrary to completely new monumental cities that the firm is now planning and realising in China and Mexico, in which the forest structure lushly runs through and covers all the constructional and spatial dimensions, the variant of cultivating urban forests in existing cities is linked in Tirana Riverside with the strategy of also integrating agricultural production into the urban context. In addition, this project aims to provide contributions in the area of architecture, landscape architecture and urban design after the earthquake of 2019 in Albania and in the context of the coronavirus pandemic.[93] Cooperation was once again with the Milan landscape architecture and horticulture studio of Laura Gatti, as well as with the engineers from the Albanian SON Group and the German air conditioning and energy technology experts from Transsolar.[94]

The master plan for Tirana Riverside of 2020 refers to a new build area for multicultural population groups with different economic and social backgrounds, as well as a 29-hectar area to the north of the inner city along the course of the Tirana river. The overarching main goal of creating an open, sustainable and lively district and of generating biodiversity is expressed in comprehen-

sive greenery on facades and roofs designed for collective usages on the

18–19   Redevelopment along Tirana river providing lush green spaces on ground and roof levels and façades

FOREST CITY: TIRANA RIVERSIDE   Als ein Vorhaben, um Landschaft wiederzugewinnen, bezeichnete Stefano Boeri den übergreifenden Masterplan seines Büros zur Neudefinition der albanischen Hauptstadt Tirana 2030.[92] Zu den Arealen, die dazu beitragen, dass die geplante Verdreifachung des öffentlichen Grünraums realisiert werden wird, zählt das Projekt Tirana Riverside (Abb. 17). Es kann zugleich als Beispiel für die städtebauliche Dimension des Wald/Stadt-Konzepts stehen wie es seit dem Biomilano-Projekt artikuliert wurde. Im Unterschied zu gänzlich neuen monumentalen Städten, die das Büro mittlerweile in China und Mexico plant und realisiert, in denen die Waldstruktur alle baulich-räumlichen Zusammenhänge üppig durchzieht und übergreift, ist die Variante, in existierenden Städten urbane Wälder zu kultivieren, in Tirana Riverside verknüpft mit der Strategie, auch landwirtschaftliche Produktion in den städtischen Kontext zu integrieren. Zudem ist dieses Projekt mit dem Ziel verbunden, für die Wohnungsnot nach dem Erdbeben von 2019 in Albanien sowie im Kontext der Corona-Pandemie Beiträge aus dem Bereich von Architektur, Landschaftsarchitektur und Städtebau zu erbringen.[93] Die Zusammenarbeit erfolgte hier erneut mit dem Mailänder Landschaftsarchitektur- und Gartenbaustudio von Laura Gatti sowie mit den Ingenieuren der albanischen SON-Group und den deutschen Klima- und Energietechnikexpert:innen von Transsolar.[94]

Der Masterplan für Tirana Riverside von 2020 bezieht sich auf ein Neubaugebiet für multikulturelle Bevölkerungsgruppen mit unterschiedlichem wirtschaftlichem und sozialem Hintergrund sowie auf ein 29 Hektar großes Areal nördlich der Innenstadt am Flusslauf des Flusses Tirana. Das übergreifende Hauptziel, einen offenen, nachhaltig lebendigen Stadtteil zu schaffen und Biodiversität zu erzeugen, findet Ausdruck in umfangreicher Begrünung von Fassaden und für kollektive Nutzungen vorgesehenen Dächern der Wohn- und Bürogebäude sowie in großzügigen Freiräumen, die darüber hinaus mit einer Aufforstung verbunden sind (Abb. 18–19). Zudem ist eine Selbstversorgungsstrategie geplant, die Energie, Wasser und Lebensmittel ebenso einschließt wie

20 Self-sufficiency includes farming and horticulture

residential and office buildings, as well as in generous outdoor spaces with reforestation (fig. 18-19). In addition, a self-sufficiency strategy is planned that includes energy, water and food, as well as public services, articulated for example in solar panels on the roofs or areas for farming and horticulture (fig. 20).[95] Vegetation is also planned for areas such as co-working spaces, sport and leisure facilities and pedestrian bridges. Many ground level areas are designed for commercial usages and public services (fig. 21). A school open 24 hours with community rooms and a university centre are also intended to contribute to a diverse urbanity. The spatial arrangement of the buildings and their composition is adapted to the dominating wind directions and incidence of sunlight, allowing the creation of permeable spaces and the avoidance of shade. Decentralised energy production with power generation through photovoltaics and geothermal heat are networked across the buildings with an intelligent energy exchange system. The accompanying guideline stated the mix of different works and companies for the programme of new architectures and specific local materials such as timber construction for the design.[96]

In consideration of pandemic situations, a quantitively large area was planned for public, semi-public, collective and private outdoor spaces, mixing zones with different degrees of publicness and privacy. With the trees and the further vegetation, a total of 12 thousand plants from a wide range of regional species will be planted in the new urban area, just as many as people, creating an urban forest. The territorial project Tirana Riverside with the big densely and lushly planted areas and spaces, public parks and agricultural and horticultural areas can thus generate a contemporary interpreted landscape, according to the designers from the architecture office, a contemporary landscape that mixes nature and technology in the interests of the well-being of those people who are here occasionally or permanently.[97]

21 Commercial and public uses are integrated on ground floor levels

öffentliche Dienstleistungen, was sich beispielsweise in Solaranlagen auf den Dächern oder Flächen für Landwirtschaft und Gartenbau artikuliert (Abb. 20).[95] Vegetation ist außerdem auch vorgesehen für Bereiche wie Co-Working, Sport- und Freizeiteinrichtungen sowie für Fußgänger:innenbrücken. Viele Erdgeschossbereiche sind für kommerzielle Nutzungen sowie öffentliche Dienstleistungen vorgesehen, und auch eine 24 Stunden geöffnete Schule mit Gemeinschaftsräumen und ein Universitätszentrum sollen zu einer vielfältigen Urbanität beitragen (Abb. 21). Die räumliche Anordnung der Gebäude und ihre Komposition sind an die dominierenden Windrichtungen und den Sonneneinfall angepasst, die durchlässige Räume entstehen lassen und Verschattungen vermeiden. Dezentrale Energiegewinnung mit Stromerzeugung durch Fotovoltaik und geothermische Wärmeherstellung sind mit einem intelligenten Energieaustauschsystem über die Gebäude netzartig verknüpft. In der begleitenden Guideline wurden für die Programme der neuen Architekturen die Mischung unterschiedlicher Gewerke und Unternehmen und für die Gestaltung lokalspezifische Materialien beispielsweise die Holzbauweise benannt.[96]

In Bezug auf pandemische Situationen wurde eine quantitativ große Fläche für öffentliche, halb öffentlich-kollektive sowie private Außenräume vorgesehen, Zonen verschiedener Öffentlichkeits- und Privatheitsgrade wurden gemischt. Mit den Bäumen und der weiteren Vegetation sollen insgesamt 12.000 Pflanzen unterschiedlichster regionsspezifischer Spezies im neuen Stadtgebiet verortet werden, ebenso viele wie Menschen, und damit den urbanen Wald erzeugen. Das territoriale Projekt Tirana Riverside mit den großen dicht und üppig begrünten Flächen und Räumen, den öffentlichen Parks sowie den landwirtschaftlichen und gartenkulturellen Bereichen kann damit eine zeitgenössisch interpretierte Landschaft generieren, so die Entwerfenden des Architekturbüros – eine zeitgenössische Landschaft, die Natur und Technologie zum Wohlbefinden der Menschen mischt, die sich hier zeitweise oder permanent aufhalten.[97]

The special characteristic of the concept of the vertical forest in the projects by Stefano Boeri Architetti is the planting in front of the entire façade surface of the high-rise buildings. It is conceived as lush and dense, as a three-dimensional area of vegetation and a habitat for flora and fauna, which in addition acts as a CO_2 balance and noise protection and is intended to contribute in a special way to the physical and mental well-being of the people. On an urban design scale, the notion of a forest in the design is associated in particular with the planting of trees and bushes and with municipal forestation, as well as the planning of roof gardens and urban farming, parks, hanging gardens and vegetation alongside paths, roads and bridges. An important role in the realisation of the vertical and urban forest ideas is played by various experts, especially Laura Gatti, who has been contributing her agricultural, landscape architectural and botanical expertise since the first Bosco Verticale project in Milan. It is not the first time that trees have been used in the context of architecture and urban development, but the difference is the intensity with which this is happening. Stefano Boeri names as references the architectural visions of the 1960s and 1970s in Italy of the so-called architettura radicale, which interpreted architecture from a utopian perspective in their visions within the context of the environment. He refers to the artist Friedensreich Hundertwasser, who integrated little groups of trees in his house projects on the roof and facades, and to Joseph Beuys, who

with his ecological intervention at documenta 7 in 1982, City Forestation

Die besondere Charakteristik des Konzepts des vertika-
len Waldes in den Projekten von Stefano Boeri Architects sind die Pflanzungen vor den gesamten Fassadenflächen der Hochhausbauten. Sie werden
üppig und dicht als dreidimensionaler Vegetationsraum und Habitat für Flora und Fauna imaginiert, der zudem als CO_2-Ausgleich und Lärmschutz wirkt
und in besonderer Weise zum physischen und psychischen Wohlbefinden
der Menschen beitragen soll. Im städtebaulichen Maßstab ist die Vorstellung des Waldes in den Entwürfen wiederum insbesondere mit Baum- und
Strauchpflanzungen bzw. städtischer Aufforstung verbunden, ohne andere Wertsetzungen auszuschließen. So werden außerdem Dachgärten und
urbane Landwirtschaft, Parks, hängende Gärten sowie Wege, Straßen und
Brücken begleitende Vegetationen geplant. Ein gewichtiger Anteil der Realisierung der Ideen zu vertikalen und urbanen Wäldern wird dabei von unterschiedlichen Expert:innen erbracht, insbesondere von Laura Gatti, die ihre
landwirtschaftliche, landschaftsarchitektonische und botanische Expertise seit
dem ersten Bosco-Verticale-Projekt in Mailand einbringt. Es ist nicht das erste
Mal, dass Bäume im Kontext von Architektur und Städtebau eingesetzt werden, aber die Intensität, mit der dieses geschieht, unterscheidet sich. Stefano
Boeri benennt als Referenzen die Architekturvisionen der 1960er und 1970er
Jahre in Italien der sogenannten Architettura radicale, die Architektur mit uto-
pischer Haltung in ihren Visionen im Maßstab von Umwelt interpretierten. Er
verweist auf den Künstler Friedensreich Hundertwasser, der in seinen Haus-
projekten auf dem Dach und an Fassaden kleine Baumgruppen integrierte,
und auf Joseph Beuys, der mit seiner ökologischen Intervention im Rahmen
der documenta ‚7000 Eichen. Stadtverwaldung statt Stadtverwaltung‘, von

instead of City Administration, planted 7,000 oak trees, each with a basalt stone on the side, over the course of several years in different locations in Kassel.[98] The planted high-rise already occupied the imagination of architects before in different ways. For example with the project 'High-rise of Homes' (1973), James Wines and his firm SITE presented a mix of building and vegetation on all floors and Ken Yeang had realised various architecture projects since the 1990s in Singapore that include planting.

With the idea of the vertical and urban forest, Boeri is also aiming, however, to create a forest biosystem. Even if the goal of having a climate-neutral effect and thus increasing biodiversity has not yet optimally succeeded, the projects and concepts show thet form that 'Green Architecture: Green City' may take in the future. They also show how the combination of biological and technological possibilities could be tested and integrated into the design, without making a claim to have already found the perfect solution.[99] The examples can provide stimuli as a starting point for further developments and also for architecture and urban building designs by other designers, as well as convey impulses and know-how. For further projects that are embedded in the urban ecological network, urban forests could also be accorded their own development potential, for example, and a share of the care suggested to the inhabitants.[100] The vertical and urban forests are ultimately both images as well as a desired character of places and modalities that characterize them, as a new type

of urban architecture that is associated with the idea of landscape-ness.

1982 an im Verlauf mehrerer Jahre 7000 Bäume mit jeweils einem Basaltstein an der Seite an unterschiedlichen Standorten in Kassel pflanzte.[98] Auch das bepflanzte Hochhaus hat die Imagination von Architekturschaffenden zuvor bereits in unterschiedlicher Weise beschäftigt. So beispielsweise hatten James Wines und sein Büro SITE mit dem gezeichneten Projekt ‚Highrise of Homes' (1981) in allen Geschossen eine Vermischung von Bauten und Vegetation präsentiert, und Ken Yeang hatte in Singapur seit den 1990er Jahren verschiedene Architekturprojekte in Singapur realisiert, die Bepflanzungen einschließen.

Mit der Idee des vertikalen und urbanen Waldes zielt Boeri allerdings zudem darauf, ein Waldbiosystem zu erzeugen. Auch wenn das Ziel, klimaneutralisierend zu wirken und Biodiversität in dieser Weise zu steigern, zurzeit noch nicht optimal gelungen ist, zeigen die Projekte und Konzepte exemplarisch, wie ‚Grüne Architektur:Grüne Stadt' in der Zukunft gestaltet sein könnte. Sie zeigen auch, wie dabei die Verbindung biologischer und technologischer Möglichkeiten getestet und in den Entwurf integriert werden könnte, ohne den Anspruch zu erheben, die perfekte Lösung bereits gefunden zu haben.[99] Die Beispiele können als Ausgangspunkt für weitere Entwicklungen auch für Architektur- und Städtebauentwürfe anderer Entwerfender Anstöße geben sowie Impulse und Know-how vermitteln. Für weitere Projekte, die in das städtische ökologische Netz eingebettet sind, könnte so beispielsweise den urbanen Wäldern auch ein eigenes Entwicklungspotenzial zugestanden und den bewohnenden Menschen ein Pflegeanteil vorgeschlagen werden.[100] Die vertikalen und urbanen Wälder sind letztlich sowohl Bilder als auch ein gewünschter Charakter von Orten und Modalitäten, die sie charakterisieren, als ein neuer Typus städtischer Architektur, der mit der Idee von Landschaftlichkeit verbunden ist.

AUSBLICK: LANDSCHAFTLICHKEIT MIT GRÜNER ARCHITEKTUR
OUTLOOK: LANDSCAPE-NESS BY GREEN ARCHITECTURE

Regardless of the specifics of the practices and projects presented here, what the basic concepts of the architectural offices have in common is that they incorporate the function and structure of environmental systems into the design process as important conditions. This includes the integration of local climate characteristics and resources as well as a cooperation between experts that goes beyond conventional collaborations. This allows new, practical possibilities to develop. The differentiated framework for these various environmental problems, components and effects thereby becomes a setting for architectural thinking, and at the same time forms a part of the systematic conceptual orientation, the design building blocks and the evaluations. References to sustainability – as described in discourses and reflected in certification systems, such as embodied material energy, energy efficiency, water consumption and other aspects of building performance that can be measured and simulated – are transcended in the further linking to various dimensions of biodiversity and biophilia, which are also incorporated relationally into the complex processes of design, development, realisation and evaluation. However, these can only be measured to a limited extent and can rarely be predicted.

The special aspect of these concepts and projects is vegetation and the integration of fauna. As a significant integral part of the multifactorial, complex and transdisciplinary design and realisation process, they open up a design level that can be developed even further. Contrary to solid building materials, the 'living' materials are characterised by dynamic growth and change. These components change architectural and urban development typologies and extend the design repertoire. The history of the environmental tangent and the integration of plants in architecture and urban building is diverse and goes back a long way. It can refer to types of courtyard house, roof and

Ungeachtet der Spezifizität der hier vorgestellten Praktiken und Projekte haben die Grundkonzeptionen der Architekturbüros gemeinsam, dass sie Funktion und Struktur von Umweltsystemen als wichtige Konditionen in den Entwurfsprozess einbeziehen. Dies schließt die Integration lokaler Klimaeigenschaften und Ressourcen ebenso ein wie eine Zusammenarbeit mit Expert:innen, die über konventionelle Kollaborationen hinausgehen. So können sich neue, praktische Möglichkeiten entwickeln. Die differenzierte Rahmung diverser umweltbezogener Probleme, Komponenten und Wirkungen wird dabei zu einem Setting für das architektonische Denken und bildet zugleich Anteile der systematischen konzeptuellen Ausrichtung, der Entwurfsbausteine und der Evaluationen. Referenzen zu Nachhaltigkeit, wie sie in Diskursen beschrieben und in Zertifikationssystemen abgebildet werden, beispielsweise verkörperte Materialenergie, Energieeffizienz, Wasserverbrauch und andere Aspekte der Gebäudeperformanz, die gemessen und simuliert werden können, werden dabei überschritten in der weiteren Verbindung mit diversen Dimensionen von Biodiversität und Biophilie, die ebenfalls relational in die komplexen Prozesse des Entwerfens, Entwickelns, Realisierens und Evaluierens einbezogen werden. Diese sind aber durch Messungen nur eingeschränkt zu erfassen und selten vorherzusagen.

Den besonderen Aspekt dieser Konzepte und Projekte bildet die Vegetation und im Weiteren die Integration von Fauna. Als signifikanter integraler Anteil des multifaktoriellen, komplexen und transdisziplinären Entwurfs- und Realisierungsprozesses spannen sie eine noch weiterentwickelbare Entwurfsebene auf. Im Unterschied zu soliden Baumaterialien, sind die ‚lebenden‘ Materialien durch dynamisches Wachstum und durch Veränderung charakterisiert. Mit diesen Komponenten werden architektonische und städtebauliche Typologien verändert und das Entwurfsrepertoire erweitert sich. Die Geschichte des Umweltbezugs sowie der Integration von Pflanzen in Architektur und Städtebau ist eine weit zurückreichende und vielfältige. Sie kann bezogen werden auf Hofhaustypen, Dach- und Landhausgärten, den Gebrauch von

country house gardens, the use of local materials and of transparency, or natural ornaments and planted areas in foyers and atria, as well as boulevards, parks and 'flowing' green open spaces, to name just a few examples. The current developments are now bound up with contemporary challenges due to climate and environmental crises and to increasing densification in cities.

Of course, projects in which greater attention is paid to environmental conditions contribute more towards the reduction of environmental problems than those in which this only plays a minor role. 'Green architecture' and 'green city', along with the contextualisation within a tangible and controllable concept of sustainability, also act as branding for a specific architectural and urban building perspectivation, as well as for clients and investors. These approaches are thereby also situated in the context of a perhaps too strongly economically dominated architectural and urban development, but which at the same time is transcended by pioneering spirit in the presented examples. Questions about the energy consumption of building materials, transport and maintenance also seem to be justified and could be integrated to an even greater extent in future, along with design components.

The potential these approaches harbour is a variety of concepts and metaphors, as well as creative architectural design competence, which contribute to strengthening the flexibility and the wealth of visions and further developments with regard to environmental qualities. Not least, the built projects are attractive in many aspects for the inhabitation of and well-being within the world. Particular emphasis is to be placed on opening up the basic understanding of architects to a notion of landscape-ness as an architectural idea that goes beyond the object character of individual architectures or a city of singularities. Whether with metaphors and analogies such as garden city of the future, jungle or forest, associated with measurements of air, noise, energy consumption or biodiversity, the interpretations, evaluations and methods here point to a conglomerate of relations in which functionality, relationality and poetry are connected. Working on this, venturing and risking something, while also offering solutions with an improvement potential and thereby stimulating alternatives, is one of the qualities of this form of landscape-ness as architectural idea.

lokalen Materialien und von Transparenz oder naturbezogene Ornamente und Pflanzbereiche in Foyers und Atrien sowie auf Alleen, Parks und ‚fließende' Grünräume, um nur einige Beispiele zu nennen. Die aktuellen Entwicklungen nun sind eingebettet in zeitgenössische Herausforderungen durch Klima- und Umweltkrisen ebenso wie durch zunehmende Verdichtungen in Städten.

Selbstverständlich tragen Projekte, bei denen eine größere Aufmerksamkeit auf Umweltkonditionen gerichtet wird, in einem stärkeren Maße zur Minderung von Umweltproblemen bei als solche, bei denen dies nur eine geringfügige Rolle spielt. ‚Grüne Architektur' und ‚Grüne Stadt' sowie die Kontextualisierung zu einem greifbaren und kontrollierbaren Konzept von Nachhaltigkeit fungieren dabei auch als Branding für eine spezifische architektonische und städtebauliche Perspektivierung wie auch für Auftraggebende, für Investor:innen. Damit sind diese Herangehensweisen auch situiert im Kontext einer vielleicht zu stark ökonomisch dominierten Architektur- und Stadtentwicklung, die von den hier dargebotenen Beispielen aber zugleich durch Pioniergeist überschritten wird. Fragen nach dem Energieverbrauch von Baumaterialien, Transport und Unterhalt scheinen ebenfalls berechtigt und könnten ebenso wie gestalterische Komponenten zukünftig noch stärker integriert werden.

Das Potenzial, das in diesen Ansätzen steckt, sind verschiedene Konzepte und Metaphern sowie kreative architektonische Entwurfskompetenz, die dazu beitragen, die Beweglichkeit und den Reichtum von Visionen und Fortentwicklungen im Hinblick auf Umweltqualitäten zu bestärken. Nicht zuletzt sind die gebauten Projekte in vielen Aspekten attraktiv für das Bewohnen von und das Wohlbefinden in der Welt. Insbesondere hervorzuheben ist das Grundverständnis der Architekturschaffenden, eine über den Objektcharakter einzelner Architekturen oder einer Stadt aus Singularitäten hinausreichende Imagination von Landschaftlichkeit als Architekturidee zu öffnen. Ob mit Metaphern und Analogien wie Gartenstadt der Zukunft, Dschungel oder Wald, mit Messungen von Luft, Lärm, Energieverbrauch oder Biodiversität verbunden, die Interpretationen, Wertsetzungen und Methoden weisen hier auf ein Konglomerat von Relationen hin, in dem Funktionalität, Rationalität und Poesie verbunden sind. Daran zu arbeiten, etwas zu wagen und zu riskieren sowie darüber hinaus auch Lösungen mit Verbesserungspotenzial darzubieten und damit Alternativen zu stimulieren, ist eine der Qualitäten dieser Form von Landschaftlichkeit als Architekturidee.

1 Cf. on this | Vgl. hierzu https://www.worldgbc.org/about-green-building 29.12.2021 **2** Cf. on this | Vgl. hierzu Hans Blumenberg, Lebenswelt und Technisierung unter Aspekten der Phänomenologie in: id., Wirklichkeiten, in denen wir leben, Stuttgart: Reclam 2020, 9–58, 50–53 **3** Cf. | Vgl. John Vogler, Globale Umweltpolitik, in: Ulrich Beck (ed.), Perspektiven der Weltgesellschaft, Frankfurt am Main 1998, 293–331; Margitta Buchert, Simply design. Five descriptions, in: id./Laura Kienbaum (eds.), Simply design. Ways of shaping architecture, Berlin: Jovis 2013, 13–35, 26 **4** Cf. | Vgl. https://www.netzwerk-n.org/wp-content/uploads/2017/04/0_Brundtland_Report-1987-Our_Common_Future.pdf 28.12.2021 **5** Cf. | Vgl. Amory B. Lovins/L. Hunter Lovins/Ernst Ulrich von Weizsäcker (eds.), Faktor Vier. Doppelter Wohlstand – halbierter (Natur-)Verbrauch. Der neue Bericht an den Club of Rome, München: Droemer Knaur 1995, passim; Susannah Hagan, Taking shape. A new contract between architecture and nature, Oxford et al.: Architectural Press 2000, XII–XV; Helen Bennets/Antony Radford/Terry Williamson, Understanding sustainable architecture, London et al.: Spon 2003, 4–8 **6** Cf. | Vgl. https://www.un.org/en/site-search?query=agenda+2050 28.1.2021 **7** Cf. | Vgl. Catherine Slessor, Eco-Tech. Sustainable architecture and Eco-Tech, London: Thames and Hudson 1998, passim; Susannah Hagan, Five reasons to adopt environmental design, in: William S. Saunders (ed.), Nature, landscape and building for sustainability, Minneapolis, MN: University of Minnesota Press 2008, 100–113, 104–105 **8** Cf. | Vgl. Atelier Kempe Thill, New prototypes for a global society, Rotterdam: 010 2005, 8–16, 104–109; Peter Buchanan, Ten shades of green. Architecture and the natural world, New York, NY: Architectural League of New York 2005, 30–39; Anja Thierfelder/Matthias Schuler, Gebäude als Systeme begreifen – der Ort als Identitätsstifter, in: Institut für Internationale Architektur-Dokumentation (ed.), Positionen zur Zukunft des Bauens: Methoden, Ziele, Ausblicke, München: Detail 2011, 82–93 **9** Cf. on this for example | Vgl. hierzu beispielsweise Hélène Frichot. Creative ecologies: theorizing the practice of architecture, London: Bloomsbury Visual Arts 2019, 40–41; 55–64 and | und passim; Daniel M. Abramson, Obsolence. An architectural history, Chicago, IL et al.: University Press 2016, 153–155; Peg Rawes, Introduction, in: id. (ed.), Relational architectural ecologies. Architecture, nature and subjectivity, London et al.: Routledge 2013, 1–18, 1–2 and | und 10 **10** Cf. on this for example | Vgl. dazu beispielsweise Jana Söderlund, The emergence of biophilic design, Cham: Springer 2019, 1–12; Chris Trott, Biophilia in design, on: | auf: https://www.fosterandpartners.com/plus/biophilia-in-design 1.10.2021 **11** Cf. | Vgl. Erich Fromm, The heart of man, New York: Harper and Row 1964, 110 **12** Cf. | Vgl. Edward O.Wilson, Biophilia, Cambridge, MA: Harvard University Press 1984, passim; Stephen R. Kellert, Nature by design. The practice of biophilic design, New Haven, CT et al.: Yale University Press 2018, IX and | und 17-22 and further | und im Weiteren Donna Haraway, Staying with the trouble. Making kin in the Chthulucene, Durham, NC: Duke University Press 2016, 16 **13** Cf. fundamentally the comprehensive scientific study and analysis | Vgl. hierzu grundlegend die umfassende wissenschaftliche Studie und Analyse William D. Browning/Catherine O. Ryan/

Joseph O. Clancy, 14 patterns of biophilic design, New York, NY: Terrapin Bright Green 2014, 4–12 and | und passim and | sowie Marc G. Berman/John Honides/Stephen Kaplan, The cognitive benefits of interacting with nature, in: Psychological Science 19(2008), 1207–1212   **14** Cf. | Vgl. Robert McDonald/Timothy Beatley, Biophilic cities for an urban century. Why nature is essential for the success of cities, Berlin: Springer 2020, 63–85; William D. Browning/Catherine O. Ryan/Joseph O. Clancy 2014 op. cit. (note | Anm.13), 18; Jana Söderlund 2019, op. cit. (note | Anm. 10), XIII   **15** Cf. | Vgl. William D. Browning/Catherine O. Ryan/Joseph O. Clancy 2014, op.cit. (note | Anm. 13), 13; Stephen R. Kellert, Dimensions, elements and attributes of biophilic design, in: id./Judith H. Heerwarden/Martin L. Madar (eds.), The theory, science and practice of bringing buildings to life, Hoboken, NJ: Wiley 2008, 3–20   **16** Cf. | Vgl. https://www.wellcertified.com, 30.12.2021; https://www.german-gba.org/well 30.12.2021   **17** Cf. on this | Vgl. hierzu Anna L. Tsing, Der Pilz am Ende der Welt, 3. ed. Berlin: Mattes & Seitz 2021, 204–205   **18** Cf. on this also | Vgl. hierzu auch Peter Buchanan 2005, op. cit. (note | Anm. 8), 12, 19–20 and | und 30–39   **19** Cf. | Vgl. Rudi Scheuermann/Peter Cachola Schmal/Hilde Strobl (eds.), Why building greenery?, in: ids. (eds.), Einfach Grün. Greening the city, Frankfurt am Main: DAM 2021, 4–9, 8   **20** Cf. on this also | Vgl. hierzu auch François Roche/Etienne Turpin, Matters of fabulation on the construction of realities in the Anthropocene (interview | Interview), in: Etienne Turpin (ed.), Architecture in the anthropocene, Encounters among design, deep time, science and philosophy, Ann Arbor, MI: Open Humanities press 2013, 197–208, 201; Iñaki Ábalos/Juan Herreros, Journey through the picturesque, in: Mohsen Mostafavi (ed.), Landscape urbanism. A manual for the machinic landscape, London: Architectural Association 2003, 52–57, 56   **21** Cf. on this and the following | Vgl. hierzu und zum Folgenden https://www.ingenhovenarchitects.com/office/about-us 20.12.2021   **22** Cf. | Vgl. Christoph Ingenhoven/Martha Thorne, Practicing architecture today. Creating unexpected opportunities (Interview), in: Nobuyuki Yoshida (ed.), Ingenhoven architects – supergreen, Tokio: a+u 2015, 19–27, 24   **23** Cf. for example | Vgl. beispielsweise Christoph Ingenhoven (2019), Preisträgerrede Semperpreis 2019 (speech | Rede 26.9.2019), Dresden: Hochschule für bildende Künste, on: | auf: https://www.youtube.com/watch?v=s6BLKUCMxxg, 23.11.2021; Christoph Ingenhoven/Martha Thorne 2015, op.cit. (note | Anm. 22), 20   **24** Cf. on this | Vgl. hierzu Till Briegleb (ed.), Hochhaus RWE AG Essen. Ingenhoven, Overdiek und Partner, Basel et al.: Birkhäuser 2000, passim   **25** Cf. | Vgl. N. N./Christoph Ingenhoven, In another life, I can well imagine myself as a landscape architect, in: Kristin Feireiss/Hans-Jürgen Commerell (eds.), Green Heart Marina One. Architecture for tropical cities, Berlin: Aedes 2017, 16–42, 39–40   **26** Cf. | Vgl. Stefan Altenschmidt/Christoph Ingenhoven (eds.), Praxishandbuch Green Building, Berlin et al.: De Gruyter 2018   **27** Cf. | Vgl. Christoph Ingenhoven, Supergreen®. Zur Bedeutung von nachhaltigem Entwerfen von Gebäuden, in: ibid., 16–19   **28** Cf. | Vgl. Christoph Ingenhoven, How architect Christoph Ingenhoven improved the standards for sustainable buildings, on: | auf: https://www.friendsoffriends.com/architecture/ingenhoven-architects-sustaina-

ble-architecture, 28.12.2021   **29** Cf. on this | Vgl. hierzu N. N., Kö-Bogen II, in: Hilde Strobl/Peter Cachola Schmal/Rudi Scheuermann (eds.) 2021, op. cit. (note | Anm. 19), 224–231, 246–247 and | und 251–253, 253; cf. | vgl. Peter Cachola Schmal, Warum wurde für den Kö-Bogen II die Hainbuche ausgewählt?, Gespräch im Rahmen der Ausstellung ʻEinfach Grün – Greening the cityʻ (talk | Gespräch 2021), on: | auf: https://dam-on-line.de/veranstaltung/einfach-gruen, 1.12.2021   **30** On ACROS in Fukuoka cf. | Zu ACROS in Fukuoka vgl. Stefano Boeri/Guido Mussante/Azzurra Muzzonigro, A vertical forest. Un bosco verticale, Mantua: Corraini 2015, 50   **31** Cf. on this and the following | Vgl. hierzu und zum Folgenden Frank Kaltenbach, Kö-Bogen II in Düsseldorf. Gebäudehülle ais 30.000 Pflanzen, in: Detail 9(2020), on: | auf: https://www.detail.de/artikel/au-tos-zu-hainbuchen-ingenhoven-fk/, 28.12.2021   **32** Cf. | Vgl. Martin Reuter mit Rudi Scheuermann/Hilde Strobl (Interview), in: Peter Cachola Schmal/Rudi Scheuermann/Hilde Strobl (eds.) 2021, op. cit. (note | Anm. 19), 248–250, 249   **33** Cf. on this | Vgl. hierzu Masaioshi An/Kisaburo Ishii/Ng Lang, The future of the city. Urban development in Singapore and Japan, in: Nobuyuki Yoshida 2015, op. cit. (note | Anm. 22), 225–228, 225   **34** Cf. | Vgl. Hwang Yu-Ning, Greening Singapore, in: Thomas Schröpfer/Sacha Menz (eds.), Dense and green building typologies. Design perspectives, Singapore: Springer 2019, V–VI, V   **35** Cf. on this | Vgl. hierzu Martina Thorne, Going above and beyond, in: Kristin Freireiss/Hans-Jürgen Commerell (eds.) 2017, op. cit. (note | Anm. 25), 7–9, 7   **36** Cf. | Vgl. N. N./Christoph Ingenhoven 2017, op. cit. (note | Anm. 25), 28 and | und 31   **37** Cf. | Vgl. Kathryn Gustafson, It is not that the city has a garden, the city is the garden itself, in: Kristin Freireiss/Hans-Jürgen Commerell (eds.) 2017, op. cit. (note | Anm. 25), 105–111, 105–106 and | und 109   **38** Cf. | Vgl. N. N./Christoph Ingenhoven 2017, op. cit. (note | Anm. 25), 35   **39** Cf. on this | Vgl. hier-zu Herbert Wright, The jungle block. Marina One by Ingenhoven architects and Gustafson, Porter + Bowman, in: Design/curial 8 (2018), on: | auf: https://www.designcurial.com/news/the-jungle-block-marina-one-6716694, 27.10.2021   **40** Cf. | Vgl. Nobuyuki Yoshida, Marina One, in: id. (ed.) 2017, op. cit. (note | Anm. 22), 42–53, 51   **41** Cf. | Vgl. WOHA, About, on: | auf: https://www.world-architects.com/en/woha-singapore, 12.1.2022   **42** Cf. on this and the following | Vgl. hierzu und zum Folgenden Vladimir Belogolovsky/Richard Hassell/Wong Mun Summ, The only way to preserve nature is to integrate it into our built environment (interview | Interview 25.11.2016), on: | auf: https://www.archdaily.com/800182/interview-with-woha-the-only-way-to-preserve-nature-is-to-integrate-it-into-our-built-environment, 3.1.2022   **43** Cf. | Vgl. Patrick Bingham-Hall/Ri-chard Hassell/Wong Mun Summ, Garden City Mega City, Singapore: Pesaro 2016   **44** Cf. on this and the fol-lowing | Vgl. hierzu und zum Folgenden Richard Hassell mit Sacha Menz/Thomas Schröpfer (Interview), in: Sacha Menz/Thomas Schröpfer (eds.), Dense and green city. Design perspectives, Singapore: Springer 2019, 33–34   **45** Cf. | Vgl. Richard Hassell, ibid.   **46** Cf. on this and the following | Vgl. hierzu und zum Folgenden Patrick Bingham-Hall/Richard Hassell/Wong Mun Summ 2016, op. cit. (note | Anm. 43), 280, 287–301 and | |

und 308   **47** Cf. | Vgl. Hwang Yu-Ning, Greening Singapore, in: Sacha Menz/Thomas Schröpfer (eds.) 2019, op. cit. (note | Anm. 44), IV-VI, V; Masatoshi An/Kisaburo Ishii/Ng Lang 2015, op. cit. (note | Anm. 33), 225; on Green branding cf. also | zu Green branding vgl. auch Natalie Marie Gulsrud/Saskia Gooding/Cecil C. Konijnendijk van den Bosch, Green space branding in Denmark in an era of neoliberal government, in: Urban Forestry & Urban Greening 12 (2013)/3, 330–337, 330–331   **48** Cf. | Vgl. Peter Cachola Schmal/Schirin Taraz, Grün als Greenwashing oder echte Chance? Gespräch im Rahmen der Ausstellung ‚Einfach Grün – Greening the city' (talk | Gespräch 2021), on: | auf: https://www.youtube.com/watch?v=JfhC96gapuc, 10.1.2022   **49** Cf. | Vgl. WOHA, Singapur-Pavilion Expo 2020 Dubai, on: | auf: https://www.world-architects.com/en/woha-singapore/project/singapore-pavilion, 13.1.2022; Andreea Cutieru, Singapore's pavilion at Expo 2020 Dubai illustrates the vision of architecture in nature, on: | auf: https://www.archdaily.com/969262/singapores-pavilion-at-expo-2020-dubai-illustrates-the-vision-of-architecture-in-nature, 9.1.2022   **50** Cf. | Vgl. N. N., Singapore pavilion Expo 2020, Dubai, Vereinigte Arabische Emirate, on: | auf: https://transsolar.com/de/projects/singapore-pavilion-at-expo-2021, 10.1.2022   **51** Cf. on this and the following | Vgl. hierzu und zum Folgenden Michaela Busenkell/Richard Hassell/Wong Mun Summ, Skyville @ Dawson, Singapur I Singapore (Interview), in: id./Peter Cachola Schmal (eds.), WOHA. Breathing architecture, München et al.: Prestel 2011, 58–59   **52** Cf. | Vgl. Wee H. Koon, Bigness und die Suche nach Identität, in: Archplus 243(2021) 178–189, 183–184   **53** Cf. | Vgl. Patrick Bingham-Hall, Beneath the Banyan tree, in: Michaela Busenkell/Peter Cachola Schmal (eds.) 2011, op. cit (note | Anm. 51), 28–37, 31 and | und 37   **54** Cf. on this and the following | Vgl. hierzu und zum Folgenden N. N., Skyville @ Dawson, on: | auf: https://www.world-architects.com/en/woha-singapore/project/skyville-dawson, 13.1.2022   **55** Cf. | Vgl. Richard Hassell/Simon Morrison mit Sacha Menz/Thomas Schröpfer (Interview), in: Sacha Menz/Thomas Schröpfer (eds.) 2019, op. cit. (note | Anm. 44), 70–71   **56** On visual and acoustic possibilities cf. | Zu den visuellen und akustischen Möglichkeiten vgl. Patrick Bingham-Hall/Richard Hassell/Wong Mun Summ 2016, op. cit. (note | Anm. 43), 68   **57** Cf. | Vgl. Michaela Busenkell/Richard Hassell/Wong Mun Summ (interview | Interview) 2011, op. cit. (note | Anm. 51), 58   **58** Cf. | Vgl. Patrick Bingham-Hall 2011, op. cit. (note | Anm. 53), 28–37, 31 and | und 34   **59** Cf. on this also | Vgl. hierzu auch Patrick Bingham-Hall/Richard Hassell/Wong Mun Summ 2016, op. cit. (note | Anm. 43), 110–112 and | und 124   **60** Cf. | Vgl. Richard Hassell mit Sacha Menz/Thomas Schröpfer (interview | Interview) 2019, op. cit. (note | Anm. 44), 34   **61** Cf. | Vgl. Tan Shao Yen (Consultant and president of the Board of Architects Singapore | Consultant und Präsident des Board of Architects Singapore) mit Sacha Menz/Thomas Schröpfer (Interview), in: Sacha Menz/Thomas Schröpfer 2019, op. cit. (note | Anm. 44), 21   **62** Cf. | Vgl. https://tierradesign.com.sg/projects/parkroyal-on-pickering, 12.1.2022   **63** Cf. also | Vgl. auch https://www.stxla.com/page_media/oasia-downtown-hotel, 15.1.2022; https://patriciaurquiola.com/architecture/oa-

sia 15.1.2022   **64** Cf. on this also | Vgl. hierzu auch Patrick Bingham-Hall/Richard Hassell/Wong Mun Summ 2016, op. cit. (note | Anm. 43), 134   **65** Cf. | Vgl. Thomas Geudner, Oase in luftiger Höhe. Hochhaus Oasia Downtown Hotel in Singapur von WOHA, on: | auf: https://www.german-architects.com/de/architecture-news/praxis/oase-in-luftiger-hoehe 12.1.2022   **66** On biodiversity cf. | Zur Biodiversität vgl. N. N., Oasia Downtown Hotel, in: Hilde Strobl/Peter Cachola Schmal/Rudi Scheuermann (eds.) 2021, op. cit. (note | Anm. 19), 264–269, 267   **67** Cf. on this also | Vgl. hierzu auch Patrick Bingham-Hall/Richard Hassell/Wong Mun Summ 2016, op. cit. (note | Anm. 43), 76   **68** Cf. also | Vgl. auch ibid., 13 and | und 285   **69** Cf. | Vgl. Richard Hassell mit Michaela Busenkell/Peter Cachola Schmal (Interview), in: ids. (eds.) 2011, op. cit. (note | Anm. 51), 70   **70** Cf. on this also | Vgl. hierzu auch Patrick Bingham-Hall/Richard Hassell/Wong Mun Summ 2016, op. cit. (note | Anm. 43), 285   **71** Cf. on this and the following | Vgl. hierzu und zum Folgenden https://www.stefanoboeriarchitetti.net/en/about, 27.1.2022   **72** Cf. on this for example | Vgl. hierzu beispielsweise Stefano Boeri, Seven inspirations, in: Stefano Boeri/Guido Mussante/Azzurra Muzzonigro 2015, op. cit. (note | Anm. 30), 3–23, 6–9   **73** Cf. for example | Vgl. beispielsweise Stefano Boeri/Arturo Lanzani/Edoardo Marini, Il territorio che cambia. Ambienti, paessagi e immagini della regione Milanese, Mailand: Abitare Segesta 1993   **74** Cf. for example | Vgl. beispielsweise Stefano Boeri, Eklektische Atlanten, in: Daidalos 69/70(1998) 102-113; Stefano Boeri/Multiplicity, Uncertain States of Europe, in: id./Rem Koolhaas/Sanford Kwinter/Hans Ulrich Obrist/Nadia Tazi, Mutations, Barcelona: Actar 2001, 338–483   **75** Cf. | Vgl. https://www.stefanoboeriarchitetti.net/project/expo-2015-2 20.1.2021   **76** Cf. | Vgl. Stefano Boeri/Michele Brunello/Sara Pellegrini, Biomilano. Glossary of ideas for a metropolis based around biodiversity. Glossario di idee per una metropoli della biodiversitá, Mantua: Corraini 2011   **77** Cf. | Vgl. https://www.wfuf2018.com/en-ww/scientific-committee.aspx, 24.1.2022; https://www.wfuf2018.com/en-ww/call-for-action.aspx, 24.1.2022   **78** Cf. | Vgl. Stefano Boeri 2015, op. cit. (note | Anm. 72), 20–21   **79** Cf. | Vgl. Stefano Boeri/Michele Brunello/Sara Pellegrini 2011, op. cit. (note | Anm. 76), 107–115; Stefano Boeri/Guido Mussante/Azzurra Muzzonigro 2015, op. cit. (note | Anm. 30), 65   **80** Cf. | Vgl. Sirkka Heinonen/Matti Minkkinen, Interpreting the built city. Deconstructing the metaphorical messages of futuristic buildings, in: Futures 84(2016) 163–177, 169   **81** Cf. | Vgl. Stefano Boeri/Guido Mussante/Azzurra Muzzonigro 2015, op. cit. (note | Anm. 30), 52,112 and | und 116   **82** Cf. on this also | Vgl. hierzu auch Stefano Boeri 2015, op. cit. (note | Anm. 72), 14–17   **83** Cf. on this | Vgl. hierzu N. N., Bosco Verticale, in: Hilde Strobl/Peter Cachola Schmal/Rudi Scheuermann (eds.) 2021, op. cit. (note | Anm. 19), 224–231,

230–231 **84** Cf. on this for example | Vgl. hierzu beispielsweise Gerald Raunig, Factories of knowledge. Industries of creativity, Cambridge, MA: MIT Press 2013, 33 and | und 132; Jana VanderGoot, Architecture and the forest aesthetic. A new look at design and resilient urbanism, New York, NY et al.: Routledge 2018, 224; Max Visser, The geography of vertical forests. Exploring the green city, Utrecht: Utrecht University Faculty of Geography 2019, 42, 51–53 and | und 55, on: | auf: https://dspace.library.uu.nl/handle/1874/393704, 26.1.2022 **85** Cf. | Vgl. Max Visser, ibid. 49 and | und 53 **86** Cf. | Vgl. Stefano Boeri/Guido Mussante/ Azzurra Muzzonigro 2015, op. cit. (note |Anm. 30), 132–139 and | sowie 144 **87** Cf. | Vgl. https://www. stefanoboeriarchitetti.net/en/project/trudo-vertical-forest, 16.1.2022 **88** Cf. on this and the following | Vgl. hierzu und zum Folgenden Bianca Pichler, In the Netherlands the first vertical forest applied to social housing, on: | auf: https://www.domusweb.it/en/news/gallery/2021/10/05/in-holland-the-first-vertical-forest-applied-to-social-housing.html, 17.1.2021 **89** Cf. | Vgl. Stefano Boeri/Christele Harrouk, People have a strong demand for a new proximity to nature (Interview 6.10.2021), on: | auf: https://www.archdaily.com/969614/people-have-a-strong-demand, 18.1.2022 **90** On criticism cf. | Zur Kritik vgl. Daniel A. Barber/Erin Putalik, Forest, tower, city. Rethinking the green machine aesthetic, in: Harvard Design Magazine 45(2018) S/S, 234–243, 236–237 and | und 243 **91** Cf. | Vgl. Peter Cachola Schmal/Stefano Boeri, Bosco verticale, Gespräch im Rahmen der Ausstellung ‚Einfach Grün – Greening the city' (talk | Gespräch 2021), auf: https://dam-online.de/veranstaltung/einfach-gruen, 10.1.2022; Stefano Boeri, https://www.stefanoboeriarchitetti.net/en/project/foret-blanche, 25.1.2022 **92** Cf. | Vgl. https://www.stefanoboeriarchitetti.net/en/project/tirana-030-2, 17.1.2022 **93** Cf. | Vgl. https://www.stefanoboeriarchitetti.net/project/tirana-riverside, 25.1.2022 **94** Cf. on this and the following | Vgl. hierzu und zum Folgenden N.N., Tirana 2030 Masterplan Stadtteil am Flussufer, Tirana, Albanien, on: | auf: https://transsolar.com/de/projects/masterplan-tirana-riverside, 21.1.2022 **95** Cf. on this and the following | Vgl. hierzu und zum Folgenden ibid. **96** Cf. | Vgl. op. cit. (note | Anm. 93) **97** Cf. | Vgl. ibid. **98** Cf. | Vgl. Stefano Boeri 2015, op. cit. (note | Anm. 72) 22–23; Stefano Boeri/Guido Mussante, Illustrated dictionary of the vertical forest in 100 items, in: Stefano Boeri/Guido Mussante/ Azzurra Muzzonigro 2015, op. cit. (note | Anm. 30), 49–103, 44–45, 78–79 **99** Stefano Boeri, His methodology and how success is sometimes a problem, in: ArchDaily (2019), on: | auf: https://www.youtube.com/watch?v=AiSN31y8S_4, 30.12.2021 **100** Cf. on this also | Vgl. dazu auch Harry van Helmond, Ökologie und ein Waldturm, on: | auf: https://biotope-city.net/ecologie-en-een-bostoren, 18.1.2021

RAUMFORMATION
UND MATERIAL
SPACE FORMATION
AND MATERIAL

Design-related perspectives and ways of shaping design are thematised here explicitly as an important facet in the field of interpretating landscape as the action and interaction of natural and human factors, and as a mix of natural and cultural effects.[1] They both touch on core elements of architecture and describe attributions of value. In particular, references, correspondences or analogies emerge that are associated with the formation of building volumes and space, as well as with locational references and materiality, and therefore explicitly have aesthetic layers. This is framed by questions about components of constellations that contribute to landscape characteristics, as well as about various scales of conception, experiential aspects and perception. Observation and reflection are also accompanied by an orientation towards topological and atmospheric dimensions of the production and reception of spaces and architectural ensembles to which increasing significance has been attributed in recent decades in various disciplinary and interdisciplinary perspectives. Relations, as well as transitions and interconnections of phenomena and formations, come to the fore. Design theory themes of modern architecture, such as those referred to as 'flowing space' or 'promenade architecturale', form part of this. This focus does not exclude, however, that various sustainable concepts and social components are also considered as relevant and are incorporated in the architectural approaches and projects. More specifically than the concept of bionics associated with the transferral of natural structures and constructions, or the often very wide topic of an organic architecture, properties that are linked to the phenomena of topology and atmosphere can enrich and intensify the observation of the idea of landscape-ness and illuminate its facets as an open system of formation and effect of architectural concepts and projects.

Aus dem Interpretationsfeld von Landschaft als Aktion und Interaktion natürlicher und humaner Faktoren und als Mischung natürlicher und kultureller Wirkkräfte werden hier gestaltungsbezogene Perspektiven und Entwurfswege explizit als gewichtige Facette thematisiert.[1] Sie berühren gleichzeitig Kernbestände von Architektur und beschreiben Wertsetzungen. In besonderem Maße treten dabei Bezugnahmen, Korrespondenzen, Referenzen oder Analogien hervor, die mit der Formation von Baukörperformulierung und Raumformation sowie mit Ortsbezug und Materialität und damit explizit mit ästhetischen Ebenen verbunden sind. Eine Rahmung erfolgt durch Fragen nach Komponenten von Konstellationen, die zu landschaftlicher Charakteristik beitragen, sowie nach unterschiedlichen Maßstäben der Konzeption, Erfahrbarkeit und Wahrnehmung. Begleitet werden Beobachtung und Reflexion zudem von einer Orientierung an topologischen und atmosphärischen Dimensionen der Produktion und Rezeption von Räumen und architektonischen Ensembles, denen in verschiedenen disziplinären und interdisziplinären Perspektiven in den letzten Dekaden zunehmend Bedeutung beigemessen wurde. In den Vordergrund treten dabei Relationen sowie Übergänge und Verschränkungen von Phänomenen und Formationen. Entwurfstheoretische Themen der modernen Architektur wie die als ‚fließender Raum' oder ‚promenade architecturale' bezeichneten, bilden einen Teil davon. Diese Schwerpunktsetzung schließt allerdings nicht aus, dass in den architektonischen Ansätzen und Projekten verschiedene nachhaltige Konzeptionen sowie soziale Komponenten ebenfalls als relevant erachtet werden und einbezogen sind. Spezifischer als das mit der Übertragung natürlicher Strukturen und Konstruktionen verknüpfte Konzept der Bionik oder die oft sehr weit gefasste Thematisierung einer Organik der Architektur können Eigenschaften, die mit den Phänomenen Topologie und Atmosphäre verbunden werden, die Beobachtung der Idee von Landschaftlichkeit bereichern und intensivieren und deren Facettierung als offenes System der Formation und Wirkung architektonischer Konzepte und Projekte veranschaulichen. 217

TOPOLOGY   Topology differs from topography, understood as a perception, description and representation of the earth's surface, in a wide sense through the primary reference to location and positional relations, as well as spatial and structural properties. A variant of the conceptualis-ation of topological dimensions refers to notions of topos, interpreted as places and spaces of locational relations, associated with a situated-ness on the site or in the place. Apart from thinking of spatium as metrical space, this notion has a particular significance not only in the tradition of European philosophy, which also influenced architectural interpretation.[2] Today, at a time when networking and interactivity generate experiences of unprecedented extent in virtual worlds characterised by dematerialisa-tion and placelessness, a culturally significant orientation function is at-tached to the perception and experience of a factual material environment in places and their spatial relations.[3] A spatial and local conception and realisation of being – a localisation – is given by a physical presence in the 'here and now', as well as by the existential need of people to experi-ence with all their senses realities that consist of a sense-related combina-tion of constitutive physical elements. Architecture and urban design can make a significant contribution to this. Furthermore, landscape architecture proposes a design method interpretation of topology.[4] This is character-ised by the linking of microstructural and multilayered survey and rep-resentations of sites on various scales through virtual point cloud models of a terrain with ecological, historical and especially aesthetic qualities.

Regarding spatial arrangements, the development of modern architecture features conceptual characterisations that contribute prominently and con-tinuously to the formulation of specific topological spatial configurations, such as an open plan, flowing space or 'promenade architecturale'. This focusses on properties that go beyond Euclidean geometries and tradition-al notions of spaces, as well as quantitative relations. Not least, a hodo-logic understanding of space can be considered as part of this. In environ-mental psychology, the behavioural sciences and the phenomenological

TOPOLOGIE   Von Topografie, verstanden als Anschauung, Beschreibung und Darstellung der Erdoberfläche, unterscheidet sich Topologie in
einem übergreifenden Sinne durch den vorrangigen Bezug auf Lage und
Anordnungen sowie räumliche und strukturelle Eigenschaften. Eine Variante
der Konzeptualisierung topologischer Dimensionen bezieht sich auf Vorstellungen von Topos, interpretiert als Ort und als Raum von Lagebeziehungen,
der mit einem Situiert-Sein am Ort oder im Ort verbunden ist. Diese Auffassung hat, neben dem Denken von Spatium als metrischem Raum, nicht nur
in der europäischen Philosophietradition eine hervorgehobene Bedeutung,
die auch in die Architekturinterpretation hineinwirkte.[2] Heute, in einer Zeit,
in der Vernetzung und Interaktivität Erfahrungen in bis dahin unbekannten
Ausmaßen in virtuellen, durch Entmaterialisierung und Ortlosigkeit geprägten Welten erzeugen, kommt der Wahrnehmung und Erfahrung faktischer
materialer Umwelt an Orten und ihren räumlichen Relationen eine kulturell
bedeutsame Orientierungsfunktion zu.[3] Eine räumliche und lokale Konzeption und Realisation des Seins, eine Verortung, ist mit körperlicher Präsenz
im ‚Hier' ebenso gegeben wie das existenzielle Bedürfnis der Menschen,
mit allen ihren Sinnen Realitäten zu erfahren, die aus einer sinnesbezoge-
nen Kombination konstitutiver physischer Elemente bestehen. Architektur
und Städtebau können wesentlich dazu beitragen. In der Landschaftsarchitektur wird zudem eine entwurfsmethodische Lesart von Topologie vorgeschlagen.[4] Diese ist charakterisiert durch die Verbindung mikrostruktureller
und vielschichtiger Erfassung und Darstellung von Standorten in unterschiedlichen Maßstäben durch virtuelle Punktwolkenmodelle eines Terrains
mit ökologischen, historischen und insbesondere ästhetischen Qualitäten.

Im Blick auf Raumanordnungen zeigen sich in der Entwicklung der modernen Architektur begriffliche Charakterisierungen, die prominent und an-
haltend zur Formulierung spezifischer topologischer Raumkonfigurationen
beitragen wie offener Grundriss, fließender Raum oder ‚promenade architecturale'. Damit werden Eigenschaften fokussiert, die über euklidische Geo-
metrien und klassische Raumauffassungen sowie quantitative Verhältnisse
hinausreichen. Nicht zuletzt kann hierzu ein hodologisches Raumverständnis gezählt werden. In der Umweltpsychologie, den Verhaltenswissenschaf-
ten und auch im phänomenologischen Architekturverständnis wird diese
Raumvorstellung im Sinne einer Erfahrungsräumlichkeit vorgeschlagen,
die aus den Bewegungen und Handlungen Einzelner oder von Gruppen

understanding of architecture, this notion of space in the sense of a sphere of experience is proposed, emerging and taking effect from the movements and actions of individuals or groups.[5] The conceptualisation and design of route spaces and places, as well as their sequential formations in the architectural design context, form an equivalent to this. Morphologies of a more complex kind, that are plastically formed, folded, curved or interlinked – as well as their continuities, connectivities and transformation potentials, as studied systematically especially in a specialised mathematical field and in IT – can also be found in the field of topology concepts. The morphological qualities, in particular, probably formed the reason for corresponding interpretations taken up in architecture since the 1990s, especially in connection with parametric design and the generation of complex figurations.[6] In part, this can also be characterised as a type of 'topographisation' of architectural space, whereby the formations evoke coasts, caves, hills or valleys, or the shifts of tectonic plates.[7] Locational references can also become relevant when handling material, due to its availability on-site and its economic aspects, due to regional traditions and methods, or due to the striving for correspondence with the surroundings. Material-related context relations, however, are not necessarily bound up with topological dimensions. In the foreground of concepts of topology, there are structural arrangements and abstractions, as well as horizontality and a certain degree of heterogeneity.[8]

ATMOSPHERE   A specific aspect of the discourses on space in recent decades has also been the thematisation of atmospheres, a term which also includes notions of ambience, milieu, aura and mood. The concept, which originated in physics and meteorology, refers in the everyday and aesthetic context to a phenomenon that is associated with emotional perceptions of things, spaces or situations.[9] Subjectively tinged experiences, which are neither measurable nor quantifiable with natural science methods, stimulate and prime perceptions and their interpretations. Atmospheres are perceived as spatially associated and enveloping and also as in-between phenomena, which are intertwined with multisensory

entsteht und wirksam wird.[5] Das Denken und Gestalten von Weg- und Orträumen sowie ihrer sequenziellen Formationen im architektonischen Entwurfskontext bilden dazu ein Äquivalent. Auch plastisch geformte, gefaltete, gebogene oder verknüpfte komplexere Morphologien sowie deren Kontinuitäten, Konnektivitäten und Transformationspotenziale, wie sie vor allem in einem mathematischen Spezialgebiet und in der Informatik systematisch untersucht werden, finden sich im Feld von Topologiekonzepten. Die morphologischen Qualitäten vor allem bildeten wohl den Anlass für das Aufgreifen entsprechender Interpretationen in der Architektur seit den 1990er Jahren insbesondere in Verbindung mit parametrisch basiertem Entwerfen und dem Generieren komplexer Figurationen.[6] In Teilen kann dies auch als eine Art ,Topografisierung' des architektonischen Raumes charakterisiert werden, wobei die Formbildungen beispielsweise an Küsten, Höhlen, Hügel und Täler oder die Verwerfungen tektonischer Platten erinnern.[7] Ortsbezüge können auch im Umgang mit Material relevant werden, wenn sie beispielsweise aufgrund ihrer Verfügbarkeit vor Ort und ökonomischer Aspekte, aufgrund regionaler Traditionen und Techniken oder aufgrund des Strebens nach einer Korrespondenz mit der Umgebung aufgegriffen und behandelt werden. Materialbezogene Kontextbezüge sind jedoch nicht zwangsläufig mit topologischen Dimensionen verbunden. Im Vordergrund von Topologiekonzepten stehen strukturelle Anordnungen und Abstraktionen sowie Horizontalität und ein gewisses Maß an Heterogenität.[8]

ATMOSPHÄRE   Eine Spezifik in den Raumdiskursen der letzten Jahrzehnte bildete ebenfalls die Thematisierung von Atmosphären, in deren Begriffsumfeld auch Ambiente, Milieu, Aura oder Stimmung enthalten sind. Das ursprünglich in Physik und Meteorologie beheimatete sphärische Konzept bezeichnet im alltäglichen wie im ästhetischen Kontext eher ein Phänomen, das mit emotionalen Wahrnehmungen von Dingen, Räumen oder Situationen verbunden wird.[9] Subjektiv gefärbte Erfahrungen, die weder messbar noch mit naturwissenschaftlichen Methoden zu erfassen sind, stimulieren und grundieren Wahrnehmungen und ihre Interpretationen. Atmosphären werden dabei als räumlich verbindende und umhüllende bzw. als Zwischenphänomene aufgefasst, die mit multisensorischer Wahrnehmung und damit verkörperter Erfahrung (embodiment) verwoben sind.[10]

perception and embodiment.[10] In terms of building and space, they can be described as a dynamic interaction between objectifiable architectural and urban design aspects and their subjective perception, as well as multimodally caused effects and the possibility to experience spatial syntheses. They appear as a linking of personal and emotional impressions of spaces, co-produced by 'objective' constellations and modulations of a physical formation of material, light and shade, proportion and rhythm, or narrowness and expanse, to name just a few design elements and relations from the multitude of aspects that flow into the atmospheric whole.[11] The handling of material and its sensual qualities that come to the fore in an interplay with geometry and light in the spatial compositions as a whole is also explicitly thematised. Atmospheres form characteristic ways of co-presence appearing in the spatial context, whose specifics can also be seen in movement suggestions.[12]

The atmospheric was discussed with regard to both analytical and projective design levels and then in the context of reception. What is circumscribed as atmospheric is not foreign and completely novel in architecture. For example, in French architecture theory of the 18th century, discussions about the effects of buildings and the possibilities of generating special affects were accorded particular importance.[13] Terminologically, this was referred to as expression and character (caractère) in an aesthetic production context, as well as sensation and affect regarding the influence on people. Expression and character remain preserved as ways of describing architecture and are still widely used today. Beyond that, in everyday and informal conversations about architecture and urban spaces, the atmospheric is regularly mentioned. The sensitisation for the properties and gradations of this quality are perceived as a continuous unity, which brings various components of a context together as a whole, with an enriching effect. It can contribute to developing and extending capacities, sounding out various elementary environmental conditions and integrating them into the architectural design, as well as 222 into the individual and collective understanding of the world and the self.

Baulich-räumlich können sie als dynamische Interaktion zwischen objektivierbaren architektonischen und städtebaulichen Aspekten und ihrer subjektiven Wahrnehmung sowie als multimodal bedingte Wirksamkeit und Erfahrungsmöglichkeit räumlicher Synthesen beschrieben werden. Sie erscheinen als Verbindung persönlicher und emotionaler Eindrücke von Räumen, die mitproduziert werden durch ‚objektive' Konstellationen und Modulationen physischer Formation aus Material, Licht und Schatten, Proportion und Rhythmus oder Enge und Weite, um nur einige gestalterische Elemente und Relationen aus der Vielfalt von Aspekten zu nennen, die in das Ganze des Atmosphärischen einfließen.[11] Die Behandlung des Materials und seine insbesondere im Zusammenspiel mit Geometrie und Licht erscheinenden sensuellen Qualitäten in den Raumkompositionen werden dabei ebenfalls ausdrücklich thematisiert. Atmosphären bilden charakteristische Erscheinungsweisen der Ko-Präsenz im Räumlichen, deren Spezifik zudem in Bewegungssuggestionen gesehen werden kann.[12]

Das Atmosphärische wurde sowohl im Hinblick auf analytische wie auf projektive Entwurfsebenen und schließlich im Kontext der Rezeption diskutiert. Das, was dabei mit dem Atmosphärischen umschrieben wurde, ist in der Architektur nicht fremd und vollständig neuartig. So erhielten beispielsweise in der französischen Architekturtheorie des 18. Jahrhunderts Diskussionen um Wirkungsweisen von Bauwerken und die Möglichkeiten der Erzeugung spezifischer Affekte eine hervorgehobene Bedeutung.[13] Begrifflich wurde dies gefasst mit Bezeichnungen wie Ausdruck (expression) und Charakter (caractère) im produktionsästhetischen Zusammenhang sowie Empfindung (sensation) und Affekt (affect) im Zusammenhang der Wirkungen auf die Menschen. Ausdruck und Charakter blieben als Beschreibungsweisen von Architektur erhalten und werden bis heute vielfach verwendet. Darüber hinaus wird in alltäglichen und informellen Gesprächen über Architektur und Stadträume immer wieder vom Atmosphärischen gesprochen. Die Sensibilisierung für die Beschaffenheit und für Gradationen dieser als Einheit empfundenen, durchgängigen Qualität, die verschiedene Komponenten eines Kontextes in ein Ganzes bringt, wirkt bereichernd. Sie kann dazu beitragen, Kapazitäten auszubilden und zu erweitern, verschiedene elementare Umweltkonditionen zu erspüren und in den Architekturentwurf sowie in das eigene und kollektive Welt- und Selbstverständnis zu integrieren.

LANDSCAPE-NESS   Topology and atmosphere are proposed in connection with space formation and materiality to explore landscape-ness as an architectural idea. Through features such as continuities and connectivities, they already harbour in themselves a relation to landscape-ness, sometimes with a more morphological or a more modulatory character. In addition, with the suggestion of movement and therefore the imagination of movement sequences, they form promising perspectives for understandings of architecture. It is the positions of Peter Zumthor, Snøhetta and SANAA, which are integrated as examples not least because the architects themselves point out in different ways a high relevance of landscape references for their design work. Through the prism of their aims, their practical experiences and their knowledge, landscape-ness is presented as a variously articulated aesthetic and ethical quality. In the case of Peter Zumthor, a high value is attributed to landscape mood qualities, which he also wants to achieve in architecture. The firm Snøhetta, founded by Craig Dykers and Kjetil T. Thorsen, has been working from the beginning with the approach of entangling landscape architecture and architecture. In their works, various layers of perception and appropriation are opened up, from the tactile level of handling material to the multilayered correspondence with the surroundings. The architects Kazuyo Sejima and Ryue Nishizawa, working together at the office SANAA, each have their own interpretations of nature, landscape and public space, which mediate between in situ, physically present and technological, virtual experiences of reality. Their thinking and their understandings of architectural articulations are, in addition, shaped by Japanese cultural traditions which they integrate with contemporary modifications. In individual projects, they co-operate with landscape architects, as does Peter Zumthor. In differing ways, various positions and approaches break down the contrasts between active bodies and passive architecture, bringing

their connections to the landscape and a variety of relations to the fore.

LANDSCHAFTLICHKEIT   Topologie und Atmosphäre werden hier im Zusammenhang mit Raumformation und Materialität zu einer Erkundung von Landschaftlichkeit als Architekturidee vorgeschlagen. Durch Eigenschaften wie Kontinuitäten und Konnektivitäten bergen sie bereits in sich einen Bezug zu Landschaftlichkeit, einmal mehr morphologisch geprägt und das andere Mal mehr modulatorisch. Zudem bilden sie mit der Bewegungssuggestion und damit der Imagination von Bewegungsabfolgen für Architekturverständnisse vielversprechende Perspektiven. Es sind die Positionen von Peter Zumthor, Snøhetta und SANAA, die exemplarisch als besondere integriert werden, nicht zuletzt, da die Architekturschaffenden selbst in unterschiedlicher Weise auf eine hohe Relevanz von Landschaftsbezügen für ihr entwerferisches Schaffen verweisen. Durch das Prisma ihrer Ziele, ihrer praktischen Erfahrungen und ihres Wissens zeigt sich Landschaftlichkeit als unterschiedlich artikulierte ästhetische und ethische Qualität: Bei Peter Zumthor findet sich eine hohe Wertschätzung von landschaftlichen Stimmungsqualitäten, die er auch in der Architektur erreichen möchte. Das von den beiden Partnern Craig Dykers und Kjetil T. Thorsen gegründete Büro Snøhetta arbeitete von Beginn an mit dem Ansatz einer Verschränkung von Landschaftsarchitektur und Architektur. In ihren Arbeiten werden von der taktilen Ebene der Materialbehandlung bis zur vielschichtigen Korrespondenz mit der Umgebung diverse Layer der Wahrnehmung und Aneignung eröffnet. Die im Büro SANAA gemeinsam arbeitenden Architekturschaffenden Kazuyo Sejima und Ryue Nishizawa haben je eigene Interpretationen von Natur, Landschaft und öffentlichem Raum, die zwischen in situ physisch präsenten und technologischen, virtuellen Wirklichkeitserfahrungen vermitteln und zudem in ihrem Denken und ihren architektonischen Artikulationen durch die japanische Kulturtradition geprägte Verständnisse zeitgenössisch modifiziert einbringen. Zusammenarbeit mit Landschaftsarchitekt:innen findet sich bei ihnen in einzelnen Projekten ebenso wie bei Peter Zumthor. In zum Teil auch nur graduell unterschiedlicher Weise werden durch die verschiedenen Positionen und Vorgehensweisen Gegensätze zwischen aktiven Körpern und passiver Architektur und deren Verknüpfungen zur Landschaft aufgebrochen, und unterschiedliche Relationen treten in den Vordergrund. 225

RAUM IN RÄUMEN
SPACE IN SPACES
ATELIER PETER ZUMTHOR

The thinking and work of the Swiss architect Peter Zumthor offers an excellent way of approaching this. He received high recognition and awards worldwide for his projects in European countries, such as the shelter structures in Chur, the thermal spa in Vals, the Kunsthaus Bregenz or the Kolumba-Museum in Cologne. They are specifically tailored to the respective local context, are distinctive and at the same time subtle, and show spatial formations that are characterised by the precise working and modulations of geometry, material and light, as well as by various links between inside and outside, the architectural work and the surroundings. Zumthor's publications 'Thinking architecture' and 'Atmospheres', which were derived from presentations, also found widespread resonance. Landscape-ness as an architectural idea can be recognised in the consonance of the concepts, projects and reflections in a variety of interwoven layers. The entering into a nuanced interpretation of landscape for architecture in the imagination and as a space, place and environment, modulated by light, material, form and culture, is enabled by the various articulations, also showing that the relations of these components can only in part be rationally grasped and explained.

Das Denken und Schaffen des Schweizer Architekten Peter Zumthor bietet dafür eine hervorragende Möglichkeit der Annäherung. Für seine in europäischen Ländern realisierten Projekte wie die Schutzbauten in Chur, die Therme in Vals, das Kunsthaus Bregenz oder das Kolumba-Museum in Köln erhielt er weltweit hohe Anerkennung und Auszeichnungen. Sie sind auf den jeweiligen lokalen Kontext spezifisch zugeschnitten, wirken prägnant und gleichzeitig zurückhaltend und zeigen Raumformationen, die durch präzise Bearbeitung und Modulationen von Geometrie, Material und Licht sowie durch unterschiedliche Verknüpfungen von Innen und Außen, von Architekturwerk und Umgebung nachdrücklich charakterisiert sind. Ebenfalls die aus Vorträgen entstandenen Veröffentlichungen Zumthors ‚Architektur denken' und ‚Atmosphären' fanden weitreichende Resonanz. Landschaftlichkeit als Architekturidee kann aus dem Zusammenklang der Konzepte, Projekte und Reflektionen in unterschiedlichen, auch miteinander verflochtenen Layern erkannt werden. Das Hineintreten in ein nuanciertes Bedeutungsfeld von Landschaft für die Architektur als Raum, Ort und Umgebung, moduliert durch Licht, Material, Form und Kultur, sowie als Imagination wird durch die verschiedenen Artikulationen ebenso ermöglicht wie deutlich wird, dass dabei die Relationen dieser Komponenten nur in Teilen rational zu erfassen und zu erklären sind.

CONCEPTS   The various interweavings of architecture and landscape presented by Zumthor can be viewed as transferable key concepts, as a relation to the natural landscape, as a relation to the urban setting and as an extended understanding of architecture as space in spaces shaped by spatial formations. The architect mentioned these aspects repeatedly in presentations and interviews, forming part of the basis of his design stance. In interviews and in brief texts, he described a well-understood concept of architecture that was founded in professional experience and gained further from the everyday involvement in inhabiting the world. Trained as a cabinet maker, interior architect and architect, Zumthor worked for almost 10 years in monument preservation before opening his architecture atelier in 1979 in Haldenstein, near Chur in Switzerland. Concerned in particular with the creation of inventories of homesteads and village structures in Graubünden, Zumthor recognised during this research the strength of architecture that results from locational and usage references, as well as from the meaning of principles behind the typologies.[14] The topological properties of landscape as a region or as an urban ensemble; as part of a wide-ranging natural environment; as a specific ensemble and spatial scenery; and as a context with history and meaning are some of the description modes with which the architect later presents substantial degrees of place relation for his designs. Intensively perceiving the existing and seeing it anew form the starting point and can create a multilayered image of the local, a fabric that allows design decisions to be made. For example, for the design of the thermal spa in Vals, which is

characterised by an interplay of mass and emptiness and a kaleidoscope

KONZEPTE   Die verschiedenen von Zumthor dargebotenen Verwebungen von Architektur und Landschaft können als übertragbare Schlüsselkonzepte betrachtet werden, als Relation zur natürlichen Landschaft, Relation zum urbanen Setting und als ein durch Raumformationen geprägtes und erweitertes Verständnis von Architektur als Raum in Räumen. Der Architekt äußerte sich in Vorträgen und Interviews selbst wiederholt zu diesen Aspekten, die einen Teil der Grundlagen seiner Entwurfsposition bilden. In Interviews sowie in kurzen Texten beschreibt er gut verständlich ein Architekturverständnis, das in der beruflichen Erfahrung gründet und im Weiteren aus dem alltäglichen Involviert-Sein in das Bewohnen von Welt gewonnen wurde. Als Möbelschreiner, Innenarchitekt und Architekt ausgebildet, arbeitete er fast zehn Jahre lang in der Denkmalpflege bevor er 1979 in Haldenstein bei Chur in der Schweiz sein Architekturatelier eröffnete. Vor allem befasst mit der Inventarisation von Gehöften und Dorfstrukturen in Graubünden erkannte Peter Zumthor bei diesen Forschungsarbeiten die durch Bezug zum Ort und zum Gebrauch potenziell entstehende Stärke der Architektur sowie die Bedeutung von Prinzipien hinter den Typologien.[14] Die topologischen Eigenschaften von Landschaft als Region oder städtisches Gefüge, als Teil einer weitgespannten natürlichen Umgebung, als spezifisches Ensemble und räumliche Szenerie und als Zusammenhang mit Geschichte und Bedeutung sind einige der Beschreibungsmodi, mit denen der Architekt dann später substanzielle Ebenen des Ortsbezugs für sein Entwerfen darlegt. Das Bestehende intensiv aufzunehmen und auch neu zu sehen, bildet den Ausgangspunkt. Dies kann ein vielschichtiges Bild des Lokalen entstehen lassen, ein Gewebe, das es ermöglicht, Entwurfsentscheidungen zu treffen. So beispielsweise bildeten für den Entwurf der Therme in Vals, die durch das Wechselspiel von Masse und Leere sowie ein Kaleidoskop von Raumfolgen,

1 Therme Vals 1996

of spatial sequences, light modulations and landscape views, and is clad-
ded with Vals gneiss, inspiration was provided by the engineered structures in the area, such as avalanche protection galleries and reservoir
walls, which are perceived as powerful. The artefacts built with stone into
and out of the rock in the mountain, with impressive interior spaces in
a nuanced semi-darkness, acted here as impulse-giving 'images' for atmospheres and principles of action, as described by Zumthor (fig. 1).[15]

In his lecture for the 2013 RIBA Gold Medal Award, the architect emphasised the experience of landscape as a possibility to strengthen and enrich
his aim, which is the presence of the physical-corporeal being in the world
and its ability to be differentiated through an intensive articulation of the
material presence of architectural projects. In this context, the qualities
he seeks could also be characterised, in the sense of qualities that touch
one's own being.[16] Experiences of nature as a landscape – especially the
forms of appearance of natural light and its interplay with materials, as
well as the feeling of being surrounded by landscape – represent design
starting points for Zumthor.[17] Secluded natural landscapes with their calm-
er qualities or cultural landscapes, especially municipal ones with their
traces of time, can act equally as impulses. In the design process, Zumthor
enriches the landscape imagination by layering it with images and moods
from his own biography; such as places that once impressed him that
bear a similarity, kinship or even otherness to the situation on-site, as well
as by impressions of spatial scenarios from art, literature, film.[18] Designing on site is therefore bound up with knowledge of many other places.

Lichtmodulationen und Landschaftsausblicken charakterisiert und mit Valser Gneis ummantelt ist, die als kraftvoll erfahrenen Ingenieurbauwerke in der Umgebung wie Lawinenschutzgalerien und Staumauern eine Inspiration. Die mit Stein und im Stein in den Berg hineingebauten und aus ihm herausgebauten Artefakte mit eindrucksvollen Innenräumen im nuancierten Halbdunkel wirkten hier als impulsgebende ‚Bilder' für Stimmungen und Prinzipien des Machens, beschreibt Zumthor (Abb. 1).[15]

In seinem Vortrag zur RIBA-Gold-Medal-Verleihung 2013 hob der Architekt das Landschaftserlebnis als Möglichkeit hervor, sein Anliegen, die Präsenz des körperlich-leiblichen In-der-Welt-Seins und seiner Differenzierungsfähigkeit durch eine intensive Artikulation der materiellen Präsenz architektonischer Projekte zu stärken und zu bereichern. In diesem Kontext könnten auch die von ihm gesuchten Qualitäten charakterisiert werden, im Sinne von Qualitäten, die das eigene Sein berühren.[16] Erlebnisse der Natur als Landschaft, insbesondere die Erscheinungsformen des natürlichen Lichtes und ihr Zusammenspiel mit Materialien, sowie das Gefühl, von Landschaft umgeben zu sein, bilden für Zumthor Ausgangspunkte für das Entwerfen.[17] Abgelegene naturräumliche Landschaften mit ihren ruhigeren Zeitqualitäten oder Kulturlandschaften, insbesondere städtische mit ihren Spuren der Zeit in den Dingen, können dabei gleichermaßen impulsgebend wirken. Im Entwurfsprozess wird die landschaftliche Imagination zudem bereichert durch Überlagerungen mit Bildern und Stimmungen aus der eigenen Biografie beispielsweise von Orten, die ihn einmal beeindruckt haben, die eine Ähnlichkeit, Verwandtschaft oder auch Fremdheit zu der Situation vor Ort zeigen, sowie durch Eindrücke räumlicher Szenerien aus Kunst, Literatur und Film.[18]

This background texture varies from place to place, as do the specific levels of understanding of the location, space and nature as influential factors that stimulate ideas, whereby the meanings of nature and landscape also merge. It should be emphasised that Peter Zumthor associates thinking about landscape-ness with the notion of buildings that appear as a natural part of their surroundings while also creating beauty, an aesthetic quality that he would also like to achieve with his architecture.[19] Zumthor understands architecture as a completion of landscapes.[20]

Spatial relationality, material presence and temporality as an ephemeral presence are desired phenomena that, in this context, are especially associated with landscape as architectural features. They enable the acquisition of a reservoir of aesthetic competence from perceptions of the current local surroundings, as well as their layering with conscious and preconscious memories, which can also form a knowledge pool for handling atmospheres. Zumthor often uses the terms atmosphere, mood and presence to answer the question of what architectural qualities can be.[21] He sees atmosphere as a spatial property that is associated with emotional perception, for the producer as well as for the people experiencing and living in the architecture. The tools and instruments of design that he presented in the book 'Atmospheres' again include inter alia material presence and the consonance of materials, the tension between inside and outside, and the incidence of light on objects. There is also a special emphasis on the anticipation of possible movements, which are opened up sequentially through the shape of architectural design and can create a multimodal and multilayered perception of surrounding spatiality.[22]

So ist das Entwerfen vor Ort mit dem Wissen um viele andere Orte verbunden. Von Ort zu Ort unterscheidet sich diese Hintergrundtextur ebenso wie die spezifischen Verständnisebenen von Ort, Raum und Natur als einflussreiche ideenstimulierende Faktoren, wobei die Bedeutungen von Natur und Landschaft sich auch vermischen. Besonders hervorzuheben ist, dass Peter Zumthor mit dem Denken von Landschaftlichkeit die Vorstellung von Bauten verbindet, die als selbstverständlicher Teil ihrer Umgebung wirken, und zudem Schönheit erscheinen ließen – eine ästhetische Qualität, die er ebenfalls mit seinen Architekturen erreichen möchte.[19] Letztlich begreift Zumthor Architektur als Vervollständigung von Landschaften.[20]

Räumliche Relationalität, Materialpräsenz und Zeitlichkeit als ephemere Präsenz sind gewünschte Phänomene, die in diesem Zusammenhang als architektonische Eigenschaften mit Landschaft besonders verbunden werden. Sie ermöglichen es, aus Wahrnehmungen der aktuellen Standortumgebung sowie ihrer Überlagerung mit eingespeisten bewussten und vorbewussten Erinnerungen ein Reservoir ästhetischer Kompetenz zu erwerben, das auch einen Wissensspeicher für den Umgang mit Atmosphären bilden kann. Zumthor selbst nutzt häufig die Begriffe Atmosphäre, Stimmung und Präsenz, um sich die Frage zu beantworten, was architektonische Qualität sein kann.[21] Er sieht Atmosphäre als räumliche Eigenschaft, die mit emotionaler Wahrnehmung verbunden ist, beim Produzenten ebenso wie bei den die Architektur erfahrenden und bewohnenden Menschen. Zu den Instrumenten und Werkzeugen des Entwerfens, die er in dem Buch ‚Atmosphären' vorstellte, zählen wiederum unter anderem die materielle Präsenz und der Zusammenklang der Materialien, die Spannung zwischen Innen und Außen und das Licht auf den Dingen. Ebenso besonders hervorgehoben wird die Antizipation von Bewegungsmöglichkeiten, die durch die architektonische Gestaltung sequenziell eröffnet werden und multimodale und vielschichtige Wahrnehmung von umgebender Räumlichkeit gestalten können.[22]

2 Kunsthaus Bregenz 1997 Exhibition and office building

CREATING ATMOSPHERES: KUNSTHAUS BREGENZ

The Kunsthaus built in Bregenz, Austria, not far from the shore of Lake Constance and close to the inner city for alternating exhibitions in the fields of art and architecture, allowed Zumthor a relatively wide freedom of interpretation of the task. In an in-between space adjacent to the historical old town that was not densely built up, the new building, completed in 1997 as a 30-metre-high cube, appeared both modest and emphatic in the municipal context, with its height and with a monolithic clarity of the geometric volume (fig. 2).[23] It is a building without windows, without a base and roof closure, surrounded evenly on all sides by additively structured glass walls. Standing on metal consoles and only held in its slightly inclined position on two levels by brackets, the translucent, vertically rectangular glass panels overlapping slightly on the sides appear as a mere shell. This architecture appears thin and weightless, elaborately and precisely worked and positioned, but even so, it creates an impression of being provisional. The changing play of light on the matte white glass encasing, sometimes shimmering blueish green, reinforces this effect. In fog it can scarcely be seen; in sunshine it shimmers like plumage.

Contrary to experience-orientated, open museum buildings with generous connections between inside and outside, and in some cases art exhibition concepts with a consumerist orientation, Zumthor excluded the café, library and administration here. On the city side, a three-storey building volume with dark materials was set in front of the cube of the exhibition building at a right angle. This gave the street area the appearance of a square that could be used as public space but was asphalted without joins and with some lighter lines running through it, with little specific articulation. Due to the

ATMOSPHÄREN GESTALTEN: KUNSTHAUS BREGENZ

Das in Bregenz unweit des Bodenseeufers und innenstadtnah für Wechsel-ausstellungen aus den Bereichen Kunst und Architektur gebaute Kunsthaus ließ dem Architekten in der Aufgabenstellung eine relativ große Interpre-tationsfreiheit. In einem baulich wenig verdichteten, an die historische Alt-stadt grenzenden Zwischenbereich tritt der 1997 vollendete Bau als 30 Meter hoher Kubus im stadträumlichen Zusammenhang mit seiner Höhe und mit der monolithischen Klarheit des geometrischen Körpers gleicher-maßen zurückhaltend wie nachdrücklich hervor (Abb. 2).[23] Es ist ein Bau ohne Fenster, ohne Sockel und Dachabschluss, an allen Seiten durch ad-ditiv strukturierte Glaswände gleichmäßig umgrenzt. Auf Metallkonsolen lagernd und in ihrer in zwei Ebenen leicht geneigten Position nur durch Klammern gehalten, wirken die transluzenten, hochrechteckigen, sich an den Seiten leicht überlappenden Glastafeln wie eine bloße Hülle. Dünn und gewichtslos, aufwendig präzise gearbeitet und platziert erscheint die-se Architektur und dennoch stellt sich auch der Eindruck des Provisorischen ein. Das wechselnde Spiel des Lichts auf dem matt-weißen, manchmal blaugrün schimmernden Glasmantel verstärkt die Wirkung. Bei Nebel ist es kaum zu erkennen, bei Sonne schimmert es wie ein Gefieder.

Im Abstand zu erlebnisorientierten, offenen Museumsbauten mit großzügi-gen Verbindungen von Innen und Außen und in Teilen auch konsumistisch ausgerichteten Kunstausstellungskonzepten gliederte Zumthor hier Café, Bibliothek und Verwaltung aus. Stadtseitig wurde dem Kubus des Ausstel-lungshauses ein in dunkler Materialität gehaltener dreigeschossiger Ge-bäuderiegel rechtwinklig vorgelagert. In dieser Weise wurde der Straßen-raum platzartig ausgeprägt und als öffentlicher Raum nutzbar, blieb aber gleichwohl, fugenlos asphaltiert und mit einigen helleren Linien durchzo-gen, wenig spezifisch artikuliert. Durch die städtebauliche Setzung wur-den nicht nur Beziehungen gestiftet zwischen historischer und zeitgenös-sischer Bebauung sowie den heterogenen Elementen des Stadtraums. Es bleibt ein nicht überbauter, offener Raumkörper, der Licht und Luft vom See über diesen Zwischenbereich in Richtung Stadt leitet und das Wahrneh-mungsfeld zum naturräumlichen Umfeld hin erweitert. Der Übergang zwi-schen Außen und Innen erfolgt über einen kurzen fensterlosen Eingang. 235

urban positioning, relations were forged between historical and contemporary buildings and the heterogeneous elements of the urban area. It remains a not-overbuilt, open spatial volume that guides light and air from the lake through this intermediate area towards the city, extending the field of perception towards the natural surroundings. The transition between outside and inside is by means of a short windowless entrance. The square 25 m x 25 m and relatively high exhibition space, with a polished concrete floor and bulky wall panels made of concrete, is illuminated on one side by milky, floor-to-ceiling glazing. Its strictly geometric whole can be perceived immediately upon entering. Behind the concrete slabs, arranged in an interspace to the outer shell, are the vertical access elements.

Movement through the building gains a clarity determined by the usage. The main stairs present themselves as an ascent space with a stepped ceiling, delineated on both sides by concrete walls. At the top, a further exhibition space opens up in the same direction as the lower one, also offering an immediate overview of its totality upon entering. Contrary to the ground floor, the relations of light and walls are different. Here the space is enclosed by concrete walls all around and a skylight ceiling. The spatial concept continues in the same manner on two further floors. Only the heights and the colour nuances of the polished terrazzo floors vary slightly.

Light is experienced emphatically as a distinctive design component. By means of a lighting design thought out in detail, natural light is guided laterally into the exhibition spaces through opaque outer walls in mezzanines, and from there through translucent ceilings made of glass panels. In accordance with the outdoor light, the light modulation varies and, if necessary, computer-controlled artificial light can supplement it. Through the changing but always muted light quality, both maximum contrasts between light and dark as well as the formation of shadows are weakened. The light as an unstable, immaterial design material is intensified in a certain manner by the interplay with the lateral matte concrete slabs and the shiny terrazzo floor. It appears as a temporally mutable and corporeal spatial quality, as if the outdoor space and the natural light qualities of the Lake Constance area were guided inside, changing with the times of day and seasons – an interplay of a 'cosmic' nature and artefact.[24] The spatial qualities appear as presentations of a distinctive landscape phenomenon at the Lake Constance site; of a diffuse spatial illumination over the often moving and rippling surface of the lake. It creates the impression of landscape-ness. It is an attempt to capture a lived and experienced reality that is generated not from what is learnt but more from subjective and individual perceptions and memories while at the same time taking on and reflecting anthropological constants.

Der quadratische, 25 x 25 Meter große und relativ hohe Ausstellungsraum mit poliertem Betonboden und mit wuchtigen Wandscheiben aus Beton wird an einer Seite durch raumhohe, milchige Verglasungen belichtet und ist in seiner streng geometrischen Gesamtheit unmittelbar nach Betreten erfassbar. Hinter den Betonscheiben ausgegliedert in einem Zwischenraum zur äußeren Hülle befinden sich die vertikalen Erschließungselemente.

Die Bewegung durch das Gebäude erhält eine durch die Nutzung bestimmte Eindeutigkeit. Die Haupttreppe zeigt sich als durch Betonwände beidseitig begrenzter Aufstiegsraum mit abgestufter Lichtdecke. Oben öffnet sich ein weiterer Ausstellungsraum in derselben Richtung wie der untere und ist ebenfalls in seiner Gesamtheit unmittelbar nach Betreten überschaubar. Im Unterschied zum Erdgeschoss sind die Relationen von Licht und Wand verändert. Hier wird der Raum von einer vollständigen Betonumwandung und einer Oberlichtdecke eingefasst. Die räumliche Konzeption setzt sich in zwei weiteren Geschossen gleichartig fort. Allein die Höhen und die farblichen Nuancierungen der polierten Terrazzoböden variieren leicht.

Nachdrücklich wird Licht als prägende Gestaltungskomponente erfahren. Mittels einer bis ins Detail durchdachten Lichtführungskonstruktion wird natürliches Licht seitlich über opake Außenwände in Zwischengeschosse und von dort über transluzente Decken aus Glasplatten in die Ausstellungsräume geführt. Der Außenhelligkeit entsprechend variiert die Lichtmodulation und bei Bedarf kann computergesteuert Kunstlicht zugeschaltet werden. Durch die zwar wechselnde, doch stets gedämpfte Lichtqualität werden Maximalkontraste zwischen Hell und Dunkel ebenso wie Schattenbildungen abgeschwächt. Das Licht wird als instabiles, immaterielles Gestaltungsmaterial in gewisser Weise intensiviert durch das Zusammenspiel mit den matten seitlichen Betonscheiben und dem glänzenden Terrazzoboden. Es tritt als zeitlich wandelbare und körperhafte Raumqualität so hervor, als würde der Außenraum, würden die natürlichen Lichtqualitäten des Bodenseeraums hier nach Innen geleitet, wechselnd mit den Tages- und Jahreszeiten – ein Zusammenspiel von ‚kosmischer' Natur und Artefakt.[24] Die Raumqualitäten erscheinen wie Darbietungen eines prägenden landschaftlichen Phänomens am Standort des Bodensees, eines diffusen räumlichen Leuchtens über der oft sich bewegenden und kräuselnden Seeoberfläche. Der Eindruck von Landschaftlichkeit entsteht. Es ist ein Versuch, gelebte und erfahrene Wirklichkeit zu erfassen, die nicht aus Erlerntem, vielmehr durch subjektiv individuelle Wahrnehmungen und Erinnerungen generiert wird und dabei auch gleichzeitig anthropologische Konstanten in sich aufnimmt und spiegeln kann.

OUTSIDE-INSIDE SPACE CONFIGURATION: MUSEUM KOLUMBA
Accentuations and interpretations of space can make a location context
a specific spatial configuration with a powerful effect. This characterises
the museum Kolumba in Cologne, Germany, which opened for exhibitions
of religious and contemporary art in 2007. Through the existing buildings
and designs, as well as through choreographies of perception and appropriation, one can experience here overarching connections between
the environs and social environment, guided by the architectural articulation, which integrates various objects and spaces, along with the various
layers of outdoor and indoor space, architecture, city and open space.

The site of the St. Kolumba Church, which was destroyed between 1943
and 1945, is now orientated towards the discovered layouts and is partly
built on the remaining wall. This solid building made of warm grey bricks
was created with some window surfaces spanning the wall that appear to
be lying on the façade like screens. At the site limits, the slightly kinked
architectural volume rises like a tower (fig. 3). It does not evoke an analogy to landscape-ness initially, nor does the slightly changing colour of
the façades in varying light reflections. The more evident term for the
intensely corporeal effect of this building appears to be monumentality.[25]

Peter Zumthor presented his design in the beginning as essentially defined
by light and shadow effects. The spatial configuration was intensified in
many respects during the design development and realisation and associated with a wider spectrum of effects, offering a series of scenic components
and echos.[26] This can be understood through the choreography of the spaces. Based on the basic orientation of the person, as well as their movements
and actions in the space, choreographing as a design action refers to the

3 Kolumba Cologne 2007

AUSSEN-INNEN – RAUMKONFIGURATION: MUSEUM KOLUMBA

Akzentuierungen und Ortsinterpretationen können einen Standortkontext auch erst zu einer spezifischen baulich-räumlichen Konfiguration mit starker Wirkung werden lassen. Dies kennzeichnet das Museum Kolumba in Köln, das 2007 für Ausstellungen religiöser und zeitgenössischer Kunst eröffnet wurde. Über die Bestände des Gebauten und Gestalteten, über Choreografien der Wahrnehmung und Aneignung können auch hier, geleitet durch die architektonische Artikulation, übergreifende Zusammenhänge der Um- und Mitwelt erfahren werden, die verschiedene Objekte und Räume, die unterschiedliche Schichtungen von Außenraum und Innenraum, Architektur, Stadt und Freiraum integrieren.

Über dem Gelände der 1943 und 1945 zerstörten Kolumbakirche, orientiert an aufgefundenen Grundrissen und teilweise aufbauend auf den vorhandenen Mauerresten entstand dieses massiv gemauerte Gebäude aus warmgrauem Ziegelstein und mit einigen wandgroßen Fensterflächen, welche auf der Fassade wie Schirme aufzuliegen scheinen. An den Grundstücksgrenzen steigt der leicht geknickte Baukörper jeweils turmartig auf (Abb. 3). Eine Analogie zu Landschaftlichkeit kommt hier zunächst nicht in den Sinn. Auch die leicht wechselnde Einfärbung der Fassaden bei verschiedenen Lichtreflexionen bewirkt das zunächst nicht. Die naheliegendere Begrifflichkeit für die intensiv körperhafte Wirkung dieses Bauwerks scheint Monumentalität zu sein.[25]

Peter Zumthor präsentierte seinen Entwurf zu Beginn als wesentlich durch Licht- und Schattenwirkungen geprägt. Im Zuge der Entwurfsentwicklung und Realisierung wurde die Raumartikulation in mehrfacher Hinsicht intensiviert und verbunden mit einem breiteren Wirkungsspektrum, das eine Reihe landschaftlicher Anteile und Anklänge darbietet.[26] Dies kann über

anticipation of this physical-corporeal experience of space and the structure and distribution of active design elements, through which this is guided and stimulated.[27] There is a central focus on design qualities that in connection with movement are also characteristic of the experience of landscape, landscape gardens and outdoor spaces. The entrance to the Kolumba was designed simply as a subtle glass area with a door. Immediately after entering, movement is directed past a narrow passage by the ticket counter on one side and the cloakroom on the other around the corner, where a large glass wall with a door forms a first widening of the otherwise rather dark area.

According to the designs by the landscape architect Günter Vogt, an enclosed tree courtyard was created here above the medieval Kolumba cemetery, surrounded on the two open sides by a tamped concrete wall and on a farther side framed by the north wall of the church ruin.[28] With the water-bound surface made of Jurassic limestone, the hill-like, modulated, gravelled ground area corresponds with the beige-yellow colour of the façade. The design appears concentrated and austere with the loose grouping of 11 Christ's thorn trees, as well as the lying sculpture by the Swiss sculptor Hans Josephsohn on a low stone bench as an accent. The tree courtyard forms that is both outdoors and inside, and appears in the spatial sequence as a space open to the sky and mediating with the urban surroundings.

The choreography leads on to a high-roofed excavation landscape space surrounded by filter masonry. The structure is also penetrated by a natural incidence of light, as well as by air from the outdoor area that furthermore encases a chapel by Gottfried Böhm from the 1950s. A jagged walkway leads through it and into the outdoor area to the ruin of the former vestry, which is open to the sky. The previously erected sculpture by the American artist
Richard Serra, with its articulation as a standing rectangle, makes it possible

die Choreografie der Räume verstanden werden. Ausgehend von der Grundorientierung des Menschen sowie seinen Bewegungen und Aktionen im Raum bezieht sich Choreografieren als Entwurfshandlung auf die Antizipation dieses leiblich-körperlichen Raumerlebens und die Struktur und Verteilung aktiver Gestaltungselemente, mittels derer dieses gelenkt und ermuntert wird.[27] Ins Zentrum treten dabei Gestaltungsqualitäten, die im Zusammenhang mit Bewegung auch für das Erleben von Landschaft, von Landschaftsgärten und von Freiräumen charakteristisch sind. Der Eingang des Kolumba Museums wurde als zurückhaltendes Glasfeld mit Tür schlicht gestaltet. Unmittelbar nach dem Betreten wird die Bewegung gelenkt über einen schmalen Gang am Tickettresen einerseits und dem Garderobenraum andererseits vorbei um die Ecke, wo eine große Glaswand mit Tür eine erste Aufweitung des ansonsten recht dunklen Bereiches bildet.

Nach den Entwürfen des Landschaftsarchitekten Günter Vogt ist hier ein umschlossener Baumhof über dem mittelalterlichen Kolumbafriedhof entstanden, umgeben an den beiden offenen Seiten von einer Stampfbetonmauer und an einer weiteren Seite gerahmt von der Nordwand der Kirchenruine.[28] Mit dem wassergebundenen Belag aus Jurakalk korrespondiert die hügelartig modulierte, bekieste Bodenfläche zur beigegelben Farbigkeit der Fassade. Mit der lockeren Gruppierung von elf Christusdornbäumen sowie der Skulptur einer Liegenden des Schweizer Bildhauers Hans Josephson auf einer niedrigen Steinbank als Akzent wirkt die Gestaltung konzentriert und karg. Der Baumhof bildet ein Außen, das doch auch ein Innen ist und in der Raumfolge als zum Himmel offener, zum städtischen Umfeld vermittelnder Ortraum wirkt.

Die Choreografie leitet weiter zu einem hohen, von Filtermauerwerk umgebenen überdachten Grabungslandschaftraum. Auch hier durchdringt natürlicher Lichteinfall und zudem Luft des Außenraums das Gebaute, das darüber

to understand support and loads and shows a changeable patina within its Corten steel material. The controversally debated built palimpsest that Peter Zumthor realised here does not only reinterpret local formations anew through this multilayering, but also establishes relations to their materiality, to the tuff, basalt and bricks of the ruin and to the texture and colour spectrum of buildings of the near and distant surroundings from different construction eras.

The way leads back then through the relatively narrow stairway area surrounded by high walls past various exhibition spaces, in nightly darkness or with muted light, or which open up with floor-to-ceiling windows to the tree courtyard and the surrounding city. All the rooms differ in dimensions and degrees of lightness. The common reduced materiality of brick, mortar, plaster and terrazzo has a unifying effect. In increasingly large curves of movement, the choreography leads through pathways and interspaces to the height of the main storey. Here, rectangular cabinets and exhibition halls of varying dimensions and proportions – with steep and high plenums and lateral translucent skylights, or as dark modulated interspaces – are grouped around a large trapezoid exhibition area, whose square-like spatial structure was created by the existing layout boundaries.

The main space, where free movement is encouraged, reaches in the north, south and east to the edge of the building, where floor-to-ceiling glass wall slabs appear to draw in the urban environment very directly: the Dischhaus by the architect Bruno Paul from the 1920s; the opera house by Wilhelm Riphahn, with a big forecourt from the 1950s; the surrounding heterogeneous urban landscape, as well as the nearby Cologne Cathedral. In this interior spatial ensemble, there are alternating degrees of lightness, changing material effects, narrowness, expanse and height, as well as proximity to and distance from the surrounding urban area, with its buildings and horizons.

hinaus eine Kapelle von Gottfried Böhm aus den 1950er Jahren umhaust. Ein gezackter Steg führt hindurch und wieder hinaus in den Außenraum zur himmeloffenen Ruine der ehemaligen Sakristei mit der bereits zuvor aufgestellten Skulptur des amerikanischen Künstlers Richard Serra, die in ihrer Artikulation als stehendes Rechteck Tragen und Lasten erlebbar macht und in ihrer Cortenstahlmaterialität eine veränderliche Patina zeigt. Das kontrovers diskutierte gebaute Palimpsest, das Peter Zumthor hier realisierte, interpretiert mit dieser Mehrschichtigkeit nicht nur Formationen des Ortes neu, sondern stellt auch Relationen zur deren Materialität her, zu den Tuffen, Basalten und Ziegeln der Ruine und zu dem Textur- und Farbspektrum von Bauten der näheren und weiteren Umgebung aus unterschiedlichen Entstehungszeiten.

Zurück führt der Weg dann weiter über den von hohen Wänden begrenzten relativ schmalen Treppenraum an verschiedenen Ausstellungsräumen vorbei, die nachtschwarz oder abgedämpft beleuchtet sind bzw. sich mit raumhohen Fenstern öffnen zum Baumhof und der umliegenden Stadt. Alle Räume unterscheiden sich in ihren Zuschnitten und Helligkeitsgraden. Verbindend wirkt die gemeinsame reduzierte Materialität aus Ziegelstein, Mörtel, Putz und Terrazzo. In größer werdenden Bewegungskurven führt die Choreografie über Weg- und Orträume bis zur Höhe des Hauptgeschosses. Hier gruppieren sich um einen großen trapezförmigen Ausstellungsbereich, dessen platzartige Raumstruktur durch die am Ort vorhandenen Grundrissgrenzen geprägt wurde, mehrere unterschiedlich geschnittene und proportionierte rechteckige Kabinette und Ausstellungssäle mit steilen hohen Lufträumen und seitlichen transluzenten Oberlichtern oder als dunkler modulierte Zwischenräume.

Der Hauptraum, in dem zu einer freien Bewegung ermuntert wird, führt im Norden, Süden und Osten bis an die Gebäudekante heran, wo raumhohe gläserne Wandschirme sehr unmittelbar das städtische Umfeld heranzuziehen scheinen: das Dischhaus des Architekten Bruno Paul aus den 1920er Jahren, die Oper von Wilhelm Riphahn mit großem Vorplatz aus den 1950ern und die umliegende heterogene Stadtlandschaft sowie den nahegelegenen Kölner Dom. In diesem inneren Raumgefüge wechseln Helligkeitsgrade, changieren Materialwirkungen, Enge und Weite und Höhe sowie die Nähe und Ferne des umgebenden Stadtraums und seiner Bauten und Horizonte. Neben den Licht- und Materialqualitäten werden insbesondere Verknüpfungen zu Außenräumen in die Wahrnehmung gerückt und wird eine Entgrenzung der Innenräume

Apart from the light and material qualities, attention is drawn in particular to links to outdoor spaces and the dissolution of boundaries between interior spaces. This can be experienced in a corporeal spatiality, an in-between area of potential appropriation and action and an expanse opening up beyond the staggered roof areas, which appear to stretch beyond the view into the distance. In this manner, the architectural promenade, the layout of routes based on human experience, as well as qualities of so-called flowing space, are incorporated into the surroundings through literal transparency as an opening of architectural interior space.

The varied relations of various aggregate conditions of light and shade, of spatial constitutions and sequences of indoor and outdoor spaces – as well as the structural allusions to urban squares and fabrics in an irregular figuration, as known for example from contexts of old European cities – emphasise topological features of this architecture. The dialogue with close and distant urban areas of Cologne through the big window screens and connections to the outdoors also show landscape properties; not only those of the views but rather those of spatial extension and spatial linking. Even the material choice of the brick walls with a warm effect could be interpreted as an expression of the landscape character in relation to the surroundings, extending to the city and its history; for example, the church buildings in yellow-beige sandstone or the brick architecture of the Cologne architect Rudolf Schwarz. Not least, Zumthor's Kolumba exerts an especially strong and at the same time natural presence on-site. The interlinking of various spaces and those they contain, as well as the experiential qualities that go beyond the dimensions of the individual spaces, can also be described as characteristic of the 'space of landscape', whose contours and boundaries

244 remain largely diffuse and can furthermore reach beyond the very present.[29]

vorgenommen. Dies wird erlebbar in einer körpernahen Räumlichkeit, einem mittleren Bereich der potenziellen Aneignung und Aktion und einer über die gestaffelten Dachbereiche hinaus sich öffnenden Weite, die auch über die Ausdehnung des Fernblicks noch hinauszureichen scheint. So wurden hier die architektonische Promenade, die von der menschlichen Erfahrung ausgehende Gestaltung von Routen durch Weg- und Orträume sowie Qualitäten des sogenannten fließenden Raumes als Öffnung von architektonischem Innenraum in das Umfeld durch buchstäbliche Transparenz einbezogen.

Die abwechslungsreichen Relationen verschiedener Aggregatzustände von Licht und Schatten, von Raumkonstitutionen und Abfolgen von Innen- und Außenräumen und mit den strukturalen Anspielungen an städtische Plätze und Gefüge in unregelmäßiger Figuration, wie sie beispielsweise aus Kontexten alter europäischer Städte bekannt sind, betonen topologische Eigenschaften dieser Architektur. Auch durch den Dialog mit den dicht heranrückenden und den weiter entfernteren Stadträumen Kölns durch die großen Fensterschirme und Freiraumbezüge zeigen sich landschaftliche Eigenschaften, nicht nur der Ausblicke, vielmehr der Raumerweiterung und räumlichen Verknüpfung. Selbst die Materialwahl der warm wirkenden Ziegelwände könnte als Ausdruck des landschaftlichen Charakters in Bezug zum Umfeld und im Weiteren der Stadt und ihrer Geschichte, beispielsweise der Kirchenbauten aus gelbbeigem Sandstein oder der Ziegelbau-Architekturen des Kölner Architekten Rudolf Schwarz, gedeutet werden. Nicht zuletzt entwickelt Zumthors Kolumba am Standort eine besonders starke und gleichzeitig selbstverständliche Präsenz. Das Ineinandergreifen verschiedener Räume und die darin enthaltenen, die Dimensionen der Einzelräume überschreitenden Erfahrungsqualitäten können auch als charakteristisch für den ‚Raum der Landschaft' beschrieben werden, dessen Konturen und Begrenzungen übergreifend diffus bleiben und zudem über das Gegenwärtige hinausreichen können.[29]

REPERTOIRE   Landscape-ness appears here as the presentation of an idea associated with multimodal sensory experience and emotions, and as an interpretation of reality that guides and accompanies the design interest of the architect. The places designed in connection with the buildings are generated by creative analyses of rational and intuitively perceived topological, typological and atmospheric properties of the multilayered territories and spaces that are materially present on-site, or that flow into the concepts through the imagination. The choreographing of series of spaces in the horizontal sequence of a level and in vertical succession form important design strategies. They are related to a hodological understanding of space, as is the case in English landscaped gardens, and in the 'promenade architecturale' that the Swiss architect Le Corbusier realised after the 1920s in many of his projects.[30] Further design components that interact with the surroundings and therefore with the landscape in Zumthor's understanding of architecture are presented by the spatial extensions through large windows. These bring the outside into the building, framed and accentuated, and extend interior spaces and in particular natural light, through which landscape-ness and the environment can be perceived, even if the light enters through translucent architectural elements, skylight ceilings or masonry with light- and air-transmitting openings. Substantial and scenic understandings of landscape are therefore interwoven on many levels.[31] The lighting design is formed by a specifically articulated design tool, as well as by the handling and effect of material and materiality developed individually from in-depth on-site analyses. The relational connection, which takes account of dimensions and interim situations, gains significant relevance here regarding qualitative spatial relations formed essentially through presentist physical perception and action. The webs of relations, newly created through harmonised structures and design methods, generate special ensembles that show landscape qualities, with design continuity and an intensity of configuration, that can also be seen in natural environments.

246

Landschaftlichkeit erscheint hier als Präsentation einer mit multimodaler sinnlicher Erfahrung und mit Emotionen verbundenen Idee und Wirklichkeitsinterpretation. Sie leitet und begleitet das Gestaltungsinteresse des Architekten. Die im Zusammenhang der Bauten entworfenen Orte werden generiert durch kreative Analysen aus rational sowie intuitiv erfassten topologischen, typologischen und atmosphärischen Eigenschaften der vielschichtigen Territorien und Räume, die am Standort materiell präsent sind oder über Imaginationen in die Konzeptionen einfließen. Das Choreografieren von Raumfolgen in der horizontalen Sequenz einer Ebene und in der vertikalen Sukzession bilden wichtige Gestaltungsstrategien. Sie sind einem hodologischen Raumverständnis verwandt wie es in englischen Landschaftsgärten hervortritt, aber auch in der ‚promenade architecturale‘, die der schweizer Architekt Le Corbusier seit den 1920er Jahren in vielen seiner Projekte realisierte.[30] Weitere Gestaltungskomponenten, die mit der Umgebung und damit im Architekturverständnis Zumthors mit der Landschaft korrespondieren, bilden die Raumerweiterungen durch große Fenster, die Außenliegendes gerahmt und akzentuiert in das Gebäude holen und Innenräume ausdehnen, sowie insbesondere das natürliche Licht, durch das Landschaftlichkeit und Umgebung erfahrbar werden, auch dann, wenn das Licht über transluzente Architekturelemente, Oberlichtdecken oder Filtermauerwerk einfällt. Somit sind substanzielles und szenisches Landschaftsverständnis vielschichtig verwoben.[31] Die Lichtinszenierung bildet ein je spezifisch artikuliertes Gestaltungsinstrument ebenso wie die sich aus vertieften Ortsanalysen individuell entwickelnde Behandlung und Wirkung von Material und Materialität. Die relationale Verknüpfung, die Ausdehnung und Zwischenzustände aufnimmt, gewinnt hier große Relevanz in Bezug auf qualitative Raumbeziehungen, die sich wesentlich erschließen durch präsentische körperliche Wahrnehmung und Handlung. Die durch abgestimmte Strukturen und Gestaltungsmittel neu entstandenen Beziehungsgeflechte erzeugen räumliche Ensemble, die in gestalterischer Kontinuität bei gleichzeitiger Intensität der Konfiguration landschaftliche Qualitäten zeigen wie sie auch in naturräumlichen Gegenden wahrzunehmen sind.

ARCHITEKTONISCHE LANDSCHAFTEN
ARCHITECTURAL LANDSCAPES
SNØHETTA

Multilayered interweaving of architecture and landscape can also be found in the architecture of Snøhetta. The office, whose name is derived from the snow-covered brow of a mountain range in Norway, was founded at the end of the 1980s in Oslo and New York by Norwegian architect Kjetil Trædal Thorsen and US-American architect Craig Dykers. It was formed from a syndicate for architecture and landscape design started a few years earlier. Today it has various regional branches, for example in Paris, Innsbruck and San Francisco, each with international teams. From the beginning, the architecture, landscape and interior design works, as well as product and graphic design projects, have been developed in mixed teams and through collective, open and transdisciplinary collaborations with artists, artisans, philosophers and sociologists.[32] From the beginning, the design activities have also been intensively and fundamentally guided by a close linking of architecture and landscape, of architectural space and the local physical and social context. Snøhetta indicate this also as the reinvention of a place.[33]

Vielschichtige Verschränkungen von Architektur und Landschaft finden sich auch in den Architekturen von Snøhetta. Das Büro, dessen Name sich von der schneebedeckten Bergkuppe eines Gebirgszugs Norwegens ableitet, wurde Ende der 1980er Jahre in Oslo und New York von dem norwegischen Architekten Kjetil Trædal Thorsen und dem US-Amerikaner Craig Dykers gegründet. Es ist hervorgegangen aus ihrer einige Jahre zuvor begonnenen Arbeitsgemeinschaft für Architektur und Landschaftsgestaltung und hat heute verschiedene regionale Niederlassungen, beispielsweise in Paris, Innsbruck oder San Francisco, mit jeweils international zusammengesetzten Teams. Von Beginn an wurden die architektonischen, landschafts- und innenarchitektonischen Arbeiten sowie Produkt- und Grafikdesignprojekte in gemischten Teams und auch in externen Kooperationen mit Künstler:innen, Handwerker:innen Philosoph:innen oder Soziolog:innen in kollektiv offener transdisziplinärer Zusammenarbeit entwickelt.[32] Ebenfalls von Beginn an war es die enge Verknüpfung von Architektur und Landschaft, von architektonischem Raum und lokalem physischem und auch sozialem Kontext, die intensiv und grundlegend die Entwurfstätigkeit leitete. Snøhetta bezeichnen das auch als Neuerfindung eines Ortes.[33]

1–2 Norwegian Wild Reindeer Centre Pavilion Hjerkinn 2011

The architectural office gained international renown through cultural projects resulting from competition successes, such as the library in Alexandria, in Egypt, or the opera house in Oslo, Norway. They have also realised numerous architecture projects with different characters. These include small-scale conceptual-artistic works such as the pavilions for the Kivik Art Center in Rörum, Sweden, with its minimalist, open and cubic concrete structures that frame the surroundings in a targeted manner; the Dovrefjell observatory pavilion for observing animal and plant habitats on Norway's Dovre mountain plateau; or the restructuring of Times Square in New York City.[34] In these projects, as well as in their culture, infrastructure, urban development and design projects currently realised worldwide on various continents, they furthermore feel obliged to social and ecological sustainability.[35]

CONCEPTS   How the idea of landscape-ness is articulated is significantly evident in the configuration of the Norwegian Wild Reindeer Centre Pavilion in Hjerkinn, built in 2011 for the observation of wild reindeer, musk oxen, polar foxes and a string of endemic botanical species on the Norwegian Dovrefjell Massif (fig. 1). It also shows how Snøhetta work with the latest digital and robot-controlled technologies inspired by artisanal traditions. The wooden seating object – as a dominant artefact in the interior, taking up nearly the full breadth and height of the cuboid pavilion box – has a continuously curved shape by means of 3D technologies and appears as part of a landscape formed through the movement of natural forces (fig. 2). It accentuates the keyless shelter and invites one to linger. A fully glazed side of the Corten steel box enables a variety of observations from the interior, as well as panoramic views out to the nearer and more distant surroundings. Through the materiality and organic morphology in the interior,

International bekannt wurde das Architekturbüro mit renommierten Kultur-projekten, die auf Wettbewerbserfolge zurückgingen, wie die Bibliothek im ägyptischen Alexandria oder das Opernhaus in Oslo. Zudem verwirklichten sie eine Vielzahl unterschiedlich charakterisierter Architekturprojekte, unter ihnen auch kleinmaßstäbliche konzeptuell-künstlerisch geprägte Arbeiten, darunter die Pavillons für das Kivik Art Center in Rörum als minimalistische, die Umgebung gezielt einrahmende offene kubische Betonstrukturen, der Dovref-jell-Observatoriumspavillon zur Beobachtung von Tier- und Pflanzenhabitaten auf dem Dovre-Bergplateau oder die Restrukturierung für den Times Square in New York.[34] In diesen wie auch den aktuell weltweit auf verschiedenen Kon-tinenten realisierten Kultur-, Infrastruktur-, Städtebau- und Designprojekten fühlen sie sich zudem sozialer und ökologischer Nachhaltigkeit verpflichtet.[35]

KONZEPTE   Wie sich die Idee von Landschaftlichkeit artikuliert, zeigt sich signifikant in der Konfiguration des Wild Reindeer Pavilion auf dem Hjerkinn zur Beobachtung wilder Rentiere, Moschusochsen, Polarfüchse und einer Reihe endemischer botanischer Spezies im norwegischen Dovre-fjell-Massiv von 2011 (Abb. 1). Dabei wird zudem deutlich, wie Snøhetta auch in Anlehnung an Handwerkstraditionen mit neuesten digitalen und robotergesteuerten Technologien arbeiten. Das als dominantes Artefakt im Innenraum nahezu die Breite und Höhe der quaderförmigen Pavillonbox einnehmende hölzerne Sitzobjekt ist mittels 3D-Technologien kontinuierlich geschwungen geformt und wirkt wie ein Teil von bewegter bzw. durch die Bewegung natürlicher Kräfte geformter Landschaft (Abb. 2). Es akzentuiert den schlüssellosen Schutzraum und lädt ein zum längeren Aufenthalt. Über eine vollständig verglaste Seite der Cortenstahlbox werden vom Inneren aus sowohl differenzierte Beobachtungen wie auch Panoramablicke in das nä-here und weitere Umfeld ermöglicht. Durch die Materialität und organische Morphologie im Innenraum wetteifert die architektonische Gestaltung in gewisser Weise mit der landschaftlichen Umgebung und fügt sich zugleich

the architectural design vies to an extent with the surrounding landscape while at the same time integrating with it to only minimally disturb the natural habitat.[36] Of a more complex nature, there are often comparable dialogical connections of the architectural work with the surroundings repeatedly in larger projects by Snøhetta. In this type of relation between architecture, nature and place, they adhere to a basic approach referred to as a specifically Norwegian tradition of modernity, as presented in the theories and projects of Sverre Fehn and Christian Norberg-Schulz.[37]

Snøhetta's goal of enabling a plural openness to appropriation, and to stimulate it through changing perceptions, emphasised repeatedly in interviews and presentations, can be illuminated by the example of the intervention in Times Square. A dense, confused and unsafe traffic area was transformed into a public space for leisure and encounter. Through the dynamic structures of the ground paving of concrete with varying surface materials and round, nickelled and light-reflecting inlays, as well as with elongated, dynamically formed granite seating benches, a larger area was restructured into a place with sojourn quality.[38] New perceptions of the area and the city, as well as new appropriation possibilities, were thereby opened. They try to integrate in all their projects, if possible, comparable qualities of the new formation of experience layers and of shaping public space.

In connection with the concept of landscape-ness as architectural idea, it is also to be highlighted that Snøhetta link thinking about beauty in architecture with architectural means, such as proportions, materials, movement of light on the building structure or in the space, and connections of ideas with morphologies of the buildings and spaces that shape perception.[39] They also see an additional value, with which architecture can reinterpret or emulate nature, in the attention to the various possibilities for people to localise in architecture, the possible positions and relations of the body to something physically created, as well as the movement of people in the spatial ensemble.[40] For the architects, this means thinking from the beginning of the design process about what experiences are potentially associated with the design decisions and how these are sequenced in the sense of paths or travel routes, such as in landscapes, which are physically or metaphorically imagined and can be experienced.[41]

auch in sie ein, um das natürliche Habitat nur minimal zu stören.[36] In komplexerer Ausbildung finden sich vergleichbare dialogische Verknüpfungen von Architekturwerk mit der Umgebung wiederholt auch in größeren Projekten von Snøhetta wieder. In dieser Form des Bezugs von Architektur, Natur und Ort referenzieren sie eine als spezifisch norwegische Tradition der Moderne bezeichnete Grundhaltung, wie sie insbesondere in den Theorien und Projekten von Sverre Fehn und Christian Norberg-Schulz dargeboten wurde.[37]

Das in Interviews und Vorträgen von den Architekten ebenfalls wiederholt hervorgehobene Ziel, plurale Aneignungsoffenheit zu ermöglichen und diese über einen Wahrnehmungswechsel zu stimulieren, kann am Beispiel der Intervention am Times Square in New York vorgestellt werden. Hier wurde ein dichter, konfuser und unsicherer Verkehrsraum zum öffentlichen Aufenthalts- und Begegnungsraum transformiert. Durch die dynamischen Strukturen der Bodenpflasterung aus Beton mit verschiedener Oberflächenmaterialität und runden, vernickelten und lichtreflektierenden Inlays sowie mit lang gestreckten dynamisch geformten Granitsitzbänken wurde ein größeres Areal zur Platzfläche mit Begegnungs- und Aufenthaltsqualität umgestaltet.[38] Neue Wahrnehmungen des Ortes und der Stadt sowie neue Aneignungsmöglichkeiten wurden damit eröffnet. Vergleichbare Qualitäten der Neubildung von Erfahrungslayern und der öffentlichen Raumbildung versuchen sie, wenn möglich, in allen Projekten zu integrieren.

Im Zusammenhang des Konzepts von Landschaftlichkeit als Architekturidee ist zudem besonders hervorzuheben, dass Snøhetta das Denken von Schönheit in der Architektur mit architektonischen Mitteln in Verbindung bringen wie Proportionen, Materialien, Bewegung von Licht auf dem Baukörper oder im Raum sowie mit Verknüpfungen von Ideen mit Morphologien der Baukörper und Räume, die Wahrnehmung gestalten.[39] In der Aufmerksamkeit für die Vielfalt von Möglichkeiten zur Verortung des Menschen in der Architektur, den möglichen Positionen und Relationen des Körpers zu etwas physisch Kreiertem sowie der Bewegung der Menschen im räumlichen Gefüge sehen sie zudem einen zusätzlichen Wert, mit dem Architektur Landschaften neu interpretieren sowie der Natur ähneln kann.[40] Für die Architekturschaffenden bedeutet das im Entwurfsprozess von Beginn an, daran zu denken, welche Erfahrungen mit den gestalterischen Entscheidungen potenziell verbunden werden und wie diese aufeinanderfolgen im Sinne von Wegen oder Reiserouten wie in Landschaften, die physisch oder metaphorisch imaginiert und erfahren werden können.[41]

3   Norwegian National Opera & Ballet Oslo 2008 West façade, entrance and inclined public space

IN MOTION: OSLO OPERA   In 2000, the city of Oslo developed an idea to repurpose the embankment and port areas of Oslo, which had been freed up by deindustrialisation and economic change, for housing, commerce, leisure and culture. The plans included housing and workspace, an opera house, library, museums and parks as well as public spaces designed to link the city and the fjord.[42] With the opera house, which expresses many facets of Snøhetta's central concepts, the urban transformation was given an exceptional landmark. While the architectural volume of the building situated right by the water reflects an industrial character to the east – with workshops and rehearsal rooms, that evoke the character of the former industrial port area where the building is now situated – the complex has a dynamic and light public image to the west and south (fig. 3).[43] This happens in a way that can also be described as a typological transformation of the opera house. A roof surface spanning the foyer and the auditoria, rising with a dynamic incline, creates the effect of a continuity between the surrounding landscape and the architecture. It is also designed as a walkable, ramp-like area. Where the modest entrance is placed, there are also seamless transitions between outdoor and indoor space, external ground and flooring. The design articulation, according to the architects, has a topographical effect that creates its own identity (fig. 4–5).[44] It also has a topological and programmatic character. The fifth façade, homogeneously clad with white Carrara marble rising right by the embankment area, was created by Snøhetta together with the artists Jorunn Sannes, Kristian Blystad and Gralle Krude. Ordered as a relief area composed of a series of panels running oblique to each other and appearing lightly layered, their arrangement creates both a balanced

254

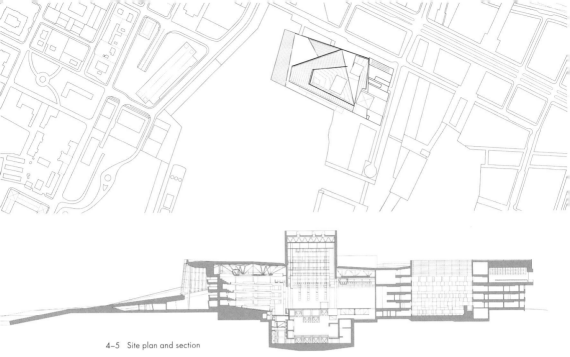

4–5 Site plan and section

IN BEWEGUNG: OPER OSLO   Die im Jahr 2000 entwickelte Idee
der Stadt Oslo, die nach Deindustrialisierung und ökonomischem Umbruch
frei gewordenen Ufer- und Hafengebiete für Wohnen, Wirtschaft, Erholung
und Kultur umzunutzen, schloss neben der Planung von Wohnungen und Arbeitsplätzen den Bau eines Opernhauses, einer Bibliothek, von Museen sowie
Parks und öffentlichen Räumen ein, welche Stadt und Fjord miteinander verbinden sollten.[42] Mit dem Opernhaus, das die Grundkonzeption des Architekturbüros Snøhetta in vielen Facetten zum Ausdruck bringt, erhielt die städtische
Transformation ein hervorragendes Wahrzeichen. Während das architektonische Volumen des direkt am Wasser gelegenen Gebäudes nach Osten hin
mit Werkstätten und Proberäumen einen industriellen Charakter reflektiert,
der auch an den Charakter des ehemaligen Industriehafenbereichs erinnert,
in dem das Gebäude nun lokalisiert ist, zeigt der Komplex zum Westen und
Süden hin ein dynamisches und hell leuchtendes öffentliches Image (Abb. 3).[43]
Dies geschieht in einer Weise, die auch als typologische Transformation des
Opernhauses beschrieben werden kann. Eine das Foyer und die Auditorien
übergreifende Dachfläche, die mit einer dynamischen Schräge ansteigt, erzeugt die Wirkung einer Kontinuität zwischen umgebender Landschaft und
Architektur. Sie ist gleichzeitig als begehbare rampenartige Platzfläche ausgebildet. Dort, wo der zurückhaltende Eingang platziert ist, gehen zudem
Außenraum und Innenraum, Außenfläche und Fußboden schwellenlos ineinander über. Die gestalterische Artikulation hat, so die Architekten, eine topografische Wirkung, die eine eigene Identität erzeugt (Abb. 4–5).[44] Und sie
ist topologisch und programmatisch geprägt. Die mit weißem Carrara-Mar-
mor homogen verkleidete, unmittelbar vom Uferbereich ansteigende fünfte
Fassade wurde von Snøhetta zusammen mit den Künstlern Jorunn Sannes,

255

6–7   The fifth façade as an inclined walkable public area suggests movement and leisure activities

and complex geometric structure.[45] This construction, which also integrates glazed compartments for lighting, is conceived as a public space and is fully accessible (fig. 6–7). Movement and exploration are explicitly stimulated through the varied design of the rising level, from which individual building compartments such as the stage tower protrude, thereby allowing a variety of possible experiences of the architecture and the urban surroundings. The basic concept of the architectural office of closely linking architecture and landscape suggests to associate the building form with a glacier rising out of the water or a coastal landscape (fig. 8).[46] However, the design gesture was bound up with the intention of giving visitors the possibility of their own experiences and creating an impulse for a variety of associations.[47] This idea of openness also applies to the appropriation that includes strolling, promenading and enjoying views, as well as sports activities such as tai chi, skating or jogging, or picnics and simply watching the world go by. As a public auditorium, the area is also used for staging by the opera and ballet, and for open-air events. This allows the opera experience to be extended from an elitist tendency to a pluralistic, open cultural event.[48] The foyer, generously transparent towards the southern waterfront and continuously accessible to both the public and the city, also contributes to this. It allows a commerce-free, pleasant stay even without an interest in opera, comparable to a public square. It is formed as a high and elongated space, and as a threshold and access area towards

256

8   Rising from the coast and the water, the opera house evokes images of a glacier or coastal landscapes

Kristian Blystad und Gralle Krude kreiert. Als Relieffläche aus einer Reihe schräg zueinander verlaufender, leicht geschichtet wirkender Plattenformen gegliedert, entwickelt deren Anordnung eine zugleich ausgeglichene wie komplexe geometrische Struktur.[45] Diese Konstruktion, die zudem verglaste Kompartimente zur Belichtung integriert, ist als öffentlicher Raum konzipiert und vollständig begehbar (Abb. 6–7). Bewegung und Erkundung werden durch die Vielgestaltigkeit der ansteigenden Ebene, aus der auch einzelne Baukörperkompartimente wie der Bühnenturm herausragen, nachdrücklich stimuliert – und damit unterschiedliche Erfahrungsmöglichkeiten der Architektur und des städtischen Umraums. Die Grundkonzeption des Architekturbüros, Architektur und Landschaft eng zu verbinden, legt die Assoziation nahe, die Baukörperfomulierung im Sinne eines sich aus dem Wasser erhebenden Gletschers oder einer Küstenlandschaft zu interpretieren (Abb. 8).[46] Die entwerferische Geste aber war mit der Intention verknüpft, den Besuchenden die Möglichkeit zu eigenen Erfahrungen zu eröffnen und einen Impuls für unterschiedlichste Assoziationen zu kreieren.[47] Die Idee der Offenheit betrifft auch die Aneignung, die hier Flanieren, Promenieren und Ausblicke erleben ebenso einschließt wie die sportlichen Betätigungen in Form von Tai-Chi, Skaten oder Joggen beispielsweise oder Picknicken und Zuschauen. Als öffentliches Auditorium wird die Platzfläche zudem von Oper und Ballett für die Übertragung von Inszenierungen oder für Open-Air-Events eingesetzt. So kann sich die Opernerfahrung von einer elitären Färbung zum pluralistisch offenen Kulturereignis erweitern.[48] Dazu trägt auch das durchgängig der Öffentlichkeit zugängliche, zur Stadt ebenso wie zur südlichen Wasserseite hin großzügig transparente Foyer bei. Es ermöglicht einen kommerzfreien, wohltemperierten Aufenthalt auch ohne Operninteresse,

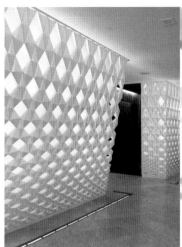

9 The publicly accessible foyer is a commerce-free indoor space for all. Installation on   10   Installation by Olafur Eliasson

the auditoria, spanning the whole height of layered wooden lamellas with a wavy shape (fig. 9). Opposite this is a space and light installation by the artist Olafur Eliasson, made of curved wall elements with a honey-combed and filigreed structure towards the cloakroom and refreshment areas (fig. 10). An open spatial atmosphere with an inviting design and an exceptional quality were thereby created here. The resulting aesthetic and programmatic-ethical quality can also be found condensed in the external appearance and effect, which looks light and bright. It also varies surpris-ingly over the course of the day and seasons, as well as in different weath-er conditions. This 'quiet' motion is reinforced further by the changing uses and free access to the water, which also shows performatively changing and various effects and allows a range of experiences.[49]

The transformation of the opera house typology created here can also be interpreted as prototypical: The basic building blocks of the walkable roof and the generous foyer as public spaces – which Snøhetta imple-mented variously in the architecture of the opera houses of Busan, North Korea, and Shanghai, China, as well as the links between outdoor and indoor spaces, particularly the varying atmospheric experience qualities of the building associated with light modulations and the changing times of day and seasons – deviate from the conventionally introverted opera house architecture (fig. 11). Landscape-ness as architectural idea is asso-ciated with morphological components that evoke geotectonics, with an expressive outward appearance through materiality and light, as well as

with overarching suggestions of movement and public sojourn qualities.

11 The appearance changes with the course of the day, with an accessible and open expression

einem öffentlichen Platz vergleichbar (Abb. 9). Es ist als hoher und lang gestreckter Raum ausgebildet und mit einem die gesamte Höhe übergreifenden, aus geschichteten Holzlamellen wellenartig geformten Schwellen- und Erschließungsraum zu den Auditorien hin ausgestattet. Diesem gegenüber ist eine Raum- und Lichtinstallation des Künstlers Olafur Eliasson situiert aus leicht gebogenen, durch Waben filigran strukturierten Wandelementen zu den Garderoben- und Erfrischungsbereichen hin (Abb. 10). So wurde hier eine offen und einladend gestaltete Raumatmosphäre von außergewöhnlicher Qualität geschaffen. Die entstandene ästhetische und programmatisch-ethische Qualität findet sich ebenfalls verdichtet in der Erscheinung und Wirkung des Äußeren, das hell und leicht erscheint und sich mit dem Lauf der Tages- und Jahreszeiten sowie den Wetterbedingungen trotz homogener Wirkkräfte auch überraschend vielgestaltig zeigt. Diese ‚ruhige' Bewegtheit wird noch verstärkt durch die sich verändernden Nutzungen und den freien Wasserzugang, der ebenfalls performativ sich wandelnde, unterschiedliche Wirkungen zeigt und verschiedenste Erfahrungen ermöglicht.[49]

Die hier erzeugte Transformation der Opernhaustypologie kann als prototypisch interpretiert werden: Die Grundbausteine des betretbaren Daches und des großzügigen Foyers als öffentliche Räume, die Snøhetta in der Architektur der Opernhäuser von Busan, Nord Korea, und Schanghai, China, variierte, ebenso wie die Verknüpfungen von Außen- und Innenräumlichkeit sowie insbesondere die mit Lichtmodulationen verbundenen und sich im Wechsel von Tages- und Jahreszeiten verändernden atmosphärischen Erfahrungsqualitäten des Gebäudes verändern die konventionell introvertierte Opernhausarchitektur (Abb. 11). Landschaftlichkeit als Architekturidee wird dabei verbunden mit morphologischen Komponenten, die an Geotektonik erinnern, mit einer nachdrücklichen Gestaltung der Erscheinung durch Materialität und Licht sowie mit übergreifenden Bewegungssuggestionen und öffentlichen Aufenthaltsqualitäten. 259

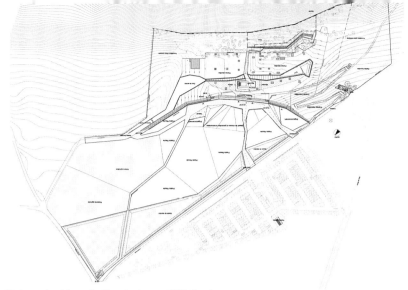

12 International Centre for Cave Art Lascaux 2016 Site plan

ATMOSPHERE PARCOURS: INTERNATIONAL CENTRE FOR CAVE ART LASCAUX At the International Centre for Cave Art in the Dordogne department in France, it is also various levels of conceptualisation and design that are associated with landscape-ness as an architecture idea. In the little village of Montignac, the office Snøhetta was given the task of creating a facsimile production and of designing a cultural institution to present the 20,000-year-old cave paintings of Lascaux to the public as a cultural asset. The caves discovered by children in 1940 are among the first testimonies to human artistic and cultural activity.[50] The 1,900 paintings and scratched drawings representing aurochses, bulls, horses and stags in various movement studies, in black, red, brown and yellow ochre tones, are considered an important example of the art of the Old Stone Age. For conservation reasons, they have not been accessible since 1963. In 1987, replicas of some parts of the cave system were created for visiting. Around the year 2000, further reproductions were created for an international touring exhibition. The International Centre for Cave Art (Centre International de l'Art Pariétal) designed by Snøhetta was opened in situ in 2016 (fig. 12–13).[51] Analyses of geomorphological, topological and historical aspects of the location, as well as of the cultural assets belonging to the UNESCO World Heritage List, were developed with the Parisian office Duncan Lewis Scape Architecture. In the later realisation and scenography, they worked with the French contact office SRA Architectes, Paris, and the London exhibition specialists from Casson Mann. The facsimile of the cave paintings was also created with a team of archaeologists and artists using a method in which the basic forms were scanned with the latest 3D technologies and cast; the paintings were then applied by hand with the same pigments as the original representations. The acoustic and interior climate conditions were also reproduced.[52] The artefacts therefore have a layer of authenticity in the context of experience, though not in the objects themselves.

13　View onto the museum complex and the village of Montignac

ATMOSPHÄRENPARCOURS: ZENTRUM FÜR HÖHLEN-KUNST LASCAUX

Beim Höhlenkunst-Zentrum im französischen Département Dordogne sind es ebenfalls verschiedene Ebenen der Konzeptualisierung und Gestaltung, die mit Landschaftlichkeit als Architekturidee verbunden sind. Im kleinen Dorf Montignac erhielt das Büro Snøhetta den Auftrag, eine Faksimile-Produktion zu kreieren und eine Kulturinstitution zu entwerfen, mit der die vor ca. 20.000 Jahren entstandenen Höhlenmalereien von Lascaux als Kulturgut für die breite Öffentlichkeit vermittelt werden können. Die 1940 auf einer Wanderung von Kindern entdeckten Höhlen zählen zu den ersten Zeugnissen menschlicher malerischer Kulturtätigkeit.[50] Mit 1900 Malereien und Ritzzeichnungen, die in Schwarz-, Rot-, Braun- sowie gelben Ockertönen Auerochsen, Bullen, Pferde und Hirsche in unterschiedlichen Bewegungsstudien darstellen, gelten sie als wichtigstes Beispiel der Kunst der Altsteinzeit. Aus konservatorischen Gründen waren sie nur bis 1963 zugänglich. 1987 entstanden vor Ort Nachbildungen einiger Teile des Höhlensystems zur Besichtigung sowie um 2000 weitere Reproduktionen für eine internationale Wanderausstellung. Das von Snøhetta entworfene Internationale Zentrum für Höhlenkunst (Centre International de l'Art Pariétal) in situ wurde 2016 eröffnet (Abb. 12–13).[51] Analysen zu geomorphologischen, topologischen und historischen Aspekten des Standorts sowie des zum UNESCO-Weltkulturerbe zählenden Kulturguts entwickelten sie mit dem Pariser Büro Duncan Lewis Scape Architecture. In der späteren Ausführung und Szenografie arbeiteten sie mit dem französischen Kontaktbüro SRA Architectes, Paris, und den Londoner Ausstellungsspezialist:innen

14　The landscaping and architecture form an integrated design, merging with the surrounding landscape

The architectural version of this cave facsimile, as well as the didactic annex and the infrastructure of the centre, are formed by a horizontally elongated, folded building volume partly integrated into the earth (fig. 14). Its building structure can be described as landscape-like architecture. In the hollow of a border area between a broad expanse of agricultural land in the Vézère Valley and hilly, densely forested territory with limestone rocks, it is incised like a linear, slightly jagged cut corresponding with the geomorphological properties of the topography, as a deep crack. This topological formation is surrounded by a landscape architecture design of the wider surroundings, which also includes the roof area as a ramp of flat steps, as a viewing plateau and as part of the spatial access route to the caves. The architecture is thus entangled with the landscape in many ways. The building almost appears as part of the existing landscape and the new outdoor space design complements this fluidly. The layered materiality of exposed concrete and glass surfaces, which form a continuous transparent strip on the front side and a subtle entrance situation, mark the contemporary constructional conception (fig. 15). The structure of the landscape architecture design, also by Snøhetta, extends up to the village in a large area with water basins and planted areas, with grasses and flowering plants in an angular formation (fig. 16).

The most important element of forging the architectural experience is an atmospherically sequenced route guidance. It leads from the foyer via a lift to the roof promenade with a view (fig. 17) and then down through a narrow passage along a stone wall to the tighter cave complex and through the various painted cave spaces in semi-darkness (fig. 18–20). Along this discovery route, the visitors then reach exhibition rooms, where the history

15–16   A ramp of flat steps leads to the roof area with a view on the landscape design

von Casson Mann zusammen. Das Faksimile der Höhlenmalereien wurde zudem mit einem Team von Archäolog:innen und Künstler:innen in einer Weise geschaffen, bei der die Grundformen mit neuesten 3D-Technologien gescannt und gegossen erzeugt und die Malereien dann von Hand mit gleichen Pigmenten wie die der ursprünglichen Darstellungen aufgetragen wurden. Zudem wurden auch die akustischen und raumklimatischen Bedingungen nachgebildet.[52] Damit verfügen die Artefakte über einen Layer von Authentizität im Kontext der Erfahrung, wenn auch nicht im Objektbestand.

Die architektonische Fassung dieses Höhlenfaksimiles sowie der didaktischen Annexe und der Infrastruktur des Zentrums wird von einem horizontal erstreckten, in Teilen in die Erde integrierten, gefalteten Baukörper gebildet (Abb. 14). Seine bauliche Struktur kann als landschaftliche Architektur beschrieben werden. In die Senke eines Grenzbereichs zwischen weitflächigem Agrarland des Vézère-Tals und bergigem, dichtem Waldgebiet mit Kalksteinfelsen ist diese wie ein linearer, leicht gezackter, mit den geomorphologischen Eigenschaften der Topografie korrespondierender Schnitt als tiefe Spalte eingefügt. Diese topologische Formation wird umgeben von einer landschaftsarchitektonischen Gestaltung des weiteren Umfelds, die auch den Dachbereich als Rampe aus flachen Stufen, als Aussichtsplateau und als Teil des räumlichen Erschließungsparcours zu den Höhlen einschließt. So ist die Architektur mehrfach mit der Landschaft verschränkt. Das Gebäude erscheint nahezu als Teil der bestehenden Landschaft und die neue Freiraumgestaltung ergänzt dies fließend. Die geschichtet gestaltete Materialität aus Sichtbeton und Glasflächen, die ein durchgehend transparentes Band an der Vorderseite und eine zurückhaltende Eingangssituation ausbilden, markieren die zeitgenössische bauliche Konzeption (Abb. 15). Die Struktur des landschaftsarchitektonischen Entwurfs, ebenfalls von Snøhetta, erstreckt sich bis zum Dorf hin auf einer großen Fläche mit Wasserbecken und ebenfalls in eckiger Formation gehaltenen Pflanzarealen aus Gräsern und Blütenpflanzen (Abb. 16).

17　Wide panoramic views of the surrounding landscape open up the tour

and the construction of the facsimile are shown, as well as presentations of examples of modern and contemporary art with artistic articulations of the experience of palaeolithic paintings and graphics. A particular architectural emphasis is given to an elongated interspace, which as an atrium is formed like a gorge with steeply slanted high walls. It was designed using varying natural and artificial light modulations (fig. 21–22). Here it is especially the zenithal incidence of light from above, together with the use of materials, that create a relatively evenly illuminated and calm interior atmosphere. The materiality of the walls appears layered due to the alternation of smooth, wider wall surfaces and narrower, horizontal strips with a rough texture. It can evoke associations with the layers of the adjacent and underground rocks. This reinforces the landscape character of the spatial choreography even further. Apart from the relative darkness in the caves and the natural horizontal incidence of light in the façade area, it is the light entering from above in varying situations that leads in particular to intense changes in atmosphere.

The interweaving of physical and conceptual-interpretative spatial formations transforms the tension between a prehistoric cultural asset ensemble, site and new architecture into a discovery route in which the various conditions can be experienced not as contrasts but more as relations; physically and mentally, they are experienced as transitions linking time and space through the spatial and material-related, as well as through atmospheric interpretation. The topological and atmospheric design open up the possibility of multifaceted experiences, which can be similar to perceptions of nature and landscape.[53]

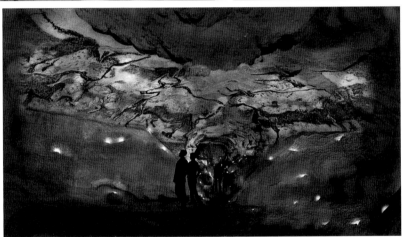

18–20 A narrow passage leads to the cave facsimiles

Wichtigstes Element der architektonischen Erfahrungsgestaltung bildet eine atmosphärisch sequenzierte Wegeführung, die vom Foyer über einen Aufzug zunächst auf die Dachpromenade mit Aussicht (Abb. 17) und dann im Abstieg über einen schmalen Wegraum entlang einer Steinmauer in das engere Höhlengefüge führt und durch die verschiedenen der im Halbdunkel gehaltenen bemalten Höhlenräume (Abb. 18–20). Auf dieser Erkundungsroute gelangen die Besuchenden danach zu Ausstellungsräumen, in denen die Geschichte und die Konstruktion der Faksimiles aufgezeigt sowie 265

21–22 The atrium design evokes associations to natural landscapes.

Beispiele moderner und zeitgenössischer Kunst mit künstlerischen Artikulationen der Erfahrung paläolithischer Malerei und Grafik präsentiert werden. Eine architektonisch hervorgehobene Bedeutung kommt einem lang gestreckten Zwischenraum zu, der als Atrium wie eine Schlucht mit steil gekippten hohen Wänden gebildet ist und durch unterschiedliche Natur- und Kunstlichtmodulationen gestaltet wurde (Abb. 21–22). Hier bewirkt insbesondere der zenitale Oberlichteinfall zusammen mit der Materialbehandlung eine relativ gleichmäßig erhellte und ruhige Raumatmosphäre. Die Materialität der Wände wirkt durch den Wechsel von glatten, breiteren Wandflächen und schmaleren horizontalen Streifen mit rauer Textur, als sei sie geschichtet. Damit können Assoziationen zu den Gesteinsschichtungen der benachbarten und unterirdischen Felsen evoziert werden. Damit wird der landschaftliche Charakter der räumlichen Choreografie noch verstärkt. Neben der relativen Dunkelheit in den Höhlen und dem natürlichen horizontalen Lichteinfall im Fassadenbereich ist es das in verschiedenen Situationen von oben eintretende Licht, das insbesondere zu intensiven Veränderungen von Atmosphären beiträgt.

Das Verweben physischer und konzeptuell-interpretativer Raumformationen verwandelt die Spannung zwischen prähistorischem Kulturgutensemble, Ort und neuer Architektur in eine Entdeckungsroute, in der die verschiedenen Zustände durch die räumliche und materialbezogene sowie atmosphärische Interpretation, nicht als Gegensätze, vielmehr als Relationen präsentiert und physisch und mental als Übergänge und Verknüpfungen von Zeit und Raum erfahrbar werden. Durch die topologische und atmosphärische Gestaltung werden dabei facettenreiche Erfahrungsmöglichkeiten geöffnet, die Natur- bzw. Landschaftswahrnehmungen ähnlich sein können.[53]

REPERTOIRE   The designs by Snøhetta are based on multilayered analyses, which prioritise place-related and programmatic dimensions. They show complex shifts and mixes of layers of the location and the function-related conditions. At the same time, these are conceptually abstracted in the designs and made architecturally into creative syntheses. The spatial concepts that shape perceptions are often densified with flowing transitions between the surroundings and the building structure, as well as between inside and outside, to form an ambience of architectural landscape-ness.[54] There is a specific development of horizontality of the spatial structures and transitions, as well as of choreographies with intensive changes in the sequential spatial articulation. These incorporate in many ways the so-called fifth façade of the roof as a platform, movement level, place of encounter and viewpoint, which is ramp-like in itself or is accessed by means of ramps. The coming together of a variety of tactile materiality with transparency and a natural incidence of light through different types of light openings creates modulated and also changing atmospheres. Together with the sequential spatial configurations, the design elements and strategies physically and metaphorically create a wide field of possibilities for landscape experiences and imaginations, in subtle creative syntheses. The orchestrated sequence of open and closed spaces, as well as the setting of the scene through consciously designed effects of light and shadow, along with the material appearance, are accorded particular attention in current discourses on architecture and atmosphere, as well as in the garden and architecture theories of the 18th century.[55] Like in these contexts, for Snøhetta it is spatial compositions that have been conceived and interpreted with regard to human experience. Through the spatial, cultural and temporal effects, various gradations of sensory experience can be generated. Not least, this also harbours the possibility of strengthening anthropological-geographical relational spheres.[56]

REPERTOIRE   Die Entwürfe von Snøhetta gründen in vielschichtigen Analysen, die ortsbezogene und programmatische Dimensionen priorisieren. Sie zeigen komplexe Verschiebungen und Mischungen von Layern des Standorts und der funktionsbezogenen Bedingungen. Gleichzeitig werden diese in den Entwürfen konzeptuell abstrahiert und architektonisch zu kreativen Synthesen geführt. Die Wahrnehmungen gestaltenden Raumkonzepte werden mit oftmals fließenden Übergängen von Umfeld und baulicher Struktur sowie von Innen und Außen zu einem Ambiente architektonischer Landschaftlichkeit verdichtet.[54] Spezifisch ist die Ausbildung von Horizontalität der Raumstrukturen und Übergängen, aber auch von Choreografien mit intensiven Wechseln in der sequenziellen Raumartikulation. Diese schließen vielfach auch die sogenannte fünfte Fassade des Daches ein als Plattform, Bewegungsebene, Begegnungsort und Aussichtspunkt, die in sich rampenartig ausgebildet oder durch Rampen erschlossen wird. Das Zusammentreffen unterschiedlicher taktiler Materialität mit Transparenz und natürlichem Lichteinfall über verschiedenartige Lichtöffnungen bewirkt modulierte und auch sich wandelnde Atmosphären. Zusammen mit den sequenziellen Raumkonfigurationen erzeugen die Entwurfselemente und -strategien in subtilen kreativen Synthesen physisch und metaphorisch ein breites Möglichkeitsfeld für landschaftliche Erfahrungen und Imaginationen. Der orchestrierten Abfolge von offenen und geschlossenen Räumen sowie der Inszenierung durch bewusst gestaltete Licht- und Schattenwirkung und der materialen Erscheinung wird sowohl in den aktuellen Diskursen zu Architektur und Atmosphäre als auch in Garten- und Architekturtheorien des 18. Jahrhunderts besondere Aufmerksamkeit geschenkt.[55] Wie in diesen Kontexten sind es bei Snøhetta räumliche Kompositionen, die im Hinblick auf menschliche Erfahrungen konzipiert und interpretiert wurden. Durch die räumlichen, kulturellen und zeitlichen Wirkungen können verschiedene Gradationen sinnlicher Erlebbarkeit hervorgerufen werden. Nicht zuletzt liegt darin auch die Möglichkeit, anthropologisch-geografische Bezugsräume zu stärken.[56]

FLIESSENDE RÄUME
FLOWING SPACES
SANAA

The projects by the Japanese architectural office SANAA enable further differentiations of landscape-ness as architectural idea. In spatial formation and material treatment, they appear as maximally reduced but at the same time evoke a range of sensory and usage-related experiences. They are characterised by complex simplicity and are firmly associated with various ideas of landscape-ness. SANAA was founded in Tokyo in 1995 by Kazuyo Sejima and Ryue Nishizawa, who had previously worked at Sejima's office. Both also work individually outside of the shared office on other projects, especially in the area of housing. Many of their light, glass and white architectures have been commissioned and completed in the last two decades in Europe, America and Australia, based on the radiance of such Japanese projects as the 21st Century Museum of Contemporary Art in Kanazawa or the Koga Park Café in Ibaraki. These include many public buildings such as museums and libraries, as well as social housing.

Die Projekte des japanischen Architekturbüros SANAA ermöglichen weitere Differenzierungen von Landschaft-lichkeit als Architekturidee. In Raumformation und Mate-rialbehandlung erscheinen sie maximal reduziert und evozieren doch gleichzeitig eine Vielfalt an sinnlichen und nutzungsbezogenen Erfahrungen. Sie sind durch komplexe Einfachheit gekennzeichnet und dezidiert mit verschiedenen Ideen von Landschaftlichkeit verbunden. SANAA wurde 1995 von Kazuyo Sejima und Ryue Nishi-zawa, der zuvor im Büro von Sejima gearbeitet hatte, in Tokio gegründet. Beide arbeiten zudem außerhalb des gemeinsamen Büros individuell an Projekten vor allem im Bereich des Wohnungsbaus. Zahlreiche ihrer leichten, gläsernen und hellen Architekturen wurden in den letzten beiden Dekaden ausgehend von der Strahlkraft japani-scher Bauten wie dem Museum für zeitgenössische Kunst in Kanazawa oder dem Koga Parc Café in Ibaraki auch in Europa, Amerika und Australien vollendet und beauftragt. Darunter finden sich viele öffentliche Gebäude wie Museen und Bibliotheken, aber auch soziale Wohnungsbauten.

The basic design concept of SANAA is linked with the notion of creating a type of boundless spatial configuration that can form a neutral background for people and their activities. This is repeatedly associated by Sejima and Nishizawa in presentations and interviews with the characterisation of architecture as landscape. The 'harmonious' interplay of architectural spatiality with the surroundings and nature is of great relevance to them. It is connected to a wide range of explorations of phenomenal properties of continuous spatial formation, lightness, transparency, material texture and lighting concepts. In addition, anticipations of appropriation, of experience and of human encounter form constants in the design processes of these architects. There are also cooperations with landscape architects, correlations of landscape conception and constructional-spatial interpretation in designs and in the physical presence of architectural projects and outdoor spaces that can reveal overlaps and transitions of architecture and landscape architecture in various ways.

CONCEPT   In the theory and practice of Kazuyo Sejima and Ryue Nishizawa, landscape forms the central orientation as a level of perception, as a public space and as a multimodal phenomenon that can be experienced by movement through the space. In presentations and interviews, they repeatedly emphasise that their projects seek to express contemporary experiential qualities of continuums and transitions, as they occur, particularly in connection with the increasing relevance of information and communication media. On the other hand, Sejima and Nishizawa highlight as a primary goal their aim to design architecture that feels like a park.[57] In these notions – as well as in more specific descriptions by the two of the basic concept that guides and accompanies their thinking and work – one can find references to social options of outdoor space qualities and to phenomenal landscape-ness as architectural ideal.

Die entwerferische Grundkonzeption von SANAA ist mit der Vorstellung verknüpft, eine Art grenzenlose Raumkonfiguration zu schaffen, die einen neutralen Hintergrund für Menschen und ihre Aktivitäten bilden kann. Diese ist von Sejima und Nishizawa in Vorträgen und Interviews wiederholt mit der Charakterisierung von Architektur als Landschaft assoziiert. Das ‚harmonische' Zusammenspiel von architektonischer Räumlichkeit mit der Umgebung und der Natur ist für sie von großer Relevanz und mit verschiedensten Erkundungen der phänomenalen Eigenschaften von kontinuierlicher Raumformation, von Leichtigkeit, Transparenz sowie Materialtextur und Lichtführung verbunden. Da zudem Antizipationen der Aneignung, des Erlebens und der menschlichen Begegnung Konstanten in den Entwurfsprozessen dieser Architekturschaffenden bilden sowie Kooperationen mit Landschaftsarchitekten und Landschaftsarchitektinnen zu finden sind, können Wechselwirkungen von Landschaftskonzeption und baulich-räumlicher Interpretation in Entwürfen und in der physischen Präsenz architektonischer Projekte und Freiräume beschrieben werden, die Schnittstellen und Übergänge von Architektur und Landschaftsarchitektur in unterschiedlicher Weise erkennen lassen.

KONZEPT   In der Theorie und Praxis von Kazuyo Sejima und Ryue Nishizawa bildet Landschaft als Wahrnehmungsebene, als multimodal durch die Bewegung in Raum und Zeit zu erlebendes Phänomen sowie als öffentlicher Raum die zentrale Orientierung. In Vorträgen und Interviews betonen sie wiederholt, mit ihren Projekten einen Ausdruck für zeitgenössische Erfahrungsqualitäten von Kontinuen und Übergängen zu suchen, wie sie insbesondere im Zusammenhang mit der zunehmenden Relevanz von Informations- und Kommunikationsmedien auftreten. Andererseits heben sie als primäres Ziel hervor, Architektur entwerfen zu wollen, die wie ein Park sein und wirken soll.[57] In diesen Vorstellungen sowie in spezifischeren Beschreibungen der beiden zur Grundkonzeption, die ihr Denken und Schaffen leitet und begleitet, lassen sich Bezüge zu sozialen Optionen von Freiraumqualitäten sowie zu phänomenaler Landschaftlichkeit als Architekturideal finden.

1 Architecture Biennale Venice 2010 Exhibition design at the Corderie halls

For Kazuyo Sejima, the main emphasis is on programmatic flexibility and diversity, as can be found in particular in municipal parks, in the open encounter of a variety of people and in their different individual and collective activities.[58] The metaphor of the park represents the opening of possibilities through specific properties of the outdoor space design and configurations of public space. The architects repeatedly describe their intention of creating spaces and enabling situations with the architecture in which different people can move freely and meet each other.[59] The Architecture Biennale in Venice in 2010 curated by Kazuyo Sejima with the title 'People meet in architecture' was also conceived with a focus on this aim.[60] Especially in the self-understanding of Ryue Nishizawa, the ideal of landscape is concentrated on features of phenomenal park and nature experience. It is associated more specifically by him with soft formations and natural light qualities, with lightness and with continuities and similarities between inside and outside. The architectural concept should exceed the scale of a building to create a larger landscape-like world and environment (fig. 1).[61] In this aim, one can recognise an architectural ideal that is associated with various levels of experience of landscape-ness and of mimetic ambitions.

When Valerio Olgiati asked the two architects to send up to ten important images that could convey the essence of their approach to their architectural designs for an installation at the Architecture Biennale in Venice in 2012, they exclusively sent photographs of anonymous landscape sceneries on various scales; for example, a close-up shot of a vortex, a view of a wild meadow or a panorama. Of these, some can be recognised as Japanese

Für Kazuyo Sejima liegt dabei das Hauptgewicht auf der programmatischen Flexibilität und Vielfalt, wie sie insbesondere in städtischen Parks zu finden seien, in der offenen Begegnung verschiedener Menschen und in ihren unterschiedlichen individuellen und kollektiven Aktivitäten.[58] Die Metapher des Parks steht für die Öffnung von Möglichkeiten durch spezifische Eigenschaften der Freiraumgestaltung und Konfigurationen des öffentlichen Raums. Wiederholt beschrieben die Architekten ihre Intention, mit der Architektur Räume zu schaffen und Situationen zu ermöglichen, in denen unterschiedliche Menschen sich frei bewegen und begegnen können.[59] Die von Kazuyo Sejima 2010 kuratierte Architekturbiennale in Venedig mit dem Titel ,People meet in architecture' war ebenfalls mit dem Fokus dieses Anliegens konzipiert.[60] Vor allem im Selbstverständnis von Ryue Nishizawa ist die Idee von Landschaft konzentriert auf Eigenschaften phänomenaler Park- und Naturerfahrung und wird von ihm spezifischer verbunden mit weichen Formationen und natürlichen Lichtqualitäten, mit Leichtigkeit und mit Kontinuitäten und Ähnlichkeiten von Innen und Außen. Das architektonische Konzept solle dabei den Maßstab eines Bauwerks überschreiten, um eine größere landschaftsähnliche (Um-)Welt zu gestalten und der Wahrnehmung darzubieten (Abb. 1).[61] In diesem Ziel werden ein Architekturideal, das mit verschiedenen Erfahrungsebenen von Landschaftlichkeit verbunden ist, und auch mimetische Ambitionen erkennbar.

Als Valerio Olgiati die beiden Architekturschaffenden gebeten hatte, für eine Installation auf der Architekturbiennale in Venedig 2012 bis zu zehn wichtige Bilder zu schicken, die als Fundament ihrer Architekturentwürfe verstanden werden können im Sinne einer Essenz ihrer Haltung, sandten beide jeweils ausschließlich Fotografien anonymer landschaftlicher Szenerien in verschiedenen Maßstäben, als Nahaufnahme eines Wasserstrudels beispielsweise, als Blick auf eine wilde Wiese oder als Panorama. Von diesen sind einige durch geografische Charakteristik und Zusammenhänge, beispielsweise zu einem kleineren Gebäude in japanischer Bautradition oder im Kontext von Inselgruppen, als japanische Landschaften erkennbar.[62]

landscapes through geographical characteristics and references, such as a smaller building in a Japanese building tradition or in the context of groups of islands.[62] It seems as though the rather unspectacular simplicity of the natural integration into an environment, characterised especially by natural contexts, is the key contributing component in their work. The specific architectural design levels of individual project concepts are aimed at repeatedly expressing the aspects associated with the described notions of park and landscape, in the sense of approaching this ideal. The generation of continuities and interactions between the architecture and surroundings, between architecture and outdoor space and between people and the environment are prominent recurring themes in their work.

In the Asian cultural circle, there are notions of space and place that not only include space, place, area, emptiness, cultural context and social encounter, but also a fundamental connection to nature, to which the people themselves belong. These concepts of space and place, articulated among others in the character 'MA' and its sphere of meaning, include time and movement, especially in the sense of overlapping 'flowing' perception content and experiential qualities.[63] Flowing space as an architectural idea became a frequently repeated topos in Western-international modernity, in connection with new building materials and construction methods.[64] The stated architecture stances develop in relation to these notional fields. For the architects, it is no contradiction to relate landscape-ness equally to natural phenomena, to situational notions of space based on individual and in-
tersubjective actions, and to changeable virtual spaces of digital culture.[65]

Es scheint, als sei das eher Unspektakuläre und Schlichte der selbstverständlichen Eingebundenheit in eine vor allem durch naturnahe Kontexte geprägten Umwelt die im Schaffen dieser Architekten grundlegend mitschwingende Komponente. Die spezifischen architektonischen Gestaltungsebenen einzelner Projektkonzeptionen sind darauf gerichtet, den mit den beschriebenen Vorstellungen von Park und Landschaft verbundenen Aspekten immer wieder Ausdruck zu verleihen im Sinne von Annäherungen an dieses Ideal. Wiederkehrend wird dabei die Erzeugung von Kontinuitäten und Korrespondenzen von Architektur und Umgebung, Architektur und Freiraum, Mensch und Umwelt zu einem herausragenden Thema.

Im asiatischen Kulturkreis treten Raum- und Ortsbegriffe hervor, die nicht nur Raum, Ort, Platz, Gegend, Leere, kulturellen Kontext und soziale Begegnung einschließen, sondern eine grundlegende Verbindung zur Natur, der auch die Menschen selbst angehören. Diese unter anderem in dem Schriftzeichen ‚MA' und seinen Bedeutungsfeldern artikulierten Auffassungen von Raum und Ort schließen Zeit und Bewegung ein, vor allem im Sinne ineinander übergehender ‚fließender' Wahrnehmungsinhalte und Erfahrungsqualitäten.[63] Fließender Raum als Architekturideal wurde insbesondere in Verbindung mit neuen Baustoffen und Konstruktionsweisen in der westlich-internationalen Moderne zu einem oft wiederholten Topos.[64] Im Zusammenhang dieser Vorstellungsbereiche entwickeln sich die genannten Architekturpositionen. Für die Architekturschaffenden ist es dabei kein Widerspruch, Landschaftlichkeit gleichermaßen auf Naturphänomene, auf situative Raumvorstellungen aus individuellem und intersubjektivem Agieren und auf veränderliche virtuelle Räume der digitalen Kultur zu beziehen.[65]

2 Rolex Learning Center Lausanne 2009

CONTINUUMS: ROLEX LEARNING CENTER LAUSANNE

The building of the École Polytechnique Fédérale de Lausanne (EPFL), completed in 2009 near Lake Geneva in Switzerland, is a significant example of the attempt to architecturally articulate corresponding qualities in the interior with alternating open spaces and enclosed spatial ensembles, as well as with locational references. Beyond visual perception, a multimodal perception of movement is especially motivated.[66] The EPFL wanted a campus centre for their disparate institutes, which were physically, contentually and socially separate from each other, on a college site with existing building stock from the 1960s and 1970s. It would be a public and identity-forging place of learning, communication and encounter, combining a library with various additional areas for a learning laboratory, an auditorium, a cafeteria, a restaurant, a bookshop, a job centre and a bank.[67] The concept was to combine the properties of an innovative representation building with a wide range of usages, further integrating the qualities of a public space. The reply by the architects can be characterised as a calm and modest interpretation that offers landscape-ness as a potential experience in an unusual manner.

The design integrated these programmatic objectives into a unique, undulating spatial form (fig. 2–3). When approaching the building, it appears as a flat, one-storey rectangular volume partly detached from the terrain, formed by means of partly curved floor and ceiling slabs made of exposed concrete, whose formation is described by Sejima and Nishizawa as hills, mountains, geography and landscape.[68] Almost full glazing of the external walls and atria in a circular shape reinforce the impression of a specific

3 The volume partially detaches from the ground, creating outdoor spaces

KONTINUEN: ROLEX LEARNING CENTER LAUSANNE

Das 2009 vollendete, unweit des Genfer Sees gelegene Gebäude der École Polytechnique Fédérale de Lausanne in der Schweiz kann als signifikantes Beispiel für einen Versuch gesehen werden, entsprechende Qualitäten im Innenraum, mit einem Wechsel von Freiräumen und umschlossenen Raumgefügen sowie im Ortsbezug architektonisch zu artikulieren. Dabei wird über die visuelle Wahrnehmung hinaus die multimodale Bewegungswahrnehmung in besonderer Weise motiviert.[66] Die EPFL wünschte ein Campuszentrum für ihre verstreuten, physisch, inhaltlich und sozial voneinander getrennten Institute eines Hochschulgeländes mit einem Bestand aus den 1960er und 1970er Jahren, einen öffentlichen und identitätsstiftenden Lern-, Kommunikations- und Begegnungsort, in der Verbindung mit einer Bibliothek mit verschiedenen zusätzlichen Bereichen für ein Lernlabor, ein Auditorium, eine Cafeteria, ein Restaurant, einen Buchladen, ein Jobcenter und eine Bank.[67] Damit waren Eigenschaften eines innovativen Repräsentationsbaus mit einem vielfältigen Nutzungsangebot zu konzipieren, der ebenfalls Qualitäten eines öffentlichen Raumes integriert. Die Antwort der Architekten kann als eine ruhige zurückhaltende Interpretation charakterisiert werden, die in einer ungewohnten Weise Landschaftlichkeit als Erfahrungspotenzial darbietet.

Der Entwurf integrierte diese programmatischen Ziele in eine einzige ondulierende Raumgestalt (Abb. 2–3). Bei der Annäherung zeigt sich das Gebäude als flach gelagerter und teilweise vom Terrain gelöster eingeschossiger Rechteckkörper, gebildet mit teilweise geschwungenen Boden- und Deckenplatten aus Sichtbeton, deren Formation von Sejima und Nishizawa

4 The undulating volume stimulates movement through the building

mobility, through the variously opened visual axes and connections between interior areas, building volumes and the surrounding, as well as
between near and far and through overlapping and layering (fig. 4).

Apart from the visual aspect, physical movement is motivated by architectural gestures; for example, in the design of the entrance. Within a green
area on the site, a terracotta-coloured ground surface forms a type of platform for the learning centre.[69] This, as well as informally distributed seating
furniture and white plant pots with bushes, mark an area that at the same
time remains publicly accessible from all sides (fig. 5–6). It stimulates a
movement impulse to walk through the ensemble of modulated building volume and open space formations, which spread out with its dynamic design.
Through darker areas under the organically undulating, mighty fortified
steel floor slabs and through smaller, lighter atria, you reach a larger interior courtyard comparable to a clearing. The central building entrance is
situated here, leading to a foyer area in which one can find various service
usages, as well as an abstract architecture model that facilities orientation,
instead of using a site map to indicate individual areas. The interior structure has no subdivisions through solid walls. It is formed instead by gently
and irregularly rising and falling floor formations, to which the shape of
the ceiling corresponds. This generates a continuous linking of various
spaces. A stepped auditorium, closed glazed workspaces, pedestals with
workplaces and other functions are arranged in various areas (fig. 7–8).

5–6 The public areas invite people to linger and move across the terracotta coloured terrain

als Hügel, Berge, Geografie und Landschaft beschrieben werden.[68] Eine nahezu vollständige Verglasung der Außenwände und kreisähnlich geformte Lichthöfe verstärken durch die unterschiedlich eröffneten Blickachsen und Verbindungen von inneren Bereichen, Baukörper und Umgebungsraum, von Nähe und Ferne und Überlagerung die Anmutung einer spezifischen Beweglichkeit (Abb. 4).

Neben dem visuellen Aspekt wird die körperliche Bewegung durch architektonische Gesten motiviert, beispielsweise in der Gestaltung des Zutritts. Innerhalb einer Grünfläche auf dem Gelände des Standorts bildet ein terrakottafarbiger Bodenbelag eine Art Plattform für das Lernzentrum.[69] Durch diese und mittels informell verteilten Sitzmobiliars sowie weißen Pflanzkübeln mit Buschwerk wird ein Areal markiert, das gleichzeitig von allen Seiten öffentlich zugänglich bleibt (Abb. 5–6). Es wird ein Bewegungsimpuls angeregt, durch das sich in seiner dynamischen Gestaltung ausbreitende Ensemble aus modulierten Baukörper- und Freiraumbildungen hindurchzugehen. Über dunklere Bereiche unter den organisch aufschwingenden mächtigen stahlbewehrten Bodenplatten und über kleinere hellere Lichthöfe wird ein größerer, einer Lichtung vergleichbarer Innenhof erreicht. Hier befindet sich der zentrale Gebäudeeingang, der zu einem Foyerbereich führt, in dem verschiedene der Servicenutzungen zu finden sind sowie ein abstraktes Architekturmodell, das anstatt eines Lageplans die Orientierung erleichtert und einzelne Areale ausweist.

7–8   Sequences of interior spaces motivate both movement and lingering

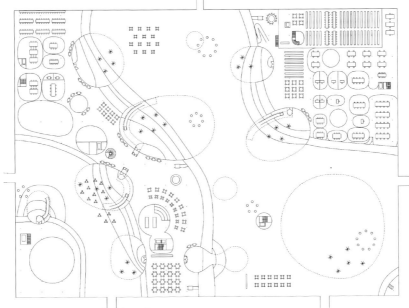

9 Ground floor plan Inside and outside

Die Innenraumstruktur besitzt keine Unterteilungen durch massive Wände, ist vielmehr aus sich sanft und unregelmäßig hebenden und senkenden Bodenformationen gebildet, zu denen die Deckenführung korrespondiert. So wird eine kontinuierliche Verknüpfung verschiedener Raumbereiche erzeugt. Ein abgestuftes Auditorium, geschlossene gläserne Arbeitsräume, Podeste mit Arbeitsplätzen und andere Funktionen sind in verschiedenen Arealen angeordnet (Abb. 7–8). Die scheinbar überall offenen Raumfolgen motivieren nicht nur zu vom Gebrauch gelösten Bewegungen durch das Gebäude, sondern in verschiedenen Bereichen auch zur flexiblen Verortung durch Aneignung und zum Aufenthalt. Darin finden sich rekreative Potenziale wie in einem städtischen Park oder in einer nicht zerstörten und nicht bedrohlichen, mit positiven Eigenschaften verbundenen Landschaft (Abb. 9).

Überall gibt es einen großzügigen Tageslichteinfall und damit eine Modulation der Lichtqualitäten, die vorwiegend durch die Tages- und Jahreszeiten sowie Wetterbedingungen geprägt wird. Die Wahrnehmung des Kontinuierlichen wird durch die Sparsamkeit gestalterischer Details und eine relativ homogene und helle Farbpalette unterstützt. Sie wird vorrangig durch weiße Decken, Wände, Einbauten und Mobiliar sowie helle und teilweise reflektierende Grautöne und transparente Materialien gebildet. Das Ensemble erinnert damit an Landschaften, die weniger von Unterbrechungen und Vielgestaltigkeit des Terrains und der Vegetation und mehr durch eine gewisse Homogenität geprägt sind wie begrünte Berghänge oder Landschaften unter Schnee. Das Blindenleitsystem ist ebenfalls in leichten Schwingungen integriert, und die in Zickzack geführten Rampen für mobilitätseingeschränkte Menschen mit Eckrundungen sind geschwungenen Bergpfaden vergleichbar.

The sequences of spaces that seem to be open everywhere not only motivate movement through the building independently of purpose, but in various areas also flexible localisation through appropriation and lingering. This harbours recreational potential, like in a municipal park or in an undestroyed and unthreatening landscape associated with positive qualities (fig. 9).

There is a generous incidence of daylight everywhere and therefore a modulation of light qualities, determined primarily by the times of day and the seasons, as well as by weather conditions. The perception of a continuity is enhanced by the sparing of design details and a relatively homogeneous and light colour palette. It is composed primarily of white ceilings, walls, installations and furniture, as well as light and partly reflecting grey tones and transparent materials. The ensemble thus evokes landscapes that are characterised less by interruptions and diversity of the terrain and the vegetation and more by a certain homogeneity, like green mountain slopes or landscapes under snow. The orientation system for the blind is also integrated with gentle undulations, while the zigzagging ramps with rounded corners for persons with reduced mobility are comparable to curving mountain paths.

This description mode using landscape metaphors implies a characterisation of architecture as an architecturally designed mimesis, which, despite the alienating abstraction, is based on the evocation of memories of already experienced, comparable landscape qualities; for example, landscapes of hills and dunes. In combination with one's own physical movement up and down or with where one pauses, the impressions change in slight variations, and with the views out. The alternation of patios and interior space, the undulating building and space formation, and the range of possible views out into the distance form the basis of the potential to perceive landscape experiences through visual and multimodal movement within the spatial constellations (fig. 10). In various contexts – from the perspective of the clients, the users, the involved architects and engineers, as well as the ensuing architecture theory and criticism – this structural ensemble prompted comparable reactions: It is repeatedly described and referred to as a landscape and as an internal landscape.[70] The analogies can also be experienced as location-specific. In the wider surroundings, one can make out specific hilly landscapes in various directions, the Jura Mountains, the vineyards of the Lavaux region and the mineral hills in front of Lake Geneva. The constructed topologies of the interior spaces – alternating with the smaller, more intimate and the larger, more public outdoor spaces of the patios – show analogies to these surroundings. Changes in position and localisation also change the perception of the space and the correspondences between inside and outside, as well as the experience of a variety of connections and of slightly varying, calm atmospheres.

10   The views through the undulating building and patios open onto the wider surrounding landscape

Dieser Beschreibungsmodus mit Landschaftsmetaphern impliziert eine Charakterisierung der Architektur im Sinne einer architektonisch gestalteten Mimese, die, trotz der verfremdenden Abstraktion, in der Evokation von Erinnerungen an bereits erfahrene vergleichbare landschaftliche Qualitäten, an Hügel- und Dünenlandschaften beispielsweise, begründet liegt. In Verbindung mit der eigenen körperlichen Bewegung hinauf und hinab oder des Aufenthalts verändern sich die Eindrücke und auch die Ausblicke in leichter Variation. Der Wechsel von Patios und Innenraum, die ondulierende Baukörper- und Raumformation sowie die vielfältig möglichen Ausblicke in die Weite begründen das Potenzial, über die visuelle und die multimodale körperliche Bewegung in den räumlichen Konstellationen einem Landschaftserlebnis nachzuspüren (Abb. 10). In verschiedenen Kontexten, aus der Perspektive der Auftraggeber, der Nutzenden wie auch der beteiligten Architekt:innen und Ingenieur:innen sowie der nachfolgenden Architekturtheorie und -kritik, rief dieses bauliche Ensemble vergleichbare Wirkungen hervor: Es wird immer wieder als Landschaft und als innere Landschaft beschrieben und bezeichnet.[70] Die Analogien können ebenfalls ortsspezifisch erfahren werden. In der weiteren Umgebung sind in verschiedenen Richtungen konkrete hügelige Landschaften zu erkennen, die Alpenkette des Jura, die Weinberge der Region Lavaux und die Mineralienhügel vor dem Genfer See. Die konstruierten Topologien der Innenräume im Wechsel mit den kleineren, intimeren und größeren, öffentlicheren Freiräumen der Patios zeigen Analogien zu diesen Umgebungen. Die Wechsel in der Position und Verortung verändern auch die Wahrnehmung des Raumes und der Korrespondenzen von Innenraum und Außenraum sowie die Erfahrung einer vielfältigen Verknüpfung und leicht variierender, ruhiger Atmosphären. 285

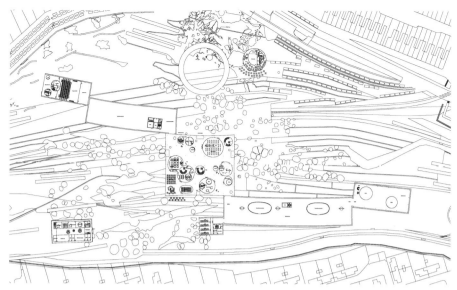

11   Louvre Lens Lens 2012 Site plan

CORRESPONDENCES: LOUVRE LENS   The example of the Louvre dependance, opened in 2012 in Lens in northern France with the intention of transforming the former coal mining region through tourism, can be used to outline a further aspect. The building that appears modest in the context, as well as the associated park, are situated on the renaturated site of a former coal mining plant, closed in 1960, on a slightly elevated and very elongated 62-hectare plateau of slag, surrounded by heterogeneous developments with little brick houses and green areas of lawns and mature trees.[71] The aim of the Japanese team of architects – which had co-operated since the competition in 2005 with the French landscape architect Catherine Mosbach and the museum expert Tim Culbert from New York – was to offer the capacity of a new public space through an open house for both visitors to and inhabitants of the city, and furthermore to articulate an effect in which architecture and the landscape architectural design of the surroundings blend.[72]

A row of five slightly offset low exhibition halls determine the formation of the building and the spatial organisation of simple geometric forms (fig. 11). The low cubes that are glazed or encased in brushed aluminium appear almost weightless in their degree of fineness and geometric precision, especially through the uniformity of the surface, which reflects in gentle nuances the colour of the sky, the outdoor space design and the wider surroundings. Thus, like comparable to a mimesis, they are only subtly distinct from the surroundings (fig. 12).

In the interior, the spatial ensembles meet in a centrally situated, large, almost square entrance hall with a light ceiling supported by very slender round struts and with a polished concrete floor (fig. 13). In this large central space,

12 Building volumes and outside landscaping

KORRESPONDENZEN: LOUVRE LENS   Das Beispiel der 2012 eröffneten Louvre Dependance im nordfranzösischen Lens, mit dem der Wandel der ehemaligen Steinkohlebergbauregion durch Tourismus befördert werden soll, kann noch eine weitere Ebene skizzenhaft verdeutlichen. Das im Kontext zurückhaltend wirkende Gebäude sowie der in diesem Zusammenhang entstandene Park befinden sich auf der renaturierten Fläche einer bereits 1960 geschlossenen Kohleabbaustätte über einem leicht erhöhten und sehr lang gestreckten, 62 Hektar großen Plateau aus Abraumschüttungen, umgeben von inhomogener Bebauung mit kleinen Backsteinhäusern und von Grünräumen aus Baumbeständen und Wiesen.[71] Ziel des japanischen Architektenteams, das seit dem Wettbewerb 2005 mit der französischen Landschaftsarchitektin Catherine Mosbach und dem Museumsexperten Tim Culbert aus New York zusammenarbeitete, war es, die Kapazität eines neuen öffentlichen Raums anzubieten durch ein offenes Haus für die Besucher, aber auch für die Bewohner der Stadt, sowie eine Wirkungstendenz zu artikulieren, bei der sich Architektur und landschaftsarchitektonisch gestaltete Umgebung vermischen.[72]

Fünf leicht versetzt aneinandergereihte niedrige Ausstellungshallen bestimmen die Baukörperbildung und Raumorganisation aus einfachen geometrischen Formen (Abb. 11). Die verglasten oder in gebürstetem Aluminium gefassten niedrigen Kuben wirken in ihrem Feinheitsgrad und ihrer geometrischen Präzision nahezu gewichtslos, insbesondere durch die Einheitlichkeit der Oberfläche, welche in leichten Nuancen die Farbigkeit des Himmels, der Freiraumgestaltung und der weiteren Umgebung reflektiert und sich so, einer Mimese vergleichbar, nur zurückhaltend von der Umgebung unterscheidet (Abb. 12).

13   The interior area with lounge, information and other functions are publicly accessible

which can be accessed and crossed from several directions from the city, several not touching, transparent, round volumes were placed as a space within a space, similar to an urban composition. Their uses as a library, shop, lounge, information centre and cafeteria are public and independent of the museum. The glass framing of these spatial situations displays changing reflections, layered with blurred images of the interior and of the surrounding foyer space like in a multiple exposure. This effect is enhanced further if several of the glass rotunda are in one's line of vision one after another (fig. 14).

The exhibition centre of the complex is formed by a large windowless gallery space, in which different artistic works are exhibited freely on pedestals and partition walls, along a timeline from 3500 BC to the 19th century, with subtle graphic markings along one of the two longitudinal walls (fig. 15). The works of art can thus be experienced in relation to each other, highlighting characteristics they have in common. The effect of this is enhanced by a daylight ceiling. The space is shaped in its effect through its enormous length, the light modulation of the floor adapted to the morphology of the terrain and especially by the homogeneous, diffusely reflecting surface quality of the slightly curved side walls made of anodised aluminium, in which one can make out a blurry image of oneself, the art and the other visitors. It creates the impression of being enveloped by the space and while also evoking an analogy to the qualities of the external building and the natural surroundings and atmospheres, characterised by the times of day and the seasons. Individual and collective courses of movement through the space are wide-ranging, as are sequences of movement into the other partly transparent and partly enclosed exhibition areas; as well as the basement that houses more rooms and workshops.

14–15   Reflections, glass walls and lighting create various atmospheres

Im Innern treffen die Raumgefüge in einer mittig angeordneten großen, fast quadratischen Eingangshalle mit leichter von sehr schlanken Rundstützen getragener Decke und poliertem Betonfußboden zusammen (Abb. 13). In diesem großen zentralen Raum, der aus mehreren Richtungen von der Stadt her betreten und durchquert werden kann, wurden mehrere einander nicht berührende transparente runde Körper ähnlich einer stadträumlichen Komposition als Raum im Raum eingestellt. Ihre Nutzungen als Bibliothek, Shop, Lounge, Information und Cafeteria sind öffentlich und können auch ohne Bezug zum musealen Zusammenhang erfolgen. Die gläserne Rahmung dieser Raumsituationen zeigt changierende Reflexionen überlagert mit den unscharfen Bildern des Innern bzw. des umgebenden Foyerraumes wie in einer Mehrfachbelichtung, verstärkt noch, wenn mehrere der gläsernen Rotunden hintereinander im Blickfeld sind (Abb. 14).

Das Ausstellungszentrum des Komplexes bildet ein großer fensterloser Galerieraum, in dem entlang einer Zeitlinie von 3500 v. Chr. bis zum 19. Jahrhundert, die in zurückhaltender grafischer Markierung an einer der beiden Längswände zu finden ist, unterschiedliche künstlerische Werke frei im Raum auf Podesten und Stellwänden ausgestellt werden (Abb. 15). Die Kunstwerke können so in Relation zueinander erfahren werden, beispielsweise auch mit der Aufmerksamkeit auf Eigenschaften, die sie gemeinsam haben. Mit einer Tageslichtdecke wird dieser Raum in seiner Wirkung durch seine enorme Länge, die leichte Modulation des der Geländemorphologie angepassten Bodens und insbesondere durch die homogene, diffus reflektierende Oberflächenqualität der leicht gebogenen seitlichen Wände aus anodisiertem Aluminium geprägt, in denen man unscharf sich selbst, die Kunst und die anderen Besuchenden wahrnehmen kann. Es entsteht der Eindruck einer Umhüllung durch den Raum, und gleichzeitig wird eine Analogie zu den Qualitäten des Außenbaus und der durch die

Apart from the central pavilion, the respective flanks are also transparent glass pavilions and thereby open up a view of the landscape architecture design and the wider surroundings in various directions (fig. 16). The landscape design by Catherine Mosbach corresponds in its longitudinal elongation to the configuration of the museum ensemble. Like many outdoor space designs that work with vegetation, the expressive quality will still vary in future. It can be perceived as a synthesis of different paths, ground modulations and a plant world that is still in the process of growing. Large, relatively linear path formations and smaller, slightly meandering paths connect the adjacent areas of the city with the building and with each other.

The arrangement and layering of the ground materials is a special feature. It consists of the existing materials such as coal slag, old tracks, areas of grass and light concrete, which spreads from a flat formation starting from the centre of the building ensemble to the east and west, like flowing material in dissolving circular formations across the terrain. Criss-crossed in part by rings of moss and areas of lawn, and enriched by low hillocks overgrown with grass and arranged individually or in groups, the building's terrain, which slopes down at the edge towards the city districts and is considered a special place. The existing trees and bushes at the edges were incorporated and supplemented by planting many trees, bushes and shrubs already present on the site, along with historical plants, some of which grow closely along the building and are reflected in the building shell, as are the lighting conditions and the wider surroundings (fig. 17–18). The layering in the handling of material of the outdoor space design can potentially be seen as a layering of different times in an analogy to the exhibition concept, referencing the past and the latest transformation of the site in accordance with the intention of the landscape design concept.[73]

In the perception of the specific spatial articulation that initiates real and virtual movement, which can be found in the interior as well as outdoors, impressions vary in gentle nuances through the kinaesthetic activity of the physical movement of people. The relatively hierarchy-free linking of the various spaces motivates not only movement through the smooth transitions and sequence of spaces that are seemingly open everywhere, but also flexible localisation that can evoke landscape experiences in both spatial designs. The significance accorded to scales and their perceptibility can also have a corresponding effect – from details, links and sequences to the conceptual incorporation of a temporal dimension. It is the shared design intentions, as well as the attention given to the design of potential spaces for the multivalent topological and atmospheric perception of this newly designed place, that intensify the ideas and effects of landscape-ness here.

16   The pavilion's glass façades open onto their surrounding landscape design by Catherine Mosbach

Tages- und Jahreszeiten geprägten natürlichen Umgebung und Atmosphären evoziert. Individuelle und kollektive Bewegungsparcours durch den Raum sind vielfältig möglich wie auch Bewegungsabläufe in die anderen teils transparent, teils geschlossen gehaltenen Ausstellungsbereiche und in das weitere Räume und Werkstätten beherbergende Untergeschoss.

Neben dem zentralen Pavillon sind auch die jeweiligen Flanken als transparente Glaspavillons ausgeführt und öffnen so in verschiedene Richtungen den Blick auf die landschaftsarchitektonische Gestaltung und die weitere Umgebung (Abb. 16). Die Landschaftsgestaltung von Catherine Mosbach korrespondiert in der longitudinalen Erstreckung mit der Konfiguration des Museumsensembles. Wie bei vielen Freiraumgestaltungen, die mit Vegetation arbeiten, wird sich die Ausdruckqualität zukünftig noch modifizieren. Sie kann als Synthese aus unterschiedlichen Wegen, Bodenmodulationen und sich noch im Wachstum befindlicher Pflanzenwelt wahrgenommen werden. Große, relativ lineare Wegeformationen und kleinere, leicht geschlängelte Wege verbinden die angrenzenden Stadtteile mit dem Gebäude und untereinander. Als Besonderheit zeigt sich die Anordnung und Schichtung der Bodenmaterialien: bestehend aus dem Materialbestand aus Kohleabraum, alten Schienenführungen, Rasenflächen und aus hellem Beton, der sich von einer flächigen Ausformung vom Zentrum des baulichen Ensembles ausgehend nach Osten und Westen hin wie fließendes Material in kreisförmigen Formationen auflösend über das Gelände ausbreitet. Zum Teil von Moosringen und Rasenflächen durchzogen und durch grasbewachsene niedrige Hügel bereichert, die einzeln oder in Gruppen angeordnet sind, wird das am Rand zu den Stadtteilen abfallende Gelände mit dem Gebäude als besonderer Ort ausgezeichnet.

17 Impressions of both building and landscaping vary with the movement

18   The façades open generously towards the surroundings while also mirroring them

Der in den Randbereichen ebenfalls vorhandene Baum- und Buschbestand wurde einbezogen und ergänzt durch viele Baum-, Busch- und Strauchpflanzungen aus bereits am Ort vorhandenen und historischen Pflanzen, von denen auch einige nahe am Gebäude entlang wachsen und wie die Lichtverhältnisse und die weitere Umgebung in der Gebäudehülle reflektiert werden (Abb. 17–18). Potenziell kann die Überlagerung in der Materialbehandlung der Freiraumgestaltung als Zeitschichtung in Analogie zum Ausstellungskonzept erkannt werden, und auf die Vergangenheit und die jüngste Transformation des Standorts verweisen, wie es Intention in dem landschaftsgestalterischen Konzept war.[73]

In der Wahrnehmung der spezifischen reale und virtuelle Beweglichkeit initiierenden Raumartikulation, die sich im Innern ebenso findet wie im Außenraum, verändern sich in der kinästhetischen Aktivität der körperlichen Bewegung der Menschen die Eindrücke in leichten Nuancen. Die relativ hierarchielose Verbindung der verschiedenen Raumbereiche motivieren nicht nur Bewegungen durch die scheinbar überall offenen Raumfolgen und die weichen Übergänge, sondern auch die flexible Verortung, die in den Raumgestaltungen an Landschaftserfahrungen erinnern kann. Als korrespondierend kann ebenfalls die Bedeutung wirken, die den Maßstäben und ihrer Wahrnehmbarkeit gegeben wird, vom Detail, über Verknüpfungen und Sequenzen bis hin zum konzeptuellen Einbezug einer zeitlichen Dimension. Es sind die geteilten Entwurfsintentionen und die Aufmerksamkeit, die dabei der Gestaltung von Möglichkeitsräumen für die multivalente topologische und atmosphärische Wahrnehmung dieses neu gestalteten Ortes geschenkt wird, die hier die Ideen und Wirkungen von Landschaftlichkeit intensivieren.

REPERTOIRE   Based on the postulation of wanting to design and create park-like structures and landscapes, Kazuyo Sejima and Ryue Nishizawa orientate their understanding of architecture and their design concepts strongly towards perception qualities of architectural spaces as well as their overlapping with the perception of the environment. Associated with the intention of offering public space that can be at the same time an individual place and a shared collective space, this is translated into topologically merging spatial formations. They often appear as continuums that are characterised by lightness, transparency and light materials. This results in light and space modulations with a low contrast, as well as changing effects of diffuse natural light that illuminates spaces in a way that is hierarchy-free but constantly varies in an interplay with the outdoor space. Atmosphere is also generated by the reflecting properties of various types of glass in mirroring, layered, translucent and shading variants. This evokes the gradations of light conditions described by the Japanese author Jun'ichiro Tanizaki in his 1933 book 'In Praise of Shadows', as a reply to Western-orientated modernisation as opposed to own ideal values of Japanese culture, based on the example of the transformative properties of shades of light and shadow.[74] This also calls to mind perceptions of virtual realities with the blurring of boundaries and fluid transitions. And at the same time, the projects incorporate various relations to local cultures and properties of the location and the region, through formations such as the floor slabs and free spatial structuring, or through visual axes and atmospheric effects. The translation takes place through abstraction and simplification in the structural spatiality, as well as through complex compositions of possible experiential reality. By contributing to the balance of oppositions between architecture and landscape, the ideas and design approaches that were associated with these projects also stimulate the development of an environmental aesthetic.

Begründet auf dem Postulat, parkähnliche Strukturen und Landschaft entwerfen und gestalten zu wollen, orientieren Kazuyo Sejima und Ryue Nishizawa ihr Architekturverständnis und ihre Entwurfskonzeptionen sehr stark auf Wahrnehmungsqualitäten von architektonischen Räumen und deren Überlagerung mit der Wahrnehmung von Umwelt. Mit der Intention verbunden, öffentlichen Raum anzubieten, der zugleich individueller Ort und geteilter kollektiver Raum sein kann, wird dies übersetzt in topologisch ineinander übergehende Raumformationen. Oft erscheinen sie als Kontinuen, die geprägt sind durch Leichtigkeit, Transparenz und helle Materialität. So entstehen kontrastarme Licht-Raum-Modulationen sowie changierende Wirkungen diffusen natürlichen Lichts, das Räume hierarchiefrei belichtet und im Wechselspiel mit dem Außenraum doch konstant variiert. Atmosphären generierend wirken ebenfalls reflektierende Eigenschaften verschiedener Glasarten in spiegelnden, geschichteten, transluzenten und schattierenden Varianten. Dies erinnert an die Abstufungen von Lichtverhältnissen, wie sie der japanische Schriftsteller Jun'ichiro Tanizaki 1933 in seinem Buch ‚Lob des Schattens' als Resonanz auf westlich orientierte Modernisierung zu eigenen idealen Werten japanischer Kultur am Beispiel der transformativen Eigenschaften von Licht- und Schattenabstufungen beschrieb.[74] Dies erinnert auch an Wahrnehmungen virtueller Wirklichkeiten mit der Verschleifung von Grenzen und fließenden Übergängen. Und gleichzeitig sind bei den Projekten verschiedene Relationen zu lokalen Kulturen und Eigenschaften des Standortes und der Region in Formationen beispielsweise der Bodenplatten und freien Raumstrukturierung oder durch Blickführungen und atmosphärische Wirkungen einbezogen. Die Übersetzung erfolgt dabei durch Abstraktion und Vereinfachung in der strukturellen Räumlichkeit sowie durch komplexe Kompositionen möglicher Erfahrungswirklichkeit. Indem sie zur Balance von Oppositionen zwischen Architektur und Landschaft beitragen, wirken die Ideen und gestalterischen Ansätze, die mit diesen Projekten verbunden waren, auch stimulierend für die Entwicklung einer Umweltästhetik.

AUSBLICK
LANDSCHAFTLICHKEIT PHÄNOMENAL
OUTLOOK
PHENOMENAL LANDSCAPE-NESS

Based on the levels of understanding that could be shown by the projects characterised here, the special focus on design and perception-related interpretations of landscape-ness and natural phenomena provides impulse-giving potentials. Understood as a design objective, landscape-ness is based on a synthesis of effect qualities that enable both human localisation in the world and design localisation.[75] Furthermore, the levels of understanding of the phenomenon of 'landscape' are imagined as relative constants in the existential and human experience of the cultural environment and are potentially extended. Landscape as a relatively universal asset can be associated with this alongside a connection to the wide-ranging appropriation potential of public spaces, which additionally plays an important role in the approaches by SANAA and Snøhetta. The dynamics of the architectural spatial formation and movement evocation contribute to this. The associated focussing of the multisensory physical and sensual experience of architectural ensembles – the physically present encounter between architecture and people, as well as between people and their cultures in architecture – forms special accents of the articulation. The conscious, intentional aesthetic design is also to be understood as a form of sustainability. This is based on a deliberate attention that essentially accompanies design beyond mere subjective reflexes or logical development and planning. Design is then perceived and practiced as an autonomous and fundamental task. This includes the reinterpretation and modification of shaping structural-spatial high-quality design developed over long periods.

Ausgehend von den Verständnisebenen, die durch die hier charakterisierten Projekte aufgezeigt werden konnten, bildet die besondere Konzentration auf gestaltungs- und wahrnehmungsbezogene Interpretationen von Landschaftlichkeit und Naturphänomenen impulsgebende Potenziale. Als gestalterisches Ziel verstanden, gründet Landschaftlichkeit auf einer Synthese von Wirkqualitäten, die das menschliche Sich-Verorten in der Welt und auch das entwerferische Sich-Verorten ermöglichen.[75] Zudem werden die Verständnisebenen des Phänomens ‚Landschaft' als relative Konstante in der existenziellen und kulturellen Umwelterfahrung des Menschen imaginiert und potenziell erweitert. Landschaft als universelles Gut kann dabei ebenso assoziiert werden wie eine Verbindung zum vielfältigen Aneignungspotenzial öffentlicher Räume, das in den Ansätzen von SANAA und Snøhetta eine zusätzlich gewichtige Rolle spielt. Dazu trägt in jedem Falle die Dynamik der architektonischen Raumformation und Bewegungsevokation bei. Die damit verbundene Fokussierung der multisensorischen körperlichen und auch sinnhaften Erfahrung architektonischer Gefüge, das meint die physisch präsente Begegnung von Architektur und Mensch sowie der Menschen und ihrer Kulturen in der Architektur, bildet besondere Akzente der Artikulation. Die bewusste, absichtsvolle ästhetische Gestaltung ist dabei auch als eine Form von Nachhaltigkeit zu verstehen. Diese gründet in einer willentlichen Zuwendung und Aufmerksamkeit, die, über bloß subjektive Reflexe oder logische Entwicklung und Planung hinausgehend, Entwerfen essenziell begleitet. Gestaltung wird dann als eigenständige und grundlegende Aufgabe wahrgenommen und praktiziert. Dies schließt die Neuinterpretation und Modifikation über lange Zeiträume entwickelter baulich-räumlicher Gestaltungsqualitäten mit ein.

This is evident specifically in the way in which place references are constituted and articulated in the shaping of design and in a wealth of complex spatial experiences, which are imagined in the design and can be perceived in the realised building. The architecture acts then as a tool for exploring and revealing the presence of the place, whereby more direct topographical aspects, in the sense of formations of the earth's surface and its physical essence, can play a role alongside more far-reaching topological and atmospheric qualities. The attentive design of the interior space is particularly intensified in this. The thinking about sequential spatial structures – whether articulated through contrast, clear transitions or as a flowing continuum – represents to varying degrees a very relevant conceptual and compositional design level that can be directly associated with experiences of landscape. The routes, parcours and sojourn areas – which are either defined through programmatic specifications, topologically or have been freely chosen – are not only articulated in an organised manner and in relation to each other, but are also characterised by modulations of the spatial effects though the designed interplay of geometry, material and natural light. The compositions then present a wide palette of nuances and allow rich sensory-physical and imaginative experiences.

The projects also show how the intensive ways of perceiving and framing of a specific site, of a landscape and the surroundings with concrete and diffuse spatial, temporal and cultural implications, are translated into ways of 'doing' and into individual spatial formations and designs. Not sculptural objectiveness, but rather complex relations of inside and outside in terms of structure and material aesthetics, as well as different degrees of diverseness, overlapping and intensification come to the fore, in the sense of spatial formations and materiality that surround the perceiving person. These are features with which the properties of landscape can be characterised.[76]

Spezifisch zeigt sich dies in der Weise, wie Ortsbezüge konstituiert und gestalterisch artikuliert werden, sowie in einem Reichtum komplexer räumlicher Erfahrungen, die im Entwurf imaginiert sind und im realisierten Bauwerk wahrgenommen werden können. Die Architektur wirkt dann als Instrument, um die Präsenz des Ortes zu erforschen und aufzudecken, wobei direktere topografische Bezüge im Sinne von Formationen der Erdoberfläche und ihres physischen Bestands ebenso eine Rolle spielen können wie weiter ausgreifende topologische und atmosphärische Qualitäten. Die sorgfältige Gestaltung der Innenräumlichkeit wird hierbei besonders intensiviert. Das Denken sequenzieller räumlicher Struktur, ob über Kontraste, deutliche Übergänge oder als fließendes Kontinuum artikuliert, bildet dabei in unterschiedlichen Gradationen eine sehr relevante konzeptionelle und kompositorische Gestaltungsebene, die mit Erfahrungen von Landschaft unmittelbar verbunden werden können. Die Routen, Parcours und Aufenthaltsareale, die teils durch programmatische Vorgaben, teils typologisch bedingt sind oder frei gewählt wurden, werden dabei nicht nur organisiert und in Relationen artikuliert, sondern zudem charakterisiert durch Modulationen der räumlichen Wirkungen durch das gestaltete Wechselspiel von Geometrie, Material und natürlichem Licht. Die Kompositionen halten dann eine breite Palette von Nuancierungen bereit und ermöglichen reichhaltige sinnlich-körperliche und imaginative Erfahrungen.

Die Projekte zeigen zudem, wie die intensiven Weisen der Wahrnehmung und Rahmung eines spezifischen Standorts, einer Landschaft und der Umgebung mit konkreten und diffusen räumlichen, zeitlichen und kulturellen Implikationen sich in die Weisen des Machens und die individuellen Raumformationen und Gestaltungen übersetzen. Nicht skulpturale Objekthaftigkeit, vielmehr strukturell und materialästhetisch komplexe Relationen von Innen und Außen sowie unterschiedliche Grade von ‚zurückhaltender' Mannigfaltigkeit, Überschneidung und Intensivierung treten in den Vordergrund im Sinne von Raumformationen und Materialität, die den wahrnehmenden Menschen umgeben. Dies sind Eigenschaften, mit denen auch die Beschaffenheit von Landschaft charakterisiert werden kann. 299

1 Cf. on this landscape interpretation | Vgl. zu dieser Landschaftsinterpretation Ian Thompsen, Afterword, in: id. (ed.), Rethinking landscape. A critical reader, London et al.: Routledge 2009, s. p. | o. S.   **2** Cf. on this | Vgl. hierzu Joachim Huber, Urbane Topologie. Architektur der randlosen Stadt, Weimar: Bauhaus Universität 2002, 39-41; Gernot Böhme, Architektur und Atmosphäre, München: Wilhelm Fink 2006, 15   **3** Cf. on this and the following | Vgl. hierzu und zum Folgenden Margitta Buchert, Entwerfen für eine Stadt wie Venedig. Wahrnehmung Wirkung Deutung, in: Katrin Schuh/Peter P. Schweger (eds.), Entwerfen für Venedig, Darmstadt: Das Beispiel 2000, 26–39 and | und 146–148, 39   **4** Cf. | Vgl. Christophe Girot, The elegance of topology, in: id./Anette Freytag/Albert Kirchengast/Dunja Richter (eds.), Topology, Berlin: Jovis 2013, 79–112, 95 and | und 112; Christophe Girot, Introduction, in: id./Anette Freytag/Albert Kirchengast/Suzanne Kirzenecky/Dunja Richter (eds.), Topology. A pamphlet, Zürich: GTA 2012, 7–8, 7   **5** Cf. on this | Vgl. hierzu Stefan Günzel, Raum, Topographie, Topologie, in: id. (ed.), Topologie, Bielefeld: Transcript 2007, 13–30, 23–24   **6** Cf. | Vgl. Manuel Gausa, L'architecture est (maintenant) géographie (d'autres ‚natures' urbaines), in: Marie-Ange Brayer/Béatrice Simonot (eds.), Archilab's earth buildings. Radical experiments in land architecture, London: Thames & Hudson 2003, 40–43; Aaron Betsky, Landscrapers. Building with the land, London: Thames & Hudson 2002, 9–13 and | und passim; on complex morphologies cf. | zu komplexen Morphologien vgl. Verena Brehm, Komplexe Morphologie in der zeitgenössischen Architektur, Hannover: TIB 2015, passim   **7** Cf. on this for example | Vgl. hierzu beispielsweise Stan Allen (2011), Landform building, (lecture | Vortrag 1.11.2011), London: Architectural Association, on | auf: https://www.youtube.com/watch?v=F8hVIDhBYtk, 4.3.2022   **8** Cf. in detail | Vgl. hierzu ausführlich David Leatherborow, Topographical stories. Studies in landscape and architecture, Philadelphia, PEN: University of Pennsylvania Press 2004, 248–255 and | und passim   **9** Cf. on this | Vgl. hierzu Mark Wigley, The architecture of atmosphere, in: Daidalos 68(1998) 18–27   **10** Cf. for example | Vgl. beispielsweise Hermann Schmitz, Atmospheric spaces, in: Tonino Griffero/Marco Tedeschini (eds.), Atmosphere and aesthetics. A plural perspective, Cham: Springer 2019, 63–76; Jean-Paul Thibaud, The urban ambiances common ground, in: Lebenswelt 4 (2014)/1, 282–294, 287; Michael Hauskeller, Atmosphären erleben. Philosophische Untersuchungen zur Sinneswahrnehmung, Berlin: Akademieverlag 1995, 33–34   **11** Cf. on the synaesthetic character of atmospheres overall | Vgl. zum synthetischen Charakter von Atmosphären übergreifend Hermann Schmitz, Atmosphären, Freiburg et al.: Karl Alber 2014, 93–94; Gernot Böhme, The aesthetics of atmospheres, Milton Parks et al.: Routledge 2014, 1–8; James Corner, Effect/affect, in: Silvia Benedito, Atmosphere anatomies. On design, weather and sensation, Zürich: Lars Müller 2021, 347–351, 348   **12** Cf. | Vgl. Hermann Schmitz, Atmosphären, Freiburg et al: Karl Alber 2014, 28 and | und 93–94; Gernot Böhme, Atmosphäre. Essays zur neuen Ästhetik, Frankfurt a.M. 1995, 31–33; Jürgen Weidinger, Atmosphären für Gestalter essenziell, in: id. (ed.), Atmosphären entwerfen, Berlin: TU 2014, 9–16, 14   **13** Cf. on this and the following | Vgl. hierzu und zum Folgenden Regine Heß, Emotionen am Werk, Berlin: Gebr. Mann 2013, 16–20; Robin Middleton, Introduction, in: Nicolas Le Camus de Mézières, The genius of architecture, Santa Monica, CA: Getty Center for the History of Art and the Humanities 1992, 16–64, 28–31 and | und 49   **14** Cf. on this | Vgl. hierzu Andreas Denk/Peter Zumthor, Die Freude, den Ort zu spüren, in: Bund Deutscher Architekten (ed.), Großer BDA-Preis. Peter Zumthor, Berlin: BDA 2017, 27–29, 28   **15** Cf. | Vgl. Peter Zumthor, Drei Konzepte. Thermalbad Vals, Kunsthaus Bregenz, ‚Topographie des Terrors' Berlin, Luzern: Edition Architekturgalerie 1997, 11   **16** Cf. | Vgl. Peter Zumthor (2013), Royal Gold Medal 2013 Lecture (lecture | Vortrag 19.2.2013), on | auf: https://vimeo.com/60017470, 24.1.2016   **17** Cf. | Vgl. Peter Zumthor, Architektur denken, 3. ed. Basel et al.: Birkhäuser 2010, 89–92   **18** Cf. | Vgl. ibid., 41   **19** Cf. | Vgl. Peter Zumthor at | bei id./Astrid Rappel, Der Kern meiner Arbeit ist eine ganzheit-

liche Betrachtungsweise, in: Bauwelt (2021)/9, 7–9, 8–9; Peter Zumthor 2010, op. cit. (note | Anm. 17), 71–75   **20** Cf. | Vgl. Peter Zumthors Kapitelüberschrift ‚Vervollständigung von Landschaften', in: Peter Zumthor 2010, op. cit. (note | Anm. 17), 17   **21** Cf. on this | Vgl. hierzu Reinhardt Knodt, Ästhetische Korrespondenzen. Denken im technischen Raum, Stuttgart: Reclam 1994, 50   **22** Cf. | Vgl. Peter Zumthor, Atmosphären, Basel: Birkhäuser 2006, 41–43   **23** Cf. | Vgl. Peter Zumthor, Kunsthaus Bregenz, in: Eduard Köb/Kunsthaus Bregenz (ed.), Peter Zumthor. Kunsthaus Bregenz. Werkdokumente, Stuttgart: Hatje Cantz 2008, 6–10; for a description and analysis of this example cf. | zur Beschreibung und Analyse dieses Beispiels vgl. Margitta Buchert, Landschaftlichkeit als Architekturidee, in: Wolkenkuckucksheim 21 (2016)/35, 109–128, 114–120   **24** Cf. on reference to place and light guiding | Vgl. zu Ortsbezug und Lichtführung auch Regine Heß, Emotionen am Werk. Peter Zumthor, Daniel Libeskind, Lars Spuybroek und die historische Architekturpsychologie, Berlin: Gebr. Mann 2013, 138–143   **25** Cf. | Vgl. Peter Zumthor, Diözesanmuseum Köln, Wettbewerbsentwurf 1997, in: id., Häuser 1979–1997, Basel: Birkhäuser 1999, 286–287   **26** Cf. | Vgl. Peter Zumthor, in: Thomas Durisch (ed.), Peter Zumthor 1985–2013: Bauten und Projekte, Bd. 1–5. Zürich: Scheidegger & Spieß 2014, Bd. 2, 166–167; Wolfgang Pehnt, Diözesanmuseum Kolumba in Köln. Peter Zumthor. Ein Haus für Sinn und Sinne, in: Hochparterre 19 (2007)/9, 48–56, 54–56   **27** Cf. | Vgl. Margitta Buchert, Mobile und Stabile, in: Annett Zinsmeister (ed.), Gestalt der Bewegung, Berlin: Jovis 2011, 50–73; Margitta Buchert, Choreographieren, in: id./Laura Kienbaum (ed.), Einfach entwerfen. Wege der Architekturgestaltung. Berlin: Jovis 2013, 126–153.   **28** Cf. | Vgl. Günther Vogt (2012), City as territory as landscape (lecture | Vortrag 4.10.2012), Cambridge, MA: Harvard University, on | auf: https://www.youtube.com/watch?v=rO3W_OieLrU, 24.1.2015   **29** Cf. on this also | Vgl. hierzu auch Martin Seel, Die Macht des Erscheinens. Texte zur Ästhetik. Frankfurt a. M.: Suhrkamp 2007, 144–147, 144   **30** Cf. on this | Vgl. hierzu Margitta Buchert 2011, op. cit. (note | Anm. 27), 61–71   **31** In academic cultural studies discourses, these two understandings of landscape are repeatedly treated as opposites. Cf. for example | In akademischen kulturwissenschaftlichen Diskursen werden diese beiden Landschaftsverständnisse wiederholt als Gegensätze behandelt. Vgl. beispielsweise Tim Ingold, Against space. Place, movement, knowledge, in: Peter Wynn Kirby (ed.), Boundless worlds. An anthropological approach to movement, Oxford: Berghahn 2009, 29–43, 29   **32** Cf. | Vgl. Gaute Brochmann, in: id./Michelle Delk/Craig Dykers/Jenny B. Osuldsen/Kjetil T. Thorsen, Gray zones and thresholds. Generosity and collective ownership, in: Snøhetta (ed.), Collective intuition, London et al.: Phaidon 2019, 212–217, 215   **33** Cf. on this for example | Vgl. hierzu beispielsweise Snøhetta, in: id. (ed.), Conditions. Architecture, interior, landscape, Baden: Lars Müller 2007, 59–61 and | und 135; Kjetil T. Thorsen, Architectural landscapes, auf: https://channel.louisiana.dk/artists/kjetil-traedal-thorsen, 1.6.2017; Kjetil T. Thorsen, Posttext, in: Conditions. Architecture, interior, landscape, Baden: Lars Müller 2007, 96–98; Kjetil T. Thorsen at | bei id./Fabian Peters, In diesem Sinne sind wir Optimisten (Interview), in: Baumeister B6(2021), on | auf: https://snohetta.baumeister.de/artikel/kjetil-traedal-thorsen-blattmacher, 5.3.2022   **34** Cf. on this | Vgl. hierzu Luis Fernández-Galiano (ed.), Snøhetta. 25 years, 25 works, Madrid: Arquitectura Viva 2014, 74, 86–87, 91 and | und 156–157; Snøhetta, in: id. (ed.), Works. Architecture, interior, landscape, Baden: Lars Müller 2009, 128   **35** Cf. | Vgl. Craig Dykers, Why (do we) bother?, in: Luis Fernández-Galiano (ed.) 2014, op. cit. (note | Anm. 34), 6–9, 9   **36** Cf. on this also | Vgl. hierzu auch Kjetil T. Thorsen at | bei Sabine Drey/id., Critical thinking is a precondition for good architecture, in: Sandra Hofmeister (ed.), Ultimately I search for clarity. Thirteen conversations with architects, München: Detail 2018, 214–241, 216, Craig Dykers at | bei id./Kjetil T. Thorsen/Hans-Ulrich Obrist, Conversation, in: op. cit. (note | Anm. 32), 128–133, 133   **37** Cf. | Vgl Kjetil T. Thorsen at | bei id./Fabian Peters 2021, op. cit. (note | Anm. 33)   **38** Cf. on this also | Vgl. hierzu

auch luis Fernández-Galiano, Times Square reconstruction, in: id. (ed.) 2014, op. cit. (note | Anm. 34), 90–93 **39** Cf. | Vgl Kjetil T. Thorsen at | bei id./Fabian Peters 2021, op. cit. (note | Anm. 33) **40** Cf. | Vgl. Snøhetta, in: id. (ed.) 2019, op. cit. (note | Anm. 36), 9; Craig Dykers/Kjetil T.Thorsen at | bei ids./Mari Lending, TeXt (Interview), in: Snøhetta (ed.), Conditions. Architecture, interior, landscape, Baden: Lars Müller 2007, 59–77, 72; Craig Dykers 2014, op. cit. (note | Anm. 35); Kjetil T. Thorsen, Concept & context, on | auf: https://snohetta.baumeister.de/artikel/context-concept, 4.3.2022 **41** Cf. | Vgl. Snøhetta 2019, op. cit. (note | Anm. 32), 9 **42** Cf. on this also | Vgl. hierzu auch Ulf Meier, Oslo als Fjordstadt, in: Archithese (2021)/4, 51–53 **43** Cf. | Vgl. Snøhetta, Norwegian National Opera and Ballet, in: id. (ed.) 2009, op. cit. (note | Anm. 34), 9–37, 26–28 **44** Cf. | Vgl. Craig Dykers/Kjetil T. Thorsen at | bei ids./Mari Lending 2007, op. cit. (note | Anm. 40), 59–61 **45** Cf. | Vgl. Snøhetta 2009, op. cit. (note | Anm. 43), 32 **46** Cf. on corresponding interpretations as glaciers, ice floes, etc. for example | Vgl. zu entsprechenden Interpretationen als Gletscher, Eisscholle etc. beispielsweise Bart Lootsma, Artificial mirages, in: Snøhetta (ed.) 2009, op. cit. (note | Anm. 34), 71–86, 78; Anselm Wagner, Architektur und Emotion. Eine Skizze, in: Archimaera 8 (2019), 9–32, 25; **47** Cf. | Vgl. Craig Dykers/Kjetil T. Thorsen at | bei ids./Mari Lending 2007, op. cit. (note | Anm. 40), 71 **48** Cf. on this | Vgl. hierzu Kjetil T. Thorsen at | bei Sabine Drey/id. 2018, op. cit. (note | Anm. 36), 224 **49** Cf. on this also | Vgl. hierzu auch Anselm Wagner 2019, op. cit. (note | Anm. 46), 26–27 **50** Cf. | Vgl. Christophe Catsaros, in: id. (ed.), Lascaux Centre International de l'Art Pariétal, Paris: Archibooks + Sautereau 2017, s.p. | o.S. **51** Cf. | Vgl. Snøhetta, Lascaux IV. The International Centre for Cave Art, 2016. Cave art in the age of digital reproduction, in: id. (ed.) 2019, op. cit. (note | Anm. 32), 32–33 **52** Cf. on this | Vgl. hierzu Casson Mann, Lascaux Centre International d'Art Pariétal, on | auf: https://www.cassonmann.com/projects/lascaux, 10.3.2022; Kjetil K.Thorsen, cit. at | zit. bei: Cate St Hill, Wonder wall. Lascaux IV by Snohetta and Casson Mann, on | auf: https://www.designcurial.com/news/lascaux-iv-by-snhetta-and-casson-mann-5858777/, 6.3.2022 **53** Cf. on this | Vgl. hierzu Casson Mann, op. cit. (note | Anm. 52); Kjetil K.Thorsen, cit. at | zit. bei: Cate St Hill, Wonder wall. Lascaux IV by Snohetta and Casson Mann, on | auf: https://www.designcurial.com/news/lascaux-iv-by-snhetta-and-casson-mann-5858777/, 6.3.2022 **54** Cf. on this also | Vgl. hierzu auch Snøhetta, Studio statement: Collective intuition, in: id (ed.) 2019, op. cit. (note | Anm. 32), 9–13, 9 **55** Cf. on this | Vgl. hierzu Regina Heß, Emotionen am Werk, Berlin: Gebr. Mann 2013, 61–63 **56** On the relevance of anthropological-geographical reference spaces cf. also | Vgl. zur Relevanz anthropologisch-geographischer Bezugsräume auch Jürgen Hasse, Heimat und Landschaft, Wien: Passagen 1993, 75 **57** Cf. for example the statements in the interview with | Vgl. beispielsweise die Aussagen im Interview mit Hans Ulrich Obrist: Ryue Nishizawa/Hans Ulrich Obrist/Kazuyo Sejima, SANAA (Interviews), Köln: König 2012, 63–72 **58** Cf. | Vgl. Kazuyo Sejima (2019), Opening Cerenomy Course 2019/2020 (lecture | Vortrag 7.10.2019), Málaga: Malaga School of Architecture, University of Malaga, on | auf: https://www.youtube.com/watch?v=XD_X9urDr2E, 12.2.2022 **59** Cf. amongst others | Vgl. u. a. Ryue Nishizawa/Kazuyo Sejima/Alejandro Zaera, Conversation, in: Fernando Márquez Cecilia/Richard Levene (eds.) Kazuyo Sejima/Ryue Nishizawa 1995–2000. Making the boundary, Madrid: El Croquis 2000, 8–21; Juan Antonio Cortés/Ryue Nishizawa/Kazuyo Sejima, Conversation, in: Fernando Márquez Cecilia/Richard Levene (eds.), Sanaa. Kazuyo Sejima. Ryue Nishizawa 2004–2008, Madrid: El Croquis 2007, 19–31; Ryue Nishizawa/Kazuyo Sejima (2011), Architecture is environment (lecture | Vortrag 31.3.2011), Cambridge, GSD: Harvard University, on | auf: www.youtube.com/watch?v=dtTo9qNrQB8, 10.08.2015; Ryue Nishizawa (2011), Arts and architecture (lecture | Vortrag 7.11.2011), San Diego, CA: Californian College of the Arts, on | auf: www.youtube.com/watch?v=hjvDGMMcJqc, 12.08.2015; Kazuyo Sejima (2015), Gathering space (lecture | Vortrag 17.9.2014), New York, NY: Columbia University, Graduate School of Architecture, Planning and Preservation, on | auf: www.youtube. com/watch?v=NiwpNM0Oo5M,

12.8.2015 **60** Cf. | Vgl. Kazuyo Sejima, Exhibition, in: id./Fondazione La Biennale di Venezia (eds.), People meet in Architecture: Biennale Architettura 2010, Venedig: Marsilio 2010, 14–15 **61** Cf. | Vgl. Kristin Feireiss/ Ryue Nishizawa/Kazuyo Sejima, Interview, in: Kristin Feireiss (ed.): Kazuyo Sejima + Ryue Nishizawa. The Zollverein School of Management and Design, Essen, München et al.: Prestel, 60–64, 62 **62** Cf. | Vgl. Valerio Olgiati, The images of architects. Luzern: Quart 2013, s. p. | o. S.; Ryue Nishizawa, Landscape-like architecture, verb-like architecture, in: Luis Fernández Galiano (ed.), Sanaa. Sejima & Nishizawa 2007–2015. Madrid: Arquitectura Viva 2015, 9–11 **63** Cf. | Vgl. Günter Nitschke, From Shinto to Ando. Studies in architectural anthropology in Japan, London: Academy Editions 1993, 49–59 **64** Cf. | Vgl. Margitta Buchert, Fließende Räume, in: Margitta Buchert/Carl Zillich (eds.), In Bewegung… Architektur und Kunst, Berlin: Jovis 2008, 102–111 **65** On the Japanese understanding of man, nature and culture, cf. overarching | Vgl. zum japanischen Mensch-Natur-Kultur-Verständnis übergreifend Kisho Kurokawa, The philosophy of symbiosis, London: Academy Editions 1994, 172–184; Augustin Berque, Japan. Nature and artifice. Northhamptonshire: Pilkington 1997, passim **66** For a description and analysis of this example cf. | Zur Beschreibung, Analyse und Deutung dieses Projekts vgl. Margitta Buchert, Landschaftsentwürfe in der Architektur von Sanaa, in: Wolkenkuckucksheim 20(2015)/34, 231–248; 239-242 **67** On the history of EPFL and the building history of the campus cf. | Zur Geschichte der EPFL und der Baugeschichte des Campus vgl. Francesco Della Casa, The Rolex Learning Center, Lausanne: 2010, 37, 45–59 **68** Cf. for example | Vgl. beispielsweise Kazuyo Sejima 2019, op. cit. (note |Anm. 58); Ryue Nishizawa (2017), Porto Academy 2017 (lecture | Vortrag 20.7.2017), Porto: Faculty of Architecture of the University of Porto, on | auf: https://www.youtube.com/watch?v=hS3gTDGP-s8, 12.2.2022 **69** In 2010 a large park was planned using species of trees, shrubs, and bushes already found on the existing campus as well as a plaza. Since 2014, a media complex for Radio Télévision Suisse (RTS) based ona design by the Brusells office of Kersten Geers David van Severen has been planned for the open space east of the building. Cf. | 2010 waren ein großer Park unter Verwendung von Baum-, Strauch- und Buscharten, wie sie auf dem vorhandenen Campus bereits zu finden sind, sowie ein Platz geplant. Seit 2014 ist auf der Freifläche östlich des Gebäudes ein Medienkomplex für Radio Télévision Suisse (RTS) nach einem Entwurf des Brüsseler Büros Kersten Geers David van Severen in Planung. Vgl. Francesco Della Casa 2010, op. cit. (note | Anm. 67), 202; Achim Reese/Anastasia Svirski, Campus RTS, in: Archplus 220(2015), 184 **70** Cf. amongst others | Vgl. u. a. Francesco Della Casa 2010, op. cit. (note | Anm. 67), 37 and | und 147–163; Daniel Jauslin, Architecture with landscape methods. Doctoral thesis proposal and SANAA Rolex Learning Center Lausanne sample field trip, on | auf: http://resolver.tudelft.nl/uuid:e413eddc-1f25-4aee-a16d-22e73963835c, 4.4.2022, 21-54, amongst others | u. a. 22 and | und 41; Manfred Grohmann/ Friedrich Kittler/Anne Kuckelkorn, Morphogenese und freier Wille (Interview), in: Helga Blocksdorf/Ute Frank/Marius Mensing/Anca Timofticiuc (eds.), EKLAT, Berlin: TU 2011, 151–168, 151; Ryue Nishizawa/Kazuyo Sejima/Hans-Ulrich Obrist, On the Louvre-Lens project. A discussion with Catherine Mosbach, in: ids. (eds.), SANAA (Interviews), Köln: König 2012, 78; Ryue Nishizawa 2015, op. cit. (note | Anm. 62), 9–11 **71** For a description and analysis of this example cf. | Zur Beschreibung, Analyse und Deutung dieses Projekts vgl. Margitta Buchert 2015, op. cit. (note | Anm. 66), 243–245 **72** Cf. for example | Vgl. beispielsweise Mosbach at | bei Ryue Nishizawa/Kazuyo Sejima/Hans-Ulrich Obrist 2012, op. cit. (note | Anm. 70); Kazuyo Sejima 2019, op. cit. (note | Anm. 58) **73** Cf. Mosbach at | Vgl. Mosbach bei Ryue Nishizawa/Kazuyo Sejima/Hans-Ulrich Obrist 2012, op. cit. (note | Anm. 72), 47–49 **74** Cf. | Vgl. Jun'chiro Tanizaki, Lob des Schattens. Entwurf einer japanischen Ästhetik, Zürich: Manesse 2017, passim; Ryue Nishizawa/Augustin Pérez Rubio/Kazuyo Sejima, Feeling at home with Sanaa (Interview), in: Museo de Arte Contemporaneo di Castilla y Léon (ed.), Houses. Kazuzyo Sejima, Ryue Nishizawa, Sanaa, Léon: Museo de Arte Contemporaneo 2007, 12–13 **75** Cf. on this and the following | Vgl. hierzu und zum Folgenden François Jullien, Von Landschaft leben oder das Ungedachte der Vernunft, Berlin: Mattes Seitz 2016, 127–129

LANDSCHAFTLICHKEIT.
Ein vorläufiges Repertoire
LANDSCAPE-NESS.
A provisional repertoire

The range of different positions presented shows that the proposal of landscape-ness is to be understood variously. It is associated with a multifaceted spectrum of possibilities for perception and appropriation, as well as for the interpretative design of technical/technological, pictorial, choreographic and programmatic variants on various scales that can be considered 'territorial'. This perspective makes it clear that a long-term, future-relevant gaining of 'building blocks' for climate-relevant, culturally and socially positive architecture is not limited to ecological and economic aspects, nor merely to questions about social compatibility. Landscape-ness as architectural idea can enable the adding of cultural value in and with the architectural design, supported by aspects of aesthetic and ethical sustainability.

Based on the preceding process of demonstration and interpretation, some of the potentials that can contribute to transformations is outlined in the following by bringing together similar aspects. The subtopics of urban landscape, urban assemblage, sustainability and biophilia – as well as topology and atmosphere as contemporary perspectives – opened up an awareness of space-related effects through programmatic overlapping and spatial connections between architecture and open spaces; as well as of the linking of the buildings with climate-effective planting and green

Die Diversität der vorgestellten Positionen zeigt: Der Vorschlag der Landschaftlichkeit ist vielschichtig zu verstehen. Ein facettenreiches Spektrum von Angeboten für Wahrnehmung und Aneignung ist damit verbunden und ebenso für die interpretierende Gestaltung von technischen/technologischen, bildhaften, choreografischen und programmatischen Varianten in verschiedenen ‚territorial' zu denkenden Maßstäben. Mit dieser Perspektive wird deutlich, dass eine langfristig zukunftsrelevante Gewinnung von ‚Bausteinen' für klimarelevante, kulturell und sozial positiv wirksame Architektur sich nicht in ökologischen und ökonomischen Aspekten erschöpft und auch nicht nur in Fragen nach der sozialen Verträglichkeit. Landschaftlichkeit als Architekturidee kann in und mit der architektonischen Gestaltung eine kulturelle Wertschöpfung ermöglichen, getragen durch Ebenen ästhetischer und ethischer Nachhaltigkeit.

Ausgehend vom vorangegangenen Prozess des Aufzeigens und der Interpretation werden durch Verdichtung ähnlicher Aspekte nachfolgend einige Potenziale konturiert, die zu Transformationen beitragen können. Die Subthemen Urbane Landschaft. Urbane Assemblage, Nachhaltigkeit und Biophilie sowie Topologie und Atmosphäre als zeitgenössische Perspektiven öffneten den Blick für raumbezogene Wirkkräfte durch programmatische Überlagerungen und räumliche Verknüpfungen von Architekturen und Freiräumen, für die Verbindung der Bauten mit klimawirksamen Bepflanzungen

areas that further contribute to human well-being, and also of aesthetic and socially efficacious design qualities for valued architectural spaces and spatial relations. To trigger what is to come in practices of design and research, the use of specific strategies is encouraged by thinking of landscape-ness as a relevant theme guiding the design. Three of the fundamental themes are outlined in the following. Quite well-known and familiar design topics and approaches come to the fore here, now modified, differently anchored and adjusted in the context of contemporary conditions.

MULTIVALENT PLACE REFERENCE   References to place and site represent a significant example of this. Thought of in terms of landscape and creatively interpreted, site specifics can be characterised as multivalent and in the sense of an architecture that is perceived in a wider context. The consideration of landscape as a milieu of geological, biological and structural substance and of human culture and climate, leads to design decisions that accord great importance to horizons, to the lines and morphologies of the terrain, and to material qualities, dimensions, horizontality, verticality and layering as design components that further incorporate cultural, social, climate and vegetation features of the situational context. Important design building blocks are also presented, for example, by panoramic views, the framing of the closer and more distant surroundings through windows or freely placed frames, as well as intensely developed modulations of natural light situations. These can enable, in particular, the experience of extended space and of interactions, as well as an awareness of the presence of a wider space in which people are situated. Between complete assimilation into an existing context and indifference, the new architectures position themselves as correspondences, abstractions and modifications. Spatial and material connectivity and continuities can be incorporated into the understanding of the environment, contemporary urban conditions, systematisations and technologies that react to ecological

properties of the site, without neglecting aesthetic architecture qualities.

und Grünräumen, die zudem zum menschlichen Wohlbefinden beitragen, sowie für ästhetisch und sozial wirksame Gestaltungsqualitäten für wertgeschätzte architektonische Räume und Raumrelationen. Um anzustoßen, was in der Praxis von Entwerfen und Forschen werden kann, wird mit dem Denken von Landschaftlichkeit als relevantem entwurfsleitendem Thema der Gebrauch spezifischer Strategien ermuntert, von denen drei grundlegende nachfolgend umrissen werden. Durchaus bekannte und vertraute Entwurfsthemen und Ausrichtungen treten dabei hervor, nun im Kontext zeitgenössischer Konditionen modifiziert, neu verankert und justiert.

MULTIVALENTER ORTSBEZUG   Der Ortsbezug bildet dafür ein signifikantes Beispiel. Landschaftlich gedacht und gestalterisch interpretiert, ist Ortspezifik als multivalent zu charakterisieren und im Sinne einer Architektur, die in einem größeren Kontext wahrgenommen wird. Die Aufmerksamkeit für Landschaft als Milieu aus geologischer, biologischer und baulicher Substanz, menschlicher Kultur und als Klima führt zu Entwurfsentscheidungen, die Horizonten, Geländelinien und -morphologien, Materialqualitäten, Größenordnungen, Horizontalität, Vertikalität und Schichtung als Gestaltungskomponenten eine gewichtige Bedeutung beimessen und zudem kulturelle, soziale, klima- und vegetationsbezogene Prägungen des situativen Kontextes einbeziehen. Zudem bilden beispielsweise der Panoramaausblick, die Rahmung von näherer und fernerer Umgebung durch Fensterflächen oder frei aufgestellte Rahmen sowie intensiv entwickelte Modulationen von natürlichen Lichtsituationen wichtige Entwurfsbausteine. Diese können im Besonderen die Erfahrung ausgedehnter Räumlichkeit und von Wechselwirkungen ermöglichen sowie die Sensibilisierung für die Präsenz eines größeren Raumes, in dem die Menschen situiert sind. Zwischen vollständiger Assimilation an einen bestehenden Kontext und Indifferenz situieren sich die neuen Architekturen als Korrespondenzen, Abstraktionen und Modifikationen. In das Verständnis von Umwelt können dabei räumliche und materiale Konnektivitäten und Kontinuitäten ebenso einbezogen sein wie zeitgenössische urbane Konditionen, Systematisierungen und Technologien, die auf ökologische Eigenschaften des Standorts reagieren, ohne ästhetische Architekturqualitäten dabei zu vernachlässigen.

TYPOLOGICAL CROSSOVERS   Apart from place-specific references, typological crossovers of inside and outside, as well as their transitions, represent design strategies that can be associated with landscape-ness as architectural idea. Through the combination, for example, of cultural and educational institutions or of housing and outdoor space typologies – which integrate the characters of a square, park, passage and street, or even of a jungle and forest – new constructional-spatial situations are formed. This allows contemporary public spaces to act as catalysts for multiple processes, to which designed roof areas and mezzanines, as well as patios, atria and generous interior layouts, open floor plans or transparency can contribute. As places of encounter, communication, recreation and experience, also of what is different and unfamiliar, they form spatial systems of connection. This integrative approach leads to crossovers between architecture, landscape architecture, infrastructure and the wider environment in different conglomerates.

PRIMACY OF CHOREOGRAPHY   This also addresses the key design strategy of spatial sequencing. Sparked by the essential meaning of creating experiences in examples of English landscape garden art, this was first prominently articulated in architecture in the 18th century. In the evolutionary process of modernity, it regained relevance with the choreographic interpretation referred to by Le Corbusier as promenade architecturale. In relation to many of the contemporary examples that integrate landscape-ness as architectural idea, spatial sequencing emerges as a central design aspect. Choreography as an architectural design strategy is based on explicit and implicit knowledge and a finely differentiated process of shaping movement within a space, which includes flows of movement, (architectural) guidance and structuring of movement as pathway spaces, as well as sojourn areas. In consideration of these multimodal spatial and spatiotemporal levels of perception, various constellations, sequences

TYPOLOGISCHE KREUZUNGEN   Neben dem Ortsbezug bilden auch typologische Mischungen von Aussen- und im Innenraum sowie deren Übergänge entwerferische Strategien, die mit Landschaftlichkeit als Architekturidee verbunden sein können. Durch die Kombination von beispielsweise Kultur- und Bildungseinrichtungen oder Wohnungsbauten mit Freiraumtypologien, die Charakteristika von Platz, Park, Passage und Straße oder auch Dschungel und Wald integrieren, bilden sich neue bauliche-räumliche Situationen. Dadurch können zeitgenössische öffentliche Räume als Katalysatoren multipler Prozesse wirken, wozu neben ‚klassischen' Außenräumen entsprechend gestaltete Dachflächen und Zwischenebenen ebenso beitragen können wie Patios, Atrien und großzügige Innenraumzuschnitte, offene Grundrisse oder Transparenzen. Als Orte der Begegnung, Kommunikation, Rekreation und der Erfahrung auch des Fremden und Anderen formen sie räumliche Systeme der Verknüpfung. Mit der integrativen Ausrichtung kreuzen sich Architektur, Landschaftsarchitektur, Infrastruktur und weiteres Umfeld in unterschiedlichen Konglomeraten.

PRIMAT DER CHOREOGRAFIE   Hier ist auch die wesentliche Entwurfsstrategie der Raumsequenzierung angesprochen. Angestoßen durch die essenzielle Bedeutung der Erfahrungsgestaltung in Beispielen englischer Landschaftsgartenkunst, wurde diese erstmals im 18.Jahrhundert prominent in der Architektur artikuliert. Im evolutionären Prozess der Moderne gewann sie nicht nur mit der von Le Corbusier als ‚promenade architecturale' bezeichneten choreografischen Interpretation erneut an Relevanz. Im Zusammenhang vieler der zeitgenössischen Beispiele, die Landschaftlichkeit als Architekturidee integrieren, tritt Raumsequenzierung als eine zentrale Entwurfsebene hervor. Choreografie als architektonische Entwurfsstrategie wird getragen von explizitem und implizitem Wissen und fein differenzierten Verfahren der Bewegungsgestaltung im Raum, die Bewegungsströme, (architektonische) Bewegungslenkungen und -strukturierungen als Wegräume sowie Räume des Aufenthalts einbezieht. Im Blick auf diese multimodalen räumlichen und raum-zeitlichen Wahrnehmungsebenen werden diverse Konstellationen, Abfolgen und Dimensionierungen der räumlichen Komposition entwickelt.[1] Diese schließen ebenfalls

and dimensions of spatial composition are developed.[1] They include both inside and outside connections and flowing, gradual or contrasting transitions in the spatial sequence, whose multidimensional appearance and experiential quality is created by basic geometric constitutions, material features and lighting design, as well as by the finer definition of details. These are experienced as a synthesis of impactful qualities of different intensities and with a variety of appropriation potential, as can also be associated with experiences of the landscape.

PERSPECTIVES   The concentration on these themes overrides some others for considering architecture and landscape, especially in times of great challenges such as global warming, viruses, floods, forest fires, extinctions and migration due to climate and war on a local and global scale. However, the presented relation systems are compatible with an extension of the field of discourse and action through further perspectives and research in the context of architecture, in order to refine the answers and widen the field; for example, with aspects of place-site-specific material use, the greater incorporation of biological realities of plants, ground or hydrological infrastructures, or various form of the recycling of resources. It is in the first instance a kind of preamble and trigger for architecture that includes a specific complexity and openness, in accordance with contemporary conditions. Thematising the idea of landscape-ness in architecture can enable a better understanding of specifics in the cultural experience of the environment. It also shows which approaches architects can take regarding sustainable transformations, as well as a set of values, strategies and design elements that contribute to this, along with multilayered locational references, public spatial qualities in indoor and outdoor areas and the dedicated creation of aesthetic experiences.

Verknüpfungen von Außen- und Innenraum ein sowie fließende, graduelle oder auch kontrastierende Übergänge in der räumlichen Abfolge, die durch geometrische Grundkonstitutionen, Materialeigenschaften und Lichtführung sowie durch feinere Ausformung von Details in ihrer multidimensionalen Erscheinung und Erfahrungsqualität gestaltet werden. In der Erfahrung erfolgt eine Synthese von Wirkqualitäten aus unterschiedlichen Intensitäten und Aneignungspotenzialen wie sie auch mit Landschaftserfahrungen verbunden sein kann.

PERSPEKTIVEN   Die Konzentration auf diese Themen stellt einige andere zurück, die eine Untersuchung zu Architektur und Landschaft zudem herausstellen könnte gerade in einer Situation der großen Herausforderungen durch Erderwärmung, Viren, Überflutungen, Waldbrände, Artensterben sowie klima- und kriegsbedingte Migrationen im lokalen und globalen Maßstab. Die aufgezeigten Relationssysteme sind jedoch anschlussfähig für die Erweiterung des Diskurs- und Handlungsfeldes durch weitere Perspektiven und Forschungen im Kontext der Architektur, um die Antworten zu verfeinern und das Feld zu verbreitern beispielsweise durch Aspekte der ortsspezifischen Materialverwendung, den stärkeren Einbezug biologischer Wirklichkeiten von Pflanzen, Böden oder hydrologischen Infrastrukturen oder verschiedener Formen des Recycling von Ressourcen. Es geht zunächst um eine Art Vorlauf und Impulsgabe für die Architektur, die eine spezifische Komplexität und Offenheit einschließt, wie sie den zeitgenössischen Konditionen entspricht. Durch die Thematisierung der Idee von Landschaftlichkeit in der Architektur kann ein besseres Erfassen von Spezifiken in der kulturellen Erfahrung der Umwelt ermöglicht werden. Sie zeigen ebenfalls, welche Ausrichtungen Architekt:innen und Architekturen in Bezug auf nachhaltige Transformationen seismografisch einnehmen können sowie ein Set von Wertsetzungen, Strategien und Entwurfsbausteinen, die dazu beitragen, beispielsweise ein vielschichtiger Ortsbezug, öffentliche Raumqualitäten im Außen- und im Innenraum sowie dezidiert ästhetische Erfahrungsgestaltungen.

LANDSCAPE-NESS AS 'FASCINOSUM'   In contemporary architecture, landscape acts as a design impulse and as a framing interpretative tool between the utilitarian perception of technical-objective rationality and sensory experiences. The basic thought behind it indicates a wider context than just that of the architectural system and the autonomous object or ensemble. Landscape as a perception construct is embedded in the ongoing search for design orientation in the context of contemporary cultural conditions and is based on the respective experience, perception and interpretation process. Although the characters of cities and regions in the world vary greatly, many other dimensions, especially urban sustainability are similar. Almost everywhere, it is about deciding how natural environments will not be devalued but rather improved, and how social equality and quality of life can be promoted, particularly through architectural projects.[2] Lastly, landscape-ness as architectural idea also means considering the physical-material, mental and social levels of architectural spatial design together and furthermore to incorporate place-specific environmental qualities, which can range on different scales from the history and vegetation of the site to urban and regional references to a cosmic scale, for example, regarding light and climate conditions. With these properties, a spatially shaped sequenced experience construct and a programmatic range of open appropriation possibilities, it can also be possible to provide alternatives to a Western world view that is too strongly materialistic, and to one-sidedness through globalisation and virtual strategies, by means of architecture that is friendly to people and to their lived environment. This is a plea for an understanding of landscape-ness as 'fascinosum'; as an attractive and captivating architectural idea that contains and brings forth an environmental aesthetic in which the contemporary interpretation of landscape alternates between a modern and contemporary context – with its challenges, circumstances and tradition – and a sensory and meaningful experiential quality.

LANDSCHAFTLICHKEIT ALS FASZINOSUM   Landschaft
wirkt in der zeitgenössischen Architektur als Entwurfsimpuls und rahmendes
Deutungsinstrument zwischen utilitaristischer Wahrnehmung, technisch-ob-
jektiver Vernunft und sinnlicher Erlebbarkeit. Der Grundgedanke verweist
auf einen größeren Kontext als nur den des Architektursystems und des au-
tonomen Objekts oder Ensembles. Landschaft als Wahrnehmungskonstrukt
ist eingebettet in die fortlaufende Suche nach gestalterischer Orientierung
im Kontext zeitgenössischer kultureller Konditionen und gründet in dem jeweiligen Erfahrungs-, Wahrnehmungs- und Deutungsprozess. Obwohl Cha-
raktere von Städten und Regionen in der Welt stark variieren, sind viele
vor allem städtische Nachhaltigkeitsdimensionen ähnlich. Fast überall gilt
es zu entscheiden, wie natürliche Umwelten nicht entwertet, sondern ver-
bessert werden sowie soziale Gleichberechtigung und Lebensqualität befördert werden können, auch und gerade mit architektonischen Projekten.[2]
Landschaftlichkeit als Architekturidee bedeutet letztlich auch, physikalisch-
materielle, mentale und soziale Ebenen architektonischer Raumgestaltung
zusammenzudenken und zudem ortsspezifische Umgebungsqualitäten einzubeziehen, die aus unterschiedlichen Maßstabskontexten von der Stand-
ortgeschichte und -vegetation über urbane und regionale Bezugnahmen
bis zum kosmischen Maßstab reichen können in der Korrespondenz beispielsweise zu Lichtverhältnissen und klimatischen Bedingungen. Mit diesen
Eigenschaften einer räumlich sequenzierten Erfahrungsgestaltung und dem
programmatischen Angebot offener Aneignungsmöglichkeiten kann es auch
möglich sein, einer zu stark materialistisch geprägten westlichen Weltsicht
und Vereinseitigungen durch Globalisierung und virtuelle Strategien Alternativen zur Seite zu stellen durch Architektur, die freundlich ist zu Menschen
und zu ihrem Lebensumfeld. Dies ist ein Plädoyer für ein Verständnis von
Landschaftlichkeit als Faszinosum, als anziehende und fesselnde Architekturidee, die eine Umweltästhetik beinhaltet bzw. hervorbringen kann, bei
der die zeitgenössische Interpretation von Landschaft zwischen modernem
zeitgenössischem Kontext mit seinen Herausforderungen und Gegebenheiten, Überlieferung und sinnlich-sinnhafter Erfahrungsqualität changiert.   315

1 Cf. on this also | Vgl. hierzu auch Margitta Buchert, Raumerleben und Raumartikulation. Experiencing and articulating space, in: id./Laura Kienbaum (eds.), Einfach Entwerfen. Simply Design, Berlin: Jovis 2013, 128–151, 128–129 **2** Cf. on this | Vgl. hierzu Timothy Beatley/Stephen M. Wheeler, Origins of the sustainability concept, in: ids. (eds.), The sustainable urban development reader, London et al.: Routledge 2014, 8–10

APPENDIX

ABBILDUNGEN INDEX OF ILLUSTRATIONS

DILLER SCOFIDIO + RENFRO **1–3, 5, 34–35** © Courtesy of Diller Scofidio + Renfro **4, 7, 11, 13, 16–17, 31** © Courtesy of Diller Scofidio + Renfro, Foto | photo: Iwan Baan **6** © Courtesy of Diller Scofidio + Renfro, Foto | photo: Michael Hundsnurcher **8** © Chun-Hung Eric Cheng, "Lincoln Center", CC BY 2.0, https://creativecommons.org/licenses/by/2.0/, entzerrt und beschnitten | rectified and cut **12** © Chun-Hung Eric Cheng, "Lincoln Center", CC BY 2.0, https://creativecommons.org/licenses/by/2.0/ **14** © Michele Ursino, "Alice Tully Hall", CC BY-SA 2.0, https://creativecommons.org/licenses/by-sa/2.0/ **15** © joevare "Alice Tully Hall at Lincoln Center - Diller, Scofidio + Renfro renovation of original Pietro Belluschi building", CC BY-ND 2.0, https://creativecommons.org/licenses/by-nd/2.0/ **18, 21–23, 25–27, 29–30** © Margitta Buchert **19** © Courtesy of Diller Scofidio + Renfro, Foto | photo: Timothy Schenck **20, 24** © James Corner Field Operations **28** © Courtesy of Diller Scofidio + Renfro, Foto | photo: Michael Montheith **32** © David Berkowitz "High Line Park - New York City", CC BY 2.0, https://creativecommons.org/licenses/by/2.0/, beschnitten | cut to size **33** © Courtesy of Diller Scofidio + Renfro, Foto | photo: Jaime Acioli BIG BJARKE INGELS GROUP **1–2, 7, 20–22** © Courtesy of BIG - Bjarke Ingels Group **3–4, 10** © Courtesy of BIG - Bjarke Ingels Group, Foto | photo: Iwan Baan **5** © Courtesy of BIG - Bjarke Ingels Group & Julien De Smedt **6** © cjreddaway "110914 BIG_8 house 12", CC BY 2.0, https://creativecommons.org/licenses/by/2.0/ **8, 12** © Courtesy of Hans Nerstu **9** © Fred Romero "København - 8Tallet", CC BY 2.0, https://creativecommons.org/licenses/by/2.0/, perspektivisch entzerrt | perspective rectified **11** © cjreddaway "110914 BIG_8 house 28", CC BY 2.0, https://creativecommons.org/licenses/by/2.0/ **13** © Courtesy of BIG - Bjarke Ingels Group, Foto | photo: Ty Stange **14, 16** © Courtesy of BIG - Bjarke Ingels Group, Foto | photo: Rasmus Hjortshøj **15, 17, 19** © SLA **18** © flöschen "Grüne Wiesen auf dem Copenhill (51494009835)", CC BY 2.0, https://creativecommons.org/licenses/by/2.0/ MVRDV **1, 8, 14–16, 18, 21** © Courtesy of MVRDV **2-3** © Courtesy of nai010 publishers, Porocity, Winy Maas/Adrien Ravon/Javier Arpa, nai010publishers 2018 **4, 7, 9–10** © Courtesy of MVRDV Foto | photo: Rob t'Hart **5** © --v "Villa VPRO", CC BY 2.0, https://creativecommons.org/licenses/by/2.0/ **6** © Marco Raaphorst "VPRO, Net 3", CC BY 2.0, https://creativecommons.org/licenses/by/2.0/ **11-13** © Bureau B+B Urbanism and Landscape Architecture **17, 19–20, 22–24** © Courtesy of MVRDV, Foto | photo: Ossip van Duivenbode INGENHOVEN ARCHITECTS **1** © Tuxyso "RWE-Turm in Essen", CC BY-SA 3.0, https://creativecommons.org/licenses/by-sa/3.0/deed.en **2–3, 7–13, 15, 17** © ingenhoven associates / HGEsch **4** © Margitta Buchert **5** © Ulrike Fischer, "Ingenhoven-Tal in Düsseldorf im Bau mit Hainbuchenhecken, Blick vom Breuninger", CC BY-SA 4.0, https://creativecommons.org/licenses/by-sa/4.0/deed.en **6** © Ulrike Fischer, "Ingenhoven-Tal in Düsseldorf im Bau mit Hainbuchenhecken, links der Kö-Bogen", CC BY-SA 4.0, https://creativecommons.org/licenses/by-sa/4.0/deed.en **14, 16** © ingenhoven associates WOHA **1** © Courtesy of WOHA, Foto | photo: a-c Patrick Bingham-Hall; d WOHA **2–4, 12, 22, 26** © Courtesy of WOHA **5–8, 10** © Singapore Pavilion, Expo 2020 Dubai / Quentin Sim **11, 13–18** © Courtesy of WOHA, Foto | photo: Patrick Bingham-Hall / Albert Lim KS **19–21, 23–25** © Courtesy of WOHA, Foto | photo: Patrick Bingham-Hall / Skyshot Pte Ltd **27–30** © Courtesy of WOHA, Foto | photo: Patrick Bingham-Hall / K. Kopter / Albert Lim KS STEFANO BOERI ARCHITETTI **1–2, 5–6, 10–11, 13, 16–21** © Stefano Boeri Architetti **3, 12** © Stefano Boeri Architetti, Foto | photo: Dimitar Harizanov **4, 7–8** © Stefano Boeri Architetti, Foto | photo: Giovanni Nardi **14–15** © Stefano Boeri Architetti, Foto | photo: Paolo Rosselli ATELIER PETER ZUMTHOR **1** fcamusd, "Therme Vals, Switzerland. Peter Zumthor, 1996", CC BY 2.0, https://creativecommons.org/licenses/by/2.0/ **2** Friedrich Böhringer, "Bregenz Hafen mit Post, CUB, Kornmarkt", CC BY-SA 2.5, https://creativecommons.org/licenses/by-sa/2.5/legalcode **3** Hpschaefer, " Museum Kolumba at Cologne, architekt Zumthor (to the right: modernist building Dischhaus)", CC BY-SA 3.0, https://creativecommons.org/licenses/by-sa/3.0/legalcode SNØHETTA **1–2** © Courtesy of Snøhetta, Foto | photo: Ketil Jacobsen **3** © Courtesy of Snøhetta, Foto | photo: Hélène Binet **4–5, 7–9, 11–12** © Courtesy of Snøhetta **6, 10** © Courtesy of Snøhetta, Foto | photo: Jiri Havran **13, 15, 18–22** © Courtesy of Snøhetta, Foto | photo: Eric Solé **14, 16** © Margitta Buchert **17** © Courtesy of Snøhetta, Foto | photo: Boegli & Grazia Photographers SANAA **1, 3–4, 7–9, 11, 15** © Courtesy of SANAA **2, 10** © Photo: Iwan Baan **5–6** Margitta Buchert **12–14, 17** © Courtesy of Julien Lanoo **16** © Courtesy of SANAA, Foto | photo: Catherine Mosbach **18** © Hisao Suzuki "SANAA - Louvre Lens Museum - Photo 13 - by Hisao Suzuki.jpg", CC BY 2.0, https://creativecommons.org/licenses/by/2.0/

IMPRESSUM

© 2022 by jovis Verlag GmbH

Das Urheberrecht für die Texte liegt bei der Autorin.

Text by kind permission of the author.

Das Urheberrecht für die Abbildungen liegt bei den Fotograf:innen/
Inhaber:innen der Bildrechte. Die Urheberrechte sind sorgfältig wieder-
gegeben; bitte informieren Sie uns im Fall eines Bildrechteanspruchs.

Copyright for all images reside with the photographers/holders of the
picture rights. The sources and owners of rights are given to the best
of our knowledge; please inform us of any we may have omitted.

Alle Rechte vorbehalten. All rights reserved.

Autorin Author: Margitta Buchert,
Architektur und Kunst 20./21. Jahrhundert Architecture and Art 20th/21st Centuries,
Leibniz Universität Hannover Leibniz University Hannover,
www.igt-arch.uni-hannover.de/a_ku

Übersetzungen Translations: Lynne Kolar-Thompson
Gestaltung Design: Margitta Buchert, Julius Krüger, Hannover
Satz Setting: Julius Krüger, Hannover
Lithografie Lithography: Bild1Druck, Berlin
Druck und Bindung Printing and Binding: GRASPO CZ, a.s., Zlín

Bibliografische Information der Deutschen Bibliothek
Bibliographic information published by Deutsche Nationalbibliothek:
Die Deutsche Nationalbibliothek verzeichnet diese Publikation
in der Deutschen Nationalbibliografie; detaillierte bibliografische
Daten sind im Internet über http://dnb.ddb.de abrufbar.

The German National Library lists this publication in the German National Bibliography;
detailed bibliographic data are available on the Internet at http//dnb.d-nb.de.

jovis Verlag
Lützowstraße 33
10785 Berlin
www.jovis.de

ISBN 978-3-86859-695-3 (Softcover)
ISBN 978-3-86859-976-3 (PDF)